Calculating Risks?

Regulation of Economic Activity

General Editors, Nancy L. Rose and Richard Schmalensee, MIT Sloan School of Management

1   *Freight Transport Regulation: Equity, Efficiency, and Competition in the Rail and Trucking Industries*, Ann F. Friedlaender and Richard H. Spady, 1981

2   *The SEC and the Public Interest*, Susan M. Phillips and J. Richard Zecher, 1981

3   *The Economics and Politics of Oil Price Regulation: Federal Policy in the Post-Embargo Era*, Joseph P. Kalt, 1981

4   *Studies in Public Regulation*, Gary Fromm, editor, 1981

5   *Incentives for Environmental Protection*, Thomas C. Schelling, editor, 1983

6   *United States Oil Pipeline Markets: Structure, Pricing, and Public Policy*, John A. Hansen, 1983

7   *Folded, Spindled, and Mutilated: Economic Analysis and U.S. v. IBM*, Franklin M. Fisher, John J. McGowan, and Joen E. Greenwood, 1983

8   *Targeting Economic Incentives for Environmental Protection*, Albert L. Nichols, 1984

9   *Deregulation and the New Airline Entrepreneurs*, John R. Meyer and Clinton V. Oster, Jr., with Marni Clippinger, Andrew McKey, Don H. Pickrell, John S. Strong, and C. Kurt Zorn, 1984

10   *Deregulating the Airlines*, Elizabeth E. Bailey, David R. Graham, and Daniel P. Kaplan, 1985

11   *The Gathering Crisis in Federal Deposit Insurance*, Edward J. Kane, 1985

12   *Perspectives on Safe and Sound Banking: Past, Present, and Future*, George J. Benston, Robert A. Eisenbeis, Paul M. Horvitz, Edward J. Kane, and George G. Kaufman, 1986

13   *The Economics of Public Utility Regulation*, Michael A Crew and Paul R. Kleindorfer, 1987

14   *Public Regulation: New Perspectives on Institutions and Policies*, Elizabeth E. Bailey, editor, 1987

15   *Deregulation and the Future of Intercity Passenger Travel*, John R. Meyer and Clinton V. Oster, Jr., with John S. Strong, José S. Gómez-Ibáñez, Don H. Pickrell, Marni Clippinger, and Ivor P. Morgan, 1987

16   *Private Antitrust Litigation: New Evidence, New Learning*, Lawrence J. White, editor, 1988

17   *The Dilemma of Toxic Substance Regulation: How Overregulation Causes Underregulation*, John M. Mendeloff, 1988

18   *Privatization: An Economic Analysis*, John Vickers and George Yarrow, 1988

19   *Informational Approaches to Regulation*, Wesley A. Magat and W. Kip Viscusi, 1992

20   *Regulatory Reform: Economic Analysis and British Experience*, Mark Armstrong, Simon Cowan, and John Vickers, 1994

21   *Calculating Risks? The Spatial and Political Dimensions of Hazardous Waste Policy*, James T. Hamilton and W. Kip Viscusi, 1999

Calculating Risks?
The Spatial and Political Dimensions of Hazardous Waste Policy

James T. Hamilton and W. Kip Viscusi

The MIT Press
Cambridge, Massachusetts
London, England

This book was set in Times New Roman by Asco Typesetters, Hong Kong.

Printed and bound in the United States of America.

Library of Congress Cataloging-in-Publication Data

Hamilton, James T. (James Towler), 1961–
  Calculating risks? : the spatial and political dimensions of
  hazardous waste policy / James T. Hamilton and W. Kip Viscusi.
     p.   cm. — (Regulation of economic activity ; 21)
  Includes bibliographical references and index.
  ISBN 0-262-08278-0 (alk. paper)
  1. Hazardous wastes—Government policy—United States.
2. Hazardous waste site remediation—Government policy—United
States. 3. Environmental policy—United States. 4. United States.
Environmental Protection Agency. 5. Hazardous waste sites—Law and
legislation—United States. 6. Risk—United States. I. Viscusi,
W. Kip. II. Title. III. Series.
HC110.E5H315   1999
363.72′87′0973—dc21   99-17964
                                                                              CIP

Contents

Series Foreword   vii

Preface   ix

1
Introduction   1

2
Measuring Individual Risks   25

3
Assessing Conservatism in Individual Risk Estimates   59
with P. Christen Dockins

4
Populations at Risk   91

5
Costs of Conservatism: Cost-Effectiveness of Site
Remediations   109

6
Are Risk Regulators "Rational"?   129

7
Environmental Equity at Superfund Sites   157

8
Market Reactions to Site Risks   189
with Ted Gayer

9
Implementing Risk Reforms in Site Remediations   211

Appendix A: Assessing Human Health Risks and Remediation
Costs   245

Appendix B: Sample Description   269

Notes   281
Bibliography   301
Index   321

Series Foreword

Government regulation of economic activity has undergone dramatic change during the course of the past century, radically transforming the economic roles of government and business as well as relations between them. Economic regulation of prices and conditions of service was first applied to the transportation sector and to public utilities roughly one hundred years ago. Similar regulatory policies were later extended to energy, financial services, health care, and other sectors. In other nations, government intervention more frequently took the form of nationalization and government ownership of productive enterprises.

The past quarter-century has been marked by regulatory retrenchment in the United States, and by large-scale privatization of government-owned enterprises elsewhere. These reforms have ranged from dismantling the regulatory apparatus in sectors such as transportation and energy, to substantially relaxing regulatory restrictions in industries such as financial services, to large-scale restructuring of markets and regulatory mechanisms as in the electric utility industries around the world. There is tremendous excitement about these changes, although the aims, methods, and results of many of these regulatory initiatives remain controversial.

"Regulatory reform" has attracted much attention, but it is far from universal. Social regulation, directed toward workplace safety, environmental preservation, consumer protection, and related goals, has grown rapidly, even as economic regulation has been pared back or eliminated. The pursuit of economic efficiency, a long-standing rallying point in economic deregulation and restructuring debates, has made but a few recent inroads into the design and implementation of social regulatory policy.

For the past several years James Hamilton, Kip Viscusi, and their students have used economic tools to analyze the Environmental Protection Agency's hazardous waste clean-up program known as "Superfund." This important book presents their results. Taken together, their findings represent a clear and comprehensive examination of this complex and far-reaching regulatory policy.

In the first part of the book, the authors provide a careful analysis of the risks associated with hazardous waste at Superfund sites. They detail the assumptions, methods, and outcomes of the EPA's risk assessment techniques and compare the EPA's estimates to their best estimates of risks for affected populations. The authors describe the economic consequences of the techniques that EPA uses to estimate risks and to target sites for clean-up priority, and they present new evidence on the cost-effectiveness of clean-up policies.

In the second part of the book, Hamilton and Viscusi try to explain why EPA policy takes the form that it does. This part of their research is grounded in the rapidly growing literature on the political economy of regulatory policy. The authors use rational choice models to explore the political economy of Superfund legislation and its associated enforcement policies. They develop and apply new techniques to evaluate the impact of EPA policies on environmental equity across demographic groups, and show how the "neighbors" at various Superfund sites affect EPA's decisions regarding site remediation policies.

The Regulation of Economic Activity series is intended to inform the ongoing debate on regulatory policy by making significant and relevant research available to scholars and policy makers. Books in this series present new insights into individual agencies, programs, and regulated sectors. They also address important economic, political, and administrative aspects of the regulatory process that cut across those boundaries. Hamilton and Viscusi's work is a significant contribution in this tradition. This important book should find a broad audience among scholars and policy makers concerned with the operation and political economy of government regulation in general, as well as those interested in the particulars of environmental regulation. It also is essential reading for anyone concerned with risk assessment methods and risk analysis in policy making.

Nancy L. Rose
Richard L. Schmalensee

Preface

The debate over cleanup of hazardous waste sites in the United States is dominated largely by anecdotes. Opposing parties in this debate have often been guilty of using distorted stories to bolster their arguments. Those urging stringent cleanup propagate exaggerated estimates of cancer epidemics, while industry trade associations anxious to reduce expenditures have greatly overstated the biases in government risk assessments and policies.

This book offers the first comprehensive analysis of the efficacy of the Environmental Protection Agency's Superfund program. How substantial are the risks posed by hazardous waste sites? Are there real risks to exposed populations? How do the risks vary by site? Who is at risk? Are hazardous waste risks particularly likely to affect minorities and the disadvantaged? Are those people affected by hazardous wastes risks adversely affected in other ways as well, such as by depressed housing prices? What determines Superfund site remediation decisions? What role do political economy influences such as local political activity play in site-level remediation choices? These are the types of questions we will address in our exploration of the Superfund program.

Our analysis in this book provides the first extensive examination of U.S. environmental policy based on a combination of agency decision data, geographic information systems (GIS) technology, and census figures. The site-level analysis involved six years of research, the efforts of over twenty research assistants, and substantial research support from the U.S. Environmental Protection Agency (EPA). The result is a detailed empirical assessment of the cleanup of hazardous waste sites that demonstrates how rational choice models can be used both to evaluate the Superfund program and explain the political economy of its implementation. Our analysis of site remediation decisions also reveals how reforms in risk assessment and management could significantly reduce expenditures in the Superfund program without reducing the protection of human health. The scope of this book is more ambitious than simply an analysis of a particular risk policy. Many of the substantive concerns that we examine have fundamental implications for risk policy more generally. The data we compiled for the Superfund program afford the most detailed examination to date of several central topics in the risk analysis literature.

This book should be of interest to regulatory economists, political scientists, policy analysts, and others involved in debates over environmental policy and risk analysis generally. Many of the substantive issues examined in the book have been the subject of recent congressional debates about the reauthorization of the Superfund program and the design of regulatory reform policies. The research presented will also be of interest to those concerned with risk assessment, for our analysis derives unique estimates of the magnitude of conservatism in EPA's risk assessment policies. We also demonstrate how census data can be combined with GIS technology to measure populations exposed to particular risk levels, which will broaden debate about what measures of risk should generally be considered in regulatory decisions.

We received partial research support for this project under cooperative agreements CR-817478-02, -03 between the U.S. Environmental Protection Agency and Duke University. Hamilton's work was aided by research support from the Sanford Institute of Public Policy, and Viscusi's research was also supported by the Harvard Law School Olin Center for Law, Business, and Economics and by the Sheldon Seevak Research Fund. We have benefited greatly from the comments and support of our contract officer, Alan Carlin. We received helpful comments throughout the project from other EPA staff members, especially Suzanne Giannini-Spohn and Harriet Tregoning. These officials gave us complete freedom in this research effort and should in no way be held responsible for any policy views that are expressed in this book. Through the course of our research we have also benefited from discussions with or comments from Vicki Been, Justice Stephen Breyer, Maureen Cropper, Christopher DeMuth, Don Fullerton, Bob Hahn, John Hird, Howard Kunreuther, Joel Marcus, Roger Noll, Paul Portney, Richard Revesz, Milton Russell, Chris Schroeder, William Schulze, Hilary Sigman, V. Kerry Smith, David Spence, Rob Stavins, Richard Stewart, James Stock, Cass Sunstein, Jonathan Wiener, and Richard Zeckhauser. Seminar participants at the American Economic Association, Duke University, Georgetown University, Columbia University, Harvard Law School, MIT, and Vanderbilt University also made helpful comments. Terry Vaughn and Andrea Werblin of The MIT Press helped speed the book through the review process and provided valuable suggestions from anonymous reviewers.

Collecting the site-level data from EPA regional offices, creating databases based on EPA risk assessments and cost analyses, and linking information on Superfund site locations to census data involved a large number of research assistants. We owe many analytical and organizational debts to Scott Rehmus, who for three years directed the research staff that assembled these data. Jason Bell, Kristen Blann, and Robert Malme provided expert computer and editorial aid throughout the analysis. For substantial help in constructing the databases and analysis, we also thank Joey Ams, Chris Chiang, Elizabeth Gregory, Jahn Hakes, Lisa Larson, Jennifer Montgomery, Jason Parsley, A. Este Stifel, and Zac Robinson. P. Christen Dockins and Ted Gayer, two of our former graduate students, were central to the analysis of conservatism in EPA site risk assessments (the topic of Dockins's dissertation) and the reaction of homebuyers to information about Superfund site risks (the topic of Gayer's dissertation). Chris Dockins is coauthor of chapter 3, and Ted Gayer is coauthor of chapter 8. Our analysis of the operation of the Superfund program would be incomplete without the help of all of these research assistants and colleagues.

We appreciate very much the permission of the following journals to publish parts of research that appeared in previous publications: *American Economic Review*, *Ecology Law Quarterly*, *Journal of Environmental Economics and Management*, *Journal of Policy Analysis and Management*, *The Public Interest*, *Stanford Environmental Law Journal*, and *Review of Economics and Statistics*. We also appreciate the support of Nancy Hamilton and Joni Hersch Viscusi, to whom this work is dedicated.

Calculating Risks?

1

Introduction

During the 1980s risks from hazardous waste sites ranked as the top environmental problem in popular opinion surveys. The public fears of risks from contaminated sites persisted despite the fact that environmental experts only ranked these risks as low to moderate.[1] In response to widespread public concern with hazardous wastes, the government in 1980 launched a hazardous waste cleanup effort administered by the U.S. Environmental Protection Agency known as Superfund. This effort translated public concern about health risks into both government and private expenditures to clean up hazardous waste sites.

The financial stakes were substantial. Public and private expenditures of funds to clean up nonfederal Superfund sites totaled $20 billion in the first dozen years of the program, 1981 to 1992.[2] Superfund also looms large relative to other federal efforts to protect the environment. Future costs for the nonfederal sites now currently listed or proposed for cleanups are estimated to be $6.7 billion.[3] The program accounted for nearly 25 percent of the U.S. Environmental Protection Agency's budget from 1991 to 1996.

The government's cleanup strategy remains controversial. When the program's authorization expired in 1994, legislative debate centered around the stringency of cleanup standards (e.g., "How clean is clean?") and the desirability of alternative funding mechanisms (e.g., "Who pays?"). Academic debates about Superfund have focused largely on program management and decision rules, the role of transaction costs in site remediation, the potential impact of congressional oversight or neighborhood composition on site cleanups, the way risk assessments are conducted in the program, the nature of site risks, and the effects of funding mechanisms on program operation.[4] While Congress discussed the aggregate costs of cleanup often during the reauthorization debate, researchers had not yet developed detailed evidence on how cost effective Superfund remediations were in preventing cancer and other adverse effects.

In this book we offer the first systematic evidence that links risk measures to cost data to derive estimates of the effectiveness of Superfund site remediations. How substantial are the risks posed by hazardous waste sites? What are the size and character of the populations exposed to these risks? How can the cleanup resources be targeted both to achieve the greatest degree of environmental protection as well as to strike a reasonable balance between the costs expended and the risk reduction achieved?

To address these issues, we constructed a national sample of Superfund sites for which we collected detailed information from the site-level documents used in remediation decisions. Taking the site risk estimates at face value, we find that the maximum individual cancer risks calculated by the agency are high relative to other risks regulated by the government. However, risks are only consequential if people are exposed to them. Most assessed Superfund "risks" do not now pose a threat to human health. Many of these risks will be present only if there are hypothetical changes in land use in the future. Conservative assumptions regarding exposure and risk parameter values also inflate the risks. Our Monte Carlo analysis reveals that the compounding of conservatism in current EPA guidelines results in risks that are often in the 99th percentile of the distribution of simulated risks. Thus there is less than a one percent chance that the risks are as great as the EPA estimates, even assuming that people are exposed to the hazards. If mean parameter values were used for three components of the analysis—the chemical concentration, ingestion rate, and exposure duration—we find that the percentage of sites with risks that trigger remediation based on current cleanup guidelines would drop substantially.

If the desirability of cleanup of hazardous waste sites were to be judged based on benefit-cost analysis, one obvious measure of cost-effectiveness to use at Superfund sites would be the cost per cancer case avoided. The primary focus of hazardous waste cleanups is a reduction of cancer risks. In addition, the cost per cancer case measure also affords comparability with other regulatory policies. The advent of the geographic information systems (GIS) technology enables us to match sites to detailed U.S. census data. We can then calculate the cost per case of cancer figure for Superfund sites by combining information on site location and risks with 1990 census data at the block group level. Once we combine information on individual risk levels with information on the size of populations likely to be exposed to chemical contaminants, we find that the number of expected cancer cases avoided by site remediations is relatively low at the majority of sites in our sample. Costs per cancer case averted are extremely high at most sites relative to estimates for other risk regulatory programs.

The poor performance of current remediation efforts does not imply that there is no constructive role that can be played by hazardous waste cleanups. Our analysis demonstrates that there would be large potential gains from a better targeted and more flexible Superfund program. Targeting cleanup resources based on more accurate assessments of the risks, recognizing the size of exposed populations, and basing the cleanup option chosen on the relative cost effectiveness of different cleanup remedies would greatly enhance the program's performance.

Although our work establishes that the majority of Superfund site remediations would fail a benefit-cost analysis based on health risks and costs, questions remain about why the agency's performance is so poor. The results from our analysis suggest at least five hypotheses: the costs of delegation in the principal-agent relationship between Congress and the EPA, the general focus on levels of individual cancer risk rather than the numbers of expected cancer cases in many federal risk regulation programs, the distrust of explicit calculations of the cost-effectiveness of site remediations, the potential opposition of residents surrounding Superfund sites to less costly cleanups, and the effect of alarmist public perceptions on the drafting of overly restrictive legislation. Before providing an outline of our methodology and approach, we first examine briefly how the evolution of the program may help account for the regulatory decisions we analyze at Superfund sites.

1.1 Political Economy of Superfund

The original legislation establishing the Superfund program is the Comprehensive Environmental Response, Compensation, and Recovery Act of 1980.[5] During the debate over the measure, legislators often referred to the legislation and program as "Superfund" because of the creation of a large federal fund to cleanup spills of hazardous substances and remediate hazardous sites. An impetus for this legislation was the substantial media attention devoted to highly publicized waste sites, such as Love Canal. The act became law during the waning months of the Carter administration. The definition and implementation of this national program for the cleanup of hazardous waste sites, however, was left to an EPA directed by Republican appointees who questioned the efficacy of vigorous attempts to enforce the act. Indeed, EPA administrator Anne M. Gorsuch and her colleagues developed a reputation for simply undermining the intent of environmental policies rather than implementing the programs or attempting to pursue an efficient risk-cost balancing approach. These failures took the character of obstructionist efforts and inaction rather than a more soundly based reform effort that sought to target environmental cleanup efforts in a more cost-effective manner.[6] The early years of the Superfund program were marked by a lack of clear cleanup standards, a preference for containment of waste rather than its treatment, an emphasis on the selection of the lowest cost remedies at sites, declining expenditures on agency enforcement and research and development, and mismanagement.[7]

In the first five years of the Superfund program very few hazardous waste sites were completely cleaned up. The lack of progress generated growing political support for strengthening the program.[8] The difficulty, however, was that the primary deficiency of the program rested with its implementation, whereas the principal lever manipulated by Congress was the program's legislative mandate. If the cleanup efforts were failing to deliver the promised risk reductions, the solution seemed to be a more stringent and less flexible legal directive that constrained the agency to undertake vigorous cleanups.

The Superfund Amendments and Reauthorization Act (SARA) legislation passed by Congress in 1986 was an explicit attempt by Congress to alter the pace and quality of Superfund cleanups. Reversing the EPA's revealed preference for low-cost containment remedies, the legislation stated a preference for treatment that "permanently and significantly reduces the volume, toxicity, or mobility of hazardous substances."[9] The legislation also required remedial actions at sites to comply with federal environmental standards considered to be "applicable or relevant and appropriate" requirements (ARARs) and declared that state ARARs had to be met at Superfund sites if they were stricter than federal ones, except under certain conditions where ARARs could be waived.

The language of SARA created goals for more stringent cleanups but gave the EPA discretion to implement those goals. In the years following SARA the EPA explicitly articulated these cleanup goals. The 1990 National Contingency Plan announced two criteria, overall protection of human health and the environment and the attainment (or specific waiver) of federal or state ARARs, as thresholds that every remedy would have to meet. In judging among those alternatives that passed this threshold, the EPA announced it would use criteria of long-term effectiveness and permanence, short-term effectiveness, implementability, cost-effectiveness, and reduction of toxicity, mobility, or volume. The plan also specified additional modifying criteria of the state's and community's acceptance of the remedy. Human health-related cleanup goals for noncarcinogens were established as chemical levels "to which human populations, including sensitive subgroups such as pregnant women and children, may be exposed without adverse effect during a lifetime or part of a lifetime," while for carcinogens cleanup goals were concentration levels that "represent an excess upperbound lifetime cancer risk to an individual to between 10^{-4} and 10^{-6} lifetime excess cancer risk."[10]

For the SARA amendments, the general discretion delegated to the EPA and the agency's implementation of higher levels of protection and more permanent remedies mean that it is likely that the agency chose to implement remediation policies as envisioned in the statutory bargain. As Horn and Shepsle (1989) have pointed out, however, legislative coalitions may drift even if bureaucrats stay fast on course. The EPA's implementation of its 1990 policy drew criticism from many quarters as the costs of permanence and protection became clearer. The 1994 election marked a change in the environmental ideology of the median voter and committee chairs in both the House and the Senate as Republicans gained control of both bodies. In the House, Congress members in charge of environmental committees in 1995 had League of Conservation Voters' scores of 19 percent for the 1993–94 period, compared to averages of 72 percent for 1993–94 for the Democratic representatives they replaced. The EPA's continued implementation in 1995 of the policies enunciated by the 1986 Congress guaranteed pressure for a substantive revision of the Superfund program, pressure increased by the expiration of the program's authorization in 1994 and its taxing authority in 1995.

This history of the principal-agent relationship between Congress and the agency offers one answer for why the EPA's Superfund remediation decisions may be so inefficient in terms of the cost per cancer case averted. EPA officials possess more information about site characteristics than Congress members and are able to take actions difficult for Congress to monitor. These elements of hidden action and hidden information give agents the ability to take actions different than those that principals would choose. When Congress delegated discretion in the initial design of the Superfund program, the initial Reagan appointees implementing the program chose remediations that were viewed as favorable to polluters. The 1986 SARA legislation imposed additional constraints on the agency by instructing that permanent cleanup remedies such as treatment of waste should be favored over containment and that cleanups should meet standards (ARARs) from other environmental programs. While these policies reduce the likelihood that the EPA will be able to use its delegated authority to favor polluters, they also carry a cost in terms of generating the selection of remedies with extremely high costs per cancer case averted. While one could argue that the agency currently has discretion to select less costly remedies, EPA may be reluctant to make changes in policy that could risk another reprimand by Congress for lax enforcement.

A second source of inefficiency in remediation policies is the EPA's focus on potential individual cancer risk levels generated by contamination rather than a focus on the expected number of cancer cases arising from exposure of a population to contaminant risks. For a given remediation budget, one can achieve the greatest reduction in the expected number of cancer cases averted by designing cleanups to take into account the different sizes of the populations exposed to risks across sites. Federal policies in many agencies focus on potential individual risk levels rather than actual expected population risks. A frequent stated rationale for this approach is equity concerns about groups highly vulnerable to risk, such as those who rely on well water. In willingness to pay surveys, individuals often exhibit a form of irrationality known as scope effects in their willingness to protect animals from harm; for example, they are willing to pay the same amount to protect 2,000 migratory waterfowl as for 200,000 migratory waterfowl.[11] The focus on individual risk levels in federal regulatory policies may arise from a similar scope effect in the demand for policies that involve risk reduction. Regulators may face demands to protect individuals against risk without regard to the number of individuals facing these risks. Another contributing factor is that the CERCLA legislative mandate for EPA focuses on threats to "public health or welfare," without indicating that the agency should take into account the number of individuals exposed to threats.[12] Actual biases in practice may even be more pronounced, as EPA focuses on a hypothetically exposed individual even in situations in which there may be no people actually present. Risk biases such as this "scope effect" may thus influence the formation of risk policies, a topic explored more in chapter 6.[13] Other perceptional biases may be influential as well. In examining the Superfund program's implementation, Hird (1994) relates how risk belief biases associated with "the degree of control of risk, the dread of risk, the catastrophic potential, its potential fatal consequences, and the inequitable distribution of risks" help generate support for cleanup policies despite potential inefficiencies in the program.[14]

A third hurdle to cost-effective remediations is that some officials resist the use of cost-effectiveness measures to judge the program. Problems with calculating the benefits of site remediation include the lack of data on synergistic effects among chemical contaminants, the difficulty of translating noncancer exposures into adverse outcomes and valuing these noncancer effects (e.g., monetizing the value of nerve disease averted), and the uncertainty surrounding future land uses at Superfund sites.[15] Such complexities, however, are not unique to hazardous waste cleanups. They are present in almost every risk management context. The central concern of the hazardous waste cleanup efforts remains the protection of human health. If there are in fact major health consequences of these efforts other than cancer prevention, EPA should quantify their importance or invest in research to develop more evidence on health outcomes and target policies appropriately. At present EPA does not even assess in its site cleanup decisions the total expected number of cancer cases avoided, a component that we have added in our analysis. Some environmentalists often dismiss the role of policy analysis in the environment area, arguing that it is anti-environmental protection. Yet this reaction ignores the opportunities for promoting the environment through better, more effective programs directed at those exposed to risk. The EPA could develop policies that are much more protective of both human health and the environment through a more thorough assessment of the consequences of these policies.

An additional explanation for the inefficiency of EPA remediations may lie in the distribution of benefits and costs associated with more efficient remedies. The debate over the degree that democratic institutions produce efficient results has attracted increasing academic scrutiny.[16] In the context of the Superfund program, consider how a reduction in remediation expenditures to efficient levels could have concentrated costs for residents surrounding sites which did not receive extensive cleanups and dispersed benefits for taxpayers/consumers who faced lower taxes or product prices to fund public and private cleanups. Local residents have an incentive to push for pristine cleanups, since remediation funds come from federal budgets and corporate expenditures. Politicians are naturally responsive to the political activity of those surrounding Superfund sites. Hamilton (1997) demonstrates that legislators' votes on the 1986 SARA amendments in part depended on the distribution of Superfund National Priorities List (NPL) sites in their districts. We find in chapter 6 that EPA decision makers set more stringent cleanup standards at NPL sites where residents are more politically active. When pushing for the expenditure of others' funds, residents have an incentive to push for remediations that are inefficient but result in more stringent cleanups. We find in chapter 8 that when spending their own funds in the housing market, residents surrounding Superfund sites reflect a willingness to pay to avoid risks similar to that found in value-of-life studies from labor markets.

There are thus many explanations for why the EPA's cleanup decisions have fallen short when judged by reasonable standards of performance. Our aim in this book is to analyze both the degree that remediation decisions are efficient and possible explanations for the remediation decisions chosen by agency decision makers.[17]

1.2 Outline for Analyzing Remediations

The progress of a hazardous waste site through the Superfund evaluation process generates a large amount of data. Over 36,000 sites had been reported by 1992 to the EPA as potentially of concern.[18] Using a rough index system called the Hazard Ranking System that incorporates information on contamination and potential exposure of populations the EPA had placed 1,388 sites (153 federal, 1,235 nonfederal) on the National Priorities List (NPL). Any site representing an immediate threat may qualify for removal actions. Since 1980 the EPA has conducted over 3,000 removals at both NPL and non-NPL sites at an average cost approaching $500,000 to address imminent health dangers.[19] Only sites on the NPL, however, qualify for the expenditure of federal remediation funds. Sites on the NPL progress through a process of Remedial Investigation and Feasibility studies (RI/FS), which generate detailed risk assessments and examinations of alternative remedies. This process is targeted to take 18 months at a cost of $1.1 million per site.[20] Based on risk and cost information and cleanup targets established by statute and regulation, the EPA issues a Record of Decision (ROD) detailing which remedy will be employed and what the target cleanup goals are in terms of chemical concentrations or risk levels.

Our examination of risks and costs at Superfund sites builds on the data generated by the EPA in its site decision making. The analysis focuses on the 267 nonfederal sites where RODs were signed in 1991–92, a group of sites that is representative of the full nonfederal NPL in terms of regional distribution, past site use, and the nature of contamination. Appendices A and B offer more detail on the construction of the sample and compare the sample sites to the composition of the full list of nonfederal sites on the NPL. We selected RODs from this period because the risk assessments done were generally comparable in that they were based on the 1989 U.S. EPA *Risk Assessment Guidance for Superfund.* This uniform analytic approach made meaningful comparison of risk estimates across sites feasible. We focus on nonfederal sites because cleanups at federal facilities may involve different incentives, actors, and rules than those affecting the majority of Superfund sites.

The assessment of risks at Superfund sites across the country is a decentralized process. Contractors typically perform the risk assessment at each site, and regional EPA personnel review the assessments. Although RODs are available at EPA headquarters and on line, we had to collect the more detailed information on the RI/FS from EPA regional offices. We assembled the site-level risk assessments in a human health risk database containing over 20,000 chemical-level exposure pathways at a subsample of 150 sites. Although the sample size drops from 267 to 150 sites for the risk assessment analysis, since not all sites had comparable risk assessments and resource constraints prevented data entry for all sites, the subsample of 150 sites is still representative of the full nonfederal NPL in terms of regional distribution, past site use, and the nature of contamination.

To determine population risks from exposure to groundwater and soil contamination, we used site-specific chemical concentrations and standardized exposure parameters to calculate population risks for each site. Using geographic information systems technology (GIS), we combined these risks with data on site boundaries, contaminated groundwater plume maps, and the 1990 census to estimate the expected numbers of cancers arising from site contamination over a thirty-year period. EPA does not currently consider such population statistics in the site analyses used for cleanup decisions. We also developed a separate cost database, which contains information on capital costs and operation and maintenance expenditures for over 1,700 remediation alternatives at 267 sites. Finally, at the site level we linked the costs of remediation operations selected to the expected cancer cases in order to estimate the cost per cancer case averted. Appendix B describes in detail our methodology for developing site-level estimates of risks and costs.

Concern for human health risks formed a primary basis for the development of the Superfund program. Under CERCLA, the Environmental Protection Agency has the authority to take action at hazardous waste sites "to prevent, minimize, or mitigate damage to the public health or welfare or to the environment."[21] In 1991 the EPA's Office of Solid Waste and Emergency Response further defined the role of risk assessment in remedy selection through a directive that stated in part: "Where the cumulative carcinogenic site risk to an individual based on reasonable maximum exposure for both current and future land use is less than 10^{-4}, and the noncarcinogenic hazard quotient is less than one, action generally is not warranted unless there are adverse environmental impacts."[22] The directive also stated that remedial actions could be taken at sites with risks between 10^{-4} and 10^{-6} if they were justified and that once a remediation was undertaken the cleanup goal would be in the 10^{-4} to 10^{-6} range. We refer to the range of risks between 10^{-4} and 10^{-6} as the discretionary zone because of the flexibility EPA has in choosing whether to remediate. Note that in order to change remediation policies at Superfund sites, one would need to address both the risk-based cutoffs that may trigger cleanups and the state and federal environmental standards imported into Superfund from other regulatory programs through ARARs.

For each site, EPA and its contractors detail the assumptions made by the EPA about chemical concentrations and exposure factors. Cancer risks are expressed in terms of lifetime excess cancer risks and noncancer risks from a chemical are expressed in terms of a hazard quotient, which equals the calculated exposure intake of the chemical divided by its reference dose (an estimate of the level of exposure likely to be without appreciable risk of harmful noncarcinogenic effects). Risk assessors at each site have discretion in deciding which pathways of individual risks to estimate. A given risk pathway at a site is defined by a number of assumptions, including time scenario of exposure (e.g., does the pathway involve a current or future land use), exposed population (residents? workers?), exposed age group (adult or child?), population location (on-site or off-site?), medium location (on-site or off-site?), exposure medium (soil or groundwater?), and exposure route (dermal? ingestion?). From the EPA approved baseline risk assessments, we collected data on chemical-level risk pathways at 150 sites. We then aggregated these chemical-level risks by population type to determine a cumulative risk to each population (e.g., all risk pathways for different chemicals and different exposure media that on-site adult residents encountered were aggregated to form a cumulative individual cancer risk for a person in this population group). The data from these risk assessments form the basis for our analysis of individual risks, expected cancer cases, and the cost-effectiveness of site remediations.

In chapter 2 we examine the individual cancer and noncancer risks as calculated according to the EPA's risk assessment methodology at 150 sites. We first examine risks at the exposure pathway level and then proceed to focus on the aggregate risks to an individual at the site level. Pathways that involve changes in current land uses (e.g., residential development on a currently barren site) or changes in current exposure pathways (e.g., the contamination of well water from future migration of a groundwater plume) are referred to as future scenarios. Of the total risk assessment pathways analyzed at these sites, 72 percent dealt with future risk. Nearly half of the pathways presented in the documents involved exposure by future residents living on-site in contaminated areas that generally do not have current on-site residential developments. Future risks played an even larger role in the maximum risk pathways calculated at the sample sites, accounting for 88 percent of the maximum cancer pathway risks and 89 percent of the maximum noncancer risk pathways estimated. What is surprising about the dominant role of future risks is that it stems largely from EPA's assumptions that in the future individuals will gravitate to live directly on hazardous waste sites. People would be making such decisions after these sites have been designated as sufficiently risky to be on the National Priorities List, whereas many current on-site residents presumably moved there before such a listing. Residents often view Superfund sites with alarm and may wish to flee housing areas in which there are publicized hazardous waste sites. To assume that people will be drawn to live on hazardous waste sites is contrary to this behavior. Moreover EPA can discourage such behavior through limited policy options, such as encouraging zoning restrictions that prevent such development.

Once we aggregate the pathway risks that an individual at a site may experience, it becomes clear that the calculated risk levels used in EPA decision making at Superfund sites are very large. Anecdotal discussions of the program often downplay the risks to human health, but the maximum individual lifetime excess cancer risks as calculated by the agency at these sites are extremely high relative to risks addressed under other federal regulatory programs.[23] The mean maximum cumulative lifetime risk for the 150 sites is 0.070 and the median is 0.0025. At over 85 percent of the sites, the maximum individual lifetime excess cancer risk is greater than or equal to 0.0001. Of these maximum site risks, most involve on-site populations. The calculation of large on-site risks does not mean that the populations are currently on-site or likely to ever be on-site. In fact survey data indicate that there are on-site residents at only 18 of these 150 sites.[24] The on-site risks rather are an indication that risk assessors have assumed that populations will reside or come onto the site.

This site-level analysis emphasizes how assumptions about future land use play a key role in estimating risks in the Superfund program. Of the 133 maximum site cumulative risks that involve future pathways, 130 are hypothetical because they would require a change in land use to be realized and 3 are hypothetical because they would involve a change in exposure pathways. Note that overall future on-site residents account for 60 percent of the number of cumulative maximum risks. Future risks are also estimated to be higher than current risks (the median of the maximum cumulative risks that are current is 0.00051 versus 0.0026 for the median maximum risks that are future risks). EPA's methodology in no way incorporates a probability that a future land use will occur; for example, future risks are not multiplied further by an estimate that the land use will change through the construction of residential developments in currently industrial areas.

One reason that estimated individual cancer risks are high at Superfund sites is that EPA guidance documents encourage conservative estimates of risk. The stated objective of doing so is to be protective of human health. The practical effect of using such upper-bound values for the risk is that estimated risks greatly exceed mean risks, and policy priorities may be distorted. If the policy objective is to prevent the largest expected number of cases of cancer with a given cleanup budget, then the policy guide should be the mean risk assessment and not the upper bound value of the risk. Use of conservative risk assessments also creates the potential for policy distortions by focusing attention on the risks that are least well understood as opposed to the risks that are most consequential.[25] In addition, to the extent that the degree of the conservatism bias varies across policies, it would be difficult for policy makers to make comparisons across different policy options because the degree of conservatism incorporated in the risk assessments may differ. Nevertheless, it should be noted that EPA is not an outlier in terms of using upper-bound values for risk, as this practice is quite prevalent throughout the U.S. federal government.

EPA's guidance to risk assessors at Superfund sites states, "For Superfund exposure assessments, intake variable values for a given pathway should be selected so that the combination of all intake variables results in an estimate of the reasonable maximum exposure for that pathway. As defined previously, the reasonable maximum exposure (RME) is the maximum exposure that is reasonably expected to occur at a site. Under this approach, some intake variables may not be at their individual maximum values but when in combination with other variables will result in estimates of the RME."[26] Estimating lifetime excess cancer risks involves assumptions about the values of numerous variables, including the duration of exposure, the frequency with which an individual is exposed, ingestion rates for water and soil, body weight, contaminant concentration, and chemical toxicity. The EPA default values for exposure factors include some that are mean estimates (body weight) and some parameter values that are upper bounds (e.g., exposure duration). For the concentration of the chemical at the site, the EPA guidance directs that the 95th upper confidence limit on the estimate of the mean concentration at the site or the maximum detected concentration be used, whichever is lower. Overall, there is no quantitative definition of what percentile of estimated risk the "reasonable maximum exposure" is said to represent at a Superfund site.

In chapter 3 we explore how sensitive EPA estimates of individual lifetime excess cancer risks are to variations in these assumptions. We focus first on the distribution of the maximum cumulative risk to adult residential populations from ingestion of soil or groundwater at the sites in our sample. We explored these pathways because groundwater and soil ingestion pathways account for 40 percent of the total risk pathways in the sample, are often the pathways of highest risk, and are easily modeled. The maximum pathways often are the focus of discussions surrounding remedy selection.

For 67 maximum risk pathways from soil or groundwater ingestion at sites where remediation had been chosen, the documents presented mean chemical concentrations along with the reasonable maximum exposure concentration used by the EPA. In analysis using the EPA's conservative default values for ingestion rate, exposure duration, and chemical concentration, 94 percent of the maximum pathways were greater than or equal to 10^{-4} and 5 percent were in the discretionary zone of 10^{-4} to

10^{-6}. If mean values are used for ingestion rate, exposure duration, and chemical concentration, however, then the distribution of pathways shifts to 54 percent in the range requiring remediation, 43 percent in the discretionary zone, and 3 percent in the range less than 10^{-6}. Thus under current remediation decision rules, the number of sites requiring cleanup if remediation were based on cancer risks would fall dramatically if mean values replaced conservative estimates in risk assessments.

In part because the current EPA methodology mixes a range of assumptions in its current estimate of risk parameters used at Superfund sites, it would be difficult for an EPA decision maker to determine what percentile on the distribution of estimated risks the "reasonable maximum exposure" scenario is for any particular site. Monte Carlo analysis, however, allows us to explore in chapter 3 the compounding effects of the individual assumptions made about exposure parameters and chemical concentrations at hazardous waste sites. For a subset of 86 sites in our sample, we were able to use Monte Carlo analysis at each site to generate a distribution for the maximum soil or groundwater ingestion pathway. For approximately two-thirds of the groundwater or soil ingestion risks calculated in these sites, the risk estimated using the EPA's reasonable maximum exposure scenario was in the 99th percentile of those risk distributions estimated through Monte Carlo simulations based on varying contaminant concentrations, body weight, exposure duration, and ingestion rate.

Analysis of the risk assessments at Superfund sites in chapters 2 and 3 thus reveals that individual cancer risks calculated in the site documents are high, although many of these risks are hypothetical risks based on changes in future land use. The levels of risk drop substantially if one shifts to mean values for risk assessment parameters. Monte Carlo analysis at sites also indicates there is a high degree of conservatism inherent in current Superfund policies. Reactions to the level of conservatism adopted in the risk assessment guidance will depend on the desired levels of protection and costs of remediation. At a minimum this analysis indicates that sensitivity analysis and Monte Carlo simulations should be conducted at sites to demonstrate the range of estimated risks that could arise at a site.

The EPA calculates individual lifetime excess cancer risks arising at hazardous waste sites for a hypothetically exposed individual. The agency does not go on to determine whether people are exposed, nor does it assess expected cancer cases averted through site cleanups. The size of the exposed population does not explicitly appear in EPA's analysis of site remediation alternatives.[27] In chapter 4 we develop a methodology to estimate the expected number of cancer cases that arise from site contamination by combining data on site chemical concentrations, contaminant dilution factors, plume sizes for groundwater contamination, and likely exposed populations. We use geographic information systems (GIS) technology and census data at the block group level to relate risk levels to exposed populations. For each site in our 150-site sample we estimated the cancer risks arising over a thirty-year time period from a consistent set of residential exposure pathways—soil and groundwater ingestion, inhalation, and dermal exposure pathways.

Using EPA's conservative parameter assumptions and ignoring disease latency periods, we estimate that there will be 731 cases over thirty years arising from contamination at these 150 sites. The vast majority of these cancer cases arise from soil exposure (695) rather than groundwater exposure (36). Nearly 90 percent of the total cancer cases are estimated to occur at one site, the Westinghouse Electric site in California (which had 652 expected cancer cases). The dominance of this single site highlights the importance of EPA's conservative exposure assumptions and the overstatement of the estimated cancer risks that occur using EPA risk data. Most of the hazardous waste area at this site is on land that has been paved over and is now an industrial parking lot, so the estimated individual cancer risks are unlikely to arise. This concentration of estimated cancers at one site means that the median number of cancer cases per site (0.017) may be more indicative of the population risks overall than the average number of cancer cases. We find that at the majority of sites the expected number of cancer cases averted is less than 0.1 cases per site based on conservative risk parameter estimates. Only ten sites had one or more expected cancer cases estimated to arise over thirty years from exposures to contaminated groundwater and soil. We use sensitivity analysis to demonstrate how robust the estimates of cancer cases are. If average exposure factors and concentrations are used, a ten-year cancer latency period is assumed, and a 3 percent discount rate is used, the discounted number of cancer cases drops by two-thirds.

In chapter 5 we combine our estimates of expected cancer cases averted by remediation with cleanup costs to derive estimates of cost-effectiveness. We estimate that for the 267 nonfederal sites in our sample, cleanup costs average $26 million (1993$). Overall expenditures are highly concentrated at a small percentage of the sites. The top 20 percent of sites in terms of costs accounted for 47 percent of all estimated cleanup expenditures, while the bottom 40 percent of sites totaled only 14 percent of these remediation costs. The magnitude and concentration of costs reinforce the importance of conducting site-level marginal analysis to determine the cost-effectiveness of Superfund expenditures.

Overall, at the 150 sites for which there are both risk and cost information, $2.2 billion in current and planned remediation actions are slated to be expended to avert an estimated 731 cancer cases, based on EPA cancer risk estimates and not accounting for cancer latency periods. Consequently the mean cost per cancer case averted is $3.0 million at these sites. Yet the concentration of risks and costs makes this mean figure potentially misleading. The median cost per cancer case averted is $388 million, without factoring in likely cost growth at sites. The costs per cancer case averted ranges widely from less than $20,000 to over $1 billion. Estimates using more realistic risk assumptions are even higher. Overall, 101 out of the 145 sites with costs per cancer case had costs per cancer case averted above $100 million—an amount well in excess of a sensible risk–cost trade-off. At 5 sites a cost per cancer cases averted could not be calculated either because there were no estimated cancer cases at the sites or no costs directly linked to averting cancer risks. If one factors in estimated cost growth at sites, the median cost per cancer case averted shifts to $700 million for the sites with a finite trade-off. If one assumes average concentrations rather than upper bounds and incorporates a cancer latency period as well as cost growth, the median cost per cancer case averted at the 96 sites with mean concentrations available is over $7 billion. Under these assumptions 87 out of the 96 sites with mean concentration data available would have costs per cancer case averted above $100 million.

What accounts for the high cost per cancer case averted? Part of the answer lies in the analysis of the stated basis for cleanup standards in the sites we analyzed. Examining the chemical concentration and risk levels stated as remediation objectives, we find that the requirement that site remedies meet "applicable or relevant and appropriate" requirements in other federal environmental programs (or state programs, if stricter) has a significant impact. Cleanup standards from other state and federal regulatory programs regularly affect decisions in the Superfund program. These standards address multiple objectives, including environmental protection as well as protection of human populations from cancer and noncancer risks. The individual cancer risks associated with these standards, however, indicate that state and federal regulatory requirements from programs outside of Superfund result in residual chemical concentrations much lower than those that would result if remediations were chosen solely on the basis of cancer risk analysis. While attention in the program's reauthorization debate has focused scrutiny on what level of individual risks are appropriate remediation goals, these results also suggest the importance of examining the strict remediation goals established by state and federal standards derived from regulatory programs outside of Superfund.

While chapters 2 through 5 view the Superfund program in terms of social welfare analysis, in chapter 6 we use our site-level data to examine the political economy of Superfund decision making. This chapter examines some of the origins of the agency's disappointing record of policy performance. We begin by indicating how the cleanup decisions made by regulators, such as the stringency of cleanup standards and the cost per cancer case averted, may vary depending on risk biases exhibited by regulators and political concerns about who bears what magnitudes of risk. Risk regulators may reflect "biases" in their decisions both because they may be subject to perception biases and because they may represent constituents whose perceptions are biased. Agency officials may also be responsive to political variables in their decision making, including the identity of the parties exposed to risk, the level of interest group scrutiny, the nature of congressional representation of affected constituents, and the degree of political activity by potentially exposed individuals.

In chapter 6 we test the degree to which Superfund cleanup decisions are driven by efficiency concerns, risk biases, and political factors by examining site-level data on two decisions central to the "how clean is clean" debate. For a sample of 130 sites with detailed remediation data available, we examine the selection of chemical cleanup targets and the expenditure of remediation funds at these contaminated sites. Though earlier chapters focused on the written guidelines for regulators, here we examine their actual risk management choices as embodied in cleanup decisions. We find that the target risk levels chosen by regulators are largely a function of political variables, such as voting rates, and risk perception variables. Communities with higher voter turnouts (a proxy for the likelihood of collective action) are more likely to have lower final risks remaining at sites and to receive more cleanup dollars spent to avert a case of cancer. Political factors have the most influence on the most inefficient cleanup decisions at sites. The impact of risk biases are also evident. Cleanup target selection reflects biases from the individual risk perception literature, such as the availability effect (e.g., more highly publicized chemicals that create high risks receive more stringent targets) and the anchoring phenomenon (e.g., regulators tolerate a higher cleanup target risk when the baseline risk is greater). In choosing remediation levels, regulators generally do not distinguish between current risks to actual residents and potential risks to hypothetically exposed populations. One response to the results in chapter 2 on the prevalence of future risk scenarios in site assessments could be that regulators might not treat current risks and hypothetical risks the same when making decisions. In terms of setting remediation goals, however, our results indicate that regulators generally treat current and hypothetical risks similarly in setting the goals for cleanups at Superfund sites.

Chapter 7 focuses more closely on variations in risk exposure and management by examining the degree that different demographic groups bear Superfund risks, a frequent topic in debates over environmental equity. Previous researchers have focused on potential exposures to hazardous waste sites by looking at the county, zip code, or census tract demographics of areas containing hazardous waste sites. In this chapter we use geographic information systems technology to derive multiple, more refined measures of exposure to Superfund risks. We stress that debates about environmental equity should focus on at least three indicators: general exposure as measured by proximity to sites, specific estimates of individual and population risk levels as derived from formal risk assessment models, and indicators of how both individuals exposed to risk and regulators respond. The exposure analysis focuses on the 1,173 nonfederal and federal Superfund sites that we were able to link up with detailed census data at the block-group level so that we could determine the characteristics of populations such as those living within a one-mile ring around a site. Our examination of EPA responses to risks draws on broad measures of regulatory activity at all nonfederal NPL sites and more detailed measures of EPA decisions we constructed at our sample of 150 sites with risk and cost information.

Reasoning from a single measure of exposure, one might conclude that there is no "environmental equity" problem in the Superfund program since the average percentage of white residents in the areas surrounding Superfund sites (85.6 percent) is actually higher than that of the U.S. population as a whole (80.3 percent). Superfund sites often are located in industrial areas where the residents are frequently white, blue-collar workers. Alternative risk indicators suggest there may, however, be a disproportionate minority exposure. Relative to the composition of the U.S. population as a whole, minorities constitute a higher percentage of the populations living within one mile of Superfund sites, a larger fraction at sites with current residential use, and a larger percentage of the expected cancer cases arising from these sites (although this last result depends on a few extremely hazardous sites located in areas with large minority populations).

The results also indicate that the term "environmental equity" may be misleading. Actions by the government as well as by private industry affect exposures to risk. If regulators respond to environmental risks differently depending on the nature of the community exposed, the differential treatment may give rise to inefficiencies, not just "inequities." Indeed it is the inefficiencies in policy choice with inequitable consequences that we believe are often the most objectionable inequities. The readily observed indicators of site treatment do not reveal much difference in the pace of cleanup in communities based on the racial composition of those exposed to the risks. Regulators do treat sites differently in terms of the cleanup remedies selected and the cost expended per cancer case averted based on the nature of the community exposed. As the minority percentage in the one-mile ring around a site increased, EPA regulators spent less per cancer case averted, were more likely to choose the cheapest alternative in dealing with soil contamination, and were less likely to invoke the more stringent cleanup standards provided by state environmental laws.

The question of how the distribution of risks varies by demographic group has attracted increasing academic and government attention.[28] Our results indicate that research on environmental equity should employ multiple measures of environmental outcomes to explore how risks vary with race, income, and education. Specifically, researchers should examine indicators of potential exposure, actual risks, and both private and government responses to these risks. Different definitions of minority populations are useful, since patterns of exposure may vary across different regions for groups such as blacks, Asians, Hispanics, and native Americans. Population weights for the analysis are also essential, since sites vary widely in population density. By examining different samples (e.g., quarter-mile ring, one-mile ring) to estimate potential exposures and different reference groups (e.g., county, state, U.S.), it is possible to compare relevant exposures. Ring patterns and the change in community characteristics as distance from site increases are especially helpful indicators in analyzing predictions generated by theories of environmental externalities. The increasing accessibility of geographic information systems technology and census data make it feasible to estimate the actual risks to which different demographic groups are exposed.

The results from chapters 5 through 7 indicate that the operation of the political marketplace results in highly inefficient remediation decisions. At most Superfund sites examined, the cost per cancer case averted exceeds $100 million even if one uses EPA's conservative assumptions that generate higher expected cancers and lower remediation costs. The greater the potential for political activity among site residents, the more stringent the cleanup standard chosen and the higher the expenditures per cancer case at the most inefficient sites. Note that residents might press for expensive remediations for at least two reasons. Their perceptions of risk might be much higher than those generated by formal risk assessment models, so they push for more stringent controls. When the benefits of remediation are concentrated among site residents and the costs are dispersed broadly across taxpayers and consumers, residents may prefer extremely inefficient though stringent remediations, since they do not bear appreciable costs from the site remediation expenditures.[29]

Chapter 8 indicates that when residents spend their own money to avoid Superfund risks, their trade-offs suggest that they assess risks accurately and spend to avoid Superfund risks in a manner predicted by private decisions to deal with risks in other markets. Chapter 8 examines housing market reactions to site risks by using evidence from the sale of 17,000 houses surrounding seven Superfund sites in the Greater Grand Rapids, Michigan, area from 1988 through 1993. By using information on housing prices, we are able to explore how the residents around Superfund sites respond to risks from hazardous waste. Using the EPA's risk information, we estimate through hedonic models the implicit value people place on risk reduction through the effect of risk on housing values.

Before residents receive the risk information provided by the EPA's Remedial Investigation study, their estimated value of a statistical cancer case is much higher than the value-of-life estimates found in job market studies, though still below EPA's cleanup cost per cancer case. This result is consistent with broader evidence on risk perception biases that demonstrates people tend to overestimate highly publicized low probability events.[30] After the release of the EPA's risk study, residents appear to update their risk perceptions. The postinformation release estimates of values of a statistical case of cancer implied by housing prices around sites range from $3.9 million to $4.6 million, which are very similar to value-of-life estimates found in job market studies.[31] The similarity between the risk–money trade-off for hazardous waste risks and the trade-offs for job risks suggests that there is no evidence that consumers are overreacting to Superfund site risks in their private decisions once EPA releases site risk information. Even before the release of the EPA data, the implied risk–money trade-off in housing prices is several orders of magnitude lower than the expenditures per case of cancer averted calculated in chapter 5. This discrepancy suggests that residents may successfully pressure regulators in the political marketplace to spend much more to avert human health risks than they are willing to spend in their private marketplace interactions, consistent with the fact that residents bear few costs from inefficient remediations.

Frustrations with inefficiencies and inequities across risk management programs have given rise to legislative proposals to reform risk analysis and decision-making. These risk reform efforts, however, are often viewed as a surreptitious way to achieve reductions in environmental protection. In chapter 9 we explore how proposed risk reform measures would affect the implementation of hazardous waste cleanups. For our sample of 150 sites, we compare cleanup decisions made under current decisions rules, decision rules where remediations are triggered by individual risks of 1 in 10,000 or higher, and a regime with this risk cutoff and the proviso that estimated risks do not include figures for future on-site residents. We find that a focus on current risks in remediation decisions rather than more speculative future risks would substantially reduce the number of sites remediated and reduce cleanup expenditures dramatically. EPA would still prevent the vast majority of cancer cases and noncancer effects even if risk reforms were implemented. We find that currently 95 percent of the expenditures at Superfund sites are devoted to eliminating only 0.5 percent of the cancer risks. We also find that sites with cleanups that pass a benefit–cost test have a higher mean minority percentage. Adoption of efficiency-based reforms will foster environmental equity and address what we believe is perhaps the most socially undesirable type of inequity—the failure to adopt efficient risk policies that benefit the disadvantaged.

Our analysis across these nine chapters indicates that the current policy approach used in the Superfund program is often convoluted. EPA devotes substantial effort to identifying chemicals at a site and ascertaining their potential risks. It also assesses the costs of a range of remedies in considerable detail. However, many key elements are missing in the agency's analyses. There is no explicit consideration of the size of the population at risk. Risks to a single individual often have the same weight as risks to a large population. Actual and hypothetical exposures to chemicals receive equal weight so that risks to a person who, in the future, may voluntarily choose to live near a currently uninhabited Superfund site receive the same weight as risks to large populations that currently may be involuntarily exposed. EPA reports conservative risk assessment values for each site, without focusing its policy attention on the expected risk level or most likely risk scenarios. Finally explicit trade-offs that balance benefits and costs do not enter remediation decisions. These problems arise in part because of decision-making constraints in the Superfund legislation and in part because of the manner in which regulators have implemented the program.

Sound reforms of risk assessment and risk management for the Superfund program would lead EPA to assess population risks, rather than just individual risks, from contamination at sites. The agency would present central tendency estimates and show the range of risks involved at sites. More flexible remedy decisions based on risk levels would reduce the costs associated with cleanup goals based on standards from other environmental programs and costs based on the preference enunciated in SARA for permanent remedies. Our analysis shows that there is a wide zone in which these reforms can improve efficiency without sacrificing human health considerations. The shift toward site cleanups based on risk levels alone—rather than on ARARs and calculations that include on-site future residents—would in our sample reduce the number of sites remediated from 145 to 86 and site expenditures from $2.2 billion to $1.6 billion. Yet this policy change would reduce the number of cancer cases averted by only 21 (from 731 to 710) and the number of individuals living within one mile of sites protected from noncancer exposures by 16,000 (from 113,000 to 97,000). Even those estimates of the low health gains sacrificed may be too high given the conservative character of the underlying risk estimates. Our analysis further indicates that calculation of risks based on central tendency would shift a substantial fraction of sites into the cleanup discretionary zone, where EPA site managers currently have the authority to decide whether or not to remediate a site. Removal of preference for permanence would also allow managers to consider more cost-effective alternatives, such as institutional controls.

Reform of the Superfund program ultimately rests on more than the results of policy analysis. Political questions such as to what degree the Congress will delegate decision making to the EPA, the magnitude of political influences on site-level decisions, the impact of agency decisions on different demographic groups, and the effects of overarching decisions about regulatory procedures will all influence the debate over Superfund policy. To the degree that concerns for social welfare play a role in the reform of hazardous waste policy, our analysis provides three clear policy lessons: the need for the EPA to assess risks more accurately, the importance of calculating the magnitude of populations exposed to risks, and the value of considering the cost-effectiveness of environmental expenditures. Our analysis underscores that there is wide latitude for reforms to reduce expenditures on Superfund remediation with minimal reductions in the protection of human health. Moreover, during the intervening period before all cleanups are completed, our targeted approach to policy design will be more protective than the current strategy that does not focus on exposed populations.

2

Measuring Individual Risks

A major impetus for the Superfund program was the public's fear of cancer risks from hazardous chemical wastes. The pictures of Love Canal on the evening news helped to develop popular images of dangerous chemicals seeping from the ground and threatening public health. The risks posed by exposure to contaminants from hazardous waste sites generated alarm among residents, stimulating Congress to draft cleanup legislation and regulators to design site remediation procedures that imposed costs on potentially responsible parties. The ultimate justification for any cleanup action hinges on whether chemical hazards are present, whether people are exposed to the risk, and the number of people exposed. This chapter examines the first two of these issues, which we will subsequently refine by analyzing biases in risk assessment procedures and the size of the exposed populations. The EPA currently requires a risk assessment as part of the process of analyzing remediation options at sites on the National Priorities List (NPL), the set of sites that EPA has designated as being eligible for remediation funds. A substantial amount of information exists in the administrative record for each NPL site on the quantitative assessment of cancer and noncancer risks for different populations potentially affected by chemicals from the site.[1] In this chapter we systematically explore questions about human health risks at Superfund sites using site-level data based in part on these analyses. Which population groups are most affected? How do these risks arise? What is the magnitude of the risks that are present? Are there serious threats to public health? Or are the risks in fact trivial, as in the case of sites that are only dangerous to hypothetical children who might eat large quantities of contaminated dirt?[2]

The character of the risks is in many respects quite surprising. Although risks to current residents have played a pivotal role in generating political support for the Superfund program, in most cases hazardous wastes do not pose an actual threat to existing populations. The overwhelming preponderance of the risks analyzed in EPA risk assessments is to hypothetical future populations for land uses that represent departures from current behavior. The character of this result will run throughout our entire study. We first analyze data from risk assessments at 150 NPL sites at the risk pathway level, where pathways are defined by exposure estimates of cancer or noncancer risks to specific population groups at particular times. This analysis considers 3,049 cancer and 944 noncancer pathways at these sites. We then focus on an analysis of the maximum cumulative risks estimated to arise at each site. Since these maximum cumulative risks may drive policy choices at some sites, we explore how remediation decisions might vary depending on the estimation of maximum risks.

2.1 Risk Assessments at Superfund Sites

Congress passed the Comprehensive Environmental Response, Compensation, and Liability Act (CERCLA) in 1980, amid a debate that focused on the potential health hazards posed by leaking chemicals at sites such as Love Canal. Section 104(a) of this act, which created the Superfund program, directed EPA to respond to hazardous waste sites that pose "a substantial endangerment to public health, welfare, and the environment." In the Superfund Amendments and Reauthorization Act (SARA) passed in 1986, Congress stated that remedial actions were preferable if they employed treatment methods that permanently and significantly reduced the volume, toxicity, or mobility of hazardous substances at sites. The law also required that Superfund remedial actions comply with federal standards considered to be "applicable or relevant and appropriate requirements" (ARARs) and that state ARARs be met at Superfund sites if they are stricter than federal ones.

The regulations implementing the Superfund law, called the National Contingency Plan, require that a site-specific baseline risk assessment be conducted to "characterize the current and potential threats to human health and the environment that may be posed by contaminants migrating to ground water or surface water, releasing to air, leaching through soil, remaining in the soil, and bioaccumulating in the food chain."[3] It would be financially infeasible to clean up all hazardous waste sites. As a result EPA did establish a risk-level floor that had to be met to warrant action. In a directive published in April 1991 on the role of the baseline risk assessment in the Superfund remedy selection, EPA's Office of Solid Waste and Emergency Response stated that "where the cumulative carcinogenic site risk to an individual based on reasonable maximum exposure for both current and future land use is less than 10^{-4}, and the non-carcinogenic hazard quotient is less than 1, action generally is not warranted unless there are adverse environmental impacts."[4] Regional EPA decision makers

Action Warranted
Cumulative Lifetime Excess Cancer Risk Exceeds 10e-4

Action Discretionary Cumulative Lifetime Excess Cancer Risk 10e-4 to 10e-6 or Noncarcinogenic Hazard Quotient above 1

Action Not Warranted Cumulative Lifetime Excess Cancer Risk Below 10e-6 or Noncarcinogenic Hazard Quotient below 1

Figure 2.1
Cleanup policies and risk levels

may choose to take action at sites with cancer risks smaller than 10^{-4}, but Records of Decision (RODs) with remedial actions at sites with risks "within the 10^{-4} and 10^{-6} risk range must explain why remedial action is warranted." The directive also declared that the "EPA uses the general 10^{-4} to 10^{-6} risk range as a 'target range' within which the Agency strives to manage risks as part of a Superfund cleanup." This means that once a remediation decision has been made, EPA prefers cleanups that achieve a risk closer to the more protective end of the range (e.g., 10^{-6}). Figure 2.1 summarizes the risk-based cleanup policy.

The assessment of these human health risks at Superfund sites across the country is a decentralized process. Contractors typically perform the risk assessment at each site, and EPA personnel review the studies. Recent risk assessments across sites are comparable for our analysis because they are generally conducted according to methodologies outlined in EPA's 1989 *Risk Assessment Guidance for Superfund, Volume I: Human Health Evaluation Manual (Part A)*, or RAGS. According to the RAGS, the baseline risk assessment conducted at each site has four objectives:

1. Analyze the risks that might exist if no remedial actions or institutional controls were adopted at a site (i.e., the "baseline risks") and help determine if actions are required at a site.

2. Provide information to help determine the maximum levels of chemicals that may remain on site, in order to protect public health.

3. Compare potential health impacts of remedial actions.

4. Evaluate and document public health threats at sites.[5]

The baseline risk assessment is part of the site characterization process in the Remedial Investigation/Feasibility study (RI/FS). The RI/FS provides regional EPA decision makers with a quantitative assessment of human health risks at a site, a description of remedial action objectives, and an analysis of the alternatives proposed to reach these objectives. The ROD for each site discusses the reasoning behind the eventual course of action selected by EPA.

The baseline risk assessment begins with the collection of site data, including samples taken to determine chemical concentrations at the site and to identify the potential chemicals of concern. For the exposure assessment, the risk assessor analyzes the contaminant data from the site, identifies exposed populations, determines potential exposure pathways, and estimates exposure concentrations and intakes by pathway. During the toxicity assessment, the next step, the analyst collects qualitative and quantitative information on the toxicity of the chemicals at the site, often using information from EPA's Integrated Risk Information System (IRIS). Finally, risk characterization models combine the information on exposure and toxicity to estimate cancer risks and relative noncancer hazards for the chemicals and exposure pathways at the sites. The analysis in this chapter takes these risk assessments at face value and does not explore alternative risk assessment assumptions, a topic we explore in chapter 3.

The assessed cancer risk from a chemical is the incremental individual lifetime cancer risk from exposure to a substance from the site. Chemical cancer risks within a given exposure pathway are often aggregated to yield a pathway cancer risk, which would represent the incremental individual lifetime cancer risk for exposure to a set of chemicals via a given exposure scenario. EPA summarizes the noncancer risk of a chemical in terms of the noncancer hazard quotient, which equals the exposure level or intake of the chemical divided by its reference dose. The reference dose is an estimate of the exposure level that is likely to be without appreciable risks of harmful effects over a lifetime and is based on studies identifying the highest "no-observed-adverse-effect level" (NOAEL) or the "lowest-observed adverse-effect level" (LOAEL). Hazard quotients for different chemicals are not comparable, since the health effects involved and the associated risk probabilities differ. Nevertheless, EPA sums the risk assessments for multiple chemicals within an exposure pathway to yield a pathway hazard index, which is meant to be a measure of noncancer risks associated with the pathway.

The data from the baseline risk assessments are designed in part to be used during the RI/FS process to establish remedial action objectives at the site. EPA bases its action decisions not only on the risk criteria in figure 2.1 but also on how these risks interact with other legislative guidelines, known as applicable or relevant and appropriate requirements (ARARs). Remedial actions must meet the ARARs of the Resource Conservation and Recovery Act (RCRA), Clean Water Act (CWA), Safe Drinking Water Act (SDWA), Clean Air Act (CAA), other federal statutes, and state environmental laws. ARARs generally fall into three categories:

1. Ambient or chemical-specific requirements that are generally health-based or risk-based numbers that translate into the amount or concentration of a chemical that may remain on site.

2. Performance or design requirements that limit the technologies or actions involving hazardous wastes at the site.

3. Location-specific requirements that place restrictions on the concentration of hazardous substances at a site because of its location.[6]

The remedial action objectives established are generally in terms of concentrations of particular chemicals that may remain after the remedial action is conducted. It is noteworthy that even though a lifetime incremental cancer risk of 10^{-6} is the floor at which remediation becomes potentially desirable, postcleanup risk levels are often much more ambitious.

2.2 Defining Risk Assessment Pathways

A key decision involved in conducting the baseline risk assessments is determining what pathways to evaluate to derive quantitative estimates of cancer and noncancer risks. Our database defines the pathways in risk assessments by a number of different category variables: time scenario of exposure, exposed population, age group, location of population, location of medium, exposure medium, and exposure route.

The time scenario variable refers generally to whether land use envisioned in the risk assessment corresponds to the current use or is related to a projected use in the future. The risk assessor determines current land use using site inspection data, zoning information, census data, and aerial photographs. Our designation of a pathway as a current or future scenario is determined by whether the risk assessment defined the pathway as current or future. What EPA means by "current" and "future" is a critical distinction. EPA's terminology differs somewhat from the normal usage of those terms. Current risks pertain to risks arising now or possibly in the future given current land use patterns. A subcategory of current risks consists of "current potential scenarios." In these scenarios the land use in an area does not change, but other things may change to give rise to a risk, such as a change in the size of a groundwater contamination plume so that wells not currently contaminated are assumed to become contaminated. Because such hazards do not pose current threats, we treat these "current potential" risks as future risks in the analysis in this chapter.[7]

EPA designates as future risks those hazards generally associated with changes in land use or site activities. The guidance provided by the RAGS encourages risk assessors to consider a scenario where land that is currently not residential is brought into residential use in the future. The guidance document states:

Because residential land use is most often associated with the greatest exposures, it is generally the most conservative choice to make when deciding what type of alternative land use may occur in the future. Assume future residential land use if it seems possible based on the evaluation of the available information.[8]

Thus the analysts may estimate future residential risks at sites that are currently undeveloped or industrial even though the sites may have a low probability of future residential use.

Exposed populations for which pathways are estimated include residents, workers, recreational users such as swimmers or hunters, and trespassers. Though risk assessments often pertain to specific age group designations for the particular pathway described, we have (for this analysis) generally collapsed the age groupings into adult (ages 18 and higher) and child (ages less than 18).[9] The risk assessment category for the location of population generally refers to where the particular population is exposed to the contaminant (for residents, location of population refers to where they live). Location of medium refers to whether the contaminant for which the pathway is estimated is on-site or off-site. Exposure medium describes in what medium the individual is exposed to the contaminant (e.g., air, groundwater, soil, or biota—the plants or animals containing chemicals and later consumed by humans through the food chain). Exposure route details how a person comes into contact with the chemical. For example, soil contaminants may enter the body through ingestion, through dermal contact, or through inhalation of contaminants.

In our analysis, we break down the description of cancer and noncancer pathways by risk assessment categories. Determining the relative magnitudes of current versus future risks is important in distinguishing how estimates of human health risks at Superfund sites are affected by assumptions about future land use. Designating whether risks involve residents, workers, recreational users, or trespassers is a necessary step in analyzing the efficacy of different policy options for reducing human health risks. Similarly, analyzing whether the populations exposed are on-site or off-site and whether the contaminants are on-site or off-site are a necessary part of evaluating the impact of remedies at Superfund sites. We also analyze the contribution of specific chemicals to the risks posed. Since uncertainty may exist over the toxicity of particular chemicals, consideration of the relative frequency of these chemicals at sites and their estimated contribution to pathway risks may help determine where additional resources could be devoted to defining the risks of these chemicals or developing remedies to deal with particular types of contaminants. After a brief description of the database construction, we turn in the subsequent section to an analysis of the cancer and noncancer risks by their category of risk assessment groupings.[10]

The data necessary to analyze fully the human health risks and estimated remediation costs associated with Superfund sites are spread across the country in the site administrative records maintained at the ten EPA regional offices. Though EPA has a central repository for RODs in Washington, the background documents that lead up to each ROD are only available at the regional level. We sent researchers to these regional EPA offices with instructions to collect for each site in our sample the complete baseline risk assessment, extended excerpts from the RI/FS, the complete ROD, and any modifications to the ROD.

While RODs contain extensive details of the pathway risks estimated in the baseline risk assessment, we considered it essential to go beyond the ROD to collect additional data for several reasons. The ROD does not include the full baseline risk assessment, which provides information on the parameter values used in the risk assessment calculations, the reasonable maximum exposure (RME) point concentrations of the particular chemicals employed to calculate pathway risks, and in many cases the average concentrations of these chemicals. ROD risk summaries are also sometimes presented so that pathway risks are combined to form the risks to a particular population, or so that risks are presented for different chemicals but not for particular pathways. These risks would be difficult to analyze at the pathway level if one did not go back to the baseline risk assessment. In addition the details necessary to link pathway risks to particular populations in order to develop population risks at Superfund sites are often only found in the baseline risk assessment or RI/FS documents.

As detailed in appendix A, our research assistants gathered information from the regional offices on all sites that had a ROD signed during 1991 or 1992. We chose these two years because the risk assessments conducted at these sites were likely to have been performed using the methodology outlined in EPA's 1989 *Risk Assessment Guidance for Superfund*.[11] We found that 276 RODs were signed during this period at a total of 266 sites. We have entered information on human health risks for 150 nonfederal sites, a sample similar to the distribution of total nonfederal NPL sites across the country.

We developed risk coding sheets that allowed research assistants to enter into the database human health risk assessment information from the baseline risk assessment, the RI/FS, and the ROD. We collected information such as chemical concentrations, risk assessment parameters used in the models to derive cancer and noncancer risks at the chemical and pathway levels, and descriptions of the different pathways (e.g., What scenario, exposed population, and exposure medium were associated with a particular pathway risk?). We checked the data entered in two ways. First, we compared the database figures against the original documents. Second, we did an independent calculation of the pathway risks through the use of the chemical concentration information and risk assessment parameters collected, which we compared to the figures in the original documents. By definition, the probability of cancer cannot exceed 1.0. In cases where the EPA documents reported a cancer risk to an individual as greater than 1.0, we reset the probability to 1.0. At the Silresim site in Lowell, Massachusetts, for example, the estimated cancer risk probability for groundwater ingestion of contaminants at the site was 5.1.[12] We correct this figure to 1.0 for our analysis of the EPA risk estimates. Subsequent chapters will completely reanalyze site risk assessments using chemical concentration data and consistent risk estimation practices.

The baseline risk assessment and ROD for a single site may contain pathway risks for pathways associated with extremely small risks. Our decision rules for entering risks into the database were as follows: The RODs served as the first source for pathway risk data. If a ROD contained risk information on all cancer pathway risks that were at least 1×10^{-6} and noncancer pathway risks with a hazard index greater than or equal to one, then we entered all the ROD risks that met the following risk cutoff levels: 1×10^{-7} for cancer pathway risks, 1×10^{-8} for cancer risks arising from an individual chemical within a pathway, 0.1 for the noncancer pathway hazard index, and 0.01 for the noncancer hazard quotient for each chemical. If the ROD did not present the minimum pathway risk data we required, we turned to the baseline risk assessment and entered the risk data according to the above decision rules. If the ROD risks were presented in forms other than by risk pathways (e.g., if only risks by chemical were present), then we used the baseline risk assessment figures. For each site, data on chemical concentrations and risk assessment parameters came from the baseline risk assessment.

We collected data on pathway risks smaller than the 1×10^{-6} figure—the cutoff for EPA action shown in figure 2.1—because the aggregation of these smaller risks can affect our subsequent calculation of population risks when the human health assessment figures are combined with census population figures surrounding sites. This chapter, however, focuses only on the risk information in our database for all cancer pathway risks greater than or equal to 10^{-6}, all noncancer pathway risks with hazard indexes greater than or equal to one, and all chemicals associated with these pathways. Thus we capture all information pertinent to EPA remediation decisions. Because these cutoffs eliminated one site in our sample at which the no-action alternative was chosen where pathway risks were below these thresholds, this chapter focuses on cancer and noncancer risks at 149 Superfund sites.

2.3   Risk Pathway Mechanisms

Analyzing the exposure pathways at Superfund sites illuminates how the risks arise. Do the risks arise from groundwater contamination, soil ingestion, or other mechanisms? Do current uses of the land comprising the site give rise to the risk, or is it some future use that has not yet occurred?

Questions such as these are of obvious interest from the standpoint of risk analysis, since the nature of the pathway generating the risk will influence the degree of exposure and the duration of exposure. Examination of the risk pathways, however, is also instructive since the nature of the pathway, not simply the level of the risk, may affect the policy decision.

EPA has a variety of policy options that it can adopt with respect to Superfund cleanup. If the main risk is that from groundwater contamination, households could switch to alternative water supplies to avoid the risk associated with this particular pathway. In addition to various stringent options involving treatment of the waste, there are also intermediate options that include restrictions on the use of the land, capping and fencing the site, and similar measures that may not eliminate the presence of the chemical but would eliminate the hazards associated with certain risk pathways.

An examination of the distribution of pathways is instructive to get a sense of the frequency with which alternative risk exposure mechanisms are operative. However, one should be cautious in proceeding from a pathway count to making inferences about the total level of the risk associated with a particular grouping of pathways. The risk associated with a set of pathways is governed not only by the number of such pathways but also by the magnitude of the risk associated with them. Pathways for which there is a high probability of an adverse outcome consequently pose greater risk than those with a lower probability. We will thus analyze the magnitude of risk associated with pathways, as opposed to simply the number of pathways. Another determinant of the risk is not only the probability but also the size of the exposed population. Population-weighted risk levels do not comprise a component of the EPA analysis and thus do not explicitly enter the analytical basis for Superfund policy making. In chapter 4 we will combine information on individual risk levels with data on the size of exposed populations to derive estimates of expected cancer cases. In this chapter we focus on the individual cancer and noncancer risks that form the focus of assessments at Superfund sites.

Table 2.1 provides a comprehensive overview of the distribution of the risk pathways by various categories of analysis. The columns of statistics in the table provide the pertinent breakdowns within the risk assessment categories for all 3,049 pathways, for the 2,105 cancer pathways, and for the 944 noncancer pathways at the 149 Superfund sites analyzed in the pathway analysis.[13] The first distinction in the table, which is perhaps the

Table 2.1
Distribution of pathways by risk assessment categories

Risk assessment category	Total pathways ($N = 3{,}049$)	Cancer pathways ($N = 2{,}105$)	Noncancer pathways ($N = 944$)
Scenario			
Current	28.0%	31.0%	21.3%
Future	72.0	69.0	78.7
Exposed population			
Residential	77.0	74.9	81.8
Worker	12.6	13.6	10.2
Recreational	3.9	4.4	3.0
Trespasser	5.4	6.2	3.5
Visitor	1.1	0.9	1.6
Age group			
Adult	60.4	66.1	47.8
Child	39.6	34.2	52.2
Location of population			
On-site	62.1	62.3	61.5
Off-site	34.2	34.2	34.1
Not indicated	2.3	2.2	2.6
Both	1.4	1.3	1.7
Location of medium			
On-site	80.6	80.4	81.0
Off-site	19.4	19.6	19.0
Exposure medium			
Air (from soil)	7.3	8.6	4.6
Air (from water)	11.0	12.3	8.1
Soil	30.2	33.0	24.2
Groundwater	37.6	31.1	52.1
Surface water	2.9	3.0	2.5
Sediment	5.2	6.2	3.0
Biota	4.1	4.0	4.3
Structures	0.2	0.3	—
Sludge	0.7	0.7	0.5
Leachate	0.6	0.8	0.1
Mother's milk	0.3	0.1	0.6

Table 2.1 (continued)

Risk assessment category	Total pathways ($N = 3{,}049$)	Cancer pathways ($N = 2{,}105$)	Noncancer pathways ($N = 944$)
Exposure route			
Ingestion	59.0	53.7	70.8
Dermal contact	22.3	24.9	16.3
Inhalation (vapor phase chemicals)	13.7	15.8	9.1
Inhalation (dust)	4.4	4.9	3.2
Inhalation/dermal	0.6	0.6	0.6

most salient result of this chapter, pertains to the breakdown between risks arising from current uses of the land and risks arising from future uses. This distinction refers not to the time period of the risk but rather to the nature of the context in which the risks will arise. For example, future risks to current residents are generally captured under the "current" time frame designation, but new uses, such as the decision to build a residential area on land that is now a Superfund site, would give rise to a "future" risk. The striking result of table 2.1 is that the great majority of the risk pathways pertain not to actual risk exposures but to hypothetical future risk exposures that assume a change in land use. Overall, 69 percent of the cancer pathways, 79 percent of the noncancer pathways, and 72 percent of the total pathways pertain to future as opposed to current uses.

Figure 2.2 illustrates some of the categories in table 2.1 that define how people could be exposed to site risks. In the figure one individual is being exposed to on-site hazards through dermal contact with dirt, while another is exposed to contaminants through inhalation. A third individual is exposed to contaminated groundwater by ingestion. Table 2.1 indicates how frequently these different types of exposure occur.

Of the exposed population types, the most important in terms of the risk pathways is that of residential populations. Approximately three-fourths of all pathways pertain to residential populations, with the next most important group being workers, who account for 13 percent of the pathways. Recreational users, such as those who fish in streams on Superfund sites, account for a very small fraction of all the risk pathways. In terms of the age distribution of those affected by the risk pathways, most of the risk pathways (over 60 percent) pertain to adult populations while 40 percent pertain to children (i.e., the population under 18 years of

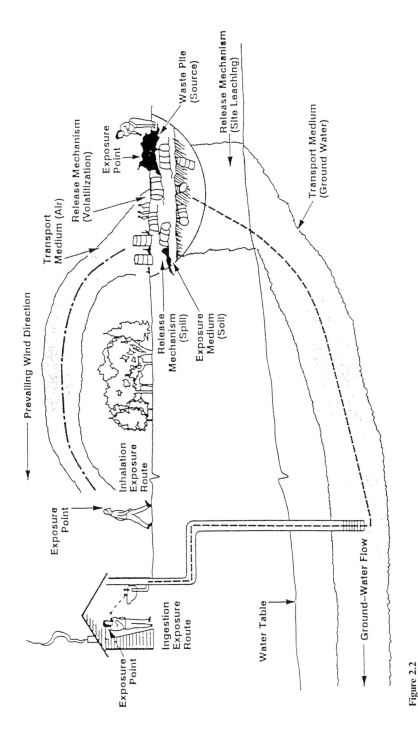

Figure 2.2
Illustrative exposure pathways at a Superfund site (source: U.S. EPA 1989a)

age). The main difference between these figures and the overall age distribution of the U.S. population is that whereas 40 percent of the risks are
to the child age population, this group comprises only 26 percent of the
U.S. population overall.[14] Thus the assumed pathways affecting children
occur almost 1.5 times as often as the representation of children in the
population.

The location where the risks arise is also of substantial interest, particularly as it relates to the potential efficacy of policy options that limit
future uses of land at or near Superfund sites. Both the location of the
populations and the location of the medium (i.e., the location of the medium from which the risk arises) are heavily concentrated toward on-site
risks. Of the total pathways, 62 percent pertain to risks to on-site populations; 81 percent of the media associated with the pathways pertain to
on-site media. The particular media that appear to be most prominent are
soil and groundwater, since each of these accounts for close to one-third
of all pathways. The other relatively important exposure media are air
(from soil), air (from water), and sediment, each of which accounts for 5
to 10 percent of all pathways. If the two air pathway mechanisms are
aggregated, they account for almost one-fifth of all pathways.

The final component of table 2.1 lists the exposure route by which the
risk arises. The dominant exposure route is that of ingestion, such as
drinking contaminated groundwater or ingesting dirt, where this category
gives rise to 59 percent of all pathways. Dermal contact accounts for 22
percent of all of the different exposure routes, and inhalation of vapor
phase chemicals and dust are next in importance. For the exposure routes
as well as for most of the other components of the table, the distribution
of pathways is fairly similar for both cancer pathways and noncancer
pathways. The major distinctions are that the noncancer pathways play a
more prominent role in the future risk scenarios, are more likely to affect
residential populations, are less likely to affect adults, are more likely to
involve groundwater exposure rather than soil, and are more likely to
arise from ingestion rather than dermal contact.

Table 2.2 analyzes the distribution of the exposed population and the
location of the exposed population for each of the two land use scenarios.
The high residential exposure rate evidenced in table 2.1 provides a misleading index of the degree to which the risks pose actual health threats.
Overall, the great majority of the pathways are accounted for by residents
based on future risk scenarios, which account for 61 percent of the pathways. In contrast, current risks to current residents, as well as future

Table 2.2
Distribution of pathways by scenario

a. Exposed population (percentage of total pathways, $N = 3{,}049$)

Scenario	Exposed population				
	Residential	Worker	Recreational	Trespasser	Visitor
Current	16.2	4.9	2.2	3.6	1.0
Future	60.8	7.6	1.8	1.7	0.1

b. Population location (percentage of total pathways, $N = 3{,}049$)

Scenario	Population location			
	On-site	Off-site	Not indicated	Both
Current	11.5	15.8	0.6	0.1
Future	50.6	18.3	1.8	1.3

populations in current residential areas, account for only 16 percent of the risk. The next most prevalent category, that of workers, also has a greater number of pathways for future scenarios as opposed to current time frames, but the difference is not as stark as in the case of the residential risks. There is also a substantial difference in the character of the risks with respect to their population location and the time frame for the analysis. On-site risks under current scenarios account for 12 percent of the total pathways, which is only somewhat smaller than the current off-site risk proportion of 16 percent. With the future-based scenarios, however, on-site risks escalate to account for 51 percent of the 3,049 pathways analyzed, which is nearly three times as great as the 18 percent of the pathways due to future off-site risks.

If one analyzes risks by time frame, the most frequently envisioned current pathways are for off-site residents, which account for 47 percent of the current pathways. On-site residential pathways account for only 10 percent of the current pathways. Because current pathways are less likely to arise in risk assessments, current off-site residential pathways account for 13 percent of the overall pathways, and current on-site residents comprise just 3 percent of the total pathways in our sample. Among future pathways calculated, on-site residents account for over 59 percent of future pathways in site risk assessments. EPA analyses consequently assume that in the future people will be drawn to live on Superfund sites much more than at present—an assumption contrary to observed behavior. These future on-site residential pathways account for 42 percent of all pathways in the sample. The dominant exposure to risks consequently arises from the expected future residential exposures on Superfund sites.

In the case of residents, the chief risks arise from ingestion of either groundwater or soil. Resident ingestion of groundwater accounts for a quarter of all total pathways. Although Superfund anecdotes frequently highlight the potential importance of children who eat dirt, it is noteworthy that ingestion of soil plays a much greater proportional role in the risk pathways for workers than it does for residents. Dermal contact with soil and ingestion of groundwater also account for a substantial share of the risks to workers. The risk pathways for recreational users and trespassers account for a very small percentage of all pathways in the sample, but the distributions for these groups are nevertheless of interest. The primary risk to recreational users is that from dermal contact with soil, with ingestion of soil or sediment also playing an important role in risk estimates for this population. For trespassers, the major risks are from ingestion of soil and ingestion of sediment, which together account for almost half of all the risks to trespassers.

2.4   Risk Levels Associated with Pathways

Although examination of the distribution of the number of pathways is instructive in providing an assessment of the mechanisms by which risks arise, the level of risks associated with the pathways is also of substantial consequence. Some pathways involve intense exposure to very hazardous chemicals, whereas others involve more minimal exposure levels. In this section we explore different features of the aspects of the risk distribution of the pathways included in our sample.

A useful starting point is the distribution of the risk pathways by risk level, which appears in table 2.3. Panel a presents the distribution of the cancer risk pathways for different risk ranges. Over half of the cancer pathways in the sample pertain to risk levels below 10^{-4}—the level of cumulative risks that triggers cleanups. However, it is quite striking that many of the pathways involve considerable risks, with 40 of the pathways posing cancer risks in excess of 0.1. Health risk levels of this kind are not unprecedented. For example, cigarettes pose a lifetime cancer risk of about one-third.[15] However, some of the large pathway risks are very large risks by comparison with the usual targets of most government risk policies. The risk threshold for most federal risk policies is either one in 100,000 or one in 1,000,000, and even annual job fatality risks for blue-

Table 2.3
Distribution of risk pathways by risk level

a. Number of cancer pathways by risk range

Cancer risk	Number of pathways
$10^{-6}-10^{-5}$	687
$10^{-5}-10^{-4}$	681
$10^{-4}-10^{-3}$	394
$10^{-3}-10^{-2}$	231
$10^{-2}-10^{-1}$	72
$10^{-1}-1$	40

b. Number of noncancer pathways by hazard index

Hazard index	Number of pathways
1–10	588
10–100	264
100–1,000	68
> 1,000	24

collar workers are below one in 10,000. In contrast, many of the risk pathways in table 2.3 are associated with risk levels orders of magnitude greater than these levels.

Such large risks arise in part because of particular risks associated with some extremely hazardous sites. The Westinghouse site in California is perhaps most noteworthy in that it accounts for two of the top ten cancer risk pathways.[16] The risks arising at that site are from high concentrations of PCBs. There are multiple pathways because there are different population groups exposed to these risks. As in the case of the overall distribution of the risk pathways, it is the future scenarios that play a dominant role. The risk pathways responsible for the high risk ranking of the Westinghouse site are the risks posed to adults on-site (dermal exposure to soil), workers on-site (dermal exposure to soil), children on-site (soil ingestion), and on-site resident children (dermal exposure to soil), where all these risks pertain to future risk scenarios as opposed to current risk pathways. As we indicated in chapter 1, the nature of this industrial site where the chemicals have largely been paved over makes the actual future threat likely to be small. This prominence of future risk pathways extends beyond this particular site. Nineteen of the top twenty pathway risks in the 150-site sample are associated with future as opposed to current risk scenarios.

Panel b of table 2.3 also presents the distribution of the relative risk levels for the noncancer pathways. These figures pertain to the hazard index associated with a noncancer risk pathway, which represents the sum of the hazard quotients for chemicals in the pathway. Chemicals differ in the potency of their health effects, so that one should be very careful in interpreting any aggregation of statistics such as hazard quotients across chemicals. For the most part the chemical exposures are less than ten times greater than the hazard index threshold, but in some cases there are apparently extremely high exposures to noncancer risks.

Table 2.4 provides a comprehensive overview of the magnitude of the risks for all the principal risk assessment categories. Whereas table 2.1 provided information on the percentage of pathways in each of the various risk assessment categories, table 2.4 provides information on the risk levels associated with these categories, where the main statistics of interest are mean risk levels and the median risk. Because of the influence of the very high risk outliers, the mean risks are consistently larger than the median risk levels, but the overall relationships are roughly similar across risk assessment categories.[17]

Earlier we found that future risks dominated in terms of the frequency with which these pathways occurred. This greater occurrence rate is reinforced by the higher-risk levels associated with future risk pathways, as the risk levels per future risk pathway exceed the risk levels per current use pathway by a factor of eight for the means and a factor of three for the medians. Not only are the future scenario risk pathways in Superfund human health risk assessments much more prevalent than existing pathways, but when future pathways do occur in the analysis, they have a much higher risk. Both the frequency and the severity of the risks of the future risk pathways are consequently greater.

The chief risks facing exposed populations are those incurred by residential populations and workers. The trespasser risk probability levels are quite small. Coupling these low-risk levels with the low frequency of trespasser pathways in risk assessments (shown in table 2.1) suggests that there may be little danger to trespassers from policy options that would not treat or remove the chemicals but simply restrict the use of the site in the future. Even without fencing or other barriers, the overall frequency of the trespasser pathways and the severity of the risks associated with these pathways is not as great as for other populations at risk.

The magnitude of the risks associated with different age groups is also somewhat contrary to general beliefs that primarily children face the

Table 2.4
Pathway mean and median cancer risks by risk assessment category

Risk assessment category	Mean	Standard deviation	Median	N
Overall	8.8e-3	6.7e-2	3.1e-5	2,105
Scenario				
Current	1.4e-3	9.4e-3	1.5e-5	652
Future	1.2e-2	8.0e-2	4.7e-5	1,453
Exposed population				
Residential	1.1e-2	7.6e-2	4.2e-5	1,577
Worker	3.9e-3	2.4e-2	2.0e-5	287
Recreational	1.2e-3	5.1e-3	6.1e-6	92
Trespasser	2.2e-4	7.3e-4	7.0e-6	131
Visitor	1.5e-5	2.0e-5	7.5e-6	18
Age group				
Adult	1.1e-2	7.4e-2	3.7e-5	1,392
Child	5.4e-3	4.9e-2	2.0e-5	713
Location of population				
On-site	8.7e-3	6.1e-2	3.1e-5	1,312
Off-site	9.6e-3	8.0e-2	3.1e-5	720
Not indicated	4.0e-3	1.9e-2	5.0e-6	46
Both	2.1e-3	4.0e-3	4.5e-4	27
Location of medium				
On-site	9.9e-3	7.0e-2	3.5e-5	1,693
Off-site	4.6e-3	5.1e-2	2.5e-5	412
Exposure medium				
Air (from soil)	2.1e-3	1.4e-2	1.2e-5	180
Air (from water)	5.5e-3	3.6e-2	4.2e-5	258
Soil	3.7e-3	4.6e-2	2.0e-5	694
Groundwater	2.0e-2	1.1e-1	2.0e-4	654
Surface water	1.4e-4	4.6e-4	7.6e-6	63
Sediment	5.0e-4	2.1e-3	4.7e-6	130
Biota	1.0e-2	4.8e-2	3.0e-5	85
Structures	3.1e-4	6.6e-4	6.2e-5	7
Sludge	8.9e-3	1.4e-2	1.0e-3	15
Leachate	7.6e-4	3.0e-3	2.9e-5	16
Mother's milk	4.7e-2	8.0e-2	2.2e-3	3

Table 2.4 (continued)

Risk assessment category	Mean	Standard deviation	Median	N
Exposure route				
Ingestion	1.2e-2	8.1e-2	4.2e-5	1,130
Dermal contact	6.0e-3	5.5e-2	1.9e-5	525
Inhalation (vapor phase chemicals)	5.2e-3	3.3e-2	3.5e-5	333
Inhalation (dust)	4.1e-4	2.4e-3	1.0e-6	104
Inhalation/dermal	6.8e-4	8.1e-4	4.4e-4	13

greatest risks. The mean level of the risks faced by adults is greater than that facing children, although the median risks are similar.

In terms of the location of the risks, the on-site populations face the greatest risks, and the on-site media pose the greatest risks. Preventing future development of the site or use of the site for other purposes would, for example, eliminate the most severe risks that arise. Of the various exposure media, many posing the largest risk (e.g., mother's milk and biota) are associated with very few pathways. The most prevalent pathways, those linked to soil and groundwater, pose mean cancer risks on the order of 0.01 and 0.001. These estimated risks are several orders of magnitude larger than those driving many other federal risk regulation efforts.

Table 2.5 distinguishes the different risk levels according to the principal dimension that influences the pathway distribution: the time frame for the risk scenario. It indicates for each of the time frames what the risk levels are for different exposed populations and different population groups. The largest population group by far is the on-site residential population for future risk scenarios. This population group accounts for 855 pathways and also faces a high mean risk level, 1.2×10^{-2}. The median future on-site resident risk level is nearly three times greater than the risks facing current on-site residents. The EPA risk analysis consequently assumes not only that on-site resident pathways will be much more prevalent than they are now but that these pathways also will pose greater risks than those faced by current on-site residents. Future workers and future recreation users also will face greater risks than their current scenario counterparts. Overall, trespassers face the lowest risk levels in the sample, and future trespassers are not only infrequent but face an extremely small median risk level.

Table 2.5
Distribution of cancer pathway risks by scenario, population location, and exposed population

Scenario	Population Location	Exposed population (count, mean, and median)				
		Resident	Worker	Recreation user	Trespasser	Visitor
Current	On-site	64	102	23	68	14
		7.7e-4	2.3e-3	1.0e-3	1.1e-4	1.9e-5
		2.0e-5	1.2e-5	1.1e-5	7.0e-6	1.4e-5
	Off-site	301	22	23	21	0
		1.6e-3	5.6e-3	8.1e-5	3.8e-4	
		2.0e-5	3.2e-5	6.0e-6	8.8e-6	
	Not indicated	3	0	6	1	2
		7.7e-5		3.0e-6	1.3e-6	2.0e-6
		8.6e-6		2.0e-6	1.3e-6	2.0e-6
	Both	1	1	0	0	0
		2.2e-6	4.6e-6			
		2.2e-6	4.6e-6			
Future	On-site	855	138	17	29	2
		1.2e-2	5.4e-3	4.9e-3	4.4e-4	3.0e-6
		5.8e-5	2.2e-5	2.9e-5	1.1e-5	3.0e-6
	Off-site	316	10	17	10	0
		2.0e-2	4.7e-5	4.7e-5	1.3e-5	
		6.8e-5	6.0e-6	6.0e-6	4.5e-6	
	Not indicated	19	7	6	2	0
		9.7e-3	1.0e-4	3.0e-6	3.5e-6	
		1.0e-4	1.0e-5	2.0e-6	3.5e-6	
	Both	18	7	0	0	0
		2.7e-3	1.4e-3			
		1.1e-3	2.0e-5			

The population locations of the different parties at risk are reflective of the nature of the exposed populations. Since future residents are in many cases on-site, the on-site future scenario group accounts for the largest number of pathways as well as the high average risk level. The future off-site risk probabilities are comparable to the future on-site risks. It is also interesting that the on-site and off-site risks for the current scenarios are similar as well. The main difference is not between the on-site and off-site location but rather whether it is a current or future scenario. The mean future resident risk (0.0139) is nearly ten times greater than the mean current resident risk (0.0014). Thus the EPA analyses are predicated not only on an assumption that future scenarios involving exposed populations will be the dominant pathways but also that these future scenarios will expose the population in a manner that will give rise to much larger risks than those now faced based on the current structure of economic development in the area.

Analysis of the frequency of risk pathways gives a sense of how often the pathways are pertinent; consideration of the risk levels associated with the pathways indicates the magnitudes of the risk per pathway. However, the overall level of the risk that will be generated at a Superfund site will reflect the combined influence of the frequency with which particular types of risk pathways occur as well as the levels of the risk associated with different types of pathways. Our analysis in chapter 4 will explicitly incorporate the size of the populations exposed to the risk. Note, however, that the current EPA mandate dictates that the risk posed from hazardous waste sites should be presented as risks to the individual, not to the population. As stated in the National Oil and Hazardous Substances Pollution Contingency Plan of 1990, "acceptable exposure levels for carcinogens are generally concentration levels that represent an excess upperbound lifetime cancer risk to an individual of between 10^{-4} and 10^{-6}."[18] As a result, baseline risk assessments focus on individual risk.

To convey information concerning both the frequency and magnitude of pathway cancer risks, table 2.6 provides statistics on the risk-weighted shares of the different cancer risk pathways. Rather than simply determining the fraction of the pathways represented by particular types of exposures, such as risk to future generations, each of these pathways is weighted by the total magnitude of the risk estimated for that pathway and the risk-weighted pathways are then summed for the entire sample. The statistics in table 2.6 provide information on the percentage of the total risk-weighted pathways accounted for by each pathway type.

The principal purpose of combining the influence of the frequency of pathway occurrence with the magnitude of the risk is to generate a hybrid of the two influences discussed above. For example, in the case of future risk scenarios, we found that future risk pathways were not only more prevalent than pathways based on current risk scenarios but that these pathways posed a greater risk level per pathway as well. The compounding of these influences is borne out in the statistics in table 2.6, as 95 percent of all total cancer pathway risks are attributable to future risk scenarios. This overwhelming emphasis on future risks is much greater than the unweighted share of future cancer pathways, which we found in table 2.1 to be only 69 percent.

The other statistics in the table are presented for total cancer pathway risks, future cancer pathway risks, and current cancer pathway risks. In terms of the distribution of risks, by far the largest risk share is for adults for current pathways and for future pathways. A very strong contrast arises with respect to risks to the various exposed populations. Residential populations account for 59 percent of the current cancer pathway risks, and this figure escalates to 95 percent for future risk pathways. Similarly, exposures to workers account for 36 percent of current cancer pathway risks, and this figure drops to only 4 percent for future risk pathways.

The location of the populations affected by these risks also changes dramatically depending on the time frame for the risk scenario. The percentage role of on-site population risks rises from 32 to 63 percent when one moves to the future risk scenarios, and the role of off-site risks drops from 68 to 36 percent. The implication of the exposed population and location of population results is that future risk scenarios put a much greater weight on risks posed to on-site residential areas. Of the exposure media listed in table 2.6, the most noteworthy pattern is that groundwater risks account for nearly three-quarters of the future cancer risk pathways, as contrasted with 7 percent of these pathways for current cancer risk assessments. Whether such a tenfold increase in the role of groundwater will actually occur depends on a broad range of hypothetical estimates, none of which are anchored in models of how people will actually behave. The role of biota drops substantially for future risk pathways.

Another way to analyze the pathway sample is to examine the top 20 carcinogenic chemicals in terms of their frequency in risk assessments at the 150 sites. Table 2.7 reports the average cancer risk per media pathway of exposure for each of these chemicals. While previous tables have aggregated the chemicals in a given exposure pathway such as

Table 2.6
Risk-weighted shares of cancer pathway risks

Risk assessment category	Total cancer pathway risk	Future cancer pathway risk	Current cancer pathway risk
Scenario			
Current	4.8%	0%	100.0%
Future	95.2	100.0	0
Age group			
Adult	79.4	79.4	78.3
Child	20.6	20.6	21.7
Exposed population			
Residential	93.3	95.1	59.1
Worker	5.9	4.4	36.4
Recreational user	0.6	0.5	2.8
Trespasser	0.2	0	1.7
Visitor	0	0	0
Location of population			
On-site	61.6	63.1	31.6
Off-site	37.1	35.5	68.3
Not indicated	1.0	1.0	0
Both	0.3	0.3	0
Exposure medium			
Air (from soil)	1.9	1.7	8.0
Air (from water)	7.6	7.4	11.6
Soil	13.8	13.4	22.0
Groundwater	70.0	73.2	6.7
Surface water	0.1	0	0.3
Sediment	0.3	0.2	3.2
Biota	4.7	2.8	42.9
Structures	0.0	0	0.2
Sludge	0.7	0.5	4.8
Leachate	0.1	0.1	0
Mother's milk	0.8	0.8	0.3
Exposure route			
Ingestion	73.4	74.2	57.8
Dermal exposure	16.9	16.6	22.6
Inhalation (vapor phase)	9.3	9.0	16.3
Inhalation (dust)	0.2	0	3.3
Inhalation/dermal combination	0	0.1	0

Table 2.7
Top 20 carcinogens

Chemical	Chemical pathway frequency	Total chemical cancer pathways	Average cancer risk
Arsenic	989	9.55%	1.5e-3
Trichloroethylene	693	6.69	1.8e-3
Benzene	541	5.22	1.2e-3
Tetrachloroethylene	541	5.22	1.3e-3
Beryllium	522	5.04	1.1e-4
Di(2-ethylhexyl)phtalate	377	3.64	1.1e-4
1,1-Dichloroethene	346	3.34	1.9e-3
Benzo(a)pyrene	330	3.19	6.8e-4
Vinyl chloride	330	3.19	1.1e-2
Chrysene	330	3.19	4.2e-4
Benzo(a)anthracene	326	3.15	4.1e-4
Benzo(b)fluoranthene	289	2.80	4.0e-4
Benzo(k)fluoranthene	267	2.58	7.8e-4
1,2-Dichloroethane	259	2.50	4.6e-3
Indeno(1,2,3-cd)pyrene	248	2.39	7.0e-5
Chloroform	233	2.25	2.7e-4
Dichloromethane	229	2.21	3.3e-3
Dibenzo(a,h) anthracene	189	1.82	2.7e-5
Aroclor 1260	188	1.81	1.3e-2
Carcinogenic PAHs	170	1.64	8.9e-6

groundwater ingestion to derive a total risk, this analysis focuses on each chemical as an individual risk pathway. The most frequently occurring chemical is arsenic, which accounts for close to 10 percent of the total cancer chemical pathways at these sites and generates on average a cancer risk of 1.5×10^{-3}. The list reads like an enumeration of chemicals targeted by the government in many regulatory programs, such as vinyl chloride and PCBs (e.g., aroclor 1260).[19] These chemicals combine relatively high frequency of appearance with high risks per pathway to play a substantial role in the risk assessments. Analysis of the chemical-specific risks may help because policy makers can focus on particular remediation technologies that are useful in dealing with substances that appear frequently and generate high risks. Moreover, if additional scientific evidence subsequently reveals that the risks of particular chemicals are more or less hazardous than was initially believed, then the effect will not be to

alter the risk distribution uniformly but rather to affect particular exposure pathways and sites in a disproportionate manner.

2.5   Site-Level Analysis of Individual Risks

Our analyses of pathway counts and magnitude of pathway risks suggest
that future risks, particularly future on-site residential risks, may play an
important role in EPA evaluation of cancer and noncancer risks. To the
extent that remediation decisions are triggered by risks to human health
rather than standards imported from other environmental programs, the
risk levels that trigger remediations are defined as cumulative risks to
individuals in a given population. In this section we focus on aggregating
the risk pathways at each site by population type (e.g, on-site adult risk)
to determine a cumulative risk to each population. In this analysis we use
the maximum of the cumulative risks (e.g., the summation of ingestion,
dermal, and inhalation risks from all media) faced by a population as our
indicator of carcinogenic risks at each site. We selected this risk indicator
in part because remediations often focus on the maximum individual risk
at sites. Focus on the maximum cumulative risks allows us to examine
how sites could shift into different categories of remediation depending on
how risks were assessed and managed.

Table 2.8 analyzes the distribution of the calculated risk levels to see
how the magnitude of risks varies with their character. These maximum
individual lifetime excess cancer risks are extremely high relative to risks
addressed under other federal regulatory programs. The mean maximum
cumulative cancer risk for the 150 sites is 0.070 and the median is 0.0025.
At over 85 percent of the sites the maximum individual cancer risk is
greater than or equal to 0.0001. Of these maximum site risks, most involve on-site populations. This designation does not mean that the populations are currently on-site. In fact survey data indicate on-site residents
are actually at only 18 of these 150 sites.[20] The on-site risks rather are an
indication that risk assessors have assumed that populations will reside or
come onto the site in the future. Assumptions about future land use
obviously play a key role in estimating risks in the Superfund program.

As in the earlier pathway analysis, in table 2.8 the maximum cumulative risks that involve changes in current land uses (e.g., residential development on a currently barren site) or changes in current exposure
pathways (e.g., the contamination of well water from future migration of
a groundwater plume) are designated future scenarios. Of the 133 maxi-

Table 2.8
Distribution of sites by maximum cumulative risk

Risk scenario	Total sites[a]	Carcinogenic risk level			Mean risk	Median risk
		$10^{-4}-1$	$10^{-4}-$ 10^{-6}	$<10^{-6}$		
All	150	130	20	0	7.0e-02	2.5e-03
On-site	106	94	12	0	6.5e-02	3.8e-03
Off-site	49	41	8	0	7.7e-02	1.0e-03
Current	19	16	3	0	1.7e-02	5.1e-04
Future	133	114	19	0	7.6e-02	2.6e-03
Future on-site resident	92	81	11	0	7.4e-02	4.0e-03
Not future on-site resident	62	53	9	0	6.3e-02	1.1e-03
Soil	29	18	11	0	5.3e-02	6.0e-04
Groundwater	121	112	9	0	7.2e-02	2.6e-03

a. Total number of sites in categories does not sum to 150 because at some sites multiple populations are exposed to the same cumulative risk level.

mum cumulative risks that involve future pathways, 130 are hypothetical because they would require a change in land use to be realized, and 3 are hypothetical because they would involve a change in exposure pathways. Note that pathways affecting overall future on-site residents account for 60 percent of the cumulative maximum risks. Estimated future risks also exceed the magnitude of current risks (the median of the maximum cumulative risks that are current is 0.00051 versus 0.0026 for the median maximum risks that are future risks). EPA's assessments never attempt to estimate a probability that a future land use will occur; for example, future risks are not multiplied further by an estimate of the probability that the land use will change through the construction of residential developments in currently industrial areas.

Table 2.9 focuses on a different question: If risks were limited to particular types of exposure pathways, what would the maximum risks look like? If one adopted a policy which excluded on-site populations from Superfund sites, the row designated as off-site populations indicates that 65 out of 150 sites would have maximum cumulative risks greater than or equal to 10^{-4}. If one focused only on cancer risks involving current land uses, the distribution of cancer risks shifts markedly into the discretionary zone (10^{-4} to 10^{-6}), and 40 sites would not have any current pathways identified or exceeding the cutoff for entry into our database

Table 2.9
Distribution of sites by maximum cumulative risk by risk scenario

		Carcinogenic risk level					
Risk scenario	Total sites	$10^{-4}-1$	$10^{-4}-$ 10^{-6}	$<10^{-6}$	N/A	Mean risk	Median risk
All	150	130	20	0	0	7.0e-02	2.5e-03
On-site	130	104	25	1	20	5.4e-02	2.2e-03
Off-site	106	65	37	4	44	4.4e-02	4.5e-04
Current	110	46	54	10	40	5.1e-03	6.9e-05
Future	142	121	21	0	8	7.1e-02	2.3e-03
Future on-site resident	110	94	16	0	40	6.2e-02	2.6e-03
No future on-site resident	135	88	45	2	15	4.0e-02	4.9e-04
No groundwater	120	58	56	6	30	1.6e-02	9.0e-05
No soil	140	123	16	1	10	6.3e-02	2.0e-03

Note: N/A = Number of 150 sample sites without applicable scenario.

(i.e., chemical pathway risks greater than or equal to 10^{-8}). Risk assessors often assume on-site residents in future land use scenarios, even though residents may not live there currently, as part of the attempt to explore reasonable maximum exposures. Of the 150 sites, at 14 sites there were current and future on-site residential risks estimated, at 2 sites there were current but not future on-site residential risks, at 96 sites there were future on-site residential risks estimated without current residential on-site risks estimated, and at 38 sites neither scenario was estimated. If EPA adopted policies that restricted residential development so that no future residents were allowed at sites that today are not residential, the maximum risk distribution shifts dramatically so that only 88 sites have maximum individual cancer site risks greater than or equal to 10^{-4}. The set of sites where maximum individual cancer risks would automatically trigger remediation thus drops substantially under policies that would restrict future residential development on Superfund sites. Without regard to future pathways, only 46 out of the 150 sites had current carcinogenic risks greater than 1 in 10,000, which is the individual risk level that may trigger remediations.

Table 2.8 indicates that of the 130 sites with maximum cumulative risks in the 10^{-4} to 1 range, 112 of these maximum cumulative risks were from groundwater exposure pathways. Table 2.9 reveals that if groundwater risks were eliminated, then the number of sites in this highest risk category

Table 2.10
Distribution of sites by maximum cumulative risk by sites with noncancer risks

Risk scenario	Noncancer HQ level	Carcinogenic risk level			
		10^{-4}–1	10^{-4}–10^{-6}	$<10^{-6}$	Total sites
All	≥ 1	113	12	0	125
	≥ 10	74	4	0	78
	≥ 100	26	1	0	27
Current	≥ 1	31	11	2	44
	≥ 10	17	2	0	19
	≥ 100	2	1	0	3

based on other risks would drop to 58. The dominance of groundwater risks among the largest assessed risks indicates the importance both of focusing attention on the likelihood of the groundwater exposure scenarios envisioned and attention on remediation measures that would reduce the likelihood of groundwater exposure.

Noncancer risks may also trigger remediations, so one must examine how these risks are distributed across sites. Table 2.10 shows that the vast majority of sites (125 out of 150) do have at least one pathway where a hazard quotient for a noncarcinogen is greater than one. If one increases the hazard quotient cutoff to 10 (e.g., to account for conservatism biases in estimation), however, a large number of sites drop out in terms of noncancer risks. Only 78 sites had chemicals with hazard quotients greater than or equal to 10. If one restricts the analysis to current pathways, only 44 out of 150 sites have chemicals with hazard quotients greater than 1 and only 19 have hazard quotients greater than 10. Table 2.11 provides information on examples of the noncancer chronic effects associated with the most frequently occurring noncarcinogens at the 150 sites in the risk sample. The table highlights the difficulty of comparing noncancer risks across chemicals, since the adverse outcomes range from drowsiness to death.[21]

Table 2.10 reveals that sites in the discretionary zone based on cancer risks were also less likely to have noncancer risks that involved hazard quotients exceeding one, an indication that cancer and noncancer risks may move together. The table indicates only a relatively small number of sites in the sample would require remediation based on noncancer risks rather than cancer risks. Measures of noncancer and cancer risks are positively correlated. The maximum hazard quotient at a site has a

Table 2.11
Top 20 chemicals by frequency of noncancer pathways exceeding a Hazard Quotient of 1

Chemical	Frequency of HQ >1	Ingestion or inhalation effects at critical levels	Other potential short-term and long-term effects at higher doses	Overall frequency at sites
Arsenic [very mild levels beneficial]	45	Vascular complications, skin hyperpigmentation	Liver, kidney, CNS, gastro-intestinal effects, nausea, injury to fetus, death	100
Chromium** [primarily Chromium (VI)]	40	No observed effects at the Rfd level	Lung damage, nasal perforation and irritation, death	85
Manganese	37	CNS effects		73
1,2-Dichloroethylene [cis- and/or trans-]	33	Liver lesions, increased blood enzyme	Lung and heart damage, decreased blood cells, death	78
Antimony	32	Increased cholesterol, blood chemistry changes, mortality		45
Lead	25	Blood enzyme changes in children	Retardation, prematurity, CNS effects, low birth weight and weight gain in children	68
Barium	22	Increased blood pressure		70
Cadmium	22	Kidney proteinuria	Lung effects, liver disease (effects on reproduction, immune system, CNS)	71
Tetrachloroethylene	21	Hepatotoxicity and increased weight	Drunkenness, short-term drowsiness, headache, eye and nose irritation	80
Trichloroethylene	19	Under review	Drowsiness, headache, sinus irritation, death; effects on kidney, liver, CNS, fetus	97
Napthalene	18		Kidney damage, cataracts	36
Nickel	16	Decreased organ and body weight	Lung effects, death (short-term effects on fetus, immune system, CNS)	69

Vanadium	16		Bronchitis	56
Toluene	14	Altered liver and kidney weight, neurological effects	Fatigue, headache, confusion, dizziness, loss of coordination, impaired memory	40
Thallium [acetate, carbonate, chloride, nitrate]	13	Blood: increased SGOT and LDH cholesterol		20
Acetone	12	Nephrotoxicity, increased liver and overall body weight		34
1,1-Dichloroethylene	12	Liver lesions	Short-term CNS disorders (death, lung effects, liver and kidney disease)	58
Xylenes	12	Hyperactivity, increased body weight, mortality		33
Carbon tetrachloride	10	Liver lesions	Kidney toxicity, nausea, headache, injury or death in sensitive individuals	25
Copper**	10	Gastro-intestinal irritation	Vomiting, diarrhea, long-term liver damage in infants (lung damage)	46

Source of critical level effects: U.S. EPA, *Integrated Risk Information System* (IRIS) database, 1995, and U.S. EPA, *Health Effects Assessment Summary Tables*, 1994b. Source of other effects: ATSDR's HazDat database; Upton and Graber (1993).

Note: Parentheses denote animal short- and long-term effects in the absence of data on human exposures. CNS = central nervous system; Rfd = reference dose; ** = minimum levels needed for adequate human nutrition.

statistically significant rank correlation of 0.54 with the maximum cumulative cancer risk. The number of chemical pathways with hazard quotients greater than or equal to one is also rank correlated (0.50) with the maximum cancer pathway risk. Though it is difficult to aggregate noncancer risks because of their different manifestations and magnitude, remediation policies focused on higher cancer risks should tend to target higher noncancer risks because of the correlation between the two types of risks.

2.6 Conclusions

Much of the political pressure that generated the impetus for the Superfund program arose because of the concern of existing populations for the risks that they believe these sites currently pose. Consideration of the risk assessments for Superfund sites indicates, however, that it is not the existing risks that are most salient. Rather, the dominant risks as calculated by EPA arise from future risk scenarios that generally involve alternative uses of the land. These future risks account for 69 percent of the cancer pathway and 95 percent of all the risk-weighted pathways for the Superfund sites in our sample. Chief among these future risks is that of future residents living on-site. The underlying assumption driving the EPA risk analyses is that there will be new residential areas on existing future Superfund sites where no people currently live. Such risks are hypothetical and are not grounded in an analysis of likely behavior.

Analysis of the structure of risks is of fundamental importance with respect to the choice of different possible modes of government intervention. If some mechanism were available that could eliminate these future risks, such as the use of various land use restrictions and containment options, then the great preponderance of the risks analyzed in human health assessments at Superfund sites would be eliminated. Indeed examination of the risk pathways suggested that many of the risks likely to remain with such containment and land use restriction options, such as that to trespassers, are very low even without adopting policies, such as fencing, to reduce these risks.

Although many observers have attempted to dismiss Superfund risks as being trivial, taken at face value many of the estimated hazards are quite substantial. Although the EPA risk threshold for considering a pathway risk is generally a lifetime cancer risk of one in a million, the mean risk level associated with pathways is typically several orders of magnitude larger than this threshold. Moreover these mean risk levels pertain not only to the site generally but also to a variety of different kinds of pathway mechanisms and different groups of exposed populations at the site. These calculated risks suggest that Superfund risks exceed the estimated risks for other federal cancer regulation efforts. Thus, even if one chooses to disregard some particular pathway mechanisms as being unlikely, the overall scale of the risks is sufficiently large that such casual dismissals of Superfund risks based on anecdotal evidence are not warranted.

Analysis of the maximum cumulative individual risk levels at sites reinforces these conclusions. These maximum individual site risks are extremely high in comparison to risks addressed in other federal regulatory programs. Yet many of these risks are based on hypothetical changes in land use envisioned in the future. If one focused only on cancer risks involving current land uses and made remediation decisions based on these figures, then many sites would shift into the discretionary zone of cancer risks from 10^{-4} to 10^{-6}, where site managers have more discretion about whether and how to remediate. Aside from assumptions about residents moving onto Superfund sites in the future, another reason that EPA risk calculations may overstate the risk is that the agency's guidance on risk assessment encourages the use of conservative parameter values in constructing the individual risk estimates. In the following chapter we focus on how conservatism in EPA's risk assessment methodology at Superfund sites distorts estimates of risks.

3

Assessing Conservatism in Individual Risk Estimates

Risk assessment is not an exact science. Risk calculations are subject to considerable uncertainty and variability. Governmental risk estimates have typically treated such uncertainties conservatively through the assumptions and default positions mandated by policy makers. In effect worst-case scenarios assume a more prominent role than more realistic risk assessments. If our objective is to save the greatest expected number of lives, however, the mean risk should be our guide. In recognition of these and other concerns, Congress has recently considered (but not to date enacted) legislation that would change the nature of risk assessment in many federal agencies, calling for "realistic" and "central" estimates of risk to be used in evaluating regulatory alternatives.[1]

Existing critiques of the effect of conservatism practices are largely conceptual or confined to narrow illustrative examples. Yet as a practical matter, how much do the conservatism practices influence risk assessment? In what ways do conservatism biases enter and which are most consequential? How would decisions change if based on more realistic risk assessments? This chapter provides the most extensive analysis to date of the consequences of conservative risk estimation that has been undertaken for any risk policy area. Because conservatism biases differ across programs and across agencies, the main generalizable principle from our results is the importance of more realistic risk assessments. Moreover, if agencies wish to be "conservative," we indicate a more rigorous procedure for doing so than the current series of ad hoc adjustments with unknown consequences. The Superfund program offers a good laboratory to study risk assessment because of the extensive data generated by site investigation and decision documents. Using data generated at 141 hazardous waste sites, we explore the implications for risk management if mean parameter values for contaminant concentrations, exposure duration, and ingestion rates are used to estimate cancer risks rather than the conservative default values presently employed by the agency. These adjustments take into account some, but not all, conservatism biases. We find that assessing risks based on mean parameter values would shift over 40 percent of the sites that now require remediation under the EPA's

This chapter was written with P. Christen Dockins.

current guidelines into the range of risks where EPA managers have greater discretion over whether to remediate or not.

By selecting a conservative value for multiple parameters within the risk equation, a regulator calculates a final risk value that is at the extreme high end of the distribution of risks. The compounding of the selection of high end input parameter values can result in risk estimates that are more extreme than the assessor intended due to the multiplicative nature of the risk equation. In the later sections of this chapter we use Monte Carlo analysis to quantify the degree of conservatism embodied in EPA's risk assessment practices. Superfund site-level risk assessments generally employ a single point estimate of individual level risks to describe the cancer risk at a site. This estimate is meant to reflect the risks arising from a reasonable maximum exposure (RME). Our Monte Carlo analysis reveals that nearly two-thirds of RME-estimated risks exceed the 99th percentile of their simulated risk distribution. If one switched from the current RME estimate to the 90th percentile of simulated risk, the number of populations facing risks that automatically trigger cleanups would drop by 26 percentage points.

These results underscore the potential benefits of exposing the assumptions used in risk assessments to greater examination and debate. Additional assessments based on mean parameter values and expanded analyses embodying a Monte Carlo approach would provide regulators, legislators, exposed populations, and other parties involved in site remediation with a more informative picture of site risks.

3.1 Conservatism and Risk Assessment[2]

The desire for caution or prudence in risk management, which we call conservatism, may arise directly from political considerations (Noll and Krier 1990) as well as from concerns regarding uncertainty and variability about the nature and magnitude of the hazard. Uncertainty reflects a lack of knowledge of the system and can be reduced through further measurement, at least in principle. Biases toward regulation (conservative choices) in the face of uncertainty reflect a "better safe than sorry" approach to risk management. Such concerns may reflect a greater weight on losses from not regulating when it is warranted than on the losses from regulating when it is not warranted.[3] Variability refers to the inherent heterogeneity in human behaviors and characteristics. Conservatism based on variability is consistent with policy that is based on protecting individuals suffering the greatest potential risk and has been characterized as a determination of "who's safe and who's sorry." If risk is monotonically increasing in the relevant variable, then this might be better phrased as "how many safe and how many sorry."

Potential difficulties may arise if policy makers use conservative risk assessment values. If, for example, the 1,000 residents near a Superfund site face a 0.5 chance that the risk of cancer is 1/1,000 and a 0.5 chance that it is 3/1,000, the conservative approach would assess the cancer risk as 3 cases rather than the 2 expected cases of cancer. Protecting society through conservative risk assessments that guard against false negatives consequently overstates the expected benefits of regulation by overestimating mean risks. There are sounder ways to be "conservative" and protective of health than distorting the true values of risk. A superior alternative would be to use a higher implicit value of life associated with the lives saved or attach a higher value to the environmental benefits. Placing a greater policy weight on the expected benefits that will occur rather than exaggerating the chance that there will be benefits will make across-program choices more comparable.

Conservatism in risk regulation is analogous to ambiguity aversion bias, which is one form of irrationality of choice under uncertainty. In situations involving lotteries to win a prize, the well-known Ellsberg paradox has documented the predilection of individuals to prefer precisely understood chances of winning a prize to less precise and more uncertain chances of winning a prize. An analogous form of irrationality affects individual decisions involving the potential for environmental losses which creates situations of ambiguity aversion.[4] In situations in which people are exposed to environmental risks, they tend to prefer policies that reduce uncertain risks to policies that reduce a more precisely understood risk, for any given mean value of risk. Other aspects of risk perception and behavior under uncertainty also seem consistent with conservative risk regulation.[5]

Advocates of the conservatism approach might suggest that conservatism is needed because of the presence of a variety of other complicating uncertainties, such as synergistic effects. If, however, one wished to adjust for other potential risk factors, one should do so explicitly. There is no reason to believe that such influences are always systematically correlated with the degree of uncertainty in the parameters in the analysis of the chemicals at the site. This more explicit adjustment procedure also would give a role to such influences in contexts in which the site risk assessments are quite precise. There would be no role for a conservatism bias, but there nevertheless would be a mechanism for recognizing synergistic effects.

Recent legislative proposals have included requirements that risk characterizations make apparent the distinction between data and policy assumptions, and that agencies give preference to model assumptions and input parameters that represent the most plausible or realistic inference from scientific data. Some proposals would have required that agencies calculate quantitative risk assessments using the "best estimate for each input parameter."[6] Superfund, under consideration for reauthorization at the time of this writing, may be subject to similar requirements, including the provision of unbiased and scientifically objective risk assessments and the estimation of central estimates of risk. Our analysis of conservatism here is thus relevant to consideration of Superfund reform and broader implementation of risk management reforms in federal agencies.

3.2   Superfund and Risk Regulation

Guidelines known as the *Risk Assessment Guidance for Superfund* (U.S. EPA 1989a) govern estimates of individual cancer risks at Superfund sites. EPA has established agencywide methodologies and default assumptions for evaluating the first two stages of risk assessment, hazard identification and the dose-response function. These default assumptions generally produce conservative estimates of toxicity. Superfund risk assessors use the toxicity estimates that result from these procedures in conjunction with exposure assessments specific to the program. The EPA uses the term reasonable maximum exposure (RME) to describe the Superfund approach to exposure assessment and provides the following information in guidance documents:

For Superfund exposure assessments, intake variable values ... should be selected so that the combination of all intake variables results in an estimate of the reasonable maximum exposure for that pathway. As defined previously, the reasonable maximum exposure (RME) is the maximum exposure that is reasonably expected to occur at a site. Under this approach, some intake variables may not be at their individual maximum values but when in combination with other variables will result in estimates of the RME.[7]

The RME therefore is clearly not meant to be a "worst-case" scenario but to be toward the upper end of plausible risk estimates. The EPA states it this way: "The intent of the RME is to estimate a conservative exposure case (i.e., well above the average case) that is still within the range of possible exposures."[8] While the EPA does not explicitly provide a percentile goal for the RME risk estimate, the agency describes a "reasonable worst case" of exposures in the 90th to 95th percentile range.[9]

Superfund risk managers use these estimates to select the appropriate site remediation strategy in accordance with agency guidelines. The emphasis on individual risk in Superfund relegates cost-effectiveness considerations to "primary balancing" criteria. The principal "threshold" criteria that must be satisfied by the selected remedial alternative are overall protection of human health and the environment. Cleanups must also comply with applicable or relevant and appropriate requirements (ARARs) from other environmental programs, but these can be waived under certain situations.[10]

As we indicated in figure 2.1, Superfund risk managers rely upon action thresholds—levels of risk that guide remediation policy at the site. Superfund incorporates what may best be termed a fuzzy threshold. Risks greater than 1×10^{-4} generally mandate remediation, risks less than 1×10^{-6} are generally considered acceptable, and risks between these two figures may or may not require action depending on the circumstances and the judgment of the manager.[11]

While the goal of Superfund risk assessment is to provide a plausibly conservative estimate of risk, a number of studies suggest that RME estimates may greatly exceed this target.[12] The compounding of conservative assumptions in the individual parameter estimates can generate risk estimates that may be considerably larger than expected through the use of upper bound, or even "plausible upper bound," parameter values.[13] The difficulty for site managers is that the degree of conservatism embodied in current Superfund risk assessment practices is uncertain. Do such estimates represent the 90th, 95th, or 99th percentile value? The extent of conservatism also varies according to the type of risk and site, but the degree to which conservatism is compounded is unknown, even to the analyst generating the risk estimate. We first compare the magnitude of EPA risk estimates to those generated by the use of mean parameter values for key variables in the equation for estimating individual cancer risks. We then use Monte Carlo analysis to quantify how conservative is the Superfund's emphasis on "reasonable maximum exposure."

3.3 Methods and Data

To assess how Superfund cleanups might be affected by a change to central estimates of risk, we recalculate RME estimates using mean parameter assumptions and evaluate these according to the Superfund policy guidelines. Consistent with the EPA policy approach, we limit ourselves to how these risk estimates compare across sites and to program thresholds. EPA does not apply them to population data and estimate expected cancer cases and we will not do so here. Since we focus on cancer risks from ingestion, we first present the lifetime excess cancer risk (LECR) equation for ingestion risks and then discuss the associated effect of conservatism. The LECR from contaminant i in pathway j is given by equation (3.1):

$$\text{LECR}_{ij} = \left(\frac{\text{ED}_j \times \text{EF}_j \times \text{IR}_j}{\text{BW}_j \times \text{AT}} \right) \times \text{CC}_{ij} \times \text{Tox}_{ij}, \tag{3.1}$$

where

LECR = lifetime excess cancer risk,

ED = exposure duration,

EF = exposure frequency,

IR = ingestion rate,

BW = body weight,

AT = averaging time,

CC = contaminant concentration, and

Tox = toxicity.

EPA estimates the risks associated with each chemical from soil and groundwater ingestion by calculating what is termed the human intake factor (HIF), (the bracketed expression in equation 3.1) which is a function of ingestion rate, exposure frequency, exposure duration, body weight, and averaging time. EPA then multiplies the human intake factor by an estimate of the concentration of the contaminant and a measure of the chemical's toxicity to determine the lifetime excess cancer risk arising from ingestion of the chemical.[14] Finally EPA sums the risks from the chemicals in a pathway to determine the pathway risk from soil or groundwater ingestion at the site.[15] This summation yields equation (3.2) which we use to calculate pathway risk:

$$\text{LECR}_j = \sum_i \text{LECR}_{ij}. \qquad (3.2)$$

In effect the lifetime excess cancer risk is a function of five components in the numerator (ingestion rate, exposure frequency, exposure duration, concentration, and toxicity), and two components in the denominator—body weight and averaging time. Agency guidelines do not advocate that either of the denominator values be estimated conservatively. Instead, each takes on average values. However, four of the five numerator components are subject to conservative adjustments, with the possible exception being exposure frequency.[16] These adjustments primarily reflect variability about the parameters (except for contaminant concentration, which primarily reflects uncertainty). As we recalculate risks in order to obtain more central estimates, the only one of these conservatively estimated parameter values that will not be adjusted is the toxicity value. Our analysis consequently does not adjust for the conservatism bias in estimates of the potency of the chemicals. Doing so would require reevaluation of EPA's interpretation of the scientific literature on a chemical-by-chemical basis.

The standard values for many components of the pathway LECR given in EPA guidance documents appear in table 3.1. The values listed pertain to ingestion rates by adults and children for both soil and groundwater as well as the exposure duration. As indicated in the final column of table 3.1, the contaminant concentration is based on information in the site documents for the reasonable maximum exposure (RME).

The typical assumption used in EPA risk assessments is the EPA default value shown in the top row of the table. The EPA default assumption for exposure duration, for example, is thirty years. The second row of information provides the EPA mean estimates for each of these values as drawn from Superfund guidance documents. In the case of exposure duration this amount is nine years. The subsequent rows in the table provide information on different percentiles based on other information in the literature indicated in the sources for table 3.1. The relationship of the EPA default values to the different percentiles varies depending on the parameter. In the case of exposure duration, the EPA default value is almost as high as the 95th percentile, whereas the adult water ingestion rate is just below the 90th percentile and the adult soil ingestion rate is between the mean and the 90th percentile. The extent of the conservatism of risk assessments consequently varies across the different parameters.

Table 3.1
Parameter values used for risk sensitivity analysis

	Adult soil ingestion rate (mg/day)	Child soil ingestion rate (mg/day)	Adult water ingestion rate (L/day)	Child water ingestion rate (L/day)	Exposure duration (years)	Contaminant concentration (mg/kg or µg/l)
EPA default	100	200	2.0[a]	1	30[a]	RME[b]
EPA mean	50	200	1.4	1	9	Site documents
Alternative mean	46.6	75	1.3	0.7 (ages 0–10) 0.9 (ages 11–18)	11	—
Alternative 90th percentile	176	1190	2.1	1.2 (ages 0–10) 1.6 (ages 11–18)	26	—
Alternative 95th percentile	196	1751	2.5	1.4 (ages 0–10) 1.9 (ages 11–18)	33	—
Alternative 99th percentile	211	—	3.5	2.0 (ages 0–10) 2.7 (ages 11–18)	47	—
Source of EPA values	1, 2	1, 2	1, 2	Most frequently used in assessments	1, 2	Site documents
Source of alternative values	3	4	5	5	6	—

Sources: 1. U.S. EPA (1989b); 2. U.S. EPA (1989a); 3. Calabrese, Stanek, Gilbert, and Barnes (1990); 4. Stanek and Calabrese (1995); 5. Roseberry and Burmaster (1992); 6. U.S. EPA (1992).
a. Value is approximately the 90th percentile.
b. Reasonable maximum exposure is the maximum detected or 95th upper confidence limit on the mean, whichever is lower.

A note about the values used in this analysis is in order. We compiled EPA mean values from a review of the guidelines that governed the Superfund risk assessments in our sample. We derived alternative mean values from the literature on risk assessment, and much of this work is more recent than the Superfund guidelines. However, since the EPA risk values are also based on the scientific literature, it is not surprising that EPA estimates often coincide with independent published estimates. There is, for example, little difference between these two sets of mean values except for the case of child soil ingestion. Recent work by Calabrese et al. (1990), Stanek and Calabrese (1995), and the review by Finley et al. (1994) provide parameter distributions. Our choices are consistent with these studies.[17]

Consider first the case of groundwater consumption. The EPA default value for adults is 2 liters per day, while the mean value determined by the EPA is 1.4 liters per day. We use the EPA's mean value to recalculate pathway risks, and we also use an alternative mean value of 1.3 liters per day drawn from the literature. Similarly we estimate the risks using different assumptions detailed in table 3.1 for groundwater ingestion rates for children and for the soil ingestion rates for adults and children.

In the case of the contaminant concentration at a site, EPA guidance directs risk assessors to use the upper end of the 95 percent confidence limit on the estimate of the mean concentration at the site or the maximum detected concentration, whichever is lower. This value, termed the RME concentration, appears in baseline risk assessments in the equations used to estimate lifetime excess cancer risks. This value may be only mildly conservative as it is an adjustment of the mean value to incorporate the uncertainty from samples. However, the variance is so large for some samples that EPA risk assessments use the maximum concentration instead.[18] Some risk assessors also provide information on the average concentrations of individual chemicals at a site. We thus vary contaminant concentration as the third variable in the assessment to see how the risk estimates change when values other than those directed by EPA guidance are used. This variation is on a chemical-by-chemical basis using information reported in the site documents.

The analysis focuses on a total of 719 pathways for soil and groundwater ingestion by residents for 141 sites. An example of such a pathway is adult water ingestion risks for off-site residents. There are several reasons for limiting ourselves to pathways of this type. Soil and groundwater ingestion pathways account for 40 percent of the total pathways for these sites, and they are often the pathways of highest risk. Also the relatively simple LECR equation has made these pathways the most consistent in terms of parameter values used at each site. For each change in assumptions, we estimate the distribution of risks based on the information in the site documents and compare these estimates with the distribution of pathway risks using alternative assumptions.[19]

For the subsequent comparison of the risk estimates, we present the original EPA risk estimates in the site documents alongside the recalculated risks using alternative parameter values since the particular number of pathways used to estimate the risk will vary by scenario. The parameters for exposure duration are varied only for adult pathways, since child pathways always assume that the exposure duration equals the number of years that a child is in a particular age group. These age groups varied substantially across Superfund sites, from as little as 2 years to over 15. As a consequence the pathways for children drop out of the analysis when exposure duration is varied. Similarly the number of pathways analyzed declines when the concentration value is varied since the average concentration parameter is not available for all sites. As a final note, we have made no adjustment for hypothetical versus actually occurring pathways; we have taken as given the EPA assumption that pathways based on changes in land use receive weight equal to those based on current land use.

3.4   Risks Based on Mean Parameter Values

To explore the effect of the conservative assumptions, we present the EPA risk estimates for the different pathway types and compare these estimates to those obtained using mean parameter values. Table 3.2 presents estimates in which these mean values are based on those estimated by EPA, and table 3.3 utilizes mean values derived from the literature. In each case the analysis distinguishes the risks associated with soil ingestion, groundwater ingestion, and the combined influence of both of these, where these exposure mechanisms constitute the three major row categories in tables 3.2 and 3.3. The additional subdivision of the rows indicates the parameters varied. After first presenting estimates based on the site documents, we also present estimates in which we vary the EPA parameter assumptions for the ingestion rate (IR), exposure duration (ED), and contaminant concentration (CC). We then present the combined influence of the variation and uncertainty of each of these parameters.

The columns in table 3.2 indicate the different risk ranges. The first set of three columns of data indicates the percentage of pathways in each of the risk policy categories based on EPA guidance documents.[20] As noted above, risks greater than 1×10^{-4} generally warrant policy action; risks in the 1×10^{-4} to 1×10^{-6} range are those for which the record of decision "must explain why remedial action is warranted."[21] For risks below 1×10^{-6} no action is warranted. The next three columns in table 3.2 present the mean and median risk values associated with the pathway type for the given assumptions, and tests for equality of mean values for EPA risk estimates as compared to those based on mean parameters. Because the sample differs as we vary parameter values (not all sites provided sufficient data to vary all parameters), the pathway mean and median risk from site documents varies accordingly. All median values were found to be significantly different according to the sign test for the difference in medians. The count of pathways associated with each of the parameter value analyses is presented in the last column. In our discussion, we sometimes refer to the ratio of the mean risk calculated using the conservative assessment to the mean risk based on the use of central parameter estimates as the ratio between conservative and central risks.[22]

Changes in the ingestion rate have a fairly modest effect. In the case of soil ingestion, the ratio between conservative and central risks is 1.17, and the number of pathways that fall under the no-action heading increases by less than 4 percentage points. Similarly, in the case of groundwater ingestion, the ratio between conservative and central risks is 1.31, and the mean parameter alternative increases the percentage of sites for which no action is warranted by 1.5 percentage points.

If, however, the ingestion rate parameter is varied based on the evidence in the literature, as is the case in table 3.3, the ratio between conservative and central risks is 2.59 for soil ingestion and 1.55 for groundwater ingestion. This shift alone increases the percentage of no action soil ingestion risk pathways by over 6 percentage points and increases the number of no action groundwater ingestion pathways by 1.5 percentage points. The combined influence of altering the ingestion rate parameters for both soil ingestion and groundwater ingestion is intermediate between these two estimates on a percentage basis.

The exposure duration assumption appears to have a much more consequential effect on the risk estimate. This change increases the percentage of pathways for which no action is warranted by over 9 percentage points for soil ingestion and over 5 percentage points for groundwater ingestion.

Table 3.2
Risk estimates with parameter values replaced with EPA means

Pathway type	Permutation (parameter varied)	Percentage no action[a]	Percentage discretionary	Percentage take action
Soil ingestion	Site documents	1.5	81.3	17.2
	IR only	5.2	79.9	14.9
	Site documents	1.2	85.9	12.9
	ED only	11.7	83.3	5.0
	Site documents	0.7	78.9	20.4
	CC only	8.8	83.0	8.2
	Site documents	1.5	83.8	14.7
	All (IR, ED, CC)	57.4	41.2	1.4
Groundwater ingestion	Site documents	0.9	35.9	63.2
	IR only	2.4	36.6	61.0
	Site documents	1.2	30.4	68.4
	ED only	7.8	39.5	52.7
	Site documents	0.7	39.1	60.2
	CC only	2.0	48.3	49.7
	Site documents	0.9	33.2	65.9
	All (IR, ED, CC)	10.7	56.1	33.9
Soil and groundwater ingestion	Site documents	1.1	52.9	46.0
	IR only	3.5	52.7	43.8
	Site documents	1.2	48.6	50.2
	ED only	9.1	53.8	37.1
	Site documents	0.6	52.4	47.0
	CC only	4.3	59.9	35.8
	Site documents	1.1	45.3	53.6
	All (IR, ED, CC)	22.0	52.5	25.5

Note: In this table IR denotes ingestion rate, ED denotes exposure duration, and CC denotes contaminant concentration.
a. According to EPA guidance, risks less than 10^{-6} require no remedial action in the Superfund program. Risks from 10^{-6} to 10^{-4} allow the site manager to use discretion with

Table 3.2 (continued)

Pathway type	Mean	Median[b]	t statistic for means[b]	Count
Soil ingestion	1.4e-3	1.5e-5	2.5	268
	1.2e-3	1.1e-5		
	9.2e-4	1.3e-5	2.3	162
	2.8e-4	3.9e-6		
	2.5e-3	1.6e-5	2.7	147
	1.5e-3	7.5e-6		
	2.1e-3	1.1e-5	2.2	68
	1.8e-4	7.2e-7		
Groundwater ingestion	1.7e-2	3.1e-4	3.9	451
	1.3e-2	2.3e-4		
	2.1e-2	5.3e-4	3.7	332
	4.6e-3	1.2e-4		
	1.3e-2	3.3e-4	2.7	294
	3.6e-3	1.0e-4		
	1.7e-2	6.0e-4	2.9	214
	5.6e-4	2.9e-5		
Soil and groundwater ingestion	1.1e-2	7.1e-5	3.9	719
	8.6e-3	5.2e-5		
	1.5e-2	1.0e-4	3.8	494
	3.2e-3	3.0e-5		
	9.7e-3	8.4e-5	2.8	441
	2.9e-3	3.4e-5		
	1.3e-2	2.0e-4	3.0	282
	4.7e-4	1.1e-5		

an explanation given if remedial action is taken. Risks greater than 10^{-4} are deemed unacceptable and require remedial action.

b. All median pairs are significantly different according to the sign test for equality of medians. All t values for means tests are statistically significant at the 95 percent confidence level.

Table 3.3
Risk estimates with parameter values replaced with means from literature

Pathway type	Permutation (parameter varied)	Percentage no action[a]	Percentage discretionary	Percentage take action
Soil ingestion	Site documents	1.5	81.3	17.2
	IR only	7.8	82.1	10.1
	Site documents	1.2	85.9	12.9
	ED only	10.5	83.3	6.2
	Site documents	0.7	78.9	20.4
	CC only	8.8	83.0	8.2
	Site documents	1.5	83.8	14.7
	All (IR, ED, CC)	55.9	42.6	1.5
Groundwater ingestion	Site documents	0.9	35.9	63.2
	IR only	2.4	37.9	59.7
	Site documents	1.2	30.4	68.4
	ED only	6.6	37.7	55.7
	Site documents	0.7	39.1	60.2
	CC only	2.0	48.3	49.7
	Site documents	0.9	33.2	65.9
	All (IR, ED, CC)	10.3	55.6	34.1
Soil and groundwater ingestion	Site documents	1.1	52.9	46.0
	IR only	4.5	54.4	41.1
	Site documents	1.2	48.6	50.2
	ED only	7.9	52.6	39.5
	Site documents	0.6	52.4	47.0
	CC only	4.3	59.9	35.8
	Site documents	1.1	45.3	53.6
	All (IR, ED, CC)	21.3	52.5	26.2

Note: In this table IR denotes ingestion rate, ED denotes exposure duration, and CC denotes contaminant concentration.
a. According to EPA guidance, risks less than 10^{-6} require no remedial action in the Superfund program. Risks from 10^{-6} to 10^{-4} allow the site manager to use discretion with

Table 3.3 (continued)

Pathway type	Mean	Median[b]	t statistic for mean[b]	Count
Soil ingestion	1.4e-3	1.5e-5	2.5	268
	5.4e-4	5.9e-6		
	9.2e-4	1.3e-5	2.3	162
	3.4e-4	4.8e-6		
	2.5e-3	1.6e-5	2.7	147
	1.5e-3	7.5e-6		
	2.1e-3	1.1e-5	2.2	68
	2.0e-4	8.2e-7		
Groundwater ingestion	1.7e-2	3.1e-4	3.8	451
	1.1e-2	2.1e-4		
	2.1e-2	5.3e-4	3.7	332
	5.6e-3	1.4e-4		
	1.3e-2	3.3e-4	2.7	294
	3.6e-3	1.0e-4		
	1.7e-2	6.0e-4	2.9	214
	6.2e-4	3.2e-5		
Soil and groundwater ingestion	1.1e-2	7.1e-5	4.1	719
	7.4e-3	3.9e-5		
	1.5e-2	1.0e-4	3.8	494
	3.9e-3	3.6e-5		
	9.7e-3	8.4e-5	2.8	441
	2.9e-3	3.4e-5		
	1.3e-2	2.0e-4	3.0	282
	5.2e-4	1.2e-5		

an explanation given if remedial action is taken. Risks greater than 10^{-4} are deemed unacceptable and require remedial action.

b. All median pairs are significantly different according to the sign test for equality of medians. All t values for means tests are statistically significant at the 95 percent confidence level.

The effects for the mean values from the literature shown in table 3.3 are comparable in the case of the exposure duration parameter. The net effect when the exposure duration assumption is varied for both soil and groundwater ingestion to the value from the literature is that the ratio between conservative and central risks is 3.85. The pathways for which no action is warranted increase by over 6 percentage points. Similarly, the percentage of pathways for which action is definitely warranted (risk greater than 1×10^{-4}) drops by almost 11 percentage points.

The final individual parameter varied is the contaminant concentration amount, which is varied based on the contaminant concentration estimates reported in the site documents in the case of both table 3.2 and table 3.3. When mean concentrations are used, the fraction of pathways for which action is warranted drops by over 10 percentage points for soil pathways, groundwater pathways, and both groundwater and soil pathways. Most of the changes in the other categories is exhibited in the intermediate discretionary action category. The number of soil and groundwater ingestion pathways now in the discretionary range increases by over 7 percentage points.

Although considering each of these parameter values in turn is useful to get a sense of their individual influence, the overall policy question is how altering all of the exposure parameters to reflect the mean values will affect the estimated risk. For concreteness, let us focus on the final set of results for which both soil ingestion and groundwater ingestion are combined. The overall effect of altering the three parameter values for which the biases are compounded in the analysis is considerable. In the case of the EPA mean estimates, the estimated pathway risk for soil and groundwater ingestion drops from an average of 1.3×10^{-2} to 4.7×10^{-4}, whereas in the case of the mean values from the literature the decline is to 5.2×10^{-4}. The average RME (e.g., the value used in EPA decisions) value is over 27 times greater than central estimates using the EPA mean parameter values and 25 times greater when mean parameter values from the literature are used.

These parameter changes greatly influence the actions warranted under the policy action guidelines. In the case of the EPA mean estimates in table 3.2, the percentage of soil and groundwater ingestion pathways for which no action is warranted increases by 21 percentage points, the percentage of pathways for which action is discretionary and must be justified increases by 7 percentage points, and the fraction of pathways for which action is required drops by 28 percentage points. Similar declines are exhibited in the case of the mean estimates from the literature shown in table 3.3. The fraction of soil and groundwater ingestion pathways for which no action is warranted increases by 20 percentage points, the percentage of pathways for which cleanup is discretionary increases by 7 percentage points, and the percentage of pathways for which cleanup action is required decreases by 27 percentage points. These implications are, of course, based solely on the residential ingestion pathways present at these sites. Other significant sources of risk may still exist, where EPA also addresses these other risks conservatively.

Although analysis of all adult (and some child) resident ingestion pathways at 141 sites is instructive, all of these pathways may not be equally influential in driving the policy choice. In particular, one might posit that the maximum risk pathways at sites play a more prominent policy role than smaller risk pathways. Table 3.4 presents the maximum pathway risks from either soil or groundwater ingestion at the different sites. Thus, only the largest risk pathway associated with the site is included in this analysis. Nearly all of the sites in the sample had a maximum risk pathway that was a soil or groundwater residential risk ingestion pathway so that our focus on these classes of risk for our sensitivity analysis for the effect of mean parameter values is instructive in indicating how maximum risk pathways will be altered. Panel a of table 3.4 excludes sites for which no action was recommended to focus attention on the potential to shift some sites where remedial actions were selected to no action status. Panel b of table 3.4 provides an assessment in which the no action sites are included to provide a comprehensive analysis for the broader sample.

The estimates of the mean risks from the site documents are extremely large for the maximum site risks—an average of 0.036 overall, excluding the no action sites. This lifetime cancer risk is almost as great as the estimated lung cancer fatality risk from cigarette smoking and, by any standard, is considerable.[23] The overall median risk is somewhat lower (1.7×10^{-3}) but is still quite large. Perhaps more striking is that conservative risk estimates for only 4 out of the 67 maximum risk pathways are less than the 1×10^{-4} remediation trigger.

Once we shift to estimates based on mean parameter values, these risk estimates drop considerably. (See the fourth and fifth columns of data in table 3.4.) Altering the ingestion rate reduces the mean by one-third, altering the exposure duration reduces the mean by over half, and altering the contaminant concentration to the mean reduces the overall mean risk by over two-thirds. The net effect on the estimated risk for maximum risk pathways is to reduce the risk value by a factor of 20, where this value drops from 3.8×10^{-2} to 1.9×10^{-3}. The proportional effect is almost

Table 3.4
Maximum risk pathways using alternative mean values

a. No-action sites not included

Permutation (parameter varied)	Value	Percentage no action[a]	Percentage discretionary	Percentage take action
Ingestion rate	Database risks	0.8	12.3	86.9
	Alternative mean	0.8	14.9	84.3
Exposure duration	Database risks	1.0	8.7	90.3
	Alternative mean	1.0	12.5	86.5
Contaminant concentration	Database risks	1.3	10.5	90.8
	Alternative mean	1.3	23.7	75.0
All	Database risks	1.5	4.5	94.0
(IR, ED, CC)	Alternative mean	3.0	43.3	53.7

b. No-action sites included

Permutation (parameter varied)	Value	Percentage no action[a]	Percentage discretionary	Percentage take action
Ingestion rate	Database risks	0.8	13.6	85.6
	Alternative mean	0.8	16.8	82.4
Exposure duration	Database risks	0.9	9.7	89.4
	Alternative mean	0.9	15.0	84.1
Contaminant concentration	Database risks	1.1	12.6	86.3
	Alternative mean	1.1	28.7	70.2
All	Database risks	1.3	6.6	92.1
(IR, ED, CC)	Alternative mean	5.3	46.1	48.6

Note: In this table IR denotes ingestion rate, ED denotes exposure duration, and CC denotes contaminant concentration.
a. According to EPA guidance, risks less than 10^{-6} require no remedial action in the Superfund program. Risks from 10^{-6} to 10^{-4} allow the site manager to use discretion with

Table 3.4 (continued)

a. No-action sites not included

Permutation (parameter varied)	Mean	Median[b]	t statistic for means[b]	Count
Ingestion rate	3.6e-2	1.7e-3	2.9	114
	2.4e-2	1.1e-3		
Exposure duration	3.8e-2	1.8e-3	3.2	104
	1.5e-2	8.1e-4		
Contaminant concentration	3.4e-2	1.7e-3	2.8	76
	1.0e-2	3.7e-4		
All	3.8e-2	1.9e-3	2.2	67
(IR, ED, CC)	1.9e-3	1.1e-4		

b. No-action sites included

Permutation (parameter varied)	Mean	Median[b]	t statistic for means[b]	Count
Ingestion rate	3.3e-2	1.2e-3	2.9	125
	2.2e-2	8.2e-4		
Exposure duration	3.6e-2	1.4e-3	3.1	113
	1.4e-2	7.2e-4		
Contaminant concentration	3.0e-2	1.2e-3	2.8	87
	9.1e-3	2.0e-4		
All	3.4e-2	1.5e-3	2.2	76
(IR, ED, CC)	1.7e-3	8.9e-5		

an explanation given if remedial action is taken. Risks greater than 10^{-4} are deemed unacceptable and require remedial action.

b. All median pairs are significantly different according to the sign test for equality of medians. All t values for means tests are statistically significant at the 95 percent confidence level.

identical for maximum risk pathways in which the no action sites are included, since their mean risk value drops from 3.4×10^{-2} to 1.7×10^{-3}.

The distribution of the maximum risk estimates shifts substantially toward lower values in the case of both parts of table 3.4. In panel a, 94 percent of sites had maximum risk pathways above the high-risk threshold value of 1×10^{-4}, where this amount drops to 54 percent based on the alternative risk assessment value. An almost identical pattern is shown in panel b of table 3.4. There is a slight increase of 4 percentage points in the number of sites with a maximum pathway that falls below the no-action threshold in panel b. From a policy standpoint the most important shift shown in table 3.4 is the substantial increase in the number of sites that fall into the range of risks where there is discretion regarding the cleanup action. Shifting to the alternative mean values puts almost half the maximum risk pathways into the intermediate 1×10^{-4} and 1×10^{-6} risk range.

It is also useful to inquire how the risk values are altered once we sum all the pathway scenarios involving soil and groundwater ingestion that may affect a population group. In particular, we sum all ingestion risks from the various pathways (e.g., ingestion of soil and groundwater containing many different chemicals) for populations specified by exposure population (worker, resident), age group, population location (on-site or off-site), and time frame scenario (present or future). These population groups may be at risk from both contaminated soil and contaminated groundwater, a fact that this measure incorporates. Again, because of complications arising from the exposure duration variable, these risks apply only to adults. We generated cumulative risks in three different ways to assess the effect of each assumption. We put each site into a remediation category based on the highest cumulative scenario risk we calculated at the site.

Table 3.5 presents these statistics, which reflect the cumulative scenario risks to individuals from Superfund sites. Consider the final row in table 3.5, which considers the combined influence of using means for these parameter values. At 80 percent of these sites, the cumulative EPA risk estimate was greater than 1×10^{-4}, as compared to 33.3 percent when mean values were used. The percentage of sites in the discretionary range jumped from 20 to 57 percent, while the percentage of sites requiring no remediation rose by 9 percentage points. Using only mean concentration estimates (in conjunction with conservative exposure values) similarly shifted many sites into the discretionary range.

Table 3.5
Cumulative scenario risks

Variables at mean value	Type of estimate	Percent no action[a]	Percent discretionary	Percent take action	Mean	Median[b]	t statistic for means	Number of sites
ED and IR	Site documents	0	20.0	80.0	3.7e-2	1.0e-3	3.0	135
	Mean risk	2.2	36.3	61.5	6.6e-3	2.4e-4		
CC	Site documents	0	19.6	80.4	2.7e-2	1.0e-3	2.1	102
	Mean risk	0.9	32.4	66.7	8.4e-3	2.1e-4		
ED, IR, CC	Site documents	0	19.8	80.2	2.8e-2	1.0e-3	2.3	96
	Mean risk	9.4	57.3	33.3	1.2e-3	4.2e-5		

Note: In this table IR denotes ingestion rate, ED denotes exposure duration, and CC denotes contaminant concentration.

a. According to EPA guidance, risks less than 10^{-6} require no remedial action in the Superfund program. Risks from 10^{-6} to 10^{-4} allow the site manager to use discretion with an explanation given if remedial action is taken. Risks greater than 10^{-4} are deemed unacceptable and require remedial action.

b. All median pairs are significantly different according to the sign test for equality of medians.

		Highest risk	Conservative ranking quantile			Lowest risk
		1	**2**	**3**	**4**	**5**
		(*n*=15)	(*n*=15)	(*n*=15)	(*n*=15)	(*n*=14)
Highest risk	**1** (*n*=15)	0.80	0.20	0	0	0
	2 (*n*=15)	0	0.47	0.53	0	0
Mean ranking quantile	**3** (*n*=15)	0.07	0.13	0.33	0.47	0
	4 (*n*=15)	0.07	0.13	0.07	0.40	0.33
Lowest risk	**5** (*n*=14)	0.07	0.07	0.07	0.13	0.64

Figure 3.1
Correspondence of site ranking by risk-level quantile: Fraction of sites from conservative ranking quantile in mean ranking quantile

Shifts in prioritization may arise by using conservative risk estimates rather than means. Would priorities be different if central estimates of risk are considered? In the Superfund program changes in risk estimates could affect which pathways at a site to focus on and which sites to prioritize. Because our analysis here focuses only on ingestion pathways we cannot fully examine distortions across pathways. However, we can look across sites for inconsistencies. We have done this by taking the maximum EPA-assessed risk for each site and ranking the sites accordingly. We then compare this ranking to a ranking using mean estimates of risk.

Rank-order correlation measures indicate how well two different rankings tend to agree. Two measures are used here. The Spearman correlation coefficient uses squared differences in rank to measure concordance, while the gamma statistic relies on the number of inversions found between the two rankings.[24] These rankings have a significant Spearman correlation coefficient of 0.74 and a gamma statistic of 0.62, indicating that a positive correspondence is found between the two rankings. The gamma statistic lends itself to a straightforward interpretation: Among untied pairs, the probability of selecting a pair with the same order is 0.62 more than doing otherwise. We can conclude that a positive relationship exists between conservative and central site priority, but the rankings are not identical.

Figure 3.1 presents these results in tabular form for a more thorough examination. The conservative rankings are measured on the horizontal axis from high (left) to low (right). The mean rankings are on the vertical axis from high (top) to low (bottom). If the rankings were perfectly consistent, we would expect to see a 5×5 identity matrix, but this is not the case. Consider the data by matrix rows. If we take the conservative case to be the baseline, we see that although there is an 80 percent agreement in the first quantile, three of the fifteen first-quantile sites have fallen to the third quantile or below in the rankings of mean risk. In the second conservative quantile three additional sites have fallen below the third mean risk quantile. Together, seven sites fall by two or more quantiles when mean estimates of risk are used for prioritization. One of these sites fell from being the eighth riskiest site (of 74) to the sixty-first. Overall, approximately 40 percent of the 74 sites fall off the diagonal and into a different quantile when central risk estimates are considered. Using central risks will result in different priorities for the policy maker.

Although there is a growing theoretical literature on conservatism in risk assessment and accompanying policy concerns, the debate over conservatism has been largely over principles. What has been missing is a firm empirical sense of the consequences of moving to a mean risk approach. Our results offer programwide evidence on the magnitude and implications of limiting conservatism in accordance with various legislative proposals. Our analysis of 141 Superfund sites indicates that current EPA use of conservative risk assessment parameters instead of mean variables leads to estimated risks that are 27 times greater than the pathway mean and 18 times greater than the pathway median. For the maximum risk pathways at the sites in our sample, the use of conservative parameter values instead of mean values generates risks that are 20 times greater at the mean and 17 times greater at the median. The use of central estimates of risk may therefore result in fewer sites requiring remediation under agency action thresholds. More sites fall into the range where managers have the greatest discretion under a central risk approach. Results using pathways of maximum risk as an indicator suggest that over 40 percent of sites requiring remediation under EPA risk assessments fall below the 1×10^{-4} cutoff when mean parameters are used. Program priorities also differ when sites are ranked based on mean parameter assumptions. Because toxicity estimates are often conservative, these results would presumably be more dramatic if we varied toxicity estimates as well.

In sum, our analysis suggests that risk assessments based on mean parameter values could affect policy judgment by substantially changing estimates of risk levels, especially for cumulative risks that mandate remediation under current guidance. Shifting to an approach based on central risk estimates would provide the risk manager with greater flexibility in addressing site hazards, since many more site risks would fall within the discretionary range of 1×10^{-4} to 1×10^{-6}.[25] A mean parameter approach also results in policies that will save the greatest expected number of lives.

In the next section we examine another method for analyzing the conservatism embraced in EPA's Superfund risk assessment methodology—the use of Monte Carlo analysis to quantify the degree of conservatism represented by the agency's focus on the "reasonable maximum exposure" at sites.

3.5   Quantifying Conservatism through Monte Carlo Analysis

A risk assessor trying to estimate the lifetime excess cancer risk for an on-site resident drinking groundwater containing multiple carcinogens is faced with many decisions about what values to use for variables that go into estimating cancer risks. Some variable values such as contaminant concentration are surrounded by uncertainty, which depends in part on the sampling of groundwater at the site. Other variables will vary because of heterogeneity of people, such as the differences across individuals in the amount of water ingested per day. This mixture of uncertainty and variability means that the "risk" of drinking groundwater can be represented as a distribution of risks. EPA guidelines encourage assessors to focus on one point on this distribution, the risk derived from assumptions about a "reasonable maximum exposure." The guidelines do not explicitly specify what percentile of risk that is meant to represent. The EPA's methodology rather encourages the use of parameter estimates which reflect a mixture of conservatism, with some parameters chosen to reflect upper bounds and others selected closer to mean values.

The multiplicative nature of the risk equation means that the compounding of conservative choices can generate risk estimates that are much higher on the final distribution of risk than the point represented by the value used in each parameter assumption. This effect is known as compounding or "cascading" conservatism and is illustrated in the following example from Burmaster and Harris (1993). Suppose that risk is estimated as the product of several independent and identically distributed (i.i.d.) lognormal parameters. If there are three such variables, each valued at its 95th percentile, the risk estimate will fall at the 99.78th percentile of the resulting distribution. The resulting estimate will be at the 99.95th percentile if there are four such parameters. This example is stylized, since distributions in practice may not be independent or identically distributed. However, it does indicate the dramatic effect that compounding conservation assumptions can have on the overall degree of the risk estimate conservatism.

Monte Carlo analysis offers a way to combine information on the shape of parameter distributions and the relationships among the distributions to generate an overall distribution for a given risk, such as the risk from consumption of groundwater by onsite residents. The first step in constructing a Monte Carlo analysis is to specify a probability density function (or, alternatively, a cumulative distribution function) for each parameter of the risk equation that is to be varied. Interdependence of these random variables must be incorporated by either modeling the process that underlies the correlation or by specifying joint distributions for the correlated parameters.[26] After the specification of distributions and relationships between input variables, a random draw is made from each parameter distribution and risk is calculated from this random draw. This process is iterated several thousand times to create a random sample of the dependent variable, risk. This allows for complete characterization of the risk distribution using standard statistical techniques.

Several case studies have employed Monte Carlo techniques to assess conservatism in point estimates of risk such as those used in Superfund. Hawkins (1991) assesses conservatism for a maximally exposed individual (MEI) using lognormal and uniform distributions. He finds that the point estimate suggested by MEI methods falls in the 99.99th percentile of potential exposures and that the conservative estimate is approximately an order of magnitude greater than the 95th percentile. Whitmyre et al. (1992) illustrate that hypothetical RME-like point estimates of exposure frequently exceed the 95th percentile. Estimates of soil ingestion risks are at the 98.1th percentile while those from dermal contact with soil are in the 99.8th percentile. Finley and Paustenbach (1994) find that RME-like point estimates often exceed the 95th percentile.

While the debate over Superfund risk assessment has continued for years, there have been relatively few studies of conservatism in risk estimates specific to this program. Elliott (1992) estimates potential risk from an existing Superfund site for over 657 individual exposure scenarios, although the only results presented in detail are for risks from inhalation of methylene chloride. The RME estimated risk exceeds the 99.9th percentile in this case.[27] Smith (1995) also estimates risks from an undisclosed Superfund site using probabilistic methods in comparison to RME risks. Using exposure scenarios of drinking water ingestion and showering, Smith finds that the cumulative RME risk is approximately the 95th percentile of distribution. In this section we offer the first programwide evidence on conservatism in Superfund. Our analysis uses actual risk assessment data from a sample of Superfund hazardous waste sites to quantify the conservatism in existing risk assessments and to assess the potential impact of this conservatism on site remediations.

We focus on a subset of 86 sites where sufficient data were available to develop reliable simulation estimates. Reasons that some sites in the earlier analysis of 141 sites are dropped from the Monte Carlo analysis include insufficient sample sizes to estimate a stable contaminant concentration and ambiguity in risk assessment parameters used. As before, we use the lifetime excess cancer risk equation specified in equation (3.1) to examine the groundwater or soil ingestion risks faced by residents. We refer to the estimates of those risks found in the site-level documents as the "RME" risks, the scenario the agency indicates they are meant to reflect. We take the toxicity values and exposure frequency as given in the site documents, though one could develop distributions for both and the agency focuses on "upper-bound" values for these. Our Monte Carlo analysis focuses on sampling from distributions for four variables: ingestion rates, exposure duration, body weight, and chemical concentration. Information on these distributions for the first three factors was derived from EPA publications or the broader scientific literature.[28]

Distributions for contaminant concentrations posed the greatest difficulty for estimation and a number of alternatives were employed so that specification sensitivity could be assessed. Ideally one would like to use full sampling data from sites to estimate these distributions by fitting the samples to a parametric distribution such as the lognormal.[29] Alternatively, one could use full sampling data as a basis for estimation through bootstrapping that draws from the sample observations (with replacement) to fill out the distribution.

Unfortunately, full sampling data were unavailable for our sample of sites so several second-best approaches were attempted based on alternative assumptions about site contamination. It is widely believed that many environmental variables including concentration of contaminants are distributed lognormally. This formulation is reasonable given that the lower bound on the concentration must be nonnegative and data are typically heavily right-skewed. EPA recognizes this aspect of contamination in its guidance and suggests methodology to estimate the 95th upper confidence level of a lognormal distribution for use in risk assessment.[30] According to guidance documents: "EPA's experience shows that most large or "complete" datasets from soil sampling are lognormally distributed. In most cases, it is reasonable to assume that Superfund soil sampling data are lognormally distributed."[31] Of course, it is possible to test for normality and EPA guidance does suggest the use of a normal distribution "if a statistical test supports the assumption that the data set is normally distributed."[32] Based on the importance apparently placed on the lognormal distribution and its wide applicability, it was assumed that concentrations are lognormally distributed for soil and groundwater unless specified otherwise in the site documentation.

Data available for estimation of the concentration term consisted of the concentration mean, the RME concentration, and the number of samples used to determine the RME concentration. These samples often included a proxy for nondetect values set at half the contract required quantification limit, the method detection limit, or some other minimum level. If these samples were used to determine the mean and RME, they were included in the sample size data. Also several specifications were clear enough so that we could determine whether an assumption of normality or lognormality was used to determine the sample statistics. In the absence of specific information, we assumed a lognormal distribution. There were four cases to be considered with the data. In all cases concentrations estimated on the basis of fewer than ten observations were dropped from the analysis in an effort to assure stability of the concentration parameter estimates.[33]

It is possible that concentrations of contaminants at a site are correlated with one another, which we explored through the use of Spearman correlation coefficients. Because the correlations could not be estimated directly from sampling data, separate simulations were run for coefficient values ranging from zero to 0.6. It was found that the final risk estimates were relatively insensitive to these specifications, and those reported here reflect a coefficient of 0.3. Correlations in other input variables were not accounted for explicitly, although neglecting weak correlations between input parameters is unlikely to have a significant effect on final risk estimates.[34]

Once the parameter distributions are specified, the Monte Carlo analysis proceeds with selection of a point on the distribution for the ingestion rate parameter, the distribution for exposure duration, the distribution for bodyweight, and the distribution for chemical concentration. These values were used to generate an estimate for the lifetime excess cancer risk arising from, for example, ingestion of contaminated groundwater. The process is then repeated to derive a second estimate. The repetition generates a risk distribution which we will refer to as the simulated risk distribution. Ten thousand iterations were run for each risk estimate, a number found to provide results that were generally stable. In particular, a comparison of runs at 10,000 iterations to those at 15,000 and 20,000 produced less than 1 percent difference in several distribution parameters, including the mean, median, standard deviation and 90th percentile. The 95th percentile estimates were found to agree within less than 2 percent. Based on these results, we judged 10,000 to be a sufficient number of iterations to ensure stability.

One way to quantify the degree of conservatism in EPA's risk assessment policy is to compare that RME pathway estimate at a site to the distribution of simulated risks derived from Monte Carlo analysis. For the 286 ingestion pathway risks estimated in documents at the 86 sites in our subsample, we can locate where each risk falls on the simulated distribution estimated for each pathway. Table 3.6 indicates the percentage of RME estimates which fall within a given percentile range on the simulated distributions

For soil ingestion pathways, 20.2 percent of EPA-estimated risks are greater than the 99.9th percentile of the corresponding simulated distribution. An additional 23.6 percent are between the 99th and 99.9th percentile, indicating that approximately 43 percent of soil ingestion pathways are greater than the 99th percentile. Of the remaining pathways, 39 percent fall between the 95th and 99th percentiles. Only 13 percent of the pathways fall within the assumed EPA target range between the 90th and 95th percentiles. Over 83 percent of soil ingestion pathways exceed this goal.

An even more striking result is seen when groundwater ingestion pathways are considered. Of the 197 pathways analyzed, only 2.5 percent are within or below EPA's target range. Approximately 28 percent of these pathways exceed the 99.9th percentile and an additional 49 percent exceed the 99th percentile. Such results indicate EPA risk assessments may greatly exaggerate groundwater risks. Considering all 286 pathways, approximately 26 percent of EPA-assessed risks are greater than the 99.9th percentile, an additional 41 percent exceed the 99th percentile and only 5.2 percent fall within the EPA target range.

Table 3.6
Location of RME estimates on the simulated risk distribution

Medium	Percentile range							EPA estimate	
	N	<75	75–90	90–95	95–99	99–99.9	>99.9	Mean	Median
Soil	89	0	3.4	13.5	39.3	23.6	20.2	2.4e-3	2.5e-5
Groundwater	197	0.5	1.0	1.0	20.3	49.2	27.9	3.3e-2	6.4e-4
both	286	0.3	1.4	5.2	25.5	41.3	26.2	2.3e-2	2.0e-4

Table 3.7
Risk thresholds and pathways of maximum risk

Count	Point	$< 10^{-6}$	$10^{-6}-10^{-4}$	$> 10^{-4}$	Mean	Median
$n = 86$	RME	0.0	26.7	73.3	4.9e-2	6.3e-4
	99th	4.7	24.4	60.9	1.0e-2	3.5e-4
	95th	5.8	39.5	54.7	3.5e-3	1.3e-4
	90th	5.8	44.9	49.3	2.2e-3	9.1e-5
	Mean	8.1	57.0	34.9	1.1e-3	4.2e-5

In table 3.7 we consider the pathway of maximum ingestion risk at each site and determine how alternative policy specifications affect this pathway. We compare specific points on the risk distribution and determine whether risks of this magnitude would trigger remediation under EPA's guidelines. Of the 86 sites in this study, the RME estimate of the maximum ingestion risk pathway indicates remediation is triggered at 73.3 percent of the sites. The remaining 26.7 percent fall within the site manager's range of discretion. If one focuses on the 95th percentile risks, only 54.7 percent of these sites mandate remediation. Nearly 40 percent would fall within the manager's discretionary range, and 5.8 percent would fall below the action threshold of 10^{-6}. Similarly, based on 90th percentile risks, 49.3 percent of sites mandate remediation, 44.9 percent fall within the discretionary range, and 5.8 percent do not meet the 10^{-6} discretionary action threshold. Basing remedial decisions on target risks of the 90th or 95th percentile rather than on the RME estimates thus would lead to a reduction of up to 20 percentage points in the number of sites mandating remediation based on ingestion risk pathways.

Because residents may face risks from both soil and groundwater ingestion, it is necessary to sum risks across pathways to assess total individual risk levels. Summing ingestion risk pathways by age group (adult or child), time frame (current or future), and location of exposure (on-site or off-site) provides estimates of total risk to populations defined by these variables. There were 164 such populations at the 86 sites in this sample, and these cumulative risk pathways are the focus of table 3.8. Under the RME assumptions, 66 percent of these populations faced cumulative risks that exceeded 10^{-4} and 34 percent faced risks in the middle range of 10^{-4} to 10^{-6}. Evaluating risks at the 95th percentile indicates a 15 percentage point drop in the number of populations facing unacceptably high risks and over seven percent face risks below the 10^{-6} threshold. At the 90th

Table 3.8
Risk thresholds and cumulative population risks

a. All populations

Count	Point	$< 10^{-6}$	$10^{-6}-10^{-4}$	$> 10^{-4}$	Mean	Median
$n = 164$	RME	0	34.1	65.9	4.0e-2	4.7e-4
	99th	6.7	29.3	64.0	8.4e-3	2.5e-4
	95th	7.9	42.1	50.0	3.1e-3	9.8e-5
	90th	8.5	51.8	39.7	1.9e-3	5.8e-5
	Mean	13.4	59.8	26.8	9.0e-4	2.8e-5

b. Maximum risk populations

Count	Point	$< 10^{-6}$	$10^{-6}-10^{-4}$	$> 10^{-4}$	Mean	Median
$n = 86$	RME	0.0	23.3	76.7	6.3e-2	1.0e-3
	99th	4.7	24.4	70.9	1.2e-2	3.8e-4
	95th	5.8	34.9	59.3	4.4e-3	1.7e-4
	90th	7.0	41.9	51.1	2.6e-3	1.0e-4
	Mean	9.3	54.7	36.0	1.3e-3	4.7e-5

percentile only 40 percent of populations face risks that are unacceptably high.

The results are similar if one considers the population that faces the maximum risk at each of the 86 sites. Panel b in table 3.8 shows that over three-quarters of these sites have at least one population that faces unacceptably high risks as opposed to approximately 60 percent if the 95th percentile is used. At the 95th percentile, 6 percent of sites have no populations that face ingestion risks greater then 10^{-6}. The 90th percentile indicates that 51.1 percent of sites have at least one population facing risks that exceed 10^{-4}.

These Monte Carlo results indicate that overall the conservatism embodied in EPA's risk assessment is quite striking. For the soil and groundwater risk pathways we examined, over two-thirds were at the 99th percentile or higher on the range of simulated risks we developed. In terms of the maximum cumulative ingestion risks for the populations at these sites, the EPA's "reasonable maximum exposure" scenarios result in 77 percent of the sites analyzed as having risks estimated to be 10^{-4} or higher. If one uses the 90th percentiles on these maximum cumulative ingestion risk distributions, however, only 5 percent of the sites would have cumulative ingestion risks automatically triggering remediation. Many more sites would be shifted into the range where site managers have more discretion about whether to remediate.

3.6 Conclusion

The Monte Carlo results indicate the fundamental weakness of the current series of ad hoc conservation adjustments. Even if one wished to avoid uncertainty, the expression of this conservatism concern should be with the distribution of the overall risk value, not the component parameters. The current approach leads to an unpredictable and quite extreme level of conservatism in risk estimation because of the compounding of the varying conservatism adjustments. A more reliable approach for setting the degree of conservatism at a specific value is to use Monte Carlo analysis to assess the shape of the overall risk distribution and to assess the risk at the percentile of interest. Ideally this exercise should be symmetric. For example, coupling examination of the 95th percentile with consideration of the 5th percentile will provide a more balanced perspective on the character of the risk than will considering the upper tail alone.

Our preference is not to focus on the extremes of the possible risk distribution but rather to obtain a more realistic assessment of what the risk is actually likely to be. That approach will be most protective in terms of the expected health benefits to populations exposed to the risk. Taken together, the analyses in chapters 2 and 3 demonstrate that the site documents overestimate individual cancer risks. Assessing the import of these individual risks should also involve examining the likelihood that they will arise (e.g., are they risks to hypothetical future residents on currently uninhabited sites?), the alternate estimates based on mean parameter assumptions, and consideration of the size and proximity of the exposed population. All of these factors would play a role in a benefit–cost analysis at site remediations. In the following chapter we take another step toward assessing the nature of hazards at sites by explicitly linking individual risk levels to the magnitude of exposed populations.

Populations at Risk

Our matching of 1990 U.S. census statistics with available site boundaries for 1,173 nonfederal and federal NPL sites indicates that over 51 million people live within 4 miles of a Superfund site. How large the risks to those populations will be depends on the proximity of these populations to the sites, the extent of contamination, and the likelihood of exposure.

EPA guidance for risk assessment has a different focus. The agency assesses levels of risks that individuals would face if exposed to harmful chemicals. Whether a person actually is exposed to the risk or simply might potentially be exposed in the future is not distinguished. Somewhat surprisingly, in EPA risk assessments people, in terms of the extent of the exposed population, do not explicitly enter final cleanup decision making. One hypothetically exposed individual and a densely populated area each receive the same weight.[1]

Our focus is more comprehensive in that it explores the full extent of the health risk consequences. A benefit–cost analysis of remediations would, at a minimum, consider the number of expected cancer cases averted at sites. A regulator with a constrained budget would use this indicator of efficiency to allocate funds across sites, if averting the greatest expected number of cancer cases were a primary objective. EPA site documents contain a key building block for this calculation—information on contaminant concentration. In this chapter we demonstrate how to assess site risks by combining these data with information on site boundaries and block-level census data. The advent of geographic information systems (GIS) technology for census data analysis enables us to make a precise linkage of exposed populations. Our methodology, described in detail in appendix A, allows us, for a sample of nonfederal sites, to calculate the expected number of cancer cases at each site and estimate the number of individuals exposed to particular levels of noncancer risks. These estimates in turn will allow us in chapter 5 to estimate the cost per case of cancer averted as a measure of program performance.

4.1 Assessing Populations

Our risk database contains information on chemical concentrations at sites for pathways where the cancer risk from the chemical reported in the

ROD or risk assessment was 10^{-8} or higher. Because of the diversity of site analyses, there was large variation across risk assessments in terms of pathways selected for evaluation, such as the population age groups considered. To make all estimated site risks comparable, we developed a standardized set of risk scenarios at each site that used the chemical concentration data from the site level documents. For each site in our 150 site sample, we estimated the cancer risks arising over a thirty-year time period from a consistent set of residential exposure pathways—soil and groundwater ingestion, inhalation, and dermal exposure pathways. We developed estimates based on three cases, defined below:

Case 1: Conservative exposures. We estimated the conservative risk value by taking the 95th percentile of the combination of two exposure factors, the intake rate and body weight, in conjunction with EPA values for other residential risk assessment parameters. The concentration used was the mean of the "reasonable maximum exposure" values for all areas (including areas of high chemical concentrations called "hot spots") at the site. We did not incorporate any cancer latency period or discount future cancer cases, consistent with EPA practices. Thus the discounted value of the risk reduction benefits will be overstated. This case incorporates the conservatism adopted by the agency in its general approach to estimating cancer cases.

Case 2: Mean concentrations. This case used the same methodology as in case 1, except that we only developed estimates for sites (99) which had mean concentration values for all contaminated media presented in the site documents. Case 2 also does not discount the risk levels. This case provides a baseline for comparison to case 3.

Case 3: Mean risks. This case extended the analysis of the 99 sites with mean concentration values available for all contaminated media. We also included the mean of the intake rate/body weight ratio in conjunction with EPA values for other residential risk assessment parameters. The concentration used was the average of the mean sampling concentrations presented in the site documents. The estimates also incorporated a ten year latency period for the onset of cancers. We discounted the cancer cases at a 3 percent rate to reflect the different values placed on avoiding harms today versus those in the future.[2] This weighting reflects assumptions a social welfare-maximizing regulator might make if he or she were trying to save the greatest discounted expected number of lives with a limited remediation budget.

The mapping of sites to populations is precise. Based on aerial photographs and on-site surveys, EPA has established the latitude and longitude values for the site boundaries. We then superimposed these site locations on a grid of 1990 block and block-group level census data to estimate the populations living in rings of various radii around a site. We estimated on-site populations using 1990 census data if the EPA survey data indicated that populations were currently living on the site.[3] To estimate cancer cases arising from soil exposures, we assumed that populations living within one mile were potentially exposed to the chemicals in the soil pathways. We varied the probability that these populations were exposed to the soil pathway with the distance from the site. In the case of dermal and ingestion exposure, the exposure probability ranged from 1 for on-site resident exposure to 0.0063 for residents within one mile. The source of these probabilities was a U.S. EPA analysis of how the probability that individuals will come into contact with a site varies with their distance from the area.[4] Multiplying the individual cancer risk estimated from soil exposure pathways by the population size within the ring and by the probability of exposure yields the expected number of cancer cases by ring for a given year.

This analysis took into account the role of population growth. We increased population size by applying a growth factor to the 1990 census figures based on the annual rate of population change in the county from 1980 to 1990. The population per ring area thus changes for each year in our estimates of the number of cancer cases arising from soil exposure over a thirty-year period. In effect this procedure takes current land uses as given and estimates the additional incidence of cancer cases that would arise over thirty years.

We estimated groundwater risks for the 142 sites where the risk assessments indicated that this pathway could potentially be present. At 74 sites, EPA had prepared plume maps in the site documents. After we digitized these maps using GIS technology, the contaminated plume could be linked to 1990 block-level census data. The census data included information on the number of people who rely on groundwater for drinking water.[5] Multiplying this population figure by the estimated individual groundwater exposure pathway risks yields an estimate of the number of cancer cases per year from exposure to groundwater. At sites where plume maps were unavailable, we combined the populations in each ring with the percentage of the ring that would be affected by a groundwater plume of average size. The average estimated ring was based on analysis of the sites where plume maps were given in site documents. Our approach for estimating cancers arising from groundwater contamination implicitly assumes that residents using public water supplies will be protected by monitoring and treatment of public water supplies. This assumption is consistent with current EPA drinking water standards.

To illustrate how we matched risks with populations, we demonstrate the approach using the Genzale Plating Company site as a case study of how cancer cases arising from soil exposure were estimated and the Bofors Nobel site to show how cases arising from groundwater consumption were analyzed.

4.2   Estimating Soil Risks

The estimation of soil exposure risks at the Genzale Plating Company site in New York illustrates our standardized methodology for calculating the population cancer risks associated with soil contamination at a site. The site is a half acre plot with two on-site residences and a metal plating facility that has contaminated soil with heavy metals. The site is located in Franklin Square on Long Island, New York. It contains leaching pits, storage buildings, and various chemical storage facilities. Previously the company had dumped the waste directly into the sewer. The soil is contaminated with heavy metals, such as chromium, cadmium, and nickel. EPA conducted a removal action at the site that removed contaminated sludge and backfilled the leaching pits. In terms of the long-term site remediation decision, the agency chose to evacuate the site and use off-site treatment and disposal of the contaminated soil.

Figure 4.1 illustrates the layout of the site based on site-level documents. Two residences flank the front of the plant, which is surrounded by a fence. The "on-site" residents must go either through the plant or over the fence to have direct contact with the leaching pits behind the plant. Similarly the EPA dermal exposure assumptions for the surrounding populations can be thought of as the probability that an individual in each ring will cross the fence and be exposed. These behavioral assumptions consequently embody an additional level of conservatism that we recognize but do not adjust for in our estimates.

Using site boundary information from the EPA, we were able to match the location of the Genzale site with information of the surrounding population. Figure 4.2 indicates the location of the site with respect to the local terrain. The network of surrounding roads is quite dense, as one

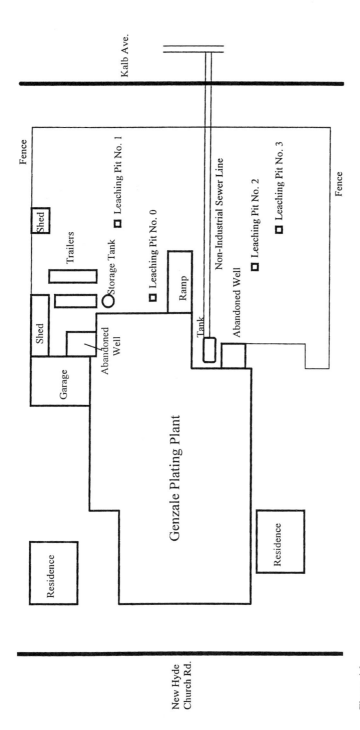

Figure 4.1
Genzale Plating Company site

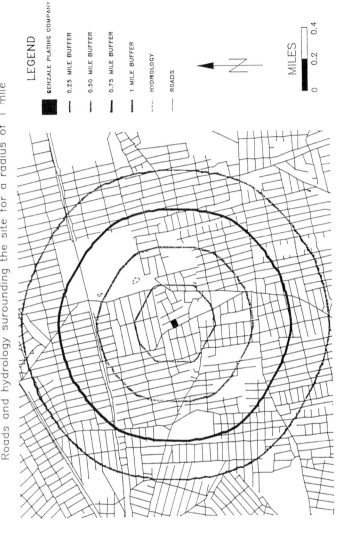

Figure 4.2
Genzale Plating Company location

would expect in this urban area. Similarly the substantial population density makes the size of the neighboring block groups relatively small, as figure 4.3 reveals the numerous census block groups surrounding the site. The size of a block group may vary and is based on household numbers. The census recommends an ideal block group be 400 housing units or about 1,500 people.[6] Thus this level of detail is much more refined than zip code or county-level analyses. The map indicates which block groups fall within a ring with a one-mile or four-mile radius. We calculated population risks from exposure to contaminated soil through ingestion, dermal, and inhalation of outdoor dust in the following manner: The site boundaries used to create rings were spaced at $\frac{1}{4}$, $\frac{1}{2}$, $\frac{3}{4}$, 1, 2, 3, and 4 miles around the site. For any block group in a ring, we calculated the fraction of the block group within the ring. Making the assumption of an even population distribution within a block group, we estimated the number of individuals in the ring by multiplying the fraction of the block group within the ring by the block-group population. The number of individuals within the ring equaled the number of individuals from the portions of each block group within the ring.

Our primary method for estimating populations residing within the rings was to begin with the 1990 census block-group population data as indicated above. The annual growth rate for populations associated with the site was the annual growth implied by the change in the county population between 1980 and 1990. For the Genzale site in Nassau county, the estimated county annual growth rate was actually negative (-0.3 percent), since the county population shrank between 1980 and 1990. We used this growth rate to estimate a population for each ring over a thirty-year period. Table 4.1 summarizes the population estimates for the Genzale site at year 1, in 15 years, and in 30 years.

We calculated the expected number of cancer cases associated with soil exposure during the first year in the following way. Table 4.2 uses the mean of the RME chemical concentrations and the 95th percentile on soil intake rates and body weight parameters. This approach represents the case 1 scenario. The individual cancer risk is the sum of the annual risks from the standardized pathways (i.e., soil and groundwater ingestion, inhalation, and dermal exposure). Each of these annual pathway risks is in turn a summation of the chemical risks in each pathway. The population for a ring follows the methodology demonstrated in table 4.1. For ingestion of soil and dermal contact, we multiply the risk for each ring by a factor to indicate the probability a resident will come on-site to come into

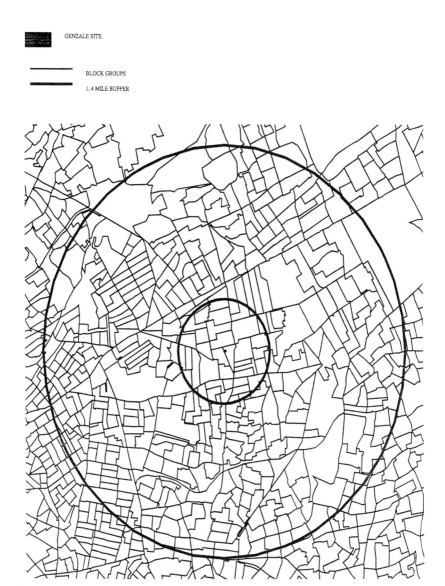

GENZALE SITE

BLOCK GROUPS

1, 4 MILE BUFFER

Figure 4.3
Block groups and 1- and 4-mile rings, Genzale Plating Company

Table 4.1
Population totals over time, by ring, at Genzale Plating Company site

Ring distance	Year = 1	Year = 15	Year = 30
On-site	11	11	11
$0-\frac{1}{4}$ mile	2,149	2,071	1,991
$\frac{1}{4}-\frac{1}{2}$ mile	5,267	5,077	4,881
$\frac{1}{2}-\frac{3}{4}$ mile	7,845	7,562	7,270
$\frac{3}{4}-1$ mile	14,257	13,743	13,212
1–2 miles	78,114	75,296	72,389
2–3 miles	133,897	129,066	124,084
3–4 miles	208,071	200,565	192,823
Total	449,611	433,391	416,661

Note: An annual growth rate of −0.3 percent was used to derive the population estimates.

contact with the soil. Using EPA estimates, the value of this factor is 1 for on-site residents, 0.025 for residents within $\frac{1}{4}$ mile, 0.0125 for residents between $\frac{1}{4}$ and $\frac{3}{4}$ mile, and 0.0063 for residents between $\frac{3}{4}$ and 1 mile.[7] For the inhalation pathway, a dilution factor multiplies the risk to account for the attenuation of concentration with distance.[8]

Table 4.2 demonstrates for the eight rings how the risks from soil ingestion, dermal exposure, and inhalation of dust yields an estimated number of 0.16 cancer cases in the first year for the adult age group. Table 4.3 shows the results of performing this calculation by age groups by ring for thirty years. For the Genzale site, the estimated number of cancer cases over a thirty-year period from exposure to soil contaminants via ingestion, dermal exposure, and inhalation is 8.88. Note that the effects of soil exposure are calculated out to 4 miles. For dermal and ingestion risks, this procedure involves the probability of on-site and off-site residents coming onto the site. Similarly for inhalation there must be exposure to on-site and off-site residents to (diluted) concentrations from the soil at their respective distances from the site.

The estimate of 8.88 expected cancer cases over thirty years from soil exposure at the Genzale Plating site is based on mean RME concentrations and 95th percentile parameter assumptions for intake rate and body weight. These numbers, however, assume that the cancer cases occur without a lag time. Consider, however, how this estimate would change if calculated under case 3 assumptions. Avoiding some of the conservatism inherent in the EPA's current methodology, we assume chemical concentrations in cancer risk calculations based on mean concentrations

Table 4.2
Example of generation of cancer cases from soil exposure, by ring and by route, for adult residents in first year at Genzale Plating Company site

Ring distance	Age	Route	Population	Soil risk	Dilution/ probability factor	Cancer cases
On-site	Adult	Inhalation	9	9.5e-5	1	8.2e-4
	Adult	Ingestion	9	4.1e-7	1	3.5e-6
	Adult	Dermal	9	8.7e-7	1	7.5e-6
					Total: 8.2e-4	
$0-\frac{1}{4}$ mile	Adult	Inhalation	1,655	9.5e-5	0.025	3.9e-2
	Adult	Ingestion	1,655	4.1e-7	0.025	1.7e-5
	Adult	Dermal	1,655	8.7e-7	0.250	3.6e-5
					Total: 3.9e-2	
$\frac{1}{4}-\frac{1}{2}$ mile	Adult	Inhalation	4,179	9.5e-5	0.0125	2.1e-2
	Adult	Ingestion	4,179	4.1e-7	0.0125	2.1e-5
	Adult	Dermal	4,179	8.7e-7	0.0540	4.5E-5
					Total: 2.1e-2	
$\frac{1}{2}-\frac{3}{4}$ mile	Adult	Inhalation	6,299	9.5e-5	0.0125	9.6e-3
	Adult	Ingestion	6,299	4.1e-7	0.0125	3.2e-5
	Adult	Dermal	6,299	8.7e-7	0.0160	6.8e-5
					Total: 9.7e-3	
$\frac{3}{4}-1$ mile	Adult	Inhalation	11,492	3.3e-6	0.0063	1.7e-2
	Adult	Ingestion	11,492	3.3e-6	0.0063	2.9e-5
	Adult	Dermal	11,492	6.8e-4	0.0160	6.3e-5
					Total: 1.7e-2	
1–2 miles	Adult	Inhalation	62,071	3.3e-6	0.051	3.0e-2
	Adult	Ingestion	62,071	3.3e-6	0	0.0
	Adult	Dermal	62,071	6.8e-4	0	0.0
					Total: 3.0e-2	
2–3 miles	Adult	Inhalation	105,014	3.3e-6	0.0023	2.3e-2
	Adult	Ingestion	105,014	2.9e-6	0	0
	Adult	Dermal	105,014	6.7e-4	0	0
					Total: 2.3e-2	
3–4 miles	Adult	Inhalation	162,716	3.3e-6	0.0014	2.2e-2
	Adult	Ingestion	162,716	2.9e-6	0	0.0
	Adult	Dermal	162,716	6.7e-4	0	0.0
					Total: 2.2e-2	
					Year 1 total: 1.6e-1	

Note: Cancer case estimates based on case 1 scenario.

Table 4.3
Cancer cases from soil exposure, by resident age group, by ring, over 30 years at Genzale Plating Company site

Ring	Expected cancer figures by age						Adult	Total
	Age 0–3	Age 3–6	Age 6–9	Age 9–12	Age 12–15	Age 15–18		
On-site	0	0	0	0	0	0	0.02	0.05
0–$\frac{1}{4}$ mile	0.46	0.27	0.16	0.10	0.06	0.07	1.14	2.26
$\frac{1}{4}$–$\frac{1}{2}$ mile	0.18	0.14	0.08	0.04	0.04	0.03	0.62	1.13
$\frac{1}{2}$–$\frac{3}{4}$ mile	0.07	0.06	0.03	0.02	0.02	0.01	0.28	0.49
$\frac{3}{4}$–1 mile	0.16	0.11	0.05	0.04	0.03	0.02	0.51	0.91
1–2 miles	0.27	0.18	0.11	0.07	0.05	0.04	0.87	1.59
2–3 miles	0.22	0.15	0.08	0.06	0.04	0.03	0.66	1.25
3–4 miles	0.22	0.13	0.07	0.06	0.04	0.03	0.63	1.18
Total	1.60	1.06	0.59	0.38	0.28	0.25	4.73	8.88

Note: Cancer case estimates based on case 1 scenario.

reported at the Genzale site. We also use the mean of the intake rate/body weight ratio in conjunction with other EPA values for residential risk assessments. Assuming a ten-year latency was assumed for the onset of cancers and a discount rate of 3 percent, the expected number of cancer cases over thirty years from soil exposure is 0.11. This substantial change in the estimates demonstrates how conservatism can boost the assessed population risks.

For the sample of 150 sites, we used this methodology to derive estimates of cancer cases from soil exposure over a thirty-year time horizon. Before reporting these results, we describe our methodology for estimating groundwater population risks.

4.3 Estimating Groundwater Risks

To ensure comparability, we also standardized estimates of expected cancer cases from exposure to contaminated groundwater across sites. The assessment of chemical concentration values followed the same procedure as for soil risks, with case 1 estimates based on the mean of RME concentrations and case 3 based on mean concentrations. The exposure pathways estimated for groundwater were ingestion, dermal while showering/bathing, and inhalation while showering. Ingestion rate and body weight parameters for the specific age groups outlined above coupled with an exposure duration of one year provided the components for estimating the annual risks of cancer arising from groundwater exposure through a particular pathway.

The challenge in estimating expected cancer cases generated from groundwater contamination arises in determining which populations are exposed to the groundwater. The RODs and RI/FSs do provide detailed information at some sites with groundwater contamination on the location and size of plumes. For 74 sites we were able to create digitized plume maps and overlay this with the 1990 census data and GIS maps. We also used the data on plume size to generate a mean plume size per site estimate. We used this information at sample sites with groundwater contamination but without plume data to estimate the fraction of each ring area contaminated by an average plume. The fraction of the population living over the contaminated area served as a base for estimating the potentially exposed population. We multiplied this figure by the fraction of households in each ring not connected to a municipal water supply, a figure derived from census data, to estimate the population exposed to contaminated water.[9]

Figure 4.4 illustrates how the groundwater methodology was applied at the Bofors Nobel site. The Bofors site is located in Egleton Township, six miles east of downtown Muskegon, Michigan. The site is a currently operating chemical production facility with an abandoned landfill and ten abandoned sludge lagoons. The groundwater surrounding the site is contaminated by volatile organic compounds and semivolatile organic compounds. According to the data in the site documents, the plume at the site measures 838,715 square meters. Figure 4.4 indicates that while the plume is mostly on-site it potentially affects groundwater out to part of the quarter-mile ring around the site. The 1990 census data from the block groups overlaid on the plume area indicate that 52 people live within a quarter mile of the site and that 96 percent of the households were not connected to municipal water supplies. For each block group we multiply the fraction of households not on municipal water supplies times the population in the area estimated to overlay the groundwater plume. For the Bofors site this procedure results in an estimate of the exposed population to groundwater contamination of 29 (see figure 4.5). This figure is increased with a constant annual growth rate of 0.09 percent over the thirty-year period, to yield an annual exposed population.

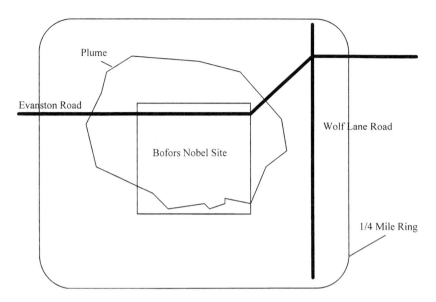

Figure 4.4
Bofors Nobel site layout and plume

The chemical concentration figures from groundwater exposure pathways at the site are used to generate estimated annual individual cancer risks, following standard EPA risk assessment guidelines (except for the use of mean values in cases 2 and 3). Multiplying the annual cancer risk probability from groundwater exposure of 0.0073 by the exposed population figures for each year and summing these figures generates an estimate for the total number of expected cancers estimated to arise over thirty years from groundwater contamination at Bofors Nobel. This figure is 6.60 for case 1, which is the scenario embodying the conservatism favored by the agency. If mean chemical concentrations had been available at Bofors Nobel, we would have combined this with a mean intake rate/body weight figure, a ten-year latency period assumed for the onset of cancers, and a 3 percent discount rate for cancer cases to derive the expected number of cancer cases arising over thirty years from groundwater contamination under our case 3 scenario. We used this methodology at the other sites with groundwater contamination in the 150-site sample to derive aggregate estimates of cancers caused by groundwater contamination.

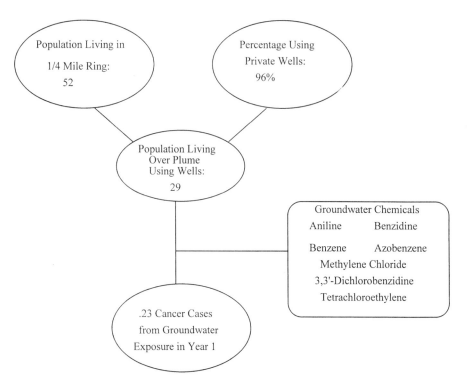

Figure 4.5
Generating cancer case numbers—Bofors Nobel site

4.4   Adding Population Risks

The combination of site-level concentration information, boundary data, census figures, and GIS technology allows us to calculate measures of cancer and noncancer risks. Under the case 1 scenario embodying con-servative EPA assumptions, we estimate that there will be 731 cancer cases over thirty years arising from exposure to contamination at our sample of 150 sites. The vast majority of these cancer cases arise from soil exposure (695) rather than groundwater exposure (36).

The substantial disparity in site risks makes this tally a somewhat mis-leading indicator of the relative frequency of groundwater and soil risks. Nearly 90 percent of the total estimated cancer cases occur at one site, the Westinghouse Electric site in California (which had 652 expected cancer cases). This concentration of estimated cancers at one site means that the median number of cancer cases per site (0.017) is more indicative of the population risks overall than the average number of cancer cases (4.87). Figure 4.6 underscores how low the number of cancer cases is at most sites. Of the 150 sites where cancer cases were estimated, only 10 had 1 or more expected cancer cases estimated to arise over a thirty-year period from groundwater and soil exposures. If agency exposure factors and concentrations are used, a ten-year cancer latency period is assumed, and a 3 percent discount factor is used for the 99 sites where average concentrations are available, the discounted number of cancer cases at these sites drops by two-thirds from 698 cases under case 2 to 204 cases under case 3.

The majority of Superfund sites in our sample thus have fewer than 0.1 cancer cases estimated to arise from exposure to soil or groundwater contamination under case 1 assumptions. Our estimation approach is conservative, in that the concentrations of chemicals used at sites were taken as the mean of the RME concentrations derived from site-level documents. Thus "hot spot" figures were included in the figures averaged to yield the exposure point concentrations in cases 1 and 2 even if it were unlikely that populations around the site would come into contact with the chemical at these elevated concentrations. The large number of expected cancer cases at the Westinghouse site derives from this assumption. At this site estimated soil exposures include exposure to high PCB concentrations from a 650-square-foot area which is mostly paved over. Even more conservative calculations are possible if, for example, one assumes that current land use patterns will change so that many areas and sites that are currently not residential become sites for new residential developments. In that case the population figures associated with the individual cancer risks would rise, and the estimated number of cancer cases would increase as well. Note also that the chemical concentration figures used at sites are postremoval action, so the cancer cases that would arise if prior Superfund removal actions had not taken place are not included.

The small number of expected cancer cases arising from unremediated exposures also indicates the potential importance of analyzing how the risks to cleanup workers and surrounding residents of remediating these sites compare to the risks at the site under alternative remedies (e.g., institutional controls, containment, or treatment of waste). Recent work on dealing with chemical risks underscores the potential that some remediations may entail larger risks than the original hazard addressed.[10]

While noncancer risks cannot be aggregated due to the differences in the severity of the adverse health outcomes associated with different

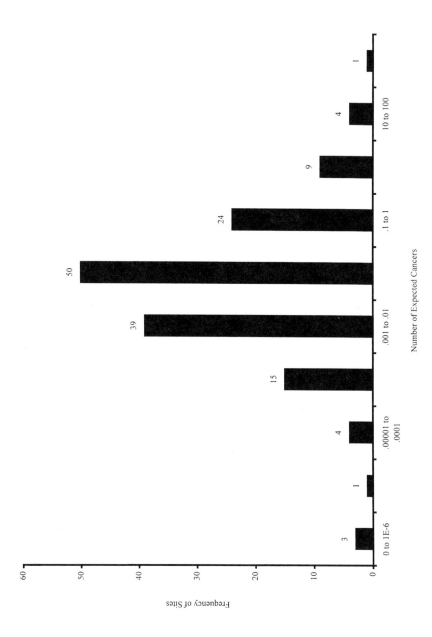

Figure 4.6
Number of cancer cases expected from site contamination

chemicals, we can use the methodology described above to estimate the expected number of people exposed to different levels of noncancer risks. At each of the 150 sites, we combined information on the level of non-cancer individual risks, the probabilities of exposure described above for soil and groundwater contaminants, and the total populations living on site and within a four-mile radius. The expected number of people exposed to noncancer hazard quotients greater than or equal to one from soil risks were 6,130 persons for dermal exposure, 6,430 via ingestion, and 109,400 for inhalation (primarily because of the low reference dose for chromium). For groundwater, these numbers were 320 people via dermal, 1,610 for ingestion, and 900 via inhalation.

If one were to use a more conservative risk estimate defining only those sites with hazard quotients greater than ten as hazardous, then the esti-mated populations exposed are substantially smaller. The expected num-ber of exposed individuals to hazard quotients greater than 10 due to soil risks drop to 2,250 for dermal exposures, 5,050 for ingestion, and 15,850 for inhalation. For groundwater risks, the expected number of exposed individuals is 40 via dermal, 860 for ingestion, and 480 for inhalation. These figures represent the expected number of people exposed to these levels of noncancer risks, not the expected number of cases of noncancer reactions. The current information used by the EPA in risk assessment does not translate exposure to varying levels of noncancer risks into the probability of an actual adverse outcome. The closest the government has come to assessing the magnitude of the risks is in work by the Agency for Toxic Substances and Disease Registry (ATSDR), which has tried to link actual human health outcomes to chemical exposures at the sites through long-term health monitoring and epidemiological studies. The agency has documented human exposures to contamination at 40 percent of the sites, determined that 35 percent of the sites are public health hazards, and classified 2 percent of the sites as imminent and urgent public health hazards.[11]

4.5 Conclusion

Overall, our analyses in chapters 2 through 4 of human health risks esti-mated to arise at Superfund sites indicate that current agency practices do not accurately assess these risks. Various conservatism biases distort the extent of the risk and the relative priority that should be given to different sites. Even though actual risk exposures are usually low, individual life-time cancer rates estimated to arise at sites under EPA's risk assessment methodology are extremely high in comparison to other risks regulated by the government. Many of these risk estimates drop to levels deemed acceptable in EPA remediation guidelines, however, if one uses more realistic parameter values in the risk assessment process. If prevention of the greatest number of expected adverse effects is the objective, central parameter estimates are superior to estimates influenced sharply by un-certainty or heterogeneity in exposure.

Our analysis reveals that once individual risk levels are combined with data on exposed populations, the magnitude of apparent cancer risks diminishes even further. These population risks, though small in magni-tude overall, may nevertheless merit stringent remediations in particular cases. Sites differ both in terms of their cleanup costs and the extent of exposed population. If one judged remediations by efficiency standards, then the agency would try to spend its remediation funds taking into ac-count the cost per expected cancer case averted at sites. In the next chap-ter we use the population risks developed here to assess the efficiency of the EPA's remediation of Superfund sites.

Costs of Conservatism: Cost-Effectiveness of Site Remediations

The costs of ill-chosen regulations can take many forms. Public and private costs of complying with a rule's requirements are one index of a regulatory impact. Alternatively, one could focus on performance measures such as the number of sites cleaned up, or better yet, the adverse health effects prevented. The performance measure that we will adopt combines both sets of concerns. By assessing the cost per cancer case prevented, we will be able to determine how well the cleanups address their principal objective. Superfund cleanup policies that are not targeted at protecting actual exposed populations may be very "costly" in terms of opportunities forgone and opportunities squandered. Ineffective cleanup efforts themselves may impose more costs than benefits, and they also divert cleanup resources from sites where cleanup would have been socially beneficial. In this case a real cost of poorly designed policies is the illnesses borne or environmental damages incurred because of lax government activity at sites where cleanups are desirable.

Regulation ultimately requires that property rights be defined and applied. Choices are restricted. The existence of constraints places regulation at the heart of many political conflicts. Regulations thus have political costs. For legislators, the political costs of a rule may entail constituent votes lost, contributions forgone, or a loss of a policy personally valued. For regulators, political costs may involve reduced funding, restricted discretion, increased public or congressional scrutiny, or diminished opportunities to pursue their own objectives. Failure to regulate effectively may squander the scarce regulatory opportunities that an agency has.

The weight that regulators give these different types of costs will often depend on signals from Congress. For the Superfund program, legislators in the 1980s focused the EPA's attention on the political costs of failing to provide extensive cleanups. The agency's original mandate in CERCLA did not mention the costs of remediation. The legislation called for "actions as may be necessary to prevent, minimize, or mitigate damage to the public health or welfare or to the environment."[1] In the SARA amendments passed in the wake of the agency's failure to implement a vigorous remediation program, Congress again did not mention costs in the statutory language. The bill stated a preference for remediations that "permanently and significantly reduc[e] the volume, toxicity, or mobility of hazardous substances" and required remediations to meet standards from other federal programs (ARARs) or, if they were stricter, state standards.[2] Unlike some more stringent environmental rules, EPA's regulations do allow cost to be one of the nine criteria used in evaluating remedies, but only after protection of human health and the environment and compliance with ARARs are met.[3] In short, Congress throughout the 1980s and into the early 1990s emphasized the political costs of lax enforcement rather than financial costs imposed by stringent remediations.

In this chapter we will examine both the cost and cost-effectiveness of remediations at Superfund sites. Since cancer prevention is the primary mission of Superfund, how well do the cleanups fare in fostering that objective? We find that at the majority of sites in our sample, EPA remediations would fail a benefit–cost analysis based only on the cost per cancer case averted.

Congress, however, never required the agency to balance benefits and costs. Indeed legislative guidance in many respects fostered neglect of such efficiency concerns, so Congress should share some responsibility for the program's performance. Dealing with inefficiencies in the agency's approach to conservatism in risk assessment, its focus on individual rather than population risk, and the failure to assess the efficiency of its remediations may require specific risk reform signals from Congress. We later explore in chapter 9 how risk reform proposals might affect the outcomes that we analyze in this chapter.

5.1 Remediation Costs and Goals

Measures of cost-effectiveness require measures of both costs and benefits. In addition to developing the benefits methodology discussed in the previous chapters, we also had to develop our own estimates of remediation expenditures. As we describe in appendixes A and B, we collected detailed cost data from site documents on the remedy selections considered and chosen at 267 nonfederal NPL sites where RODs were signed during 1991 and 1992. We also collected cost information on past remediation actions and estimated figures where documents indicated future RODs were anticipated. These data allow us to estimate a site-level cost for remediation expenditures. These figures, however, exclude transaction costs borne by the agency or private parties and do not cover the expenditure of funds for removal actions (e.g., emergency actions to avert immediate dangers at a site) that were done prior to the long-term remediations considered here.[4]

Table 5.1
Distribution of site costs

| | Percent of total cost | | |
Cost quantile	Soil costs ($N = 228$ sites)	Groundwater costs ($N = 221$ sites)	All costs ($N = 248$ sites)
0–20%	2%	3%	4%
21–40	7	10	10
41–60	14	16	16
61–80	21	23	23
81–100	56	48	47

Note: Nineteen no-action sites were excluded from this analysis.

At 19 sites in the sample, the agency formally chose not to pursue further remediation actions at a site, although some of these did entail additional costs for monitoring of potential hazards at a site. With these no-action sites included, the average cost of remediation per site was $18.1 million (7 percent discount rate, 1993$) based on estimates derived from site documents.[5] EPA data indicate, however, that actual remediation costs tend to be higher at most sites than estimated costs. When one adjusts for the projected growth in costs once a remediation is undertaken, the average cleanup cost per site rises to $25.7 million. Remediation costs for soil averaged $17.3 million (with cost growth) and are highly concentrated in capital costs (91 percent), while those for groundwater remediation averaged $13.1 million and are split between capital costs (34 percent) and operation and maintenance (66 percent). As table 5.1 indicates, these expenditures are highly concentrated at a small percentage of the sites. The top 20 percent of sites in terms of costs accounted for 47 percent of all estimated "projected" expenditures, while the bottom 40 percent of sites totaled only 14 percent of these remediation costs. The magnitude and concentration of costs reinforce the importance of conducting site-level marginal analysis to determine the cost-effectiveness of Superfund expenditures.

Table 5.2 indicates the relative frequency of choosing different cleanup options. The remedy choice pattern suggests that EPA decisionmakers have followed the instruction expressed by Congress in the 1986 Superfund Amendments and Reauthorization Act to favor more permanent remedies such as treatment rather than containment of waste. Rabe (1990) indicates that for a set of 395 CERCLA sites examined as of 1984

Table 5.2
Selected components

a. Cleanup options chosen, analysis based on 277 nonfederal RODs[a]

Medium	Component	RODs	Percentage
Soil	No action	8	4
	Institutional controls	1	< 1
	Containment	50	27
	Removal	13	7
	Treatment	63	34
	Combination	49	27
	Total soil	184	100
Groundwater	No action	10	6
	Institutional controls	28	17
	Treatment	132	78
	Total groundwater	170	100

b. Did EPA choose the cheapest option?[b]

Medium	Component selected	Decisions analyzed[b]	Selected cheapest option N	Percentage
Soil	Institutional controls	1	0	0
	Containment	39	15	39
	Removal	4	1	25
	Treatment	46	19	41
	Combination	32	8	25
	Soil total	122	43	35
Groundwater	Institutional controls	19	6	32
	Treatment	98	38	39
	Groundwater total	117	44	38
Total	All	239	87	36

a. The combination component for soil actions represents any combination of containment, removal, and treatment.
b. Cost is only one of nine criteria used by EPA in choosing a remedial action. EPA made a total of 362 decisions in 277 RODs during 1991–1992. Only those decisions that involved a choice between two or more alternatives of the same component grouping are included in this analysis.

(e.g., pre-SARA), containment remedies were employed at 99 percent of the sites and treatment of waste at only 1 percent of the sites. This policy emphasis shifted starkly in the post-SARA era. Table 5.2 shows that among groundwater ROD actions signed in 1991 and 1992, 78 percent involved treatment of the contaminated groundwater. For soil actions, 34 percent involved treatment and 27 percent consisted of some combination of containment, removal, and treatment.

In making these decisions among remedies at sites, the EPA decision makers are guided by the nine explicit criteria discussed earlier, including costs. Table 5.2 also demonstrates that when faced with multiple remedies using a given technology (e.g., two remedy options that involved treatment), the agency chose the cheapest remedy option 35 percent of the time when soil contaminants were involved and 38 percent of the instances when groundwater remedies were involved. Since remedies may vary in effectiveness, however, the EPA may have selected a higher cost remedy to increase the level of protection at some sites. The results in table 5.2 are consistent with work by Gupta, Van Houtven, and Cropper (1996) that reveals that in the selection of remediation technologies the EPA at times took cost into consideration and demonstrated a preference for more permanent remedies. These authors found that at larger sites the agency was willing to pay as much as $40 million in additional costs over and above the costs of capping contaminated wastes to incinerate soils.

EPA site documents contain detailed information on both the costs of remedies selected and the cost of remedies not selected. At each site we averaged the costs of remedies by type of policy action (e.g., institutional controls, containment, removal, treatment, and combination).[6] Some sites did not have cost estimates for a given policy option, so we weighted the cost observations for each policy by site type to produce estimates of the costs of using alternative remedies at the sites in our cost sample. Our results indicate that if institutional controls were adopted for soil and groundwater actions at the sample sites, the average cost per site, including projected cost growth, would be $2.6 million. If containment were chosen as the remedy for contaminated soils and institutional controls for groundwater actions, the costs would be $13 million. This figure would jump to $22 million if groundwater treatment and soil containment were selected. A policy of soil removals (with containment for landfill sites) and treatment for groundwater generated an estimate of $38.6 million per site, while treatment for both soil and groundwater at all types of sites would generate an average of $118.9 million. The costs of remediating Super-fund sites would thus vary widely depending on whether a permanent treatment remedy or another policy were selected. Shifting away from a policy focused on treatment, however, would require legislative changes to the language in the 1986 legislation directing the agency to pursue permanent treatment solutions.[7]

Though the basis for cleanup standards varies across Superfund sites, EPA most often uses three main standards: state standards from other environmental programs, federal standards from environmental programs other than Superfund, and risk-based goals which are translated back into the chemical concentrations that may remain after remediation. Internal EPA administrative guidance indicates that cleanups should generally be undertaken when risks are greater than or equal to 10^{-4} (with a discretionary zone up to 10^{-6}) and that the risk targets for remediation actions should be individual risks in the range of 10^{-4} to 10^{-6}. Applicable legislation indicates, however, that any existing state or federal standards (generally expressed in terms of the concentration of a given chemical that is acceptable) for exposure to a given chemical become the basis for remediation. State standards must be met if they are stricter than federal requirements. Groundwater standards exist for many chemicals from the federal Clean Water Act or state legislation, so many chemicals involved with groundwater contamination at Superfund sites have cleanup standards imported into hazardous waste remediations from these other regulatory programs. Chemical concentration standards are less common for soil exposures in federal and state regulatory programs. As a result soil remediations at Superfund sites may be based on risk analysis where allowable chemical concentrations are backed out from a given cancer risk level (e.g., what chemical concentrations would yield a site-level risk of 10^{-6} given the exposure pathways for a given population at the site?).

Table 5.3 provides information on the basis of remediation concentrations selected for the carcinogenic and noncarcinogenic chemicals that matched up in our risk and remediation databases. The justification for the remediation level chosen was coded directly from the Record of Decision at the site. For soil contaminants, state regulations were the source of 21.3 percent of the concentration goals and federal regulations accounted for 1.5 percent. Most soil concentration goals were derived from risk-based levels (e.g., what soil concentration values would yield a risk of 10^{-6}?), which accounted for 36.2 percent of the remediation goals, or modeled concentrations (25.1 percent), where risk assessors took a

Table 5.3
Basis of chemical remediation goal, cancer and noncancer risks ($N = 194$ sites)

a. Soil ($N = 111$ sites)

Basis for remediation level	Number of chemicals	Percentage of total
Federal regulations	15	1.5
State regulations	216	21.3
Site-specific levels	102	10.1
EPA directives	54	5.3
Risk-based level	367	36.2
Environmental standards	5	0.5
Modeled concentration	254	25.1
Total	1,013	100.0

b. Groundwater ($N = 151$ sites)

Basis for remediation level	Number of chemicals	Percentage of total
Federal MCLs	733	31.4
Other federal regulations	69	3.0
State MCLs	513	22.0
Other state regulations	638	27.3
Site-specific levels	85	3.6
EPA directives	52	2.2
Risk-based levels	179	7.7
Environmental standards	66	2.8
Modeled concentration	1	0
Total	2,336	100.0

Note: Federal MCLs = maximum contaminant levels as promulgated under the Clean Water Act (includes MCLs, proposed MCLs and MCLGs). Other federal regulations = levels determined by federal regulations other than those dealing with Superfund or the Clean Water Act. State MCLs = maximum contaminant levels as promulgated under state drinking water regulations. Other state regulations = levels determined by state regulations other than those dealing with drinking water. Risk-based levels = concentrations needed to produce a specific chemical or site risk level. Site-specific levels = level determined by background concentration or detection limit. Modeled concentrations = soil level based on output of model using groundwater remediation levels (one observation models groundwater levels based on soil remediation). EPA directives = levels as promulgated in OSWER directives or regional guidance documents. Environmental standard = levels established explicitly to protect the environment.

groundwater concentration standard or risk level and derived what soil concentration would be consistent with this goal if the soil contaminant leached into the groundwater. For groundwater concentrations of chemicals, however, federal MCLs (maximum contaminant levels) and standards accounted for 34.4 percent of the cleanup remediation goals, followed by other state regulations (27.3 percent) and state MCLs (22.0 percent). Site-specific risk assessment calculations thus accounted for very few of the concentration goals set for groundwater remediations at Superfund sites.

Some site documents list remediation goals that are already met at the site, such as when remediation concentrations exceed the current concentrations of chemicals. If one eliminates those "goals" that are already met prior to remediation, one can examine how the individual risk levels established by the different chemical concentration standards vary in stringency. For the 1,253 groundwater and 431 soil chemical pathways at the sites in our sample where contaminant concentrations exceeded established cleanup goals specified in site documents, we inserted these remediation goals into the risk assessment equations to calculate the individual cancer risks to human health remaining after remediation. Table 5.4 sheds light on our finding that the mean postremediation risks implied by groundwater cleanup targets established under state regulations (9.6e-6) are statistically significantly lower at the 1 percent level than those established on all other bases (6.1e-5). For soil contaminants, state standards (mean 8.1e-6) also result in more stringent cleanup goals than those based on other rationales (mean 8.0e-5) (also statistically significant at the 1 percent level).

EPA regularly imports into the Superfund program cleanup standards from other state and federal regulatory programs. These standards address multiple objectives, including environmental protection as well as protection of human populations from cancer and noncancer risks. When these standards are translated back into individual cancer risks, however, it is evident that state and federal regulatory requirements from programs outside of Superfund result in chemical concentrations that are much lower than what would result if remediations were chosen solely on the basis of cancer risk analysis. While attention in the reauthorization debate has focused scrutiny on what level of individual risks are appropriate remediation goals, these results also suggest the importance of examining the strict remediation goals established by state and federal standards derived from regulatory programs outside of Superfund.

Table 5.4
Individual cancer risk goals implied by remedial concentration standards

a. soil ($N = 44$ sites)

Basis	Number of matched chemical observations	Baseline risk assessment mean pathway risk	Implied mean remediation risk
Risk based	186	6.1e-4	3.4e-5
State	74	8.4e-5	8.1e-6
EPA directive	92	3.2e-2	2.3e-4
Site specific	61	1.6e-4	1.1e-5
Modeled	18	1.3e-5	5.7e-8
Total	431		

b. Groundwater ($N = 83$ sites)

Basis	Number of matched chemical observations	Baseline risk assessment mean pathway risk	Implied mean remediation risk
Risk based	100	2.8e-4	1.5e-5
Federal	417	8.2e-3	8.3e-5
State	644	5.7e-3	9.6e-6
EPA directive	1	1.8e-4	5.6e-6
Site specific	91	3.8e-3	1.3e-5
Total	1,253		

Note: This table focuses on chemical risk pathways where remediation levels were established below existing concentrations.

5.2 Measures of Cost-Effectiveness

The EPA has multiple objectives for Superfund site remediations, including protection of individuals from cancer risks, reduction of non-cancer risks to individuals, and protection of the physical environment (including natural resources). The primary policy trigger for remediation is the level of cancer risk at the site. This section uses one measure of cost-effectiveness, the cost per cancer case avoided at sites, to analyze EPA actions taken under current legislative mandates. Our analysis assumes that the remedy selected at each site will fully address the estimated cancer cases arising over thirty years, although the actual degree of prevention may vary with each site. We estimate the cancer cases using the conservative assumptions described in case 1 in chapter 4, and combine these estimates with costs without factoring in cost growth. These cost-effectiveness values will consequently understate the actual cost per case of cancer prevented, thus overstating the program's efficacy.

Before considering the cost per case of cancer prevented, let us establish a reference point for what level of expenditures is reasonable, assuming that cancer prevention is the primary objective. If all cases of cancer were fatal, a suitable measure would be the value of preventing an expected fatality. The generally accepted approach in the economics literature is that this amount is society's willingness to pay to avoid a statistical death. Thus it is the value society attaches to eliminating small changes in the probability of death, as would occur as a consequence of a Superfund site cleanup, that provides information on the appropriate trade-off between costs and risks.

A large economic literature has attached a dollar value to this willingness to pay amount based on market evidence regarding risk–money trade-offs. Since the most reliable and detailed data are with respect to workers' choices with respect to risky jobs, economists have focused primarily on the implications of wage–risk trade-offs.[8] Controlling for other aspects of the job, a typical worker receives $300 to $700 extra compensation per year to face an annual fatality risk of 1/10,000. The amount of compensation per expected fatality is consequently $3 million to $7 million, with a midpoint value of $5 million.

The U.S. Office of Management and Budget (OMB) has endorsed use of these values for benefit assessment throughout the federal government. Agencies differ in terms of the value they select for benefit assessment. The U.S. Department of Transportation uses a value near the low end of the range of about $3 million, whereas the U.S. EPA has used values such as $5 million and $7 million. For concreteness, we will use the midpoint value of $5 million, recognizing that there is heterogeneity in the value of life across different populations. Population groups may differ in their willingness to bear risk. Involuntary risks, such as environmental exposures, may consequently have a higher value than more voluntary job risks. Thus cleanup efforts with a cost per case of cancer prevented in the general range of $6 million or even $10 million are generally in a range of reasonableness, whereas expenditures of $50 million, $1 billion or possibly more would be outside of the range.

While the EPA and other agencies have endorsed value-of-life numbers for regulatory benefit assessment, they do not drive hazardous waste policy decisions. Superfund cleanups do not require that any benefit assessment be done or that the benefits exceed the costs. Indeed EPA never even calculates the cost per case of cancer prevented for such cleanup actions. Thus these types of policy analysis tests are not integrated into the current policy choice process.

Even in the case of major new regulatory proposals, for which OMB requires a benefit–cost test, this test is seldom binding. Agencies have an exemption if such a test is inconsistent with their legislative mandate, as is typically the case. As a result OMB has never succeeded in blocking a regulation with a cost per life under $100 million.[9] This figure will serve as a second reference point for judging Superfund cost-effectiveness.

It should be emphasized, however, that profligate expenditures of this type are not without societal costs. Risk–risk analysis indicates that wasteful government regulations impose a real opportunity cost, since these funds could have been used for better health care, improved nutrition, or more effective crime prevention. Although estimates differ widely on the levels of costs that will lead to the loss of a statistical life, all such estimates are below the $100 million per life figure, with the most reliable being near $50 million per expected life.[10] Thus, if we were to spend $50 million on policies with no direct health benefits, there would be the loss of one statistical life because these funds are not spent on the usual market basket of goods, including health care and other beneficial items. Ensuring that regulations do in fact reduce risk is not simply a matter of cost but also health; diverting taxpayer money to wasteful efforts prevents citizens from making more productive health-enhancing expenditures.

Overall at the 150 sites we examine, EPA has selected current and planned remediation actions that will cost $2.2 billion dollars (1993$) to avert 731 cancer cases. The resulting mean cost per cancer case averted is $3.0 million for remediation actions at the sites. This fairly low cost per case of cancer estimate indicates that on balance the program is cost-effective in the aggregate using a mean cost per cancer case averted. However, these figures overstate the efficacy of policies; they employ conservative risk assessments, ignore cost growth, and do not account for the discounting of deferred benefits. Moreover the average figures are very misleading. The distribution of the cancer cases is not uniform, as sites differ substantially in terms of the desirability of cleanup. Our previous analysis indicates that both risks and costs are concentrated at a small segment of sites, including one particularly hazardous site. The median cost per cancer case averted is $388 million, without factoring in cost growth, discounting of benefits, or conservatism in risk assessment. Figure 5.1 emphasizes that the cost per cancer case averted ranges widely

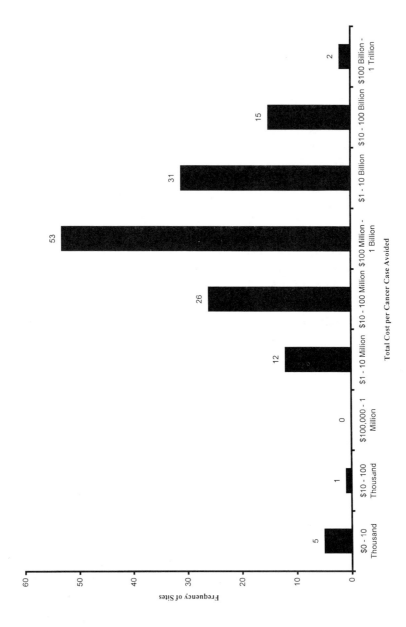

Figure 5.1
Total cost per cancer case avoided (1993$, no cost growth)

from less than $20,000 to over $1 billion. Overall, 44 out of the 145 sites with estimates had costs per cancer case averted less than $100 million—our high end reference point that is clearly out of line with a sensible risk–money trade-off. About 25 percent (26 out of 107 with soil cancers) of the soil remediations had costs per cancer case avoided less than $100 million, while the median value was $611 million. For groundwater remediations, 38 out of 127 had costs per cancer case avoided of less than $100 million, while the median was $396 million. (These mean and median figures do not include $229 million spent to remediate soil at 25 additional sites where no soil cancers were expected, nor the $115 million slated to clean up groundwater at 20 sites where no groundwater cancers were expected. These totals do, however, contribute to the aggregate cost per cancer figure). If one factors in cost growth, the median cost per cancer case averted shifts to $700 million. If average concentrations and a cancer latency period are assumed (i.e., case 3), costs and benefits are discounted at a rate of 3 percent, and cost growth is factored in, the median cost per cancer case averted at the 96 sites with mean concentrations available is $7.2 billion. Under these assumptions, only 9 out of 96 sites would have costs per cancer case averted less than $100 million.

EPA often considered less expensive alternative remedies at sites, although they may not have been judged as protective of human health and the environment, and might not reduce the additional risk of cancer to zero, as we assume the remedies will do in these figures. Nevertheless, if one looks at each site and obtains an average cost of remedy type for each site, one can compare the cost-effectiveness of alternative policies with those selected. For soil and groundwater remedies that involved institutional controls (e.g., fencing, restrictions on land or groundwater use, provision of alternative water supplies, and monitoring), at nearly half of the sites where those options were considered, the cost per cancer case avoided would be below $100 million. The provisions of SARA, however, direct the EPA toward more permanent remedies such as the treatment of groundwater and soil contaminants. For treatment options considered for soil at 10 out of 45 sites the cost per cancer case averted was less than $100 million, while for groundwater treatments the figure is 18 out of 73 sites.

What accounts for the wide variation in cost effectiveness across sites? Table 5.5 shows that the type of site can have a large impact on cost effectiveness. Sites with 0.1 or more expected cancer cases are much more likely to have remediations with cost per cancer case averted less than

Table 5.5
Cost per cancer case avoided (cost avoided, $1993 millions)

a. Number of expected cancer cases

Expected cancer cases	Total cost per cancer case avoided			Cost/Cancer < $100 M	N
	Mean	Median	Aggregate		
0.1–	58.6	30.9	1.1	30	38
0.05–0.1	241.0	171.2	219.1	2	11
0.01–0.05	853.3	538.5	650.3	8	39
0.005–0.01	1,296.8	1,156.2	1,550.5	0	8
0.001–0.005	4,812.4	2,494.8	3,926.4	3	30
0–0.001	72,910.0	17,488.3	24,108.3	1	19
Total	10,884.1	387.6	3.0	44	145

b. Cleanup standards based on ecological risk criteria

Are ecological risk standards present?	Total cost per cancer case avoided			Cost/Cancer < $100 M	N
	Mean	Median	Aggregate		
No	12,282.8	454.4	2.7	33	124
Yes	2,624.6	89.2	12.4	11	21

c. Predominant cleanup standard basis due to soil contamination

Basis of cleanup standard	Cost per cancer case avoided			Cost/Cancer < $100 M	N
	Mean	Median	Aggregate		
Federal	1,473.9	1,473.9	1,473.9	0	1
State	8,023.5	501.8	439.2	1	7
Site	2,448.1	225.9	0.46	11	34
None	153,139	2,723.2	81.9	14	65

d. Predominant cleanup standard basis due to groundwater contamination

Basis of cleanup standard	Cost per cancer case avoided			Cost/Cancer < $100 M	N
	Mean	Median	Aggregate		
Federal	4,291.8	244.8	50.8	7	25
State	63,992.2	521.7	95.5	9	38
Site	2,714.0	326.3	2.1	2	7
Combination	1,689.0	203.7	440.7	2	7
None	6,265.7	379.8	27.0	18	50

Note: N represents the number of sites for which a cost per cancer case avoided figure can be calculated for the given scenario. The aggregate cost per cancer case avoided column, however, includes costs at sites where cancers equal zero (e.g., aggregate cost per cancer case avoided = $\sum$ *costs* divided by $\sum$ *cancer cases avoided*). Cost/Cancer < $100 M indicates the number of sites with a cost per cancer case avoided less than $100 M. Estimated costs are pre-cost growth. All cancer risks use case 1 scenario.

$100 million (30 out of 38 sites in this category). The median cost per cancer for sites with 0.1 or more cancers was $31 million, which is much lower than the figures at sites with lower expected cancer cases averted. Using remediation information from site documents, we also examine in table 5.5 the cost per cancer case avoided at sites where environmental protection standards influenced remedy selection. The median cost per cancer case averted was actually lower at sites where environmental standards (e.g., those aimed at ecological/natural resource risks) were used as a basis for remediation decisions. The median cost per cancer case averted also declines at sites which have high maximum hazard quotients. Thus it is generally not the case that sites with higher cost per cancer case averted were sites with remediations based on environmental protection standards or sites with higher noncancer risks, although one site with no expected cancers did have substantial noncancer risk, and 17 sites with less than 0.1 cancers had maximum noncancer chemical pathways with hazard quotients exceeding 100.

Table 5.5 also matches up the costs of cancer cases averted by the dominant type of binding remediation standard used at the site (i.e., the most frequent basis for remediation standards where remediations were required). For both soil and groundwater remedies, the median cost per cancer case avoided is nearly twice as high when decisions were based on state standards than when remediations were based on site-level (e.g., risk-based) standards. The poor performance of EPA cleanup decisions on this measure of cost-effectiveness in part results from the importation of cleanup goals from state environmental protection programs into the Superfund program, in accordance with requirements established in the 1986 SARA legislation.

A comparison of risk and cost data does indicate that expenditures are related to measures of cancer risks on a site-by-site basis. In terms of rank-order correlations, remediation expenditures and number of cancer cases averted are positively correlated (0.36). The EPA appears to be spending more to remediate sites with current risks today than at sites where risks are hypothetical. Mean site costs (1993$, 7 percent, without cost growth) were $22.0 million at sites where the maximum cancer risk was a current risk greater than or equal to 10^{-4} versus $12.1 million at sites where the maximum risk was a future risk greater than or equal to 10^{-4} (t statistic $= 2.7$). Expenditures at sites where maximum risks were in the discretionary zone are not significantly different for current risks ($10.8 million) versus future risks ($9.8 million). For noncancer risks, the mean site cleanups at sites with current maximum hazard quotients greater than or equal to ten of $25.4 million was greater than the mean cleanup cost of $12.9 million for sites without these high current non-cancer risks (t statistic $= 1.8$). In terms of priorities, the EPA thus appears to target more resources at sites where there are higher calculated individual risks today rather than simply hypothetical risks in the future. Whether this conclusion remains true after including multivariate controls and considering the extent of exposed populations will be examined in chapter 6.

5.3   The 90–10 Principle

From the standpoint of economic efficiency, it is desirable to focus cleanup efforts on the most cost-effective sites. Many risk analysts have noted that there is substantial heterogeneity in the efficacy of risk reduction policies and that efforts with a cost per life saved value above some cutoff level, such as $5 million per life, should not be pursued if mortality risks are the sole matter of concern. Such targeting may save considerable resources at very little opportunity cost in terms of health benefits forgone.

How large these opportunity costs will be depends on the distribution of the efficacy of cleanup actions. Supreme Court Justice Stephen Breyer has hypothesized that there is often a 90–10 principle whereby society derives 90 percent of the benefit from the most effective 10 percent of the risk reduction expenditures. Justice Breyer writes:

Let me provide some examples. The first comes from a case in my own court, *United States v. Ottati & Goss*, arising out of a ten-year effort to force cleanup of a toxic waste dump in southern New Hampshire. The site was mostly cleaned up. All but one of the private parties had settled. The remaining private party litigated the cost of cleaning up the last little bit, a cost of about $9.3 million to remove a small amount of highly diluted PCBs and "volatile organic compounds" (benzene and gasoline components) by incinerating the dirt. How much extra safety did this $9.3 million buy? The forty-thousand-page record of this ten-year effort indicated (and all the parties seemed to agree) that, without the extra expenditure, the waste dump was clean enough for children playing on the site to eat small amounts of dirt daily for 70 days each year without significant harm. Burning the soil would have made it clean enough for the children to eat small amounts daily for 245 days per year without significant harm. But there were no dirt-eating children playing in the area, for it was a swamp. Nor were dirt-eating children likely to appear there, for future building seemed unlikely. The parties also agreed that at least half of the volatile organic chemicals would likely evaporate by the year 2000. To spend $9.3 million to protect non-existent dirt-eating children is what I mean by the problem of "the last 10 percent."[11]

Table 5.6
Summary of Superfund cost-effectiveness

Percentage of remediation expenditures, ranked by cancer cost effectiveness	Cumulative percentage of total expected cancer cases averted (sites = 99)	Marginal cost per cancer case averted ($ millions)
5%	99.47%	$145
25	99.86	$1,107
50	99.96	$6,442
75	99.97	$28,257
95	99.98	$241,058

Note: The following assumptions are used: average exposure concentrations and intake parameters, 3 percent discount rate and no growth factors for cost, 3 percent discount rate for cancers, and a ten-year latency period for the development of cancer.

To explore this relationship for our Superfund sample, we ranked the sites from the most cost effective to the least cost effective. Thus the comparison is across sites, given the cleanup policies selected, rather than within a site for differing gradations of cleanup.

Table 5.6 reports the distribution of these cost-effectiveness values for different 5 percentile groupings. Virtually all of the expected cancer cases to be reduced—over 99 percent—are prevented by the first 5 percent of expenditures. Although many of these initial allocations are clearly worthwhile, by the 5th percentile the marginal cost reaches $145 million. At the median site expenditure, the cost per case of cancer prevented is in excess of $6 billion, and at the least cost-effective 5 percent of the expenditures the cost per case of cancer rises to above $200 billion.

The dropoff in cost-effectiveness is consequently quite stark. A few sites, and one large site in particular, account for on overwhelming share of the cancer cases averted. Allocating resources strategically could consequently eliminate 99.5 percent of the expected cancer cases from hazardous wastes with only 5 percent of the expenditures. The disparity in cost-effectiveness is consequently much greater than Justice Breyer hypothesized but still very much in line with the general spirit of his observation. In the case of Superfund, it is not a 90–10 principle but a 95–1 principle—EPA spends 95 percent of remediation resources to eliminate under 1 percent of the risk.

Doing so is not necessarily bad policy. These efforts could be warranted based on their absolute levels of performance rather than their relative efficacy. However, even here the cleanups fall far short of any test of desirability. At the 5th percentile of most effective cleanups, the cost per case of cancer has already risen to $145 million per case. This level is more than an order of magnitude above any sensible risk–cost trade-off and the levels of performance that can be achieved with other regulatory efforts. Improved transportation safety can save more lives at far less cost.

It may be that there are other rationales for cleanup such as noncancer effects or ecological harm. However, these benefit components are not as well developed in agency analyses, since EPA has no measure of the probability or severity of the noncancer effects, only whether the concentration is above its reference dose. Ecological damages are even less well delineated in the site analyses and, in some cases, appear to be inconsequential. If these benefits are to serve as a justification for cleanup efforts, they must be quantified more thoroughly than at present.

5.4 Conclusions about Cost-Effectiveness

Our analysis does not constitute a full measure of the costs and benefits of the Superfund program but instead focuses on the primary benefit component—cancer reduction. Noncancer effects do not permit the same degree of quantification. Similarly costs pertain only to remediation costs. The transactions costs associated with cleanup, which often entail millions of dollars in litigation costs, do not enter the tally either. Our examination of sites where RODs were signed in 1991 and 1992 began after emergency removal actions had occurred at many of these sites. The early actions that EPA takes to remove imminent hazards do not enter our analysis. Existence values that people may place on pristine groundwater, potential avoidance of other natural resource damages, and the value of avoiding noncancer effects ranging from skin lesions to birth defects are not quantified here.[12] The loss in property values to society if site contamination were addressed through institutional controls or containment rather than full-scale treatment is not calculated. Whether these costs should be counted or whether doing so would represent double counting is not clear, since they may simply embody the market valuation of the benefit assessment as we will examine in the housing price effects analysis in chapter 8. Nor have we examined questions about what demographic groups bear what types of risks investigated here, a topic we explore in chapter 7.[13]

The results from our analysis of risk and cost data do demonstrate, however, the importance of site-level benefit–cost tests. Regulatory policies in general devote far too little attention to micro policy targeting and consequently sacrifice potentially major health benefits. Such analyses should, however, focus on what the risks actually are and who is really exposed to the risk. Individual cancer risk estimates at Superfund sites as calculated by the EPA are high relative to other risks regulated by the federal government. The mean maximum cumulative risk was 0.070 and the median was 0.0025. Over 85 percent of the sites had maximum individual cancer risks greater than or equal to 1 in 10,000. Yet many of these risks are hypothetical risks based on changes in land use envisioned in the future, are based on conservative parameter assumptions, and represent a combination of conservative assumptions across parameters so that the point on the distribution of risks at a site represented by the EPA's reasonable maximum exposure scenario is unclear. If mean parameter values are used for chemical concentration, ingestion rate, and exposure duration, the percentage of sites with maximum adult ingestion risks greater than or equal to 1 in 10,000 drops to 54 percent. Monte Carlo analysis reveals that the compounding of assumptions in current EPA guidance results in risks that are often in the 99th percentile of simulated risks. At a minimum these results demonstrate the need to consider what types of parameter assumptions should be used in the analysis of Superfund risks, the potential for Monte Carlo analysis to contribute to the understanding of these risks, and the need to consider the likelihood that different land uses will arise at sites where remediation is based on future risk scenarios such as future residential developments on current industrial sites.

Linking up individual risk data with census information through GIS technology shows how current Superfund information can be extended to develop estimates of population risks. Once this was done at a sample of 150 sites, we found that expected cancer cases arising from chemical exposures are high at a very small fraction of sites and relatively low at the majority of sites. The median number of expected cancer cases over thirty years at the sites in our sample is less than 0.1.

Costs per cancer case averted are very high at most of the Superfund sites in the sample, with only 44 out of 145 sites having a cost of cancer cases averted (pre-cost growth) less than $100 million. Estimates based on mean risk assumptions put the median cost per cancer in the billions. Alternative policies, such as institutional controls or containment, yielded lower estimates of costs of cancer cases averted, assuming they were equally as effective as treatment over the short run in reducing risks. Treatment policies are also aimed at risks aside from cancer, such as noncancer risks and ecological risks. If these are to be the primary justification for action at Superfund sites, however, EPA should quantify and prioritize both noncancer and ecological risks. Costs per cancer case averted are also high in part because of the state standards imported from other environmental programs, standards that result in cleanup goals that are more stringent than those based on site-level analysis of individual risks.

Though our results answer questions about the effectiveness of the EPA's Superfund remediation policies, they raise an additional question: Why are the EPA's remediation decisions so inefficient in terms of the cost per cancer case averted? In the next chapter we use our sample data to explore hypotheses about the degree that Superfund site-level decisions are driven by factors such as risk biases, politics, or concern about efficiency.

6

Are Risk Regulators "Rational"?

In the preceding chapters we have examined the cleanup of hazardous waste sites using an efficiency-based economic framework. This approach emphasizes that decisions are made under conditions of scarcity. Trade-offs are inevitable, and the task is to strike a reasonable balance between cost and safety. The results indicate that by at least one measure, the cost per cancer case averted, few Superfund cleanups in our sample would pass a benefit-cost test. In making decisions about job safety or risky products, individuals appear to be willing to spend approximately $5 million to save a statistical life.[1] Yet regulators at Superfund sites appear to make cleanup decisions that imply a cost per cancer case averted that is often in the hundreds of millions of dollars and even the billions. In this chapter we use the framework of rational choice analysis to examine *why* regulators at Superfund sites make decisions that yield such seemingly irrational results.

Risks are not always well understood. Even if perceived accurately, risks nevertheless complicate individual decisions and may lead to errors in decision making. A large literature in economics and social science focuses on how people reason about risks. Empirical evidence suggests that people frequently depart from behavior predicted by full information versions of expected utility theory.[2]

These inadequacies have implications for policy as well. Risk regulators are human and are subject to the same kinds of perceptional biases as others. Moreover they are also influenced by political pressures that are reflective of people's attitudes toward risk, and possible irrational responses to risk. As a result the public policies that regulators pursue may reflect errors in risk judgment.

Many biases stem from misperceptions of risk. Individuals overestimate small probabilities, overestimate the risks associated with highly publicized dangers, and have preferences over the manner (not just the magnitude) in which risks arise. The character of environmental risks associated with hazardous waste sites makes them particularly prone to such errors. The actual risks involved are small and highly publicized. As a consequence of this overestimation, the general public ranks hazardous waste sites as the leading environmental risk.[3]

Our analysis in this chapter is also in the spirit of a growing literature on how the decisions of risk regulators depart from choices predicted in a standard benefit–cost framework. As Noll and Krier (1990) point out, since regulators are both human and political, their decisions may reflect risk "biases."[4] Risk regulators may take into account the identity of the parties exposed to risk, the level of scrutiny by interest groups, the nature of congressional representation of affected constituents, and the degree of political activity by potentially exposed individuals.[5] Errors in risk perceptions and risk decisions cause individuals to diverge from expected utility maximization. Similar errors by policy makers and the influence of risk politics cause regulators to diverge from social welfare maximization.

This chapter examines decisions made by federal and state regulators at hazardous waste sites addressed by the Superfund program to determine how their decisions diverge from those predicted by expected utility theory and benefit–cost analysis. We explore whether risk perceptions and politics influence two decisions central to the "how clean is clean" debate at Superfund sites—the selection of chemical cleanup targets and the expenditure of remediation funds at these contaminated sites. We also analyze the interactive influence of risk perception factors and political demands.

Previous research on the regulation of chemical risks in standard setting indicates that decisions reflect evidence of risk biases and responsiveness to political factors. In assessing the determinants of the EPA's decision to cancel pesticide registration, Cropper et al. (1992) found that economic and political factors were both influential, since the EPA was more likely to cancel a pesticide in instances featuring higher risks to the maximally exposed individual user, lower benefits associated with continued use of the pesticide, higher values of intervention by environmental groups (measured by regulatory comments), and lower values of interventions by business groups. Van Houtven and Cropper (1996) stress the importance of examining regulator decisions about risk rather than simply focusing on statutory guidelines, for they find that the EPA considered both costs and risks in issuing standards even in programs where legislation indicated costs were not to be considered. In the decision of which chemicals to regulate across different agencies, Viscusi (1995) documented an irrational response to risk based on its source rather than its magnitude. Federal agencies were much more likely, for a given level of risk, to regulate risks arising from synthetic chemicals than those arising from naturally occurring sources. This result is consistent with the "reference risk effect" (Viscusi et al. 1987) and the "status quo" bias established by Samuelson and Zeckhauser (1988). In a review of 132 regulatory decisions involving cancer risks, Travis et al. (1987) found that in choosing which chemical risks to regulate, chemical risk potencies rather than the extent of population exposures were most influential in the decision to regulate. Federal agencies were strongly influenced by the levels of maximum individual cancer risks; for example, every risk above 4×10^{-3} was regulated and no action was taken (with one exception) on risks below 1×10^{-6}. There was not a "strong correlation between the size of the population exposed and the likelihood of regulation," but there was an influence of total population risks (e.g., expected annual cancer deaths) on the likelihood of regulation.[6]

Of these various classes of influences, the only ones that have received substantial scrutiny in the Superfund literature are the nature of risks and the nature of the community bearing these risks, and for these the evidence is mixed. Gupta, Van Houtven, and Cropper (1995) found that in setting cleanup targets at Superfund sites the agency did not appear to take cleanup costs into account (consistent with the congressional admonition to protect health without consideration of costs), did set more protective standards in minority areas, and left higher risks in places with higher baseline risks (interpreted as resulting from a diminishing marginal utility from cancer cases averted). Hird (1993, 1994) found that once sites were in the EPA's pipeline for remediation, the progress of the site through the phases of site investigation, record of decision (i.e., cleanup decision), and remediation did not depend on the socioeconomic characteristics of the counties containing the sites. He also found that the relevant congressional Superfund oversight committees had little or no impact on the extent or pace of cleanups of sites in the districts/states of committee members. Zimmerman (1993) found that communities with higher percentages of minorities were less likely to have cleanup decisions in place than other communities, while communities with sites that generated more controversy (as measured by news media coverage and a survey of EPA site managers) were more likely to have cleanup plans established. Lavelle and Coyle (1992) found that progress toward cleanup was slower in minority communities, which were also more likely to have less permanent remedies selected. In a larger study controlling for many factors, Gupta, Van Houtven, and Cropper (1996) found that in selecting the permanence of a site remediation, the agency was not significantly influenced by the median household income or racial composition of the surrounding population.

The analysis in this chapter advances the growing literature on agency decisions about risk in at least four ways. First, we base our analysis on a detailed assessment of the costs and benefits of hazardous waste cleanups. Using geographic information systems (GIS) technology and block-group level census data, we base our analysis on estimates of the expected number of cancer cases avoided on a site-level basis, as described in chapter 5. The risk data used in these calculations are the most comprehensive in the literature and are calculated on a consistent basis across sites. The estimated cost per cancer case avoided serves as a direct efficiency measure. Second, we analyze how a variety of risk variables affect cleanup decisions and the efficiency of cleanup decisions. These measures capture the influence of potential biases in the response to risk that have been found in various survey and laboratory settings. Thus we examine whether identified patterns of irrationality in individual decision-making influence the agency's hazardous waste cleanup decisions.

Third, we also explore the role of political factors in influencing cleanup decisions using measures of voter turnout and congressional voting records. While some previous studies have investigated whether political factors influence EPA decisions, they have noted that regulators could be concerned about the preferences of affected parties because of efficiency concerns. If one controls for certain demographic factors associated with willingness to pay to avoid risks or preserve the environment, however, one would not expect the likelihood of collective action by constituents to matter if regulators were only concerned about efficiency. Fourth, we examine the role of political factors and risk measures and their interactive effect in influencing the efficiency of cleanup decisions. Does the effect of political variables, for example, enhance the efficiency of cleanups by making them more responsive to those exposed to risks, or are political factors most powerful when the economic rationale for cleanup is weakest? Ours is the first analysis to distinguish the differential effect of such influences based on the relative efficiency of the cleanup decision.

Our results indicate that most of the significant influences on Superfund site decisions do not follow the expected pattern for efficient risk management. Policy makers sometimes respond to the expected costs of remediation and the expected number of people exposed to cancer risks in the desired economic direction. While both of these factors would be consistent with a standard benefit-cost analysis, their consideration is inconsistent with the remediation policies enunciated by the Congress (which directs the EPA to make Superfund decisions without explicitly requiring it to examine costs) and the agency (whose cleanup decisions are stated in terms of individual risk reduction without regard to the populations exposed to these levels of risk). Cleanup target selection does reflect biases from the individual risk perception literature, such as the availability effect (e.g., more highly publicized chemicals that create high risks receive more stringent targets) and the anchoring phenomenon (e.g., regulators tolerate a higher cleanup target risk the greater the baseline risk). Politics also plays a pivotal role in remediation decisions. Communities with higher voter turnouts are more likely at times to have lower final risks remaining at sites and to have more spent to avert an expected case of cancer. We find these political influences are most influential for the least cost-effective site cleanups.

6.1 Empirical Models of Superfund Decision Making

Our analysis of the response of regulators to risks uses the original data base that we developed using the extensive risk and cost data generated by the Superfund policy decision process. For the set of 267 nonfederal sites where cleanup decisions were made in 1991–92, we collected cost information on these sites and risk data on a subsample of 150 sites. This effort yielded a human health risk database with information on over 20,000 chemical level risk pathways at the 150 sites, which enabled us to develop estimates in chapters 4 and 5 of the number of cancer cases averted by remediations and the cost of cancer averted at these sites. For a subset of the sample, the Records of Decision provided detailed information on the risk levels and chemical concentrations chosen as cleanup targets. We coupled this site-specific information with a series of other variables not often available in the EPA analyses, such as population density.

In this chapter we focus on two decisions at these sites: the cancer risks selected as cleanup targets (e.g., the individual lifetime excess cancer risks that will remain after cleanup) and the implied cost per cancer case averted at each site. The primary unit of analysis in the target risk study is the chemical pathway. For a given chemical at a site where the baseline and target concentration of risk were provided in site documents, we analyze how the target risk chosen (i.e., the risk from the chemical that will remain after site cleanup) varies for the 2,888 pathways at 86 sites where these targets were announced in 1991–92. At the broader site level, we investigate how expenditures per case of cancer prevented varied across 130 sites.

To establish an efficiency reference point for the analysis, consider a regulator making a site remediation decision on the basis of a benefit–cost analysis of the reduction in cancer risks arising from contamination at the site. The regulator will consider the reduction in individual cancer risk, expressed as the baseline risk B minus the target risk T.[7] Note that B and T are the actual cancer risks as calculated from risk assessment methodology as specified by the EPA. The number of averted cancer cases from remediation is the change in individual risk $(B - T)$ multiplied by the population E exposed to the baseline risk. The value to the social welfare-maximizing regulator of this reduction in expected cancers is the number of expected cancer cases averted multiplied by the value V per cancer case averted. The cost C of the given remediation is a function of initial site contamination, the final target risk T chosen as the cleanup target, and additional chemical and site characteristics S that affect the remediation costs, such as the treatment of contaminated soil or groundwater. The social welfare-maximizing regulator will thus choose T to maximize social welfare so that marginal benefits lost from raising the target risk equal the marginal cost savings from a less stringent target for the optimally chosen policy.

There are several reasons why the target risks chosen by the EPA may diverge from those predicted in the social welfare-maximizing example. Regulators may of course not be maximizing this efficiency measure but may have other more narrowly defined objectives such as reducing risk to a reasonable level. Even if the objective is to generate policies that produce the greatest gains in societal welfare, decisions could be flawed in a number of ways. Regulators might reason on the basis of perceived risks because they are attempting to represent the risk perceptions of their constituents. Regulators also might reason on the basis of perceived risks because they exhibit the risk perception patterns evident among individuals in their daily risk choices.

Regulator decisions may also diverge from those predicted by social welfare maximization if regulators (or their constituents) value different populations differently. A well-known bias in contingent valuation studies known as the scope effect is that individual estimates of willingness to pay for some environmental amenity may be invariant to the scope of the good being purchased. For example, survey respondents report the same willingness to pay to save 2,000 migratory waterfowl as for 200,000 migratory waterfowl.[8] The practical consequence of this bias for hazardous waste cleanup decisions is that the valuation of the cleanup actions will not be sufficiently sensitive to the number of people exposed. Indeed the stated EPA risk assessment policies incorporate this scope effect since the agency expresses cleanup targets in terms of reduction of individual risk levels rather than an analysis of reduction in expected cancer cases overall. If some individuals are more highly valued by regulators, perhaps because they are more politically active and hence more likely to scrutinize regulator actions, then the nature of who bears the risk may also affect site-level Superfund decisions.

The empirical analysis here will focus on two measures of regulatory stringency—the natural logarithm of the target risk level T and the natural logarithm of the cost per case of cancer prevented. The target risks are often very small (e.g., 10^{-9}) but are not zero, so taking the logarithm of T is feasible. We estimate two different variants of a target risk model using the 2,888 chemical pathways as the unit of observation:

$$\ln T_{ij} = \alpha + \sum_{k=1}^{m} \beta_k X_{ijk} + \sum_{k=1}^{n} \gamma_k Z_{jk} + \varepsilon_{1ij}, \tag{6.1}$$

and

$$\ln T_{ij} = \alpha_j D_j + \sum_{k=1}^{m} \beta_k X_{ijk} + \varepsilon_{2ij}, \tag{6.2}$$

where T_{ij} is the risk target for chemical i at site j, X_{ijk} is a chemical pathway characteristics k for chemical i at site j, β_k is the regression coefficient for characteristic k among the set of variables in X_{ijk}, Z_{jk} is site characteristic variable k that varies only by site j not by chemical, γ_k is its coefficient, D_j is a dummy variable that takes on a value of 1 for site j and 0 otherwise, and ε_{1ij} and ε_{2ij} are random error terms. The site attributes in Z_{jk}, such as the voting rate of the community, are of independent interest, so we first estimate equation (6.1) in which we include a vector of site characteristic variables and a single constant term α rather than the site-specific constant terms. Inclusion of the site-specific constant terms in equation (6.2) makes it possible to analyze the influence of chemical characteristics controlling for all other fixed site-specific influences.

Since EPA guidance directives (U.S. EPA 1991) treat risks greater than or equal to 10^{-4} differently (i.e., risks this high trigger site remediations), we separate our analysis of standard setting into two samples. We run specifications (6.1) and (6.2) for high risk pathways, defined as those representing risks of 10^{-4} or greater, and for low-risk pathways, those with risks less than 10^{-4}. Since a given pathway at a site may contribute multiple observations to the analysis, residuals may be correlated within a pathway. We account for this by estimating robust standard errors, which take into account the presence of correlated errors within data clusters.[9]

The analysis of the log of the cost per case of cancer Q_j at site j has a similar specification except that the unit of observation is at the site level, leading to a sample of 130 sites. The site level fixed effects term drops out, and the variables depend only on the site j, not particular chemicals i. The resulting equation to be estimated is

$$\ln Q_j = \alpha_3 + \sum_{k=1}^{n} \psi_k Z_{jk} + \varepsilon_{3j}, \qquad (6.3)$$

where Z_{jk} is the value of variable k at site j, ψ_k is its coefficient, and ε_{3j} is a random error term. We exclude some site characteristics from the cost per cancer case analysis because of the much smaller sample size at the site level. For the cost per case of cancer analysis, the chemical-specific variables in X_{ijk} drop out of the analysis because the cost data are at the site level.[10]

Both T and D are jointly determined by the choice of the cleanup option and its associated cost and target risk level. These measures differ to some extent in that policy decisions involve a choice among policy options and not just the level of stringency of a particular policy option.[11] Thus, for example, there could be several policy choices that achieve the same target risk level with differing costs per case of cancer. Our analysis of target risk levels and cost per case of cancer can be viewed as a reduced form analysis in which we treat the target risk levels and cost per cancer case as functions of exogenous chemical and site characteristic measures.

The chemical pathway variables include measures that pertain to the type of chemical as well as the nature of the exposed population. We include measures of whether a chemical is a volatile organic (VOC), semi-VOC, or inorganic compound (the excluded dummy variable group) to control for differences in remediation costs that vary by these groupings. The measure for the log of chemical toxicity controls for potentially higher remediation costs associated with more toxic chemicals, so this variable should lead to a positive effect on the level of the risk target (i.e., less stringent regulation). The log of the baseline initial chemical pathway risk captures the influence of anchoring. The baseline risk will have a positive effect if a higher baseline effect leads people to tolerate a higher target, a negative effect if the higher baseline risk increases the apparent importance of reaching a zero risk level, and a positive effect to the extent that there is diminishing marginal utility to incremental cancer cases avoided or an increasing marginal cost to remediation.[12]

The number of times the chemical is mentioned in the Lexis general news file from 1988 to 1992 as hazardous or toxic and carcinogenic is the chemical media citation variable, which serves as a measure of availability bias. The more frequent the mention of a given chemical in the popular press (e.g., coverage of PCBs), the more likely it is that regulators or residents will perceive the chemical as dangerous even controlling for the level of the risk and its toxicity. More frequently cited chemicals consequently should receive lower-risk targets. We also include the number of times a site was mentioned in news coverage. Sites with more coverage should have more prominence with the general public and may appear to be riskier, leading to a lower level of T and a higher value of D.

The other chemical variables pertain to the character of the exposure. A variable for whether the chemical exposes the person through a soil pathway as opposed to groundwater may be influential to the extent that people have preferences over how a risk arises, not simply its level. Risks for which the time frame of the pathway is current should be associated with lower values of T both because of discounting and because the presence of existing populations exposed to the risk increases the likely benefits from regulation. The residential pathway variable reflects differences in risk depending on the character of the exposed population. Most of the residential pathways do not involve current residents but rather potential future residents if there is a change in land use patterns.[13] EPA may place a smaller weight on such potential future residents, since there is some nonzero probability that there will be no such residents, and if there are, their discounted losses will be less. The current resident interaction variable permits the residential exposure variable to vary with whether it is actual or potential residential risks. The final chemical pathway variable pertains to whether it is children that are exposed to the risk.

The various site characteristic variables reflect cleanup cost considerations, benefits in terms of the population at risk, political influences, and perceptional factors. The first set of eight variables pertains to basic physical characteristics of the site and its location—chemical industry site, manufacturing site, whether the site is a landfill, industrial waste site, suburban site location, rural site location, total number of operable units, and area of the site in square meters. A lower-risk target level T for a landfill could result from factors such as the representativeness heuristic to the extent that such sites conjure up media images of notorious landfill sites. Residents may perceive landfills as posing greater risk than, for example, industrial waste sites. These differences may also reflect cost factors correlated with landfills. The urban, rural, or suburban location of the site may reflect not only cost and benefit influences but also the likelihood that the risk assessors believe that a risk will actually be realized in terms of whether there will ever be people that will actually be exposed to the risk at the site. The number of contaminated cleanup areas (operable units) at a site, the total site area, and the Hazard Ranking System score control for potentially increasing or decreasing marginal remediation costs as these indicators increase.

EPA policy actions with respect to the site may also be influential, so we include whether a site was listed on the NPL in 1981 to 1984 or 1985 to 1988. The number of polluting facilities and sites tracked in five EPA regulatory programs within one mile of the site also appears as a variable in the analysis.[14] People may view sites in more polluted areas as riskier because of the availability bias. Alternatively, remediations in more polluted areas might be seen as having lower marginal returns because of the overall levels of surrounding pollution. An influence with a similar directional effect is that the high pollution levels may capture an omitted political variables bias: Polluted areas have revealed through their other pollution outcomes an inability to pressure EPA for cleanup or inability to discourage the location of polluting facilities. Remediation target concentrations based on state regulatory standards may be different than those based on human health risk assessments or federal regulatory standards, and the analysis controls for such differences explicitly. The analysis also includes a variable for the lead site authority (i.e., who is supervising the cleanup).

The population characteristic variables reflect both the size and character of the exposed population. EPA should set more stringent regulations with lower target risk levels in more densely populated areas. However, if EPA is prone to scope effects biases and ignores the number of people exposed, as its risk assessment guidelines suggest is the case, there will be no relationship to the number of exposed people. The minority population percentage will control for the extent to which EPA recognizes the nature of the exposed population. The influence of this variable is a test of the role of environmental equity in terms of whether minority populations are being comparatively ignored (leading to a higher target risk level T) or receiving more attention because of the substantial policy focus on environmental equity (leading to a lower value of T). Regulators may also set more stringent targets in minority communities because they face multiple sources of environmental risks. Multiple risks may be important on efficiency grounds (e.g., synergetic effects) or because of political concerns. The mean household income of residents should have a negative effect on the target level of the risk and a positive influence on the cost per case of cancer to the extent that the valuation of environmental amenities increases with income level.

A series of political variables may be influential as well. The variable for voter turnout in the county in the 1988 presidential election provides a measure of whether regulators are more concerned about populations that are likely to overcome collective action problems to scrutinize their actions.[15] While previous studies such as Hird (1993, 1994) and Gupta, Van Houtven, and Cropper (1996) have explored whether "politics" matters by examining site demographics and site political representatives, we explicitly test whether the likelihood that residents will be active affects behavior. We measure the nature of environmental support in the community by environmental group membership per 1,000 residents in the state. We also include League of Conservation Voters' (LCV) scores from 1988 to 1992 for the district's House representative and the state's senators to control for community environmental preferences and support, as well as likely pressure for stringency by legislators. Some of these "political" variables may also reflect efficiency concerns, since citizens who value the environment more highly will tend to elect representatives with better environmental voting records. A series of other variables controls for other aspects of a site's region.[16]

In addition to analyzing the determinants of target risk selection, we examine what influences the log of the cost per cancer case avoided. Since this analysis is at the site level, the chemical pathway variables do not enter, and the analysis is restricted to a subset of site characteristics variables.

6.2 Target Risk and Selection

As we indicated in previous chapters, the EPA officials who make the cleanup decisions at Superfund sites have a number of stated criteria to guide them. If the overall lifetime excess cancer risk to an individual from site contamination is 10^{-4} or higher, EPA guidelines suggest that the site should be remediated so that the remaining risk is somewhere within the 10^{-4} and 10^{-6} interval or below. If baseline risks are already within this range, the site manager has discretion to remediate. If there exist state or federal standards from other environmental programs that apply to a chemical (e.g., ARARs), then the remediation should meet these standards. The cleanup goals enunciated by site managers are generally not expressed at the site level. Instead, they are target chemical concentrations or chemical pathway risks that will remain after the EPA's remediation has been carried out. Our analysis thus focuses on the chemical risk pathway as the unit of analysis. We focus on cancer risks because there is not a good standard metric that allows one to compare noncancer risks (e.g., some chemicals give rise to noncancer effects such as skin rashes, while others generate liver damage).

Figure 6.1 underscores a key result from chapter 2, that if we treat the EPA Superfund risk assessments at face value and examine chemical pathway risks, these risk levels are high compared to many other regulatory programs. For 480 of the 2,888 chemical pathways, the risk is at least 10^{-4}. These risks are high in part because of conservative assumptions made about parameter values in the risk assessments, as indicated in chapter 3. The distribution of the remediation pathway risks remaining at sites shifts downward after remediation, as only 104 pathways pose a risk of at least 10^{-4}. As figure 6.1 illustrates, there is a corresponding increase in the number of pathways posing a risk of 10^{-6} or less after remediation.

The log of the chemical target risks (i.e., the individual lifetime excess cancer risk remaining from a chemical pathway after site remediation is completed) is the unit of analysis in our initial examination of reactions to risk. The 86 sites in the sample with both baseline and target risk data averaged 34 chemical risk pathways with associated baseline and target risks.

Table 6.1 reports the regression estimates of the target risk equation 6.1 and reports the counterpart fixed effects estimates of equation 6.2 for both high- and low-risk chemical pathway samples. We distinguish the high- and low-risk pathways because of the different policy criteria based on pathway risk levels. In each case the natural logarithm of the target risk after remediation is the dependent variable. Higher (lower) values of the dependent variable reflect less (more) stringent cleanup in terms of the level of risk that is permitted to remain at the site. Standard errors reported are robust to the possible presence of correlated errors across chemicals within a given pathway of a site.

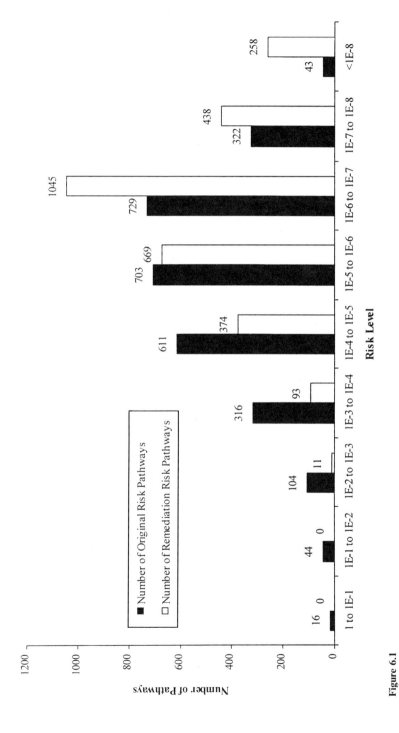

Figure 6.1
Comparison of original and remediation chemical risk pathway levels

Table 6.1
Regression estimates of the natural logarithm of the target risk level: Coefficients (standard errors)

	High risk	Low risk	High risk[a]	Low risk[a]
Chemical pathway				
Volatile organic compound	1.005	−1.011***	1.704**	−0.512**
	(0.656)	(0.222)	(0.839)	(0.204)
Inorganic compound (metals)	3.434***	0.228	3.530***	0.484***
	(0.566)	(0.196)	(0.646)	(0.153)
Log of the chemical toxicity (mg/kg-day)$^{-1}$	0.503***	0.191***	0.577***	0.194***
	(0.082)	(0.036)	(0.089)	(0.036)
Log of the initial chemical pathway risk	0.158**	0.751***	0.181**	0.783***
	(0.077)	(0.034)	(0.087)	(0.032)
Chemical media citations (in thousands), 1988–92	−0.865**	0.014	−1.007**	−0.087
	(0.399)	(0.151)	(0.465)	(0.137)
Soil pathway	0.581	−0.481	−0.007	−0.627*
	(0.739)	(0.367)	(0.809)	(0.345)
Time frame of pathway is current	1.585	−0.080	1.357	0.034
	(1.156)	(0.397)	(0.887)	(0.312)
Residential pathway	0.579*	0.663**	0.597***	0.516**
	(0.324)	(0.287)	(0.227)	(0.218)
Current resident pathway	−2.034	0.296	−2.229*	0.562
	(1.360)	(0.459)	(1.199)	(0.422)
Child pathway	−0.337	0.048	−0.310	−0.061
	(0.344)	(0.252)	(0.244)	(0.104)
Remediation target concentration based on state regulatory standards	−0.019	−0.245	−0.930*	−0.089
	(0.412)	(0.217)	(0.518)	(0.254)
Remediation target concentration based on stated human health risk	0.566	−0.444*	1.011*	−0.607***
	(0.486)	(0.262)	(0.579)	(0.228)

Site characteristics

Chemical industry site	1.242*	−0.649
	(0.658)	(0.556)
Manufacturing site	0.576	0.109
	(0.468)	(0.322)
Landfill	−1.327**	−0.336
	(0.571)	(0.356)
Industrial waste site	0.933	−0.170
	(1.000)	(0.635)
Site location—suburban	−0.237	0.576
	(0.504)	(0.434)
Site location—rural	−0.908	1.499**
	(0.852)	(0.657)
Total number of operable units	−0.698***	−0.168
	(0.249)	(0.181)
Area of the site in square kilometers	−0.082	0.026
	(0.123)	(0.056)
Hazard ranking score	−0.036	−0.016
	(0.030)	(0.020)
Site media citations, 1988–92	0.163	−0.044
	(0.134)	(0.061)
NPL listing for site between 1981–84	0.324	0.277
	(0.607)	(0.312)
NPL listing for site between 1985–88	0.304	0.110
	(0.569)	(0.330)
Federal enforcement cleanup	1.415	0.723
	(2.803)	(1.378)
State enforcement cleanup	1.289	0.505
	(2.883)	(1.535)

Table 6.1 (continued)

	High risk	Low risk	High risk[a]	Low risk[a]
Site lead being negotiated	0.597	0.605		
	(2.610)	(1.410)		
Fund-led cleanup	1.651	−0.496		
	(2.544)	(1.586)		
Number of waste-generating facilities within a 1-mile radius	0.024	−0.023		
	(0.030)	(0.020)		
Population (in thousands) per square mile, 1-mile ring	−0.211*	0.179*		
	(0.117)	(0.097)		
Minority population percentage for the 1-mile ring	−0.046***	−0.016*		
	(0.012)	(0.008)		
Mean household income of residents within 1-mile ring ($ thousands)	0.046***	0.033***		
	(0.016)	(0.012)		
County voting percentage, 1988	−0.013	−0.056**		
	(0.032)	(0.024)		
Environmental group members per 1,000 state residents	−0.475***	0.121		
	(0.172)	(0.149)		
House LCV score, 1988–92	0.016*	−0.003		
	(0.009)	(0.007)		
Senate LCV score, 1988–92	−0.065***	−0.020		
	(0.016)	(0.013)		
R²	0.582	0.662	0.700	0.756

Note: Significance levels using two-tailed tests, *** = statistically significant at 1 percent level, ** = significant at 5 percent, * = significant at 10 percent. All standard errors are robust standard errors based on the clustered model. Clusters were based on unique pathways defined by site, exposure medium (soil?), time frame (current?), exposure location (resident?), and age (child?). $N = 479$ in 132 clusters for high-risk group. $N = 2,409$ in 220 clusters for low-risk group. The robust clustered model also included indicators of site location by EPA region. Omitted dummy variables are: semivolatiles, other site types, urban, 1989–92 NPL listing date, unspecified site lead, and federal standards.
a. The model included fixed-effect variables by site for 85 of the 86 sites represented by the 2,888 chemical pathways. Omitted dummy variables were for semivolatiles and federal standards. Sample sizes as above.

Our results provide strong support for the influence of risk perceptions and politics on the selection of remediation targets at Superfund sites. Consider first the two principal measures of the potency of the chemicals. In both the overall and the fixed effects estimates, more toxic chemicals and chemicals associated with a higher initial risk level have higher target risks after remediation. Thus there is less stringent regulation in terms of the outcome of the more potent chemicals. This result could reflect efficiency concerns, since there may be increased costs for remediating more toxic chemicals; for example, these may take longer to remediate. There also may be increased marginal costs of cleanup. Other possibilities include regulators exhibiting diminishing marginal utility for cancer cases averted and perhaps anchoring so that the initial level of risk influences perceptions about what remaining risks are safe. For example, if regulators' notion of what is a "safe" level of risk is anchored by the estimation from the baseline risk assessments, they will select higher remaining risk targets at sites with higher initial levels of risk.

One risk measure that is influential in leading to more stringent risk targets is not a measure of chemical potency but rather the chemical's public notoriety. Controlling for various risk-level measures, the larger the number of mentions of a chemical in the popular press, the more stringent is the target risk selected in the case of high risk pathways. This result is consistent with the availability heuristic, since both regulators and those surrounding sites may view particular carcinogens as more dangerous if they have received more media coverage. The higher perceived baseline risks for more publicized chemicals will cause the regulators to set a lower target risk T. If a given T appears more dangerous for more highly publicized chemicals, this will also promote the selection of a more stringent cleanup level.

Perhaps the most surprising chemical pathway variable in terms of its lack of statistical significance is whether the time frame of the pathway is current. The interaction of this variable with whether the site is a residential pathway (i.e., the current resident pathway variable) is also not statistically significant, except in the high-risk fixed effects equation. These results suggest that the presence of current exposed populations to health risks generally does not enter EPA's decision with respect to the stringency of cleanup. By treating existing populations exposed to risk with the same weight as is placed on hypothetical populations based on changes in future land uses, EPA is failing to adjust the hypothetical risk scenarios for the fact that there is some probability that there will not be such future exposed populations. Moreover, if they are exposed, the discounted benefits of preventing their exposure will be less than will arise from protecting current populations now at the site. This may reflect a skepticism on the part of policy makers, who may believe that these residential scenarios are less likely to arise and consequently will have a lower expected value.[17]

The estimates in table 6.1 include risk perception variables calculated at the site level, which also influence target selection. Landfills receive more stringent risk targets in the high-risk sample, perhaps because the representativeness heuristic means that Superfund landfills are seen as similar to notorious leaking landfills. Note that the variables related to risk perception bias of availability/representativeness, such as the chemical media citations variable and the landfill dummy, are statistically significant only for the high risk sample. This result is consistent with biases coming into play when risks are large enough to command regulators' or local residents' attention. Sites that are mentioned more in the media did not receive lower chemical target risks.[18] The site characteristic variable results indicate that broad population-based concerns may affect standard settings, even though EPA guidelines focus on individual rather than population risks. For high individual risk levels the agency sets more stringent cleanup standards the greater the population density. The agency adopts the opposite course for low-level risks, where as population density rises the agency sets less stringent standards. This may be in part because as density increases scrutiny of regulator actions dealing with low-level risks may be less likely if people are less likely to monitor agency decision-making as the number of people in an area grows. Rural sites also received less stringent requirements in the low-risk sample. If regulators believed that these sites were less likely to experience residential development in the future, then this variable could be capturing some of the effects associated with distinctions between current and future residential pathways.

Although EPA appears at times to respond to economic concerns relating to the population at risk, it also reacts to political concerns. The higher the voter turnout in the area, the lower the target risk chosen when risks are low. Note that when risks are high, political activity has no effect on standards. It is when risks are low that political activity matters. This finding is consistent with previous results that indicate that differences in the potential for residents to engage in collective action affect how polluters treat the distribution of environmental risks (Hamilton 1993, 1995). Similarly the higher the membership in environmental groups per 1,000 residents in the state, the lower the target risk set for high-level risks. The higher the support (as measured by League of Conservation Voters' scores for 1988–1992) by a state's senators for environmental legislation, the lower the risk targets set by the EPA. This result may reflect responsiveness to congressional principals by regulatory agents, or if environmental constituents are represented by environmentalists, this effect may simply reflect additional responsiveness of regulators to local preferences for environmental protection.[19]

The community variable results go against some popular beliefs. At sites with higher average income levels in the one-mile ring around a site, a higher-risk target will be set. This result may be because regulators believe wealthier residents are less likely to be exposed as assumed in the risk assessments (e.g., groundwater exposures assume well water consumption, while wealthier residents may be connected to public systems). However, the finding is also consistent with environmental equity concerns focusing more policy attention on risks to the economically disadvantaged. This latter hypothesis is consistent with our estimated effects of the influence of a higher minority percentage in an area, which leads to the selection of a more stringent risk target.

Several possible factors may be at work. Since these remediation decisions were made after the policy debate over environmental equity began, regulators may have been more conscious of the treatment of risks to the poor and minorities. In addition the risk perception literature (see Flynn, Slovic, and Mertz 1994) demonstrates that minorities are more likely to perceive given levels of environmental risks as high risks to human health, which could generate more demand for risk regulation in these communities. Regulators might also believe that calculated risks in minority communities were more likely to arise (e.g., if minorities were more likely to consume contaminated groundwater). Since there are no adjustments for this influence in EPA's site-level risk analyses, regulators may treat reported risks more stringently in these communities. More broadly, environmental equity issues span a variety of concerns including where sites are located, which sites are cleaned up, how fast they are cleaned up, and how stringent the remediation policy is. While our results in this chapter pertain only to the target risk level, our analysis in chapter 7 indicates different effects of race on other dimensions of environmental equity.

Analysis of the elasticities implied by the coefficients in the first specification in table 6.1 underscores the relative impact of political factors on the determination of the risk targets. For the high-risk pathways, the elasticities of the target risk variable with respect to several of the key statistically significant variables were as follows: environmental group membership (−4.82), senators' environmental voting records (−4.12), the pathway's initial risk level (0.16), chemical toxicity (0.50), residents' income (1.84), and the minority percentage in the one mile ring (−1.06). For the low-risk pathways, the mix of statistically significant variables was somewhat different, including the following elasticities: voter turnout (−2.97), the initial risk level (0.75), chemical toxicity (−0.19), and residents' income (1.43). Overall, political factors appear to be the most influential in terms of the degree of responsiveness of the cleanup stringency to changes in the variable level.

6.3   Influences on the Cost per Case of Cancer Avoided

Another way to examine the reactions of regulators to risks at Superfund sites is to explore the determinants of the site-level expenditure of cleanup funds and the implied costs per cancer case averted by remediations. Our estimates of the costs per case of cancer utilize the results from chapters 4 and 5, which combine the site-specific risk data with block-group level census population data using the geographic information systems methodology. The site remediation costs for the sample of sites with matching risk data had a mean of $15.0 million using 1993 dollars, a 7 percent discount rate for costs, and pre-cost growth figures. The range of site costs from $57,000 to $133.9 million reflects differences in both stringency of remedy selection and degree of contamination. Superfund site documents focus only on individual risk levels. The mean number of cancer cases averted over a thirty-year period is 5.6, with a range from 0 to 652 and a median of 0.019 cancer cases averted per site. The mean cost per cancer case averted implied by the EPA expenditures at the sample of 130 sites is $11.7 billion, with a range from less than $20,000 to $961 billion. The median cost per case of cancer was $418 million, and only 36 of 130 were below $100 million per cancer case averted.[20] These estimates take EPA's conservative risk assessments at face value, assume no latency period for cancer, and do not discount future cancer cases. Making such adjustments (for a sample of 99 sites) leads to a median cost per case of cancer above $1 billion. If remediation expenditures are analyzed based on averting

Table 6.2
Determinants of log (cost per cancer case avoided)

Site characteristics	Parameter estimate	Standard error
Log of the maximum pathway risk at the site	−0.379***	0.083
Existence of cancer risk pathways at site under current scenario	−0.845	0.539
Site location—suburban	−1.308**	0.651
Site location—rural	−1.710**	0.734
Both soil and groundwater costs expended at the site	−0.863	1.162
Total number of operable units	−0.247	0.274
Area of the site in square kilometers	−0.025*	0.015
Hazard ranking score	0.012	0.030
NPL listing for site between 1981–84	1.655***	0.576
NPL listing for site between 1985–88	1.129*	0.574
Number of waste-generating facilities within a 1-mile radius	0.016	0.035
Population (in thousands) per square mile, 1-mile ring	−0.606***	0.151
Minority population percentage for the 1-mile ring	−0.009	0.014
Mean income of residents within 1-mile ring ($ thousands)	−0.008	0.024
County voting percentage, 1988	0.080**	0.040
Environmental group members per 1000 state residents	−0.208	0.150
House LCV score, 1988–92	0.0008	0.009
Senate LCV score, 1988–92	0.008	0.022
	$R^2 = 0.453$	

Note: Significance levels using two-tailed tests, *** = statistically significant at 1 percent level, ** = significant at 5 percent, * = significant at 10 percent. The model also included indicators of site location by EPA region. Omitted dummy variables are: urban site location, 1989–92 NPL listing date, and presence of soil or groundwater costs only. White heteroskedasticity-adjusted standard errors are reported. $N = 130$.

cancer cases alone, the Superfund program has relatively high regulatory costs.

Table 6.2 presents estimates of the equation for the log of the cost per cancer case averted. Many of the influences reflected in the table's analysis of the cost per case of cancer avoided are similar to those in the target risk selection estimates. Sites with a high maximum pathway risk are associated with a lower cost per case of cancer, which parallels the result from table 6.1 that cleanup levels are less stringent if the risk at the site is high. Whereas the presence of current exposed populations did not affect the target risk level, even though it should have led to more stringent regulations on an efficiency basis, in the cost per case of cancer regression estimates there is a significant negative influence. Rather than setting

more stringent standards with a higher cost per case of cancer for current exposed populations, EPA incurs a higher cost per case of cancer
when there are only potential future populations at risk. Thus the target
risk level and cost per case for cancer results are reflective of a common
pattern of influence. The higher population density leads to a lower cost
per case of cancer averted because the presence of a substantial exposed population makes cleanup more efficacious from a benefit-cost
standpoint. What should be emphasized, however, is that EPA is not pursuing a policy of equalizing the marginal cost per case of cancer avoided
across sites, which would be the efficiency dictum if cancer were the only
outcome of policy interest. Rather, by basing its policies on an individual
risk approach that does not reflect the size of the exposed population
or whether the population now exists at the site, EPA is often failing to
recognize important aspects of the overall benefit consequences of its
efforts.

Politics does influence the cost per cancer case avoided. The most influential political variable in table 6.2 is the county voting percentage in
1988. Counties with high voter turnout have sites in which the cost per
case of cancer avoided is greater, indicating a greater willingness of EPA
to expend funds on cleanup at sites with substantial political influence.
The elasticity of the cost per case of cancer with respect to voter turnout is
quite high (4.14). Political pressures exert a powerful influence on the degree of inefficiency in the cleanup expenditures. These results reflect the
same pattern of influence as in the target risk regressions, though the
magnitude of the elasticity is larger.

The presence of minority populations and people of different income
groups did not, however, affect the cost per case of cancer averted under
EPA policy decisions. The greater valuations of risk by the more affluent
also do not affect policy decisions. The cost per case of cancer avoided is
lower at large sites, which may be reflective of their greater risks and potential economies of scale in cleanup.

6.4   Distribution of Cost-Effectiveness

In chapter 5 we documented a wide range in the cost-effectiveness of
cleanup policies. The interesting economic issue is which factors drive
EPA's decisions to select particular sites from this cost-effectiveness menu
for cleanup. Does EPA choose the cleanup actions based on their level of
cost-effectiveness by working from the top down for the policy rankings in

table 5.6? If factors other than relative performance in reducing risk enter, what are these influences and do they vary across sites? Is EPA simply implementing an identical, rigid set of policy concerns for all sites or is there a different character of the influences that are operational for sites of differing efficacy? To explore these issues, we will analyze the determinants of the value of the log of the cost per case of cancer averted at different fractiles of the distribution using a quantile regression model. More specifically, the estimated coefficients of the cost per cancer D at the τth quantile satisfy

$$\text{Quant}_\tau(D_i|X_i) = X_i\beta_\tau, \qquad i = 1, \ldots, n, \tag{6.4}$$

where X_i is a $k \times 1$ vector of covariates and the vector of coefficients for the τth quantile is designated by β_τ.[21]

Table 6.3 reports the estimates of an OLS equation and quantile regression models for the analogue of the results in table 6.2. Some insignificant variables do not appear in this model so as to attain convergence. The asymptotic standard errors reported are bootstrap standard errors.

The results in table 6.3 reinforce and extend the implications of the earlier results. The maximum pathway risk reduces the cost per cancer case in a similar manner for all quantiles, since the presence of the substantial risks is always influential. Current cancer pathway risks do not affect the cost per cancer case except at the 90th percentile, where they reduce the costs per case. Site media citations are not consistently influential. The NPL listing from 1981–84 generally makes the cost per case higher, perhaps because the sites from that era that remain as cleanup targets in 1991–92 are the least cost effective. Population density enhances cost-effectiveness, where this influence is greatest for the most cost-effective sites.

The most intriguing results pertain to the effect of the dominant political variable in the analysis—the county voting percentage. The earlier analysis suggested that political factors may promote inefficiency. These results document the locus of this effect. The voting variable strongly affects the cost per cancer case and target risk selection in OLS analyses, but the quantile regression results indicate that this effect is highly selective. For sites with cost-effectiveness at the median or better, the voting percentage does not affect the cost per cancer case level selected. Influences such as the risk level and population density are more influential for these more cost-effective sites. However, at the two upper percentiles of the cost-effectiveness distribution, higher voting rates boost the cost per

Table 6.3
Quantile regression results for log (cost per cancer case avoided)

Variable	OLS	Percentile for quantile regression				
		0.10	0.25	0.50	0.75	0.90
Log of the maximum pathway risk at the site	−0.381***	−0.374***	−0.383***	−0.390***	−0.356***	−0.445***
	(0.075)	(0.140)	(0.102)	(0.074)	(0.101)	(0.128)
Existence of cancer risk pathway at site under current scenario	−0.891*	−0.192	−1.294	−0.889	−1.107	−1.747*
	(0.531)	(0.844)	(0.960)	(0.872)	(0.763)	(1.011)
Site media citations, 1988–92	−0.139	−0.245	0.054	−0.064	−0.242*	−0.160
	(0.117)	(0.255)	(0.196)	(0.125)	(0.135)	(0.232)
NPL listing for site, 1981–84	1.553***	1.889**	1.398*	1.155	2.338***	2.273***
	(0.527)	(0.862)	(0.740)	(0.851)	(0.612)	(0.706)
NPL listing for site, 1985–88	0.854*	0.765	0.350	1.033	0.984*	1.877**
	(0.507)	(0.717)	(1.004)	(0.741)	(0.569)	(0.872)
Population (in thousands) per square mile, 1-mile ring	0.600***	−1.055**	−0.825**	−0.247	−0.406*	−0.285
	(0.152)	(0.472)	(0.365)	(0.281)	(0.206)	(0.338)
County voting percentage, 1988	0.079**	−0.013	0.014	0.083	0.114**	0.139**
	(0.037)	(0.086)	(0.057)	(0.056)	(0.050)	(0.056)
Pseudo R^2 (R^2 for OLS)	0.442	0.359	0.268	0.265	0.357	0.418

Note: Significance levels using two-tailed tests, *** = statistically significant at 1 percent level, ** = significant at 5 percent, * = significant at 10 percent. All models also included a series of variables for site location (suburban, rural), minority population, income, environmental group members, Senate LCV score, both soil and groundwater costs expended, and 6 EPA region variables. To reduce convergence problems, some insignificant variables from the earlier analysis were omitted. Standard errors are in parentheses.

case of cancer averted. These political factors are consequently only influential at the most inefficient sites where the costs per case of cancer are in the billions. Moreover, at these sites, the political factors increase the extent of the inefficiency. Politics only matters through its adverse effect on the most inefficient cleanups.

6.5 Conclusions

Cleanups of hazardous waste sites in the Superfund program inevitably involve decisions about risk, since they affect the potential exposure of residents to contaminants, and decisions that are political, since they allocate limited funds across sites. Prior research on risk regulation indicates that regulator decisions may reflect biases in risk perception (Viscusi 1995) and that who bears the risks may affect how they are treated (Cropper et al. 1992). Previous work on the Superfund program has found mixed evidence on the degree that characteristics of the surrounding community or their political representatives influence cleanup selections.[22]

The analysis in this chapter has made four distinct contributions to the literature on risk regulation and Superfund decision making. We combined detailed risk information with census data to yield a direct measure of cleanup efficiency, the cost per cancer case averted. We used multiple measures describing the character of risks to establish that biases in risk perception are reflected in cleanup decisions. We demonstrated that the likelihood that residents will engage in collective action does cause regulators to adopt more stringent cleanup standards and spend more to avert cancer cases. We also revealed that differences in political power matter to push regulators toward greater inefficiency in remediation decisions.

If decision makers at Superfund sites targeted for cleanups were concerned solely with social welfare maximization, then these regulators would choose target risks for cleanups based on factors related to marginal social benefits (e.g., expected cancer cases) and marginal social costs (e.g., factors that influence remediation costs, such as site characteristics and baseline risks). Unfortunately, many of the critical economic concerns do not affect decisions in the desired manner.

Our analysis reveals that regulators' choice of risk targets is influenced by many additional factors relating both to risk perceptions and the political nature of the community bearing the risks. For high-risk pathways, chemicals with more citations in the popular press, landfill sites, and pathways with lower baseline risks all received more stringent risk targets.

These results are consistent with various phenomena found in the risk perception literature, such as the availability heuristic. Perhaps equally disturbing is the failure of key benefit variables to affect decisions in the expected manner. The presence of a risk to people based on current land use patterns rather than hypothetical future uses did not increase the stringency of the regulation. Pathways exposing current residents generally did not receive more stringent standards. EPA is thus failing to target its efforts to reflect the overall health implications of risks to currently exposed populations.

What does appear to be influential are a variety of political influences pertaining to the nature of the community. Sites in counties with higher voter turnouts, states with more environmentalists, and states with senators with stronger environmental voting records were all more likely to have stricter environmental cleanup targets. Scrutiny from the bottom up and top down may influence regulator selections. Environmental membership and legislator votes may proxy for the values individuals place on the environment, so those variables could relate to local valuations that an efficiency-minded regulator would consider. The degree of constituent political activities, measured by voter turnout, should not influence regulators unless they are affected by political concerns. A major drawback of political pressure is that it does not serve here as a mechanism for promoting efficiency-based concerns. Indeed, higher voter turnout has a greater effect in increasing stringency when the risks are small and there are not current exposed populations. These political pressures push EPA further away from an efficient policy design.

The cost per case of cancer prevented analysis yielded results that were in many respects similar. However, in this case simply the mean value of the cost per case of cancer, which was measured in billions of dollars, was quite telling. EPA cleanup policies are an outlier among government regulatory programs on any efficiency basis, assuming cancer prevention is the primary objective. The benefits of Superfund cleanup are highly concentrated at a very small percentage of sites, with most cleanup actions failing any reasonable efficiency test. The quantile regression results highlighted the pivotal role of political factors for inefficient cleanups, whereas the most desirable cleanups were not influenced by voting rates.

In sum, these results indicate that in hazardous waste cleanup decisions risk perception biases and risk politics matter. One cannot distinguish with the current information whether risk perceptions matter primarily because they reflect biases of regulators as individuals or regulators as representatives of constituents with biased perceptions, a topic with significant implications about the efficiency of regulator decisions. We can, however, indicate the impact on social welfare of the likelihood that residents will engage in collective actions. Recent debates have reprised the question on the degree that democracy promotes efficiency.[23] We find that in the Superfund program collective action is most effective when risks are small and when expenditures to avert cancer cases are many orders of magnitude greater than figures that emerge from private market decisions. In the cleanup of hazardous waste sites, our results indicate that greater scrutiny from residents pushes regulators away from decisions likely to maximize social welfare.

Environmental Equity at Superfund Sites

Environmental amenities are a normal good. If education, labor, and housing markets were functioning perfectly, one would expect individuals with lower incomes to choose, other things being equal, to live in neighborhoods with lower levels of environmental protection because housing prices would be lower there. By this theory, the areas surrounding hazardous waste sites being remediated under the EPA's Superfund program should thus be populated by residents with lower incomes. These sites, which are often active or inactive landfills, chemical plants, or manufacturing facilities, generate negative externalities that lower property values.[1] Industrial plants may have been attracted to a location by low land values, so they end up locating in low-income areas. The location of a facility generating environmental risks may also reduce housing values and lead to an in-migration of lower-income residents and blue-collar workers employed at industrial facilities.[2] Either scenario rests on efficient decisions made by residents and firms. To the extent that minorities and those with less education earn lower incomes, these demographic groups will be exposed to higher risks from Superfund sites, since their incomes will lead them to be more likely to live near these areas. Concern about the exposure of different demographic groups to environmental risks would thus be based not on efficiency terms but rather on equity considerations. The extent of the policy concern about risk equity may, of course, depend on factors other than the risk levels. Is there, for example, some form of compensation for bearing the risk? The debate over the distribution of risks by demographic groups has been termed one of "environmental equity" or "environmental justice."[3] These concerns have achieved such prominence in EPA policy that the Clinton administration established an Office of Environmental Equity within EPA and has made equity issues more prominent. Whether this prominence affects policy decisions is one of the focal points of this chapter.

Exposure of minority groups to environmental risks can sometimes result from influences other than efficient market forces. Patterns of residential location and risk may arise from discrimination in education, housing, and labor markets. If such factors give minority groups lower incomes or mobility, they may then be led to live in areas with greater levels of environmental risks. Living next to a Superfund site could thus be another manifestation of the damages arising from employment or housing discrimination. A second source of potential market failure lies within the firm. If principal-agent relations failed within a firm, those making plant location decisions might trade off profits for prejudice and explicitly locate in minority neighborhoods because of animus toward different demographic groups. One wonders, however, why one would choose to have such proximity to groups one disliked if some form of taste discrimination were driving decisions.

A more likely basis for such targeting is political influence rather than tastes. If neighborhoods around Superfund sites have a higher percentage of minority residents, a third market failure explanation for this pattern begins with the link between externalities and collective action. According to the Coase theorem (1960), the owners of plants and landfills that eventually became Superfund sites would originally choose to locate in areas where they did the least environmental damage, since that is where the expected compensation they would have to pay would be lower. Firms will respond to costs generated by expressed demands for compensation, however, which must be communicated by residents through the political process. If residents vary in the degree that they engage in collective action, minority residents may end up living near externality-generating sites if they are less likely to translate their demands for compensation into costs that firms will face in the political process.[4] The same process may be replicated in the site cleanup process. Regulators may respond to problems by adopting a strategy of police patrols, where they look for violations/remedies in the same way a police officer patrols a beat. Or regulators may adopt a strategy, which McCubbins and Schwartz (1984) call a fire alarm model, where they respond to requests for actions from constituents who "pull" an alarm. If EPA officials adopt a fire alarm model and allocate resources to sites based on community political responses, minority areas may enjoy less stringent cleanups if they are less likely to translate their demands through collective action. Community differences in the potential for collective action thus translate into differences in environmental contamination and environmental cleanups.

The implications of environmental equity for EPA policy reform are not clear-cut. A great deal depends on the source of the inequity and on whether other policy reforms, such as diminished housing market discrimination, will be more effective in reducing the inequity. A wide range of risk-related factors vary by income groups and other demographic characteristics, such as medical care, homicide rates, and smoking. Hazardous waste exposures may not be the most salient risk nor the risk associated with the greatest inefficiency. Our analysis below consequently does not resolve the fundamental issue of what role environmental equity should play in Superfund policy, but by better understanding the character of the inequities, policy makers will be able to assess the extent of the inequity and some of its causes. Our analysis consequently is intended to provide a framework for assessing the character and degree of the inequity, which should be an essential part of the policy process.

This chapter attempts to advance research in environmental equity by focusing on a single question: Do particular demographic groups bear disproportionate risks at Superfund sites? Answering this question, however, involves resolving a number of empirical issues. How are minority groups defined? What other demographic groups, such as low-income residents or those with less education, might be expected to bear higher risks? What reference standard should be used to determine whether a group bears a "proportionate" share of the risks? How far out in spatial terms do the externalities associated with Superfund sites extend? What are the multiple dimensions of risk associated with living near a hazardous waste site? Is the relevant unit of observation a community, population group, individual? We explore all of these questions to derive empirical estimates of risks to different demographic groups arising from potential exposure to contaminants at Superfund sites. Since we lack time series data on these risks, we cannot explore questions about causation in terms of the degree that these residential outcomes are the result of efficient or inefficient market operations. We can explore the degree that government responses to these risks vary, depending on the nature of the community bearing the risks.

Our analysis indicates that minority groups, low-income residents, and those with less education do bear a disproportionate risk from living near Superfund sites. Minorities have a higher probability of living within one mile or four miles of these hazardous waste sites. The minority population percentage is higher than the national percentage of minorities at about a quarter of Superfund sites, but these are the most populous sites. Thus minorities compose a higher percentage of the total potentially exposed populations, even though the majority of sites have a white population percentage exceeding the national average. The minority population percentage decreases as distance from a site increases, while incomes, education levels, and housing values increase with this distance. Since a hazardous waste site is not a positively valued neighborhood amenity and is often strongly linked to industrial activity, these patterns are not surprising. At sites where EPA surveys indicate current residential use, the average percentage of minorities and the percentage of minorities of the total populations at these sites are higher than at sites without indications of any use (e.g., residential, commercial, or other use). In terms of estimated individual risk levels, minority residents face higher levels of lifetime excess cancer risks arising from Superfund sites. Minorities constitute a higher percentage of the expected cancer cases arising from sites than their national population percentage, but this result in part depends on a few extremely hazardous sites located in areas with a large number of minorities.

These results indicate that minorities and those with less income and education are more likely to be exposed to multiple measures of risks from Superfund sites. These results do not resolve questions of causation and its efficiency. We do not know the degree that exposures result from efficient or inefficient operation of education, labor, and housing markets. The analysis does indicate, however, that notwithstanding the avowed policy commitment to environmental equity, the inefficiencies or inequities arising from market operations appear to be magnified rather than ameliorated by government action. To be remediated under the Superfund program, EPA must first place a site on its National Priorities List. Our analysis indicates that sites considered for NPL listing but rejected by the agency have a higher percentage of minorities and lower mean household incomes than sites that are accepted into the remediation program. This discriminatory result still holds if one controls for a measure of the extent of pollution in the surrounding neighborhood. In terms of the progress through the stages of the remediation pipeline, there are few differences in the treatment of sites based on the demographics of the surrounding (one-mile radius) neighborhood. However, if one examines indications of the outcomes of remediations at Superfund sites, the EPA is less likely to invoke the strictest cleanup standards, is more likely to choose the cheapest remedy if several alternatives were available, and spends less per cancer case avoided at sites with higher minority percentages. We interpret these results as consistent with the agency partially responding to sites on the basis of the extent of political mobilization at the sites. Such an explanation is consistent with our other findings regarding political factors, but we cannot test this hypothesis directly because we lack political data on the immediate neighborhoods surrounding the sites.

We begin our analysis by describing previous research on environmental equity at Superfund sites. We then develop three different measures of equity at sites based on potential exposure of different demographic groups to externalities at these hazardous waste sites, estimates of actual levels of risks at a sample of sites, and EPA responses to these risks. These results allow us to focus in the chapter's conclusion on the policy implications for regulators concerned about environmental equity at Superfund sites.

7.1 Research on Superfund and Environmental Equity

Most of the growing literature on the demographic distribution of environmental risks focuses on facilities that treat, store, or dispose of hazardous waste or manufacturing plants that release toxic chemicals or other pollutants.[5] Three studies, however, directly focus on the potential exposure of populations around Superfund sites. Analyzing county-level data, Hird (1994) found that the number of sites in a county on the National Priorities List (i.e., hazardous waste sites qualifying for federal cleanup money) increased with the percentage of the county population that was college educated, nonwhite population percentage, median house value, and percentage of the county economy composed of manufacturing. This pattern was consistent with an interpretation that counties with manufacturing were wealthier and, as a by-product of manufacturing, generated wastes that led to the creation of hazardous waste sites.

Zimmerman (1993) also found higher potential exposures for minorities at Superfund sites. Defining communities at the census place or minor civil division level, she found that in aggregate the percentages of blacks (18.7 percent) and Hispanics (13.7 percent) in the communities with NPL sites were higher than their national population percentages of 12.1 percent for blacks and 9.0 percent for Hispanics. Three-quarters of the black residents living around NPL sites are concentrated in communities with 20 percent or more black residents (which account for only 15 percent of the total NPL communities). The average population in these black communities is much higher than the average population of communities with Superfund sites. Thus for black residents, Zimmerman determined that their higher potential exposure to risks from Superfund sites arises from their living in a relatively small number of highly populated communities with hazardous waste sites.

Anderton, Oakes, and Egan (1997) use census tract data to examine potential exposure to Superfund risks. They find that in multivariate analysis a higher percentage of black residents is associated with a greater number of CERCLIS sites (i.e., NPL and non-NPL sites) in a tract but a smaller number of NPL sites. In examining the prioritization of sites that could potentially be placed on the NPL, the authors conclude:

Our analysis of the prioritization process is consistent in suggesting that neighborhoods with higher percentages of Black residents are potentially less likely to have a timely designation of NPL sites from among CERCLIS sites. Yet to definitively determine the equity of the prioritization process would require costly or even an infeasible independent assessment of site hazards.[6]

More research focuses on how the nature of the community surrounding a hazardous waste site affects its progress through the EPA's remediation pipeline. As we have previously indicated, once a site is identified as potentially hazardous, EPA undertakes a series of evaluations to determine what action, if any, will be taken at the site. If the initial assessment, known as the preliminary assessment, identifies potential risks, the site will undergo additional studies. These studies may result in the decision to take emergency removal actions and/or the development of a standardized Hazard Ranking System (HRS) score for the site. If the HRS score exceeds a predetermined level, the site qualifies for placement on the National Priorities List, the group of 1400+ sites that qualify for remediation funds from the federal government.

The agency's Hazard Ranking System used to score potential NPL sites gives higher scores to more populous sites. A study by Clean Sites (1990) found that this meant that sites in poor, rural counties were placed on the NPL at a lower rate than sites in other areas. Once sites were on the NPL, Hird (1994) found that the progress of sites through the phases of investigation, record of decision, and remediation did not depend on the socioeconomic characteristics of the counties containing the sites. Zimmerman, however, found that communities (i.e., census places or minor civil divisions) with relatively higher proportions of minorities were less likely to have records of decisions signed than other communities with Superfund sites. She found that in part this was because sites placed on the NPL earlier in the Superfund program had lower percentages of minorities (and a longer time to work their way through to the decision phase).

Lavelle and Coyle (1992) analyzed the relation between site progress and the demographics of residents in the zip code areas surrounding Superfund sites. They determined that the time from site discovery to listing on the NPL was longer for sites in the bottom quartile of white population percentage (5.6 years mean) than in the top quartile of white population percentage (4.7 years mean). They also determined that at minority sites, defined as the sites in the bottom quartile of sites in terms of white population percentage, the EPA was more likely to choose containment of waste rather than treatment of waste. In sites in the top quartile of white population percentage, the agency was more likely to select treatment rather than containment. In multivariate analysis, however, Gupta, Van Houtven, and Cropper (1995) found no evidence that the agency selected less protective cleanup risk targets in zip codes with higher minority percentages or lower median incomes. These authors (1996) also did not find any evidence that the racial composition of the zip code neighborhood surrounding sites influenced the level of permanence in the remedies chosen by the EPA.

The existing literature thus provides consistent evidence that minorities may face higher potential exposures to risks at Superfund sites and mixed evidence on whether the nature of a community bearing site risks affects the EPA's reaction to site hazards. Questions left unanswered in the literature but explored in the following sections include what are the demographics of the individuals living within the radius of externalities around a site, how estimated risks vary by demographic groups, and how site progress varies in terms of the nature of the communities directly surrounding sites.

7.2 Potentially Exposed Populations

Nearly 51 million people live within four miles of a site on the National Priorities List.[7] The extent of the potential risks borne by these people depends on the relevant radius for the externalities generated by a hazardous waste site. Whether these risks are "inequitable" requires that one define a reference group for comparison purposes. Since the EPA's risk assessments focus solely on individual risk levels, we developed the methodology outlined in chapter 4 to develop estimates of the population risks arising at these sites (e.g., the number of expected cancer cases to arise over a thirty-year period from current land use patterns). Our models incorporate EPA's assessment of the likelihood that one will come into contact with contaminated soil, which is a declining function of distance of residence from the site (e.g., residents living on-site are assumed to come into contact with contaminated soil with a probability of 1, while for those living a mile from the site the probability is 0.0063). Probability of exposure to groundwater depends on several factors, including whether a household draws water from local wells and the degree that a plume has migrated on-site and off-site. In a study of plume sizes at 74 sites, we found an average plume size of 665,000 square meters. At 68 sites, the plume had migrated into the quarter mile ring surrounding a site (though only 9 sites had plume migration into the one-mile ring surrounding a site). Aside from human health risks, sites may generate negative externalities in the form of natural resource damages and nuisance factors (e.g., industrial traffic to the site). Housing price impacts in hedonic studies at Superfund sites have found pricing impacts out to a radius of six miles from a site.[8]

Based on these data, we will primarily examine the populations of residents potentially affected by Superfund sites as those living within one mile of the site (although we also present data for rings up to four miles around sites). To calculate these populations, we obtained individual site boundary information from the EPA for close to 1,200 sites on the National Priorities List. We include federal sites in this overall population analysis. This sample does not provide the basis for our later analysis of regulatory decisions, in part because for federal sites the nature of their risks and the regulatory regime they are remediated under differs from the other sites in the Superfund program. The later analysis thus focuses on nonfederal NPL sites. Using geographic information system software, we combined the boundary data with 1990 census information to yield analysis of the demographic characteristics of residents living in successive rings around the Superfund sites. Where appropriate, we did not double count individuals when residents were found to live within particular distances of multiple Superfund sites.

What reference group should these individuals be compared to when analyzing whether given demographic groups bear a disproportionate risk from hazardous waste sites? One way to analyze the distribution of potential risks across populations is to compare the demographics of Superfund populations to demographic figures for the nation as a whole. This approach provides a salient set of reference points but does not incorporate the influence of income or efficiency-based influences on the expected risk distribution. Demographic figures can be analyzed on a site basis (e.g., what is the average of the minority percentage across sites?) and on a population-weighted basis (e.g., of the total populations living within one mile of sites, what percentage of the residents are minorities?). Yet descriptions of the allocation of risks also focus on the operation of local land markets in industrial and residential location. For this reason we also analyze how indications of exposure change across sites as one moves progressively further from a site. These figures too can be presented on a site basis and a population-weighted basis to determine how potential risks vary with race, income, education, and housing values. This exploration thus permits a more diverse exploration of the various equity effects.

Table 7.1 indicates that overall 50.9 million people live within four miles of the 1,173 nonfederal and federal NPL sites analyzed in the exposure analysis. Note that over 2 million people live within the EPA-defined Superfund site boundaries and thus fall into the on-site resident category. These exposures arise in part from western sites where extensive groundwater contamination has led the EPA to characterize large acreages as part of the sites. Overall, 18 percent of sites currently have residents on-site. Asians, Hispanics, and those designated by the census as "other races" live within the four-mile radius in higher percentages than their national population percentage.[9] Overall, minorities account for 24.2 percent of the U.S. population, compared to 35.1 percent of on-site populations and 28.9 percent of the populations living within four miles. The percentage of most nonwhite populations and minority groups as a whole declines as one moves farther from sites, indicating that these groups bear more of the potential exposures from Superfund sites.[10] Viewed in terms of probability of living within one mile of a site, minorities had a 0.05 probability compared to 0.03 for whites. At the four-mile range, a minority resident had a 0.24 probability of living in this area compared to a 0.20 probability for white residents. The probability of living within four miles was particularly high for Asians (0.31) and Hispanics (0.29), while the probability for blacks (0.21) is close to that for U.S. residents as a whole (0.20).

Minorities, particularly Asians and Hispanics, thus bear a disproportionate share of the exposures from Superfund sites, since they constitute 24.2 percent of the national population but 28.9 percent of the residents living within four miles of Superfund sites. Whether their risks are higher depends on a variety of other factors as well such as the chemicals present

Table 7.1
Potentially exposed persons

a. Total number (in thousands)

Miles from site	American Indian	Asian	Black	Hispanic	Other race	White	All minority	Total population
On-site	18	117	187	406	208	1,522	719	2,052
0–0.25	7	54	104	174	81	789	335	1,034
0.25–0.50	10	76	161	216	93	1,181	457	1,520
0.50–1	26	211	488	577	246	3,394	1,288	4,365
1–2	73	579	1,509	1,554	673	9,585	3,669	12,420
2–3	87	616	1,831	1,687	730	11,425	4,164	14,690
3–4	83	568	1,881	1,628	714	11,588	4,096	14,834
On-site to 4	305	2,222	6,161	6,243	2,743	39,483	14,728	50,914

b. Overall percentage[a]

Miles from site	American Indian	Asian	Black	Hispanic	Other race	White	All minority
On-site	0.9	5.7	9.1	19.8	10.1	74.2	35.1
0–0.25	0.7	5.2	10.1	16.9	7.8	76.3	32.4
0.25–0.50	0.6	5.0	10.6	14.2	6.1	77.7	30.1
0.50–1	0.6	4.8	11.2	13.2	5.6	77.8	29.5
1–2	0.6	4.7	12.1	12.5	5.4	77.2	29.5
2–3	0.6	4.2	12.5	11.5	5.0	77.8	28.3
3–4	0.6	3.8	12.7	11.0	4.8	78.1	27.6
On-site to 4	0.6	4.4	12.1	12.3	5.4	77.5	28.9

c. Probability of living within a given distance of a Superfund site by demographic group

Miles from site	American Indian	Asian	Black	Hispanic	Other race	White	All minority	Total
1	0.03	0.06	0.03	0.06	0.06	0.03	0.05	0.04
4	0.15	0.31	0.21	0.29	0.28	0.20	0.24	0.20

Note: Analysis in tables is based on 1,173 NPL sites and U.S. Census Bureau block group information. All minority = total population minus non-Hispanic whites.

a. The overall breakdown of the U.S. population by census group is as follows: American Indian, 0.8 percent; Asian, 2.9 percent; Black, 12.0 percent; Hispanic (all races), 8.8 percent; other, 3.9 percent; white, 80.3 percent; all minority, 24.2 percent.

Table 7.2
Distribution of sites and mean population by minority composition

Minority composition	N sites	Mean population of 1-mile ring	N sites	Mean population of 4-mile ring
0–10%	639	3,966	565	32,426
10–20	185	8,216	243	70,346
20–30	105	11,557	137	94,740
30–40	70	14,686	80	133,478
40–50	54	22,396	53	154,360
50–60	31	16,895	36	174,588
60–70	21	39,028	24	215,869
70–80	29	26,177	19	148,873
80–90	26	7,860	11	212,481
90–100	11	14,186	4	186,040

at sites and the types of exposure. The average white population percentage at Superfund sites is, however, 85.6 percent. This percentage is larger than the national white population percentage of 80.3 percent. These seemingly contradictory figures can be reconciled by table 7.2, which indicates that sites with higher minority percentages tend to be more populous. Less than one third of the sites (347 out of 1,173 sites) account for 89 percent of the minority residents living within one mile of the NPL sites. Sites with 0 to 10 percent minority populations in the one-mile ring around a site have a mean population of 3,966, while sites with 40 to 50 percent minorities in the one-mile ring had a mean population of 22,396.

Table 7.3 indicates that the conclusion that most sites have higher white population percentages than a given reference group holds whether one examines populations at the one-mile or the four-mile radius. As the reference group progresses from the ten-mile ring, county, state, and nation, a larger percentage of the sites have a white population percentage in the one-mile ring greater than the larger reference group. The same holds true for the comparison of the four-mile group. At the one-mile ring or the four-mile ring, only a quarter of the sites had minority population percentages greater than the national average. On a site basis, Superfund problems are concentrated in neighborhoods with lower minority population percentages than the national minority population average. The location of some sites in highly populous minority neighborhoods, however, means that the overall set of residents surrounding Superfund sites

Table 7.3
Racial composition of sites

a. Percentage of sites where racial composition in 1-mile ring exceeds that of a reference area

Reference	American Indian	Asian	Black	Hispanic	Other race	White	All minority
4-mile ring	41.6	35.8	38.3	43.8	36.3	56.7	44.5
10-mile ring	41.0	34.9	32.0	41.0	34.6	62.0	39.6
County	41.9	33.9	34.9	39.9	34.4	61.9	40.2
State	34.7	26.3	23.6	25.6	22.8	73.1	27.3
National	23.8	16.6	21.1	16.3	15.0	75.2	25.1

b. Percentage of sites where racial composition in 4-mile ring exceeds that of a reference area

Reference	American Indian	Asian	Black	Hispanic	Other race	White	All minority
10-mile ring	46.6	43.1	43.6	46.6	45.6	54.6	46.4
County	46.7	44.8	45.8	47.1	45.5	52.9	47.8
State	36.7	30.9	27.3	28.0	25.5	70.4	29.0
National	21.1	17.9	24.0	16.7	16.0	74.6	25.3

Table 7.4
Demographic comparisons

a. Site mean annual household income, education levels, and housing values

	Site mean household income	Mean site housing value	Site mean education levels		
			Low	Medium	High
1-mile ring	$36,930	$98,590	25.5%	58.0%	16.5%
4-mile ring	$37,690	$103,900	24.5	57.3	18.2
10-mile ring	$38,430	$107,410	23.8	56.9	19.4
NPL counties	$39,040	$110,020	23.4	56.9	19.7
United States	$38,450	$112,660	24.8	54.9	20.3

b. NPL overall annual household income, education levels, and housing values

	NPL mean household income	NPL mean housing value	NPL mean education levels		
			Low	Medium	High
1-mile ring	$37,440	$124,260	26.0%	54.6%	19.4%
4-mile ring	$40,170	$128,210	24.6	54.1	21.4
10-mile ring	$44,060	$151,700	23.7	52.4	23.9
NPL counties	$45,160	$167,180	22.5	53.5	24.0
United States	$38,450	$112,660	24.8	54.9	20.3

c. Percentage of sites where 0–1 mile value is less than 1–4 mile value

Household income	Housing value	Education levels		
		Low	Medium	High
61.4%	62.4%	44.4%	42.4%	66.4%

are more likely to be minorities than one would predict based on their national population percentages.

Table 7.4 analyzes household income, housing values, and education levels in two different ways. The table includes site-level values for these variables and the means of these values for varying distances from the site. In addition population- or household-weighted values for each of these variables appear as well. Analyzing these figures in terms of site-level means, one finds in panel a of table 7.4 that site-level mean household incomes are lower at the one-mile ring ($36,930) and the four-mile ring ($37,690) than the mean household income for the nation as a whole ($38,450). This result is reversed, however, at the county level. Thus, if one defined those potentially affected by NPL sites with a broader measure such as counties, one could conclude (as Hird did) that NPL sites were located in communities with greater wealth. Note that incomes steadily increase as one moves from one-mile to four-mile to ten-mile rings. At 61 percent of the sites, the mean household income is lower in the 0–1 mile ring than in the 1–4 mile ring (panel c). The increase in income levels with distance from the site is consistent with the prediction that the environment is a normal economic good.[11]

The site-level mean house values for residents living within one mile ($98,590) or within four miles ($103,900) were lower house values than the U.S. mean ($112,660). Such differences would be consistent with the location of NPL sites in industrial working-class neighborhoods. The ring trend is also generally consistent with the theory that the negative externalities associated with the sites and the other land uses correlated with the sites will drive down housing prices. At 62 percent of the sites, the mean housing value is lower for the 0–1 mile ring than for the 1–4 mile ring. If one defines education levels attained as low (less than high school), medium (high school or some college), and high (college or advanced degree), the site-level mean for populations living within one mile of NPL sites indicates that the percentage of residents with lower levels of education (25.5 percent) is higher than the national figure (24.8 percent), and the percentage of residents with higher education levels (16.5 percent) is lower than the national figure (20.3 percent).

Panel b of table 7.4 analyzes the demographics of potentially exposed populations on an aggregate population basis. The ring trends evident from the site-level analysis still hold true in the population- or household weighted analysis. As distance from the site increases from one to four to ten miles, the mean household income for the populations potentially exposed increases. The mean housing values also increase with distance from the site, as does the percentage of highly educated residents. However, on a population-weighted basis, residents within four or ten miles of Superfund sites have higher mean household incomes and greater housing values than those for the United States as a whole. Such income differences may arise because of the high concentration of sites in urban areas, where both incomes and housing values are higher.

Another concern about potential exposure to pollution relates to the synergistic effects of multiple exposures to different pollutants or polluting sources.[12] Risk assessments at Superfund sites do not take into account the interaction effects among chemicals, since little is currently known about the harms that arise from the particular combination of chemicals at Superfund sites.[13] We have tried to measure the potential for multiple exposures in a different way with our data. For each of 1,167 NPL sites, we counted the number of times facilities or sites within 1 mile of the site were tracked in five different EPA databases (the Toxics Release Inventory, Resource Conservation and Recovery Act [Biennial Reporting System], Aerometric Information Retrieval System, the Permit Compliance System [wastewater], and CERCLIS [which includes both NPL and nonNPL sites]). This count represents a rough proxy for the number of polluting sources in the one-mile area around a site. The correlation between the percentage minority in the one-mile ring and the number of polluting sites is 0.31. In terms of population weighted means for the populations living within one mile of Superfund sites, minorities were likely to live near a much higher number of polluting sources. The mean number of polluting sources for minority residents living within one mile of Superfund sites was 11.4 versus 6.3 for white residents surrounding Superfund sites. For particular demographic groups, the mean number of polluting sources was 5.6 for Native Americans, 8.1 for blacks, 15.2 for Hispanics, 18.1 for Asians, and 16.2 for other demographic groups. To the degree that multiple exposures lead to higher risks from a given Superfund risk, minority residents surrounding Superfund sites face higher potential risks.[14] The presence of these multiple risk exposures also suggests that concerns with risk equity should focus on multiple types of exposures.

Our analysis of the residents potentially exposed to externalities at Superfund sites thus indicates that populations living within one mile of NPL sites have higher minority percentages, lower income levels, and lower percentages of highly educated residents than the nation as a whole. The risk gradients predicted by the theory that environmental protection is a normal good also hold at these sites. On a site-level and population-weighted basis, mean housing prices, mean incomes, white population percentage, and percentage of residents with higher educations all increase as distance from the NPL site grows. In terms of local and national comparisons, one can thus conclude that minorities and those with lower incomes and educations are more likely to face potential exposures to the hazards of Superfund sites. Whether the risks are in fact greater depends on the character of the exposures, which we explore for our sample of sites rather than the larger NPL sample considered for this portion of our equity analysis.

7.3   Distribution of Estimated Cancer Risks

Proximity to a Superfund site is only a rough indicator of the potential for a person to be exposed to the human health risks arising from these areas. The EPA generates detailed information on the concentrations of chemicals at NPL sites during risk assessments conducted to aid remediation decisions. As we discussed in chapters 4 and 5, we collected this chemical contaminant information at a sample of 150 sites where remediation decisions were made in 1991 and 1992. This sample is representative of a larger sample of 1,124 nonfederal NPL sites in terms of regional distribution, past site use, and the nature of contamination. For these sites we estimated excess cancers arising from contaminated soil and groundwater for dermal, ingestion, and inhalation pathways. Estimates of soil cancers in part depended on the likelihood that residents were assumed to come into contact with contaminants (a probability which the EPA has estimated ranges from 1 for on-site residents to 0.025 for those living 0.25 miles from the site and 0.0063 for those living a mile from the site). Our estimates of cancer cases arising from groundwater ingestion are based on chemical contaminant levels, census information on use of wellwater in the tracts surrounding a site, and groundwater plume information in site documents. Though EPA's site-level risk assessments contained information on individual risks of cancer arising from site contamination, our combination of chemical data with census information through GIS software allowed us to develop estimates of the excess number of cancer cases at these sites over a thirty-year time horizon.

The results in chapter 4 indicate that there were 731 estimated cancer cases arising over thirty years from contamination at the 150 sites, with 695 attributable to contaminated soil and 36 to groundwater contamination. The cancers were concentrated in an extremely small number of sites, however. One site accounted for 652 cases and only ten sites had at least one expected case over the thirty-year horizon. The median number of cancer cases per site was 0.017. The influential site—the Westinghouse Electric site in Sunnyvale, California—which had the largest number of cancer cases is in an area with a high minority population in the one-mile ring. The 14,500 minority residents, primarily Asian and Hispanic, account for 44 percent of the population living within one mile of this site. In part because of the concentration of risks among minorities at this site, minorities account for a much higher percentage of the expected cancer cases arising from site contamination than their national population percentage. The breakdown by demographic group of the percentage of the 731 estimated cancers was minorities 43 percent, whites 68 percent, other race 9 percent, Hispanic 22 percent, black 4 percent, Asian 18 percent, and American Indian 1 percent. If the site (i.e.,Westinghouse) with the largest number of cancers is dropped from the analysis, however, the results are reversed. Minorities would account for 16 percent of the remaining 79 cancer cases, while whites (including Hispanic whites) would account for 87 percent of the expected cases. The conclusion that minorities bear a disproportionate share of the expected cancers must be tempered by the fact that this result is driven primarily by one extremely hazardous site.

EPA risk assessments at NPL sites focus on individual lifetime excess cancer risks arising from contamination, rather than the expected number of cases arising in the surrounding population. Viewed in these terms, minority residents do face higher levels of individual cancer risks than white populations surrounding hazardous waste sites. Table 7.5 indicates that the minority percentage of the potentially exposed population is higher at sites that are more densely populated. Where density is greater than or equal to 2,000 residents per square mile, minorities make up 28.3 percent of the total exposed population living within four miles of the site.[15] The mean of the maximum individual cancer risks at the less densely populated sites, where minorities account for only 15.5 percent of the total exposed population, is 0.046 (t test = 1.9). These estimated individual risk numbers are extremely high relative to other regulatory programs, as we indicated in chapter 3. These risk levels are due in part to EPA's requirement that analyses use conservative parameter values for variables such as ingestion rate or exposure duration in the calculation of individual risks.

In terms of population-weighted mean maximum individual cancer risks, minorities face higher risks than white populations surrounding the 150 NPL sites in the sample. Minority populations within four miles of the sites face a mean risk of 0.142 versus 0.125 for the white population. Asians (mean risk = 0.308), Hispanics (0.134), and members of other races (0.146) all face elevated individual cancer risks. The magnitude and distribution of the risk exposures depends to a great extent on the Westinghouse site. If this extremely hazardous site from California is dropped from the analysis, the gap between mean risks faced by minorities (0.108) and whites (0.102) nearly disappears.

Table 7.5
Percentage of potentially exposed populations, by population density and risk level

Density	Sites	Mean site risk	American Indian	Asian	Black	Hispanic	Other race	White	All minority
≥2000	32	0.155	0.4	6.7	10.3	11.5	3.5	79.1	28.3
<2000	118	0.046	0.6	1.8	7.7	5.7	2.6	87.4	15.5
Total	150	0.070	0.5	4.9	9.3	9.4	3.1	82.1	23.6

Note: The "mean site risk" is the mean of the maximum cumulative individual risks for the set of sites with the given density ($n = 150$, a subset of sites with RODs signed in 1991 or 1992). Population density is measured as the number of persons per square mile. The demographic breakdown is based on aggregate exposed populations.

In the EPA's site-level risk assessment, the agency distinguishes between current risks and future risks, which are hypothetical risks that could arise if land use changed or if likelihood of contamination changed through a mechanism such as the migration of a groundwater plume. Data on both potential exposures and estimated individual cancer levels indicate that minorities may be more likely to be exposed to current risks from Superfund sites. The maximum cumulative individual cancer risks based on current exposures are higher in minority neighborhoods. At sites where minorities account for more than 20 percent of the population within one mile, the mean of the maximum current cumulative risks is 0.013, while the mean for sites where minority population percentages are 20 percent or lower is 0.0022 ($t = 1.7$). Minorities make up a higher proportion of the population at sites where EPA survey data indicate current residential use. At the 165 sites where the EPA data indicate current residential land use, minorities constitute 45 percent of the population living within a quarter mile. At the sites ($N = 343$) where there is no current use (e.g., residential, industrial, commercial), minorities constitute 22 percent of the populations living within a quarter mile.

In terms of the estimated risks at Superfund sites, minority groups are thus disproportionately exposed. There is some evidence that minority groups account for a larger fraction of the estimated cancers than their national population percentage, evidence that the population weighted mean maximum cancer risks for minorities is higher than that of whites, and strong evidence that minorities bear larger current risks arising from present land uses at sites.

7.4   EPA Responses to Risks

Superfund cleanup decisions involve a chain of delegated decision-making. Congress has delegated to the EPA the responsibility for defining exact cleanup standards at sites. The agency delegates decisions over which remedies to choose to regional EPA officials, who in turn may transfer responsibility for risk assessments to outside consultants, responsibility for cleanup implementation and funding to the potentially responsible parties linked to the contamination at the sites, and authority to direct some site cleanups to state agencies. Significant discretion may exist within these principal-agent relationships, so responses to environmental risks may vary widely across sites. Previous research on health and safety and environmental programs indicates that both public and private sector decision makers may reach different decisions affecting the distribution of risk depending on the nature of who bears the risk.[16] This section analyzes how the EPA responded to risks from hazardous contaminants depending on the nature of the community primarily bearing these risks, the residents within a one-mile radius of these sites.

Sites enter the Superfund program through a "fire alarm" process, where interested parties notify the EPA or a state agency that an area may be contaminated.[17] EPA has not made a systematic national attempt to investigate likely sites of hazardous contamination. States vary in the degree that they have investigated potential sites. Once a site is brought to the attention of the EPA by state agencies or individual reports, the EPA enters it into a national database that currently contains over 41,000 sites. If a preliminary investigation indicates potential contamination, the agency may rate the site on a scoring system (the Hazard Ranking System) that develops an index score based on population exposed, medium of contamination, and amount of contamination. Those sites which score above 28.5 (a cutoff originally chosen to generate 400 sites for initial consideration by the agency in the early 1980s) are advanced to the National Priorities List and thus qualify for federal remediation funds.[18] Since the entry into this process entails someone to alert the agency (e.g., someone to pull a fire alarm), the question arises whether the nature of communities with potential NPL sites affects which sites are passed to the final list.

We do have information that compares communities (e.g., populations within one mile of sites) where sites were added to the NPL and those with non-NPL hazardous waste sites (see table 7.6). The mean minority percentage for sites that made it onto the NPL was 18 percent, while the minority percentage at the non-NPL sites was 24 percent ($t = 8.4$). NPL site communities had mean household incomes of \$36,730, while non-NPL communities had mean incomes of 32,880 ($t = 9.3$). This difference in NPL listing may indicate regulators were more likely to respond to risks borne by wealthier communities. Such a relationship could arise due to income effects if, for example, wealthier residents attach a higher value to preventing cancer risks. However, no government agency, including EPA, has ever adopted such a practice of differentiating benefits affecting different societal groups. Individuals in these communities may be more likely to contact regulators or regulators may be more responsive to their contacts. Another possibility is that environmental contamination was lower in minority areas, which could mean that sites hazardous enough to

Table 7.6
Comparison of CERCLA sites listed on the NPL with those not listed, controlling for number of facilities located within a 1-mile radius of the site (facilities grouped by quantile)

Number of facilities		Non-NPL mean	N	NPL site mean	N	t statistic
0	Household income	$32,600	8799	$36,680	309	4.6***
	Minority percentage	17.7%	8804	12.2%	309	5.0***
	Voting percentage	51.7%	8534	51.5%	311	0.30
1	Household income	$32,986	4997	$36,042	183	3.3***
	Minority percentage	18.0%	4998	14.3%	183	2.7***
	Voting percentage	51.0%	4914	51.1%	183	0.16
2–3	Household income	$33,527	7066	$35,111	235	1.8*
	Minority percentage	21.9%	7066	19.8%	235	1.3
	Voting percentage	50.3%	6982	51.4%	236	2.0**
4–7	Household income	$32,529	7954	$37,188	257	4.8***
	Minority percentage	23.8%	7954	20.3%	257	2.4**
	Voting percentage	50.4%	7874	51.7%	255	2.6***
≥ 8	Household income	$32,858	6883	$37,221	183	4.7***
	Minority percentage	38.5%	6885	29.2%	183	4.8***
	Voting percentage	49.3%	6863	51.0%	183	3.4***
Total sample	Household income	$32,880	35,776	$36,729	1221	9.3***
	Minority percentage	23.9%	35,784	18.4%	1221	8.4***
	Voting percentage	50.5%	35,243	51.4%	1218	3.6***

Note: *** = statistically significant at 0.01 level, ** = significant at 0.05 level, * = significant at 0.10 level.

rank on the NPL would have a lower percentage of minority residents. As a proxy for the extent of contamination at CERCLIS sites, we counted the number of facilities that appear in four different EPA tracking systems (i.e., wastewater, air pollution, hazardous waste [RCRA], and toxics release inventory [TRI]) within one mile of the site. The number of facilities serves as a measure of pollution releases in the area, which might indicate the likelihood of contamination at the potential NPL sites. Communities with NPL sites had 4.3 "facilities" within one mile, while non-NPL sites had 5.3 sites within this radius ($t = 4.2$). If one orders CERCLIS sites by quantiles based on the number of potential local polluters, for communities in the top quantile of polluting plants (average 18.0 plants), the NPL communities averaged 29.2 percent minorities, while the non-NPL communities averaged 38.5 percent. In the bottom quantile, NPL communities had a mean minority population of 12.2 percent compared to 17.7 percent for the non-NPL communities. Thus, controlling for a measure of local level of pollution, communities with higher percentages of minorities were less likely to be placed on the NPL. In each quantile, mean household income was also lower in communities where sites failed to reach the NPL. In the areas with greatest potential pollution (e.g., 2–3, 4–7, or 8+ facilities within one mile of the site) and for the sample as a whole, voter turnout was slightly higher in the NPL communities. This discrepancy is consistent with collective action being a factor which influences whether the EPA places a site on the NPL. Analyses of the Superfund program that start with the NPL list sites thus miss the potential bias in the process which generates the list of sites that qualify for federal remediation funds.[19]

A number of factors may influence the variations in EPA remediation decisions, including site types, medium of contamination, EPA region, and when the site was placed on the NPL list. Whereas the analysis in chapter 6 focused on target risk levels, here we examine other critical policy decision variables linked to different levels of action by the agency. Table 7.7 reports Poisson regression and logit results that examine the independent impact on remediation decisions of the percentage of minority residents in the one-mile ring. Removal actions can occur any time the EPA believes there is an imminent threat to human health or the environment. Table 7.7 indicates that minority population percentage did not have a statistically significant impact on the number of removal actions at a site. The logit results indicate that the minority population percentage in the one-mile ring did not affect whether a site reached the stage where the EPA issued a Record of Decision, the document containing site remediation plans. If one looks at the mean time for a site to progress through different states of Superfund remediation, there are not large differences between the time in the pipeline stages for sites in quartiles with the lowest minority community percentage and time in the pipeline for sites in the quartile with the highest minority percentage. The time between site discovery and final listing on the NPL is longer in the top minority percentage quartile of sites (5.3 years) than for the bottom minority percentage quartile (4.7 years), but this statistically significant difference is small in magnitude. Overall, progress through the Superfund NPL process is generally not linked to the racial composition of the community surrounding a site.

Table 7.7
Determinants of site remediation

	Number of removal actions at site, $n = 876$		Record of Decision issued, $n = 876$		State ARARs as cleanup standard, $n = 665$	
	Parameter estimate	Standard error	Parameter estimate	Standard error	Parameter estimate	Standard error
Chemical industry site	−1.5e-1	1.4e-1	4.7e-1	4.4e-1	−9.7e-2	3.3e-1
Industrial waste site	2.1e-1*	1.2e-1	5.6e-1	4.1e-1	−1.1e-1	3.0e-1
Landfill	−4.9e-1***	1.3e-1	5.4e-1	3.4e-1	4.5e-1	2.8e-1
Manufacturing site	−4.6e-2	1.1e-1	−4.6e-2	3.1e-1	7.2e-2	2.7e-1
Number of waste generating facilities within 1-mile radius	−3.6e-3	4.1e-3	−3.7e-2***	1.0e-2	−6.0e-3	9.8e-3
Site location—suburban	6.7e-2	1.2e-1	−1.6e-1	3.1e-1	−1.7e-1	2.8e-1
Site location—rural	−1.0e-2	1.3e-1	−2.2e-1	3.5e-1	−3.3e-1	3.1e-1
Area of the site in square meters	−1.7e-10	3.9e-10	−6.1e-12	2.4e-9	−6.4e-9	8.3e-9
Site has contaminated groundwater and soil	3.1e-1***	9.0e-2	2.8e-1	2.5e-1	3.8e-1*	2.1e-1
Hazard ranking score	1.6e-2***	3.6e-3	−1.1e-2	1.2e-2	1.7e-3	9.2e-3
NPL listing for site between 1981–84	1.3e-2	1.2e-1	1.3e + 0***	2.9e-1	−5.5e-1*	2.9e-1
NPL listing for site between 1985–88	−5.2e-2	1.2e-1	1.4e + 0***	3.2e-1	−4.3e-1	3.0e-1
Minority population percentage, 1 mile	−2.2e-4	2.2e-3	1.2e-1	8.9e-3	−1.0e-2*	5.8e-3
Total number of operable units	1.0e-1***	1.5e-2	6.7e-1***	1.6e-1	9.7e-2	6.3e-2
Mean household income of residents, 1 mile	9.1e-7	3.4e-6	2.8e-6	9.8e-6	8.2e-6	7.4e-6
County voting percentage, 1988	−7.7e-3	6.7e-3	2.1e-2	2.0e-2	−9.7e-3	1.6e-2
Population per square mile, 1-mile ring	2.2e-5	1.7e-5	−5.0e-5	5.1e-5	1.1e-5	4.8e-5
House LCV score, 1982–94	3.9e-3*	2.3e-3	−8.9e-4	6.1e-3	−6.4e-3	5.1e-3
Senate LCV score, 1982–94	−4.2e-3	3.1e-3	−1.1e-3	9.0e-3	2.1e-2***	7.5e-3
House Energy and Commerce member	1.1e-1	1.2e-1	1.4e-1	3.9e-1	2.1e-1	2.9e-1

Senate Environment and Public Works	-3.9e-2	1.1e-1	4.1e-2	3.0e-1	-5.3e-1**	2.6e-1
Environmental group members per 1,000 state residents	-5.5e-2**	2.8e-2	1.4e-2	8.4e-2	2.2e-1***	7.7e-2
	$\log L = -1045$		$\log L = -292.1$		$\log L = -397.3$	

Note: *** = statistically significant at 0.01 level, ** = significant at 0.05 level, * = significant at 0.10 level. Dependent variable in the Poisson model in column 2 equals the total number of removal actions (emergency response actions) conducted at the site. Dependent variable in the logistic regression in column 3 indicates whether any operable units in the site had reached the specified stage of the remedial process (existence of a ROD). Dependent variable in logistic regression in column 4 equals 1 if state ARARs were invoked at any site operable unit. Models in these three columns also included indicators of EPA region and site lead responsibility. House and Senate committee variables indicate the presence or absence of a Congressional district representative or Senator on the respective committee during any Congressional term from 1982 to 1994. Omitted categories are the following: indicators of other site types, urban site location, contaminated soil only, NPL listing after 1988, region 1, and site lead not determined.

The results in table 7.7 are consistent with the theory that implementation of the Superfund program is at times influenced by local and state variations in political activity and by intercession or influence of federal legislators. None of the political variables was statistically significant in the removal equation, indicating that the agency's response to acute hazards is not influenced by politics.

In the selection of cleanup standards to be used as the basis for remediation, sites with higher minority percentages were less likely to have cleanups based on state environmental standards (which often result in the most stringent cleanup targets). Sites in areas represented by senators with higher environmental voting records over the period 1982 to 1994 and sites in states with higher environmental group membership were also more likely to have state standards invoked. Note that sites where a senator served on the senate Environmental Affairs Committee during the period 1982 to 1994 were less likely to have the stricter standards invoked.[20]

For a subset of sites where the EPA made remediation decisions in 1991 and 1992, we have assembled detailed cost and risk data that allow us to examine EPA cleanup decisions in finer detail. The median number of cancer cases averted per site by the EPA was 0.017 for our sample of 150 sites. These efforts translated into a median cost per cancer case averted of $388 million (with only 44 out of 145 sites with a cost per cancer case averted less than $100 million). Table 7.8 demonstrates that the higher the minority percentage in the community, the less the EPA spent in averting cancer cases. The racial composition of the community also influenced the agency's selection among remediation alternatives. EPA guidance provides site managers with discretion to take cleanup cost into account in choosing between alternatives if both remedies adequately address human health risks. For our subsample of sites we found 98 instances where the EPA faced a choice between similarly protective alternatives that dealt with soil contamination, which the agency often enjoys more discretion in cleaning up, since there are less likely to be environmental standards from other programs that would require cleanup to a particular level of soil contamination. Table 7.8 indicates that the agency was more likely to choose the cheaper remediation option as the minority percentage increased in the one-mile ring surrounding a site. EPA officials were less likely to choose the cheaper soil remediation alternative at sites in districts where a representative served on the environment committee or at sites in states with higher environmental group memberships.

In sum, the demographic nature of the community did not appreciably affect the progress of the site through the stages of the EPA remediation process. Whether the site entered the NPL and how it was treated in terms of risk targets selected and expenditures to avert cancers did, however, vary with the racial composition of the community. We believe this differential treatment arises because these elements of the program operate in part by fire alarm; namely community pressure affects the degree that regulators take action that lead to a site being placed on the NPL and the degree they pursue stringent remediations. Progress through the stages of remediation operates according to a police patrol model; that is, EPA headquarters (and Congress) monitor the progress of sites through the remediation pipeline. If communities vary in terms of their potential for collective action, differences in treatment may arise not because of the preferences for regulators over risk reductions in different demographic communities but because regulators face different political pressures and scrutiny. We lack data on political activity at the site ring level. Voter turnout in the county, a proxy for collective action, is associated with differences in site listing. Sites that failed to make it onto the NPL had lower voter turnout rates (and the difference in voting rates was statistically significant between these NPL and non-NPL sites). The differences in EPA site treatment that vary with race may arise because the fire alarm approach to regulation means that those who are less politically active receive less environmental protection in the remediation process.

The association between higher minority population percentages and lower political activity is further evident in our data. If one divides the over 1,000 nonfederal NPL sites into quartiles based on county voter turnout, the mean voter turnout in the 1988 presidential election for the 268 sites in the lowest quartile is 41.1 percent (versus 55.1 percent for the other NPL quartiles). Of these 268 sites, 49 percent (131) were in the highest quartile of sites based on minority population percentage in the one-mile ring surrounding a site. If one compares these 131 sites that are in both the lowest voter quartile and highest minority population quartile to the other NPL sites, differences in treatment emerge that are consistent with the collective action theory. For example, the EPA has a program of technical assistance grants that is designed to help communities hire independent experts to help them understand the process of risk assessment and site remediation. The program is designed to help overcome the information imbalance between the residents bearing the risks and the regulators and responsible parties involved in the cleanup process.

Table 7.8
Measures of EPA response

	Log of cost per cancer cases averted (n = 113)		Least expensive soil alternative selected (n = 98)		Least expensive GW alternative selected (n = 94)	
	Parameter estimate	Standard error	Parameter estimate	Standard error	Parameter estimate	Standard error
Chemical industry site	5.7e-1	9.0e-1	-1.7e+0	1.4e+0	-3.3e-2	1.1e+0
Industrial waste site	-6.0e-1	1.2e+0	1.2e+0	1.1e+0	1.5e+0	1.3e+0
Landfill	-1.7e-1	5.6e-1	-1.3e-1	8.7e-1	7.8e-1	1.0e+0
Manufacturing site	-9.6e-1	7.7e-1	6.5e-1	9.2e-1	-1.7e+0*	9.6e-1
Site location—suburban	-2.1e+0***	8.3e-1	-4.9e-1	1.1e+0	2.7e-1	9.5e-1
Site location—rural	-2.9e+0***	1.0e+0	3.0e-1	1.4e+0	6.4e-2	1.1e+0
Area of the site in square meters	-3.5e-8***	1.3e-8	1.3e-7	1.9e-7	-3.2e-8	1.3e-7
Number of waste-generating facilities within 1-mile radius	1.4e-2	4.0e-2	4.4e-2	3.6e-2	5.7e-2**	2.9e-2
Site contains contaminated groundwater and soil	1.1e+0*	6.2e-1	2.1e+0**	8.6e-1	-2.5e-1	7.6e-1
Hazard ranking score	3.3e-2	3.7e-2	1.2e-2	4.7e-2	5.7e-2	4.5e-2
NPL listing for site between 1981–84	1.3e+0*	7.1e-1	1.5e+0*	8.1e-1	-6.3e-1	8.6e-1
NPL listing for site between 1985–88	1.2e+0*	6.5e-1	2.2e-1	8.1e-1	-8.2e-2	7.7e-1
Minority population percentage, 1 mile	-5.0e-2***	1.7e-2	3.8e-2**	1.9e-2	2.8e-2	2.4e-2
Total number of operable units	-1.5e-1	3.0e-1	-2.1e-1	2.9e-1	2.1e-1	2.3e-1
Mean household income of residents, 1 mile	-2.0e-5	2.6e-5	5.7e-5	3.6e-5	4.9e-5	3.2e-5
County voting percentage, 1988	-1.7e-2	4.8e-2	-3.8e-2	5.5e-2	-3.3e-2	4.8e-2
Population per square mile, 1-mile ring	-6.5e-4***	1.7e-4	-4.3e-4	2.7e-4	-3.7e-4	2.6e-4
House LCV score, 1982–94	2.3e-3	1.5e-2	-1.1e-2	1.9e-2	-1.3e-2	1.9e-2
Senate LCV score, 1982–94	-1.5e-2	2.1e-2	6.9e-2***	2.6e-2	-1.0e-3	2.1e-2

House Energy and Commerce member	-9.4e-1	6.8e-1	-3.2e$+0$**	1.4e$+0$	-5.9e-1	9.9e-1
Senate Environment and Public Works member	5.8e-2	6.0e-1	-9.3e-1	9.1e-1	-1.6e-2	8.6e-1
Environmental group members per 1,000 state residents	8.4e-2	1.8e-1	-4.1e-1*	2.5e-1	-2.9e-1	1.8e-1
	Adj $R^2 = 0.21$		$\log L = -41.8$		$\log L = -46.7$	

Note: *** = statistically significant at 0.01 level, ** = significant at 0.05 level, * = significant at 0.10 level. Dependent variable in OLS regression in column 2 is the log of the cost per cancer cases avoided. Model also included indicators of site lead responsibility and EPA region. White standard errors are reported. Dependent variable in the logistic regressions in columns 3 and 4 equals 1 if EPA chose the least expensive remedial alternative for that medium. Model also included indicators of site lead responsibility. Omitted categories in columns 2–4 are the following: indicators of other site types, urban site location, contaminated soil only, NPL listing after 1988, and site lead not determined.

Community groups, however, must apply to the EPA for funding of technical assistance grants. For the low voter turnout, high minority quartile sites, the proportion of the population living at sites that received technical grants (3.5 percent of these populations) is lower than the proportion of the population (7.9 percent) living at other NPL sites that had technical assistance grants $(Z = 2.4)$. In the selection of cleanup standards, federal environmental standards (which often generate the stricter cleanup goals than those based on risk assessments alone) were used as a basis for remediations affecting 4.8 percent of populations at the low voter, high minority sites versus 11.0 percent for the populations at other NPL sites $(Z = 2.9)$. EPA survey data also indicate that the proportion of the populations at low voter turnout, high minority sites living at sites where citizen concerns had been a factor in the selection of cleanup stadards (0.6 percent) is much lower than the 5.5 percent population percentage at other NPL sites. There is consequently strong evidence that complaints were less likely to be voiced or less likely to be heeded at these low voter turnout, high minority sites. Since communities with higher percentages of minorities are more likely to have lower rates of collective action (as proxied for by voter turnout), minorities may receive lower levels of environmental protection in the Superfund program in the parts of the regulatory process influenced by expressed community activity.

7.5 Conclusions

The question of how the distribution of risks varies by demographic group has attracted increasing academic and government attention. In 1994 President Clinton issued Executive Order 12898 which directed agencies to consider environmental equity concerns in their decision making.[21] This chapter focused on equity issues in a single regulatory effort, the Superfund program to clean up hazardous waste sites. What the policy response should be to observed inequities is a more complicated issue since one would expect, for example, to have more hazardous waste sites in industrial areas than in strictly residential areas.

To summarize, our equity focus highlighted the distribution of risks across different census racial categories. Overall, minorities are more likely to be exposed to hazardous waste sites. However, taking into account the magnitude of the risk, minorities are exposed less than whites for our sample if the Westinghouse site is excluded. This result is reversed if this large hazardous site is included in assessment of total cancer risks. Since most of this site's "risks" are not real threats, and the chemicals are now largely covered by a parking lot, in terms of expected cancer cases there is no substantial inequity in terms of the locus of the hazards. However, EPA remedial actions appear to be less stringent in some respects for sites with a higher percentage of minorities. Analysis of environmental equity should encompass both government reactions to risk as well as existing environmental exposures.

A recurring theme in the analysis is that environmental equity is a multifaceted topic that entails much more than simply identifying case studies of waste sites located in urban areas. Research on environmental equity should employ multiple measures of environmental outcomes and minority population definitions to explore how risks vary with race, income, and education. Specifically, researchers should examine indicators of potential exposure, actual risks, and market and government responses to these risks. Different definitions of minority populations are instructive, especially since patterns of exposure may vary across different regions for groups such as blacks, Asians, Hispanics, and native Americans. Population-weighted analysis is essential since sites vary widely in population density. Different samples (e.g., quarter-mile ring, one-mile ring) should be used to estimate potential exposures, and different reference groups (e.g., county, state, U.S.) should be used to compare relevant exposures. Ring patterns, the change in community characteristics as distance from site increases, are especially helpful in analyzing predictions generated by theories of environmental externalities. The increasing accessibility of geographic information systems and census data make more feasible the estimates of actual risks to which different demographic groups are exposed.

Reasoning from a single measure of exposure, one might conclude that there is no "environmental equity" problem in the Superfund program, since the average percentage of white residents in the areas surrounding Superfund sites (85.6 percent) is actually higher than that of the U.S. population as a whole (80.3 percent). Yet our analyses of multiple indicators of risk demonstrate that minorities are disproportionately exposed to hazardous waste sites. Relative to the composition of the U.S. population as a whole, minorities constitute a higher percentage of the populations living within one mile of Superfund sites, a larger fraction at sites with current residential use, and a larger percentage of the expected cancer cases arising from these sites (although this last result depends on a few extremely hazardous sites located in areas with large minority populations).

The results also indicate that the term "environmental equity" may be misleading. If regulators respond to environmental risks differently depending on the nature of the community exposed, the differential treatment may give rise to inefficiencies (not just inequities). The readily observed indicators of site treatment do not reveal much difference in the pace of cleanup in communities based on the racial composition of those exposed to the risks. Regulators do treat sites differently in terms of the cleanup remedies selected and the cost expended per cancer case averted based on the nature of the community exposed. As the minority percentage in the one-mile ring around a site increased, EPA regulators spent less per cancer case averted, were more likely to choose the cheapest alternative in dealing with soil contamination, and were less likely to invoke the more stringent cleanup standards provided by state environmental laws. Greater reliance on economic policy tests would promote environmental equity by making expected cancer cases among minorities and the poor count just as much as illnesses of the wealthy. The current policy process is influenced by political power, thus putting minorities and the poor at an additional disadvantage in the remediation of risks. In examining how the incidences of environmental risks vary across demographic groups, our analysis of the Superfund program indicates the importance of using multiple measures of potential exposure, of estimating actual risks, and of assessing the response of government to these risks.

If regulators appear to respond to risks based on the level of collective action within communities, one way to change this behavior would be to open regulator decisions to greater scrutiny. Greater reliance on the benefits and costs of cleanups rather than the political influence of those affected would enhance environmental equity. Reforms in risk assessment and risk management hold out the prospect that more information will be provided to the public and interest groups on site-level regulator decisions. In chapter 9 we will explore more in depth the potential ramifications for how greater scrutiny of regulator decisions could affect variations in government responses to risks at Superfund sites.

Market Reactions to Site Risks

Our analysis in chapter 5 indicated that Superfund remediation expenditures fail a benefit-cost test by wide margins. The estimated cost per case of cancer avoided at most sites was in the hundreds of millions of dollars, or more. The evidence from the setting of target risk cleanup standards and the willingness to pay to avert cancer cases indicates that political factors and risk biases by constituents and/or regulators influence site decision making. Even when residents assess risks accurately, the dispersion of remediation costs and the concentration of cleanup benefits will create incentives for them to press for stringent (though inefficient) cleanups. We found that the influence of collective action by residents, which can draw legislative and public scrutiny, is greatest at sites with the lowest risks and sites with the most inefficient remediation decisions.

Would residents' reaction to Superfund risks be different if they were spending their own money? How do residents and others perceive the risks at hazardous waste sites? One way to answer these questions is through surveys. When asked to evaluate the severity of environmental problems, people rank hazardous waste sites as the top priority. In answering a similar question, an Environmental Protection Agency (EPA) expert panel characterized hazardous waste sites as only a low-to-medium threat to the public.[1] A similar disparity in risk rankings was evident in the survey of health risk beliefs of homeowners near a landfill by McClelland, Schulze, and Hurd (1990). They found that the homeowners' assessments of the risk were much higher than the assessments of experts. These studies suggest that the public overestimates the low probability of hazardous waste risks. This overreaction to risk in turn may pressure the EPA to undertake unnecessarily expensive Superfund remediations.

Another way to study perceptions of and reactions to risk is to analyze the decisions of homebuyers near Superfund sites. If Superfund sites are perceived to generate health risks, then one would expect that, controlling for other factors, houses closer to sites would sell for lower prices. In this chapter we use housing price data from the greater Grand Rapids, Michigan, market to analyze how residents react to risk when they are spend-

This chapter was written with Ted Gayer.

ing their own money to avoid potential harms. These data enable us to assess the value residents place on hazardous waste risk reduction in their private decisions. The Greater Grand Rapids area contains seven Superfund toxic waste sites. We formulate residents' assessments of cancer risk from these sites as a rational learning process, though other learning models could be applicable as well. In particular, we characterize learning as a Bayesian process (described below) of updating prior assessments with information obtained from the EPA and from the local media. Using the EPA's risk information generated during the site remediation process, we estimate the implicit value people place on risk reduction through the effect of risk on housing values. We also test whether the EPA's release of risk information alters households' risk beliefs. The estimation of the marginal effect of cancer risk on housing prices allows us to calculate an implied value of a statistical case of cancer.[2]

Our exploration of the housing price effects describes the character of residents' valuations of hazardous waste risks, but these effects may not be welfare losses in addition to those already documented. In the case of perfectly informed populations, housing prices will simply reflect the value of the adverse health effects generated by the site. This principle underlies all studies of the implicit value of life and health. The effect of job risks on wages, product risks on consumer product prices, and environmental risks on housing prices will provide evidence of money–risk trade-offs. Such linkages form the basis for assessing the value of life in the economics literature. Since these trade-offs embody the valuation of health risks by those exposed to the hazard, in the full information case it would double count the individual losses if housing price consequences and risk reduction benefits were both included in the analysis.

Nevertheless, even in the case of informed consumers, there will be important distributional consequences. If people purchased the homes before the risks were known, the identification of a hazardous waste site will lower their property values, making them worse off. If people purchased land after the risks are well known, they will have already been compensated for the risks they are incurring by paying a lower purchase price. In each case hazardous waste cleanup that is financed by the government and by industry will make them better off, conferring a net gain on those who purchased property aware of the site risks. The extent of the discrepancy between how much the government spends on site cleanups and what it is worth to those affected will provide another index of the inefficiency of cleanups.

A common theme in the hazardous waste literature justifies cleanups as a mechanism for reducing the property value damages arising from the public's irrational "overreaction" to the risk. The housing price data we examine suggest that when it is people's own money that is at stake, the irrational overreaction is not great. Moreover it is the government's risk–money trade-offs, not the private trade-offs, that are excessive. Public pressure for stringent cleanups may stem in part from who is paying the bill. Risk reduction without compromising trade-offs is most attractive when it is other parties' money being spent.

Another key concern involving the possible irrationality of the public's response to hazardous waste sites is whether they respond to risk information. If so, documenting the actual extent of the risks rather than the most alarmist popular vision of what the risks could be would serve to ameliorate the effects of consumer irrationality. Hazard communication can substitute for immediately expensive and ineffective cleanups. Our housing price analysis will illuminate this linkage as well.

In this chapter we use a hedonic (i.e., quality-adjusted) housing price framework to estimate residents' reactions to risk. We find that before residents receive the risk information provided by the EPA's Remedial Investigation, their estimated value of a statistical cancer case is much higher than the value-of-life estimates found in job market studies, though still far below the cleanup cost per cancer case prevented. This result is consistent with broader evidence on risk perception biases, which demonstrates that people tend to overestimate low probability risks.[3] This overreaction could lead to a higher willingness to pay for a risk reduction. After the release of the EPA's Remedial Investigation, however, residents update their risk perceptions. These postinformation estimated values of a statistical cancer case are similar to the value-of-life estimates found in previous labor market studies. Once residents are properly informed of the risks, their choices made in the Greater Grand Rapids housing market indicate a value of hazardous waste risk similar to values of risk faced in other settings. This similarity between the risk–money trade-off for hazardous waste risks and the trade-offs for job risks suggests that there is no evidence that consumers are overreacting to the hazardous waste risks in their private decisions after the release of the EPA information.[4] Additionally, even before residents receive the EPA's information, their implied risk–money trade-off is several orders of magnitude lower than regulatory expenditures per cancer case averted in the Superfund program. Thus, while surveys demonstrate that people express a high willingness to spend public funds on Superfund risk reduction, our results demonstrate that home-buyers are much less willing to spend their own funds on risk reduction.[5]

8.1 Modeling Homebuyer Reactions to Risk

In this section we develop a model of a homebuyer's reaction to Super-fund site risks. Readers less interested in the theory behind our empirical specifications can proceed directly to section 8.2. In our model we formulate individuals' subjective perceptions of the risk of cancer (π) as a Bayesian learning process. While the assumption of a fully rational learning process is convenient analytically, other learning models could potentially be applicable as well. People update their prior probability assessment based on information provided by the EPA and by local publicity. Our learning model uses a beta distribution to characterize this Bayesian process.[6] This distribution is quite flexible and can assume a wide variety of skewed and symmetric shapes.

Individuals have a prior cancer risk assessment of p, which has associated informational content φ_0. The information weight, φ_0, is equivalent to observing φ_0 draws from a Bernoulli urn. People update their risk perceptions taking into account the probability q, which is implied by information provided by the EPA. People also update their risk perceptions taking into account the probability r, which is implied by information provided by the news media. The risk implied by the EPA information has the informational content denoted as ξ_0, and the risk implied by the news media has the informational content denoted as κ_0. For simplicity we treat φ_0, ξ_0, and κ_0 as given parameters and focus only on the risk levels p, q, and r.[7]

The cancer risk perception function takes the form,

$$\pi(p,q,r) = \frac{\varphi_0 p + \xi_0 q + \kappa_0 r}{\varphi_0 + \xi_0 + \kappa_0}. \tag{8.1}$$

By denoting the fraction of the total informational content associated with each information source as

$$\varphi = \frac{\varphi_0}{\varphi_0 + \xi_0 + \kappa_0}, \quad \xi = \frac{\xi_0}{\varphi_0 + \xi_0 + \kappa_0}, \quad \text{and} \quad \kappa = \frac{\kappa_0}{\varphi_0 + \xi_0 + \kappa_0},$$

the risk perception function is rewritten as

$$\pi(p,q,r) = \varphi p + \xi q + \kappa r. \tag{8.2}$$

Individuals maximize expected utility over two states of the world, with U_1 representing utility in the sick (cancer) state and U_2 representing utility in the healthy (non-cancer) state. We assume for any given level of income that people prefer being healthy (i.e., $U_2 > U_1$), that utility functions within states be risk-neutral or risk-averse, and that the marginal utility of income is greater when healthy. Utility in each state is a function of a vector of characteristics of the house, z, a composite good, x, and the visual disamenities of the site, s.[8] The consumer purchases one house at price h, which is a function of housing characteristics, risk perceptions, and the Superfund visual disamenities. The consumer's income is y.

Accounting for the separate health and visual aesthetic effects of Superfund sites yields a model in which consumers maximize expected utility as follows:

$$\max V = \pi(p,q,r)U_1(x,z,s) + [1 - \pi(p,q,r)]U_2(x,z,s), \tag{8.3}$$

subject to

$$y = x + h(z, \pi(p,q,r), s). \tag{8.4}$$

By construction, consumer risk perceptions, $\pi(p,q,r)$, will be an increasing function of p and q (i.e., $\xi_0/(\varphi_0 + \xi_0 + \kappa_0) > 0$, $\varphi_0/(\varphi_0 + \xi_0 + \kappa_0) > 0$). Therefore, the equilibrium conditions for the effect of higher informational risk values, p and q, on housing prices and the expected signs are

$$\frac{\partial h}{\partial q} = \frac{(U_1 - U_2)(\partial \pi/\partial q)}{\pi(\partial U_1/\partial x) + (1 - \pi)(\partial U_2/\partial x)} < 0, \tag{8.5}$$

and

$$\frac{\partial h}{\partial p} = \frac{(U_1 - U_2)(\partial \pi/\partial p)}{\pi(\partial U_1/\partial x) + (1 - \pi)(\partial U_2/\partial x)} < 0,$$

which, since $\partial h/\partial q = (\partial h/\partial \pi)(\partial \pi/\partial q)$ and $\partial h/\partial p = (\partial h/\partial \pi)(\partial \pi/\partial p)$, reduces to

$$\frac{\partial h}{\partial \pi} = \frac{U_1 - U_2}{\pi(\partial U_1/\partial x) + (1 - \pi)(\partial U_2/\partial x)} < 0. \tag{8.6}$$

Thus, as first presented by Rosen (1974), the hedonic price function reflects the locus of tangencies between the offer and bid curves. The marginal price is equivalent to the marginal willingness to pay for an incremental decrease in objective risk. Therefore one can compute the welfare effects of a marginal change in objective risk from the price gradient.[9]

The impact of the release of the Remedial Investigation on perceptions enters the hedonic price analysis by a comparison of the price gradients with respect to prior risk beliefs $(\partial h/\partial p)$ and price gradients with respect to the risk implied after the EPA Remedial Investigation $(\partial h/\partial \pi)$. The Bayesian model suggests that people will demonstrate possibly different willingness to pay for risk reduction before and after the release of the Remedial Investigation. A comparison of these gradients indicates whether the willingness to pay for risk reduction increases or decreases given the information provided by the EPA's Remedial Investigation. If the information in the Remedial Investigation raises residents' perceptions of risk, then we would expect an increase in willingness to pay for risk reduction. If the Remedial Investigation information indicates that the site is not as hazardous as previously perceived, then we would expect a decrease in willingness to pay for risk reduction.

We estimate the hedonic price function using the conventional practice of postulating the independent variable, the log of housing price (*Price*) adjusted for inflation, as a function of a vector of structural variables (*Structural*) and a vector of neighborhood variables (*Neighborhood*).[10] These structural and neighborhood variables measure the characteristics of the house, which were denoted as z in the theoretical model. The empirical model also includes measures of the overall level of the environmental condition of the neighborhood. These measures are the number of other environmental disamenities within 0.25 mile from the house (*Sites$_1$*), between 0.25 and 0.5 mile from the house (*Sites$_2$*), between 0.5 and 0.75 mile from the house (*Sites$_3$*), and between 0.75 and 1.0 mile from the house (*Sites$_4$*). Prices are also a function of the Superfund aesthetic disamenities (*Visual*), which was denoted as s in the theoretical model. The empirical model also controls for fixed time effects and city effects by using dummy variables indicating the year of the sale (denoted with a subscript $t = 1, \ldots, 5$) and the city location of the house (denoted with a subscript $i = 1, \ldots, 4$).[11] A further enhancement, as outlined in the theoretical model, is that the model includes the role of the perception of risk from Superfund sites. The semilogarithmic form of the hedonic price function is expressed as

$$\ln \text{Price} = \alpha + \beta\,\text{Structural} + \gamma\,\text{Neighborhood} + \rho_i\,\text{City}_i + \tau_t\,\text{Year}_t$$

$$+ \zeta_1\,\text{Sites}_1 + \cdots + \zeta_4\,\text{Sites}_4 + \eta\,\text{Visual} + \delta\pi(p, q, r) + u. \quad (8.7)$$

If we expand the risk-learning model and recognize its component forms from equation (8.2), we can rewrite the hedonic price function as

$$\ln \text{Price} = \alpha + \beta \text{Structural} + \gamma \text{Neighborhood} + \rho_i \text{City}_i + \tau_t \text{Year}_t$$
$$+ \zeta_1 \text{Sites}_1 + \cdots + \zeta_4 \text{Sites}_4 + \eta \text{Visual}$$
$$+ \delta_1 p + \delta_2 q + \delta_3 r + u, \tag{8.8}$$

where $\delta_1 = \delta\varphi$, $\delta_2 = \delta\xi$, and $\delta_3 = \delta\kappa$. As mentioned previously, the prior and updated probabilities have a negative effect on housing values. The relative informational content of the prior compared to the updated EPA information is $\delta_1/\delta_2 = \varphi/\xi = \varphi_0/\xi_0$, and the relative informational content of the prior compared to the updated news media information is $\delta_1/\delta_3 = \varphi/\kappa = \varphi_0/\kappa_0$. Thus the regression estimates indicate both how different risk information affects prices and also which informational source has a greater weight in consumer judgments.

We operationalize the values of p, q, and r in the following manner: In the case of perceived cancer risk arising from Superfund sites, the prior probability, p, is characterized by the information known to the residents before the EPA's release of their Remedial Investigation.[12] In capturing the prior probability p we follow two approaches. First, we set this value in the pre–Remedial Investigation release period equal to the objective risk level subsequently revealed in the EPA study. This approach assumes that people use observable signals of risk to form accurate risk judgments in much the same manner that hedonic wage studies assume that workers are aware of Bureau of Labor Statistics objective risk measures. Second, we also explore a more detailed approach in which we examine the explicit influence of the observable risk factors that could potentially affect people's prior beliefs. Although it will not be possible to construct a pre–Remedial Investigation implicit value of cancer in this instance, it will be possible to assess whether the influence of these prior signals is in the expected direction and whether the post–Remedial Investigation tradeoffs reflect plausible values per expected cancer case.

The prior signals available to residents include the area of the closest Superfund site, the ranking of the closest site on the EPA's National Priorities List (which, for all sites, occurred before the housing sales examined in this study), the elapsed time since the closest Superfund site was placed on the National Priorities List, and the type of site (e.g., landfill or industrial chemical plant). A site receives a National Priorities List ranking according to its score on the Hazard Ranking System (HRS). The HRS is a preliminary risk assessment applied to sites in order to determine if the site should be designated a Superfund site. We first examine the effects of these signals on housing prices, and then we examine the effect of the actual risk on housing prices. For the latter analysis we assume that the signals are variants of the actual risk and that the prior is thus a function of the actual risk. This allows us to estimate the dollar value people place on a reduction in Superfund risk before the release of the Remedial Investigation. Our conjecture is that people tend to over-estimate the prior risk before the release of the EPA's Remedial Investigation. People then update their risk perceptions after the release of the Remedial Investigation. There is additional updating of risk perceptions after receiving the newspaper publicity about all the Superfund sites in the Greater Grand Rapids area.[13]

We use the distance to the closest Superfund site as a proxy for the visual disamenities of the site.[14] We incorporate into the hedonic price function the variables that serve as signals of the actual risk before the release of the EPA information. We also include a variable measuring the publicity surrounding the sites, along with a dummy variable indicating if the house was sold after the release of the EPA's Remedial Investigation. Additionally we include a measure of the actual risk for those houses sold after the release of the Remedial Investigation (i.e., we interact the actual risk with a dummy variable indicating if the house was sold after the Re-medial Investigation). The first hedonic price function to be estimated is

$$\ln \text{Price} = \alpha + \beta \text{Structural} + \gamma \text{Neighborhood} + \rho_i \text{City}_i + \tau_t \text{Year}_t$$

$$+ \zeta_1 \text{Sites}_1 + \cdots + \zeta_4 \text{Sites}_4 + \eta \text{Distance}$$

$$+ \omega_1 \text{Area} + \omega_2 \text{NPL} + \omega_3 \text{Type} + \omega_4 \text{NPLTime}$$

$$+ \gamma_2 \text{News} + \theta_1 \text{After} + \theta_2 (\text{After} \times \text{Risk}) + u, \tag{8.9}$$

where *Distance* is the distance from the house to the closest Superfund site, *Area* is the area of the closest Superfund site, *NPL* is the National Priorities List ranking of the closest Superfund site, *Type* describes what operations occurred at the closest Superfund site, *NPLTime* is the number of months since the closest Superfund site was placed on the NPL, *News* is the number of words printed in the *Grand Rapids Press* about all the Superfund sites in the year previous to the sale of the house, *After* is a dummy variable indicating if the house was sold after the release of the EPA's Remedial Investigation, *After × Risk* is an interaction variable that measures the objective lifetime excess cancer risk (described in the next section) from all the sites to those individuals in a house purchased after the release of the Remedial Investigation, and the other variables are as defined earlier. The interaction variable tests whether housing prices react to the objective level of risk for houses sold after the release of the Remedial Investigation.

Our conjecture is that, before the release of the Remedial Investigation, *Area*, *NPL*, *Type*, and *NPLTime* serve as signals to the residents of the actual risks from the sites. To the degree that these signals are correlated with the actual risk from the sites, the housing prices would react to the level of the actual risk. We therefore estimate another hedonic equation that replaces the risk signals with a measure of the actual risk from the Superfund sites. This allows us to test the stability of the post–Remedial Investigation *Risk* coefficient, as well as obtain an estimate of the dollar value of a risk reduction before the Remedial Investigation. This specification also includes an interaction term of *After* and *Risk* in order to test whether the effect of the actual risk on housing prices changes after the release of the Remedial Investigation. This second hedonic price function is

$$\ln \text{Price} = \alpha + \beta \text{Structural} + \gamma \text{Neighborhood} + \rho_i \text{City}_i + \tau_t \text{Year}_t$$
$$+ \zeta_1 \text{Sites}_1 + \cdots + \zeta_4 \text{Sites}_4 + \eta \text{Distance} + \gamma_1 \text{Risk}$$
$$+ \gamma_2 \text{News} + \theta_1 \text{After} + \theta_2 (\text{After} \times \text{Risk}) + u. \tag{8.10}$$

Among other things, *Distance* serves as a proxy for the visual disamenities associated with the Superfund sites. The variable *News* measures the publicity about the Superfund sites and is thus a measure of the updating information r. The effect of this publicity on housing prices is equivalent to the joint effect of news information on perceptions and perceptions on prices (i.e., comparing equations 8.8 and 8.10 shows that γ_2 is a measure of δ_3, or the informational weight on media coverage). The effect of *Risk* on housing prices before the release of the Remedial Investigation is equal to the joint effect of prior risk information on perceptions and perceptions on prices (i.e., comparing equations 8.8 and 8.10 shows that γ_1 is a measure of δ_1, or the weight on prior risk beliefs if these beliefs equal the value of *Risk*). The effect of *Risk* on housing prices after the release of the Remedial Investigation is equal to the joint effect of updating risk information on perceptions and perceptions on prices (i.e., comparing equations 8.8 and 8.10 shows that $\gamma_1 + \theta_2$ is a measure of δ_2).

Household risk perceptions are positively related to the risk levels associated with prior beliefs and new information, since $\partial \pi / \partial p = \varphi$,

$\delta\pi/\delta q = \xi$, $\partial\pi/\partial r = \kappa$, and $0 < \varphi, \xi, \kappa < 1$. As indicated in equation (8.5), the model predicts these risk levels will have a negative impact on housing prices. The effect of risk on housing prices before the release of the Remedial Investigation (as measured by γ_1), and the effect of risk on housing prices after the release of the Remedial Investigation (as measured by $\gamma_1 + \theta_2$), are both expected to be negative. However, θ_2 can either be positive or negative depending on whether the risk analysis indicates a hazard higher or lower than prior beliefs.

We estimate a separate hedonic equation in order to determine whether publicity serves to communicate the risks of the Superfund sites. If newspaper publicity were correlated with *Risk*, then the coefficient estimate for *Risk* would be biased if *News* were omitted from the equation. Therefore we estimate a separate equation without the *News* variable to check whether this changes the price–risk relationship. The third hedonic price function estimated is

$$\ln \text{Price} = \alpha + \beta \text{Structural} + \gamma \text{Neighborhood} + \rho_i \text{City}_i + \tau_t \text{Year}_t$$

$$+ \zeta_1 \text{Sites}_1 + \cdots + \zeta_4 \text{Sites}_4 + \eta \text{Distance}$$

$$+ \gamma_1 \text{Risk} + \theta_1 \text{After} + \theta_2(\text{After} \times \text{Risk}) + u. \qquad (8.11)$$

In addition to measuring public valuations of Superfund risk, the model also tests whether willingness to pay for risk reduction is affected by the release of the EPA's Remedial Investigation. The coefficient on the interaction term estimates the influence of the Remedial Investigation on the valuation of the risks of the sites. For equations (8.10) and (8.11), a negative value for θ_2 would indicate that household perceptions of cancer risk increased after the release of the Remedial Investigation, and therefore drove down housing prices. A positive value for θ_2 would indicate that residents perceived the risks as smaller after the release of the Remedial Investigation, resulting in an increase in housing prices.

8.2 Housing Price Data

For our analysis we constructed a sample of housing prices for 16,928 houses sold in the Greater Grand Rapids area between January 1, 1988, and December 31, 1993. The Greater Grand Rapids area consists of the cities of Grand Rapids, Walker, Wyoming, Kentwood, and Grandville. The area is ideal for a hedonic analysis of Superfund risk since it is a local market which contains many Superfund sites (seven), only one of which does not have quantitative EPA risk data.[15] A local housing market with numerous Superfund sites enhances the analysis because there is a heterogeneity of risk among the households, yet there are no extraneous sites that can contaminate the analysis by contributing unmeasured risk to the households. The housing price offer curves will also be more similar within several local markets than if a national data set were used.[16]

The mean housing sale prices for each year was $60,196 for 1988, $64,436 for 1989, $68,082 for 1990, $68,983 for 1991, $70,507 for 1992, and $72,812 for 1993. The mean housing price in 1996 dollars for the entire sample is $74,176. Of the sample of 16,928 housing transactions, 16.3 percent occurred in 1988, 17.2 percent occurred in 1989, 16.5 percent occurred in 1990, 15.7 percent occurred in 1991, 16.8 percent occurred in 1992, and 17.4 percent occurred in 1993. The structural variables in the hedonic model include the number of bedrooms, the number of bathrooms, the number of fireplaces, whether or not there is a basement, the size of the lot in square feet, and whether or not there is a garage. The neighborhood variables include the median household income in the census tract, the proportion of blacks in the census tract, the proportion of people with a high school education in the census tract, the property tax rate, the distance to the Central Business District, the percentage of seventh graders in the school district who scored in the highest category for the Michigan reading assessment test, the proportion of people in the census tract under the age of nineteen, and the per capita crime rate for the city in the previous year. The estimation utilizes a fixed effects model, including annual dummy variables as well as city dummy variables.

The environmental variables include the measure of the distance to the closest Superfund site. While distance of the house to the closest Superfund site is also correlated with health risks from the site, we assume it is a proxy for the Superfund aesthetic disamenities. Additionally, four variables ($Sites_1$, $Sites_2$, $Sites_3$, and $Sites_4$) serve as proxies for the overall quality of the environment within the vicinity of the house. These variables measure the sum of the non-NPL CERCLA sites, RCRA sites, and PCS water pollution sites within quarter-mile rings around the house. These quarter-mile rings are 0 to 0.25 mile, 0.25 to 0.5 mile, 0.5 to 0.75 mile and 0.75 to 1 mile from the house.[17]

We also include variables that serve as signals for the risks from the Superfund sites. These variables measure the area (in square acres) of the closest site, the NPL ranking of the closest site, the number of months since the placing of the closest site on the NPL, and a dummy variable that is one if the closest site was a landfill and zero if it was an industrial chemical plant or battery repository.

The risk variables measure both the objective excess cancer risk to the household and the timing of the release of this information with respect to the sale of the house.[18] We adopt the methodology described in chapter 4 to measure the objective individual lifetime excess cancer risk faced by residents. This methodology standardizes the pathway definitions used in the EPA's risk assessments of the Superfund sites. Additionally we use the mean exposure and chemical concentration levels in order to determine the cancer risk at each site. To compute the cancer risk to each household in the Greater Grand Rapids area, we couple the site risk assessments with dilution estimates for soil and groundwater exposure. Soil dilution estimates come from EPA guidelines and are a function of the distances to the sites. To estimate groundwater dilution, we use maps of plumes to estimate the probability that a house is located above a contaminated plume. For each block group, we use data from the U.S. Bureau of Census to determine the proportion of households that draw their water from groundwater. Multiplying the probability of being above a contaminated plume by the probability that the house receives its drinking water from a well results in an estimate for groundwater exposure dilution. The household cancer risk from each site is the product of the soil and groundwater cancer risks of each site and the soil and groundwater dilution estimates of the house. Summing the cancer risk from each of the Superfund sites results in the total lifetime excess cancer risk to the household. The mean cancer risk to an individual in a household is 1.81×10^{-6}.[19] We do not assume that individuals living near a site can state with precision the numbers calculated in our objective risk measure. The risk measure is meant to reflect a consistently developed point estimate of cancer risks based on risk assessment assumptions consistent with EPA practices. To the extent that residents' prior assessments of site risks are related to the underlying magnitude of hazards as measured in cancer risk assessments, we expect housing prices to react negatively to the risk measure.

A dummy variable measures the timing of the risk information. This variable is a value of one if the house was sold after the EPA released its Remedial Investigation and Feasibility Study (RI/FS) for the closest site and zero if it was sold before this release. We use press coverage in the *Grand Rapids Press*, which serves the entire Greater Grand Rapids area, as the publicity measure. The publicity variable is the total number of

Table 8.1
Residents' reaction to risk, semi-log hedonic price function

	Equation 1		Equation 2		Equation 3	
	Coefficient	t statistic	Coefficient	t statistic	Coefficient	t statistic
Sites$_1$	−0.021	4.83***	−0.200	4.60***	−0.020	4.60***
Sites$_2$	−0.011	5.29***	−0.009	4.55***	−0.009	4.55***
Sites$_3$	0.001	0.96	0.003	1.85*	0.003	1.84*
Sites$_4$	0.004	3.70***	0.006	4.96***	0.006	4.95***
Distance	0.014	7.70***	0.012	5.93***	0.012	5.91***
After	−0.006	1.12	−0.012	2.26**	−0.013	2.52**
Risk			−1771.214	2.27**	−1779.076	2.28**
After x Risk	−139.135	2.13**	1635.245	2.09**	1644.076	2.10**
Area of site	−0.001	11.62***				
Type of site	0.095	15.03***				
NPL ranking	−1.62e-04	7.08***				
Months since NPL	0.001	9.27***				
News	−2.51e-6	2.46**	−2.31e-06	2.25**		
	Adj $R^2 = 0.6703$		Adj $R^2 = 0.6649$		Adj $R^2 = 0.6648$	
	$N = 16{,}928$		$N = 16{,}928$		$N = 16{,}928$	

Note: Equations also contained variables for household structure, neighborhood characteristics, and the city and annual dummy variables. *** = statistically significant at 0.01 level, ** = significant at 0.05 level, * = significant at 0.10 level, all two-sided tests.

printed words in articles about the local Superfund sites within the year before the sale of the house.

8.3   Resident Reactions to Risk

Table 8.1 presents the ordinary least-squares estimates of the hedonic price function for the relevant variables. Along with the structural and neighborhood variables, the specifications include measures of the environmental quality in the vicinity of the house. The first equation incorporates an objective risk measure only for houses sold after the release of the Remedial Investigation. This equation also includes variables that serve as signals for the actual risks of the sites. The second and third equations each incorporate an objective risk measure, along with the term interacting the objective risk and the dummy variable indicating if the house was sold after the release of the EPA's Remedial Investigation. Equations 1 and 2 of the table include a publicity measure in order to test if the probability assessment that is implied by this updating information affects housing prices. Equation 3 omits the *News* variable from the hedonic equation. This model can thus be viewed as a semi-reduced form estimate that captures both the direct effect of risk on prices as well as the effect through newspaper coverage. If newspaper coverage of the sites communicates the level of risk, then one would expect that dropping the *News* variable would result in an increase in the magnitude of the effect of the *Risk* coefficient.

As discussed previously, the hedonic price gradient with respect to a good (e.g., a structural or neighborhood attribute) is equal to the marginal value of the good. A priori expectations are that coefficients for the structural house variables are positive. The regression results of the three equations are consistent with these expectations; an increase in a structural attribute of a house increases the price of the house. All the estimates for the neighborhood variables also have the expected sign (positive for goods, negative for bads). However, the parameter estimates for school quality and for the crime rate in equation 1 are not significantly different from zero. There are no a priori expectations for the signs of the coefficients of the city and annual dummy variables. The estimated coefficient for the distance to the closest Superfund site is positive and significant for each equation, suggesting that people are willing to pay to live farther away from the visual disamenities associated with Superfund sites. All tests of significance are two-sided tests.

One of the concerns about the distance proxy used in previous studies is that it also measures the distance to other neighborhood characteristics. Multiple environmental disamenities could exist at the same distance to the house as the closest Superfund site. These other disamenities would then be reflected in the estimate of the distance gradient. The ring variables $Sites_1$, $Sites_2$, $Sites_3$, and $Sites_4$, which were described earlier, address this concern by controlling for other neighborhood environmental disamenities. The coefficient estimates of these disamenity variables indicate a negative and significant price effect of the number of such sites at a quarter-mile and half-mile from the house.

Equation 1 tests whether certain variables act as signals for the risks associated with the Superfund sites. The findings suggest that people do incorporate this prior information in the expected manner. Specifically, the size of the closest Superfund site and the NPL ranking of the closest Superfund site have negative effects on housing prices. The more time elapsed since the placing of the site on the NPL results in higher housing price, as these sites that merit lower priority may pose smaller risks. Another possibility is that alarmist responses to a site being placed on the NPL moderate over time. And homes near industrial chemical plants or the battery repository have lower prices then homes near the landfills.

As outlined earlier, we test the potential impacts that information from the EPA's Remedial Investigation and local newspaper coverage has on perceptions, and consequently on equilibrium housing prices. The hedonic price gradient with respect to total cancer risk gives the marginal valuation of cancer risk (i.e., the value of avoiding cancer risks) for households. The expected sign for this gradient is negative both before and after the release of the Remedial Investigation. Similarly, if publicity increases perceptions of risk, then we expect a negative sign for the price gradient with respect to publicity.

Equation 1 estimates the effect of *Risk* only after the release of the Remedial Investigation. The negative coefficient estimate suggests that people are willing to pay less for houses for which there is a Superfund cancer risk. For Equations 2 and 3, we assume that the prior risk is correlated with the actual risk. In using these results, it is possible to estimate the dollar value people place on risk reduction both before and after the Remedial Investigation. The negative coefficient estimates for *Risk* indicate that the public is willing to pay less for houses for which there is a Superfund cancer risk before the release of the Remedial Investigation.

The interaction variable is the product of *Risk* and the dummy variable that signifies if the house was sold after the release of the EPA's Remedial Investigation. Use of this interaction term gives the following marginal effect of *Risk* on housing prices:

$$\frac{\partial \ln \text{Price}}{\partial \text{Risk}} = [\hat{\gamma}_1 + \hat{\theta}_2(\text{After})] \text{ Price}. \tag{8.12}$$

The term $\hat{\gamma}_1$ represents the estimated *Risk* coefficient, and $\hat{\theta}_2$ represents the interaction term's estimated coefficient. The positive sign of the interaction term's estimated coefficient indicates that the negative effect of risk on housing prices was smaller after the EPA released their Remedial Investigation. Our conjecture is that the release of the EPA's Remedial Investigation provided risk information that lowered perceptions of the risk, which were initially alarmist, resulting in a decrease in magnitude of the price–risk gradient. It is also noteworthy that the post–Remedial Investigation price effect of *Risk* is comparable for these equations. The net effects on the ln *Price* variable range from −135 to −139, or a price drop that is about $220 less (for a change in *Risk* by the mean level) than the effect of risk beliefs before the completion of the EPA risk analysis.

The results also indicate that, controlling for the risk level, newspaper publicity about the local Superfund sites has a negative effect on housing prices. Previous studies have suggested that substantial newspaper coverage leads to overestimation of mortality risks (see Combs and Slovic 1979). However, this bias cannot be inferred from the gradient here since the effect of publicity on perceptions cannot be separated from the effect of perceptions on housing prices.

Equation 3 of table 8.1 presents estimates of the hedonic equation without the *News* variable. The signs, magnitudes, and significance of the estimates are virtually identical to those reported in equation 2. Dropping *News* from the regression does not significantly alter the gradients before and after the release of the Remedial Investigation. Apparently, while newspaper publicity during the time of the Remedial Investigation has a negative effect on housing prices, it does not communicate new information about the Superfund cancer risks to the residents.

To further explore the nature of the risk-dollar relationship, we use a Box-Cox transformation of the dependent variable to estimate the hedonic price function.[20] The transformation of the dependent variable, *Price*, yields the regression model

$$\text{Price}^{(\lambda)} = \alpha + \sum \beta_k X_k + \varepsilon, \tag{8.13}$$

where $\text{Price}^{(\lambda)} = (\text{Price}^\lambda - 1)/\lambda$ and X_k are the independent variables as expressed in equation (8.10). The transformation parameter, λ, is taken to be an unknown parameter, and we scan a range of values in order to determine the least squares values of λ, α, and the β_k's.

Table 8.2 presents the results of the Box-Cox model. The least-squares estimate for the transforming parameter, λ, is -0.42. The marginal effect of risk on housing price is

$$\frac{\partial \text{Price}}{\partial \text{Risk}} = (\hat{\beta}_1 + \hat{\beta}_2 \text{After}) \, \text{Price}^{(1-\hat{\lambda})}. \tag{8.14}$$

The negative value of $\hat{\beta}_1$ indicates that people are willing to pay for a reduction of cancer risk. The positive value of $\hat{\beta}_2$ indicates that the price–risk trade-off is greater before the release of the EPA's Remedial Investigation.

Remediation of Superfund sites addresses, among other objectives, the targeted reduction of cancer risks. Previous hedonic property value

Table 8.2
Regression results for the Box-Cox transformation

Variables	Coefficient	t statistic
Risk	−18.789	2.21**
After	−1.07e-04	1.86*
After x Risk	17.048	2.01**
News	2.30e-08	2.06**
Adj $R^2 = 0.6588$		
$N = 16{,}298$		
$\lambda = -0.42$		

Note: Other variables in the equation are the same as in table 8.1. ** = significant at 0.05 level, * = significant at 0.10 level, all two-sided tests.

studies computed cleanup benefits by equating remediation with movement of the houses to a certain distance in which the gradient levels out (e.g., see Kohlhase 1991; Kiel and McClain 1995). This approach captures the distance-risk relationship imperfectly since it assumes that remediation will alleviate both the (risky) health and (nonrisky) aesthetic attributes of the site. The distance gradient is also incapable of estimating the benefits of a partial reduction in the risk, which is usually the EPA's goal.

By incorporating objective cancer risk measures in the hedonic property model, we can estimate the change in housing prices given any level of risk reduction. To compare these implied benefits with the cost of remediation, we compute the change in prices before the release of the Remedial Investigation. For example, using the coefficient estimates from equation 2 of table 8.1, we find that a reduction of individual cancer risk by 1.81×10^{-6} (the mean level of Superfund site risk to an individual in a household) before the release of the Remedial Investigation results in a price increase of $238 per household (in 1996 dollars). With 42,598 households within the relevant census tracts, the total price change (an upper-bound measure of welfare benefits) is $10.1 million for reducing cancer risks at the six sites. Using the Box-Cox coefficient estimates, a reduction of household cancer risk by the mean level before the release of the Remedial Investigation results in a price increase of $232 per household, and a total price change of $9.9 million.

These estimates of the value of risk reduction are much smaller than the EPA's estimated costs of remediating the sites. The total present value cost of the EPA's remediation plans for the six Greater Grand Rapids Superfund sites is $56.8 million. By contrast, the total present value cost of only institutional controls (fencing, deed restrictions, etc.) would have been \$5.4 million had they been implemented at the six sites.[21] Using residents' valuations of cancer risk reductions, permanent remedies would not pass this test of cost versus implicit willingness to pay, while use of institutional controls to restrict access to sites would.

By evaluating the price gradient with respect to cancer risk, we can estimate the value of a statistical cancer case. The methodology is similar to value-of-life studies, where a wage hedonic is used to determine the gradient with respect to job risk (see Viscusi 1992). In the job risk literature, the wage compensation for an incremental change in job fatality risk is divided by the risk increment, resulting in the value of a statistical life. Viscusi (1981) demonstrated that value-of-life estimates are heterogeneous over different risk levels. Different members of the population attach different values to risk. People most tolerant of risk are drawn to the riskier jobs and higher wages must be paid to lure additional workers into risky jobs. Such heterogeneity of risk preferences illustrates the complexity inherent in policy applications. Value-of-life estimates obtained from a certain population of workers may not be appropriate for another population. While hedonic wage studies have been quite successful in estimating compensation to workers for job risk, values may be quite different for populations including nonworkers, white-collar workers, or children.

There have been previous attempts at obtaining risk-dollar tradeoffs in market transactions other than the job market. Unlike the labor market studies, many of these attempts rely on imputing values for at least one component of the tradeoff. For example, studies attempting to evaluate the risk–dollar trade-off associated with aspects of auto safety (see Ghosh, Lees, and Seal 1975; Blomquist 1979) assume that the wage rate equals the opportunity cost of time associated with driving fast or seat belt use.

The objective risk measures used in this study pertain to the cancer risk to an individual living in the household. To determine the value of a statistical cancer to an individual, the average household size must be divided into the risk coefficient. According to the 1990 census, the average number of members per household in the pertinent census tracts (computed by matching block group data to the sample) was 2.573.

Table 8.3 lists the estimates for the statistical value of cancer given different specifications.[22] Equation 1 only considers the effect of objective risk on housing prices after the Remedial Investigation. Using this parameter estimate, the value-of-cancer estimate after the Remedial Investigation is \$4.1 million. Using the estimates from equation 2 of table 8.1

Table 8.3
Estimates of the value of avoiding a statistical cancer case (1996$ million)

Equation estimates	Value of cancer before remedial investigation	Value of cancer after remedial investigation
Equation 1	NA	$4.1
Equation 2	$51.1	$3.9
Equation 3	$51.3	$3.9
Box-Cox	$49.9	$4.6

and dividing by the number of people per household results in a value-of-cancer estimate of $51.1 million before the release of the Remedial Investigation and $3.9 million after the release of the Remedial Investigation. To test whether the publicity picks up some of the effect of risk on housing prices, in equation 3 of table 8.1 we drop the *News* variable from the regression. The value-of-cancer estimate before the Remedial Investigation increases by only $0.2 million dollars, and there is no change in the value-of-cancer estimate after the Remedial Investigation. Using the coefficient estimates in the Box-Cox model, the value-of-cancer estimate before the Remedial Investigation is $49.9 million. After the Remedial Investigation the value-of-cancer estimate is $4.6 million.

The value-of-cancer estimates before the release of the Remedial Investigation are roughly an order of magnitude larger than the value-of-life estimates found in job market studies. This finding suggests that risk biases could affect individual reactions to Superfund risks before the EPA releases their Remedial Investigation.[23] Residents update their risk perceptions after the release of the Remedial Investigation, and the resulting value-of-cancer estimates of $3.9 million to $4.6 million are very similar to the value-of-life estimates found in job market studies.[24] Once the EPA releases the Remedial Investigation, the value people place on avoiding Superfund risks is similar to the value they place on job market risk.

The coefficient estimates of equations 1, 2, and 3, as well as the coefficient estimates of the Box-Cox equation, can determine the mean marginal willingness to pay for various attributes. The hedonic price function reflects the tangency of the consumer offer curves with the price function; thus the marginal price of an attribute is equivalent to the marginal willingness to pay. Table 8.4 presents the results for various attributes.[25]

Using the coefficient estimates from equation 1 of table 8.1, we find that the marginal willingness to pay for an additional mile from the closest

Table 8.4
Mean willingness to pay for Superfund-related attributes

Sources of estimates	Additional mile from closest site	Removal of industrial site within 0.25 mile ring	House sold before release of remedial investigation	One less word of publicity in previous year
Equation 1	$1,085	$1,588	$450	$0.19
	(145)	(323)	(409)	(0.08)
Equation 2	$859	$1,486	$661	$0.17
	(145)	(323)	(404)	(0.08)
Equation 3	$857	$1,486	$756	NA
	(145)	(323)	(402)	
Box-Cox	$627	$1,982	$520	$0.16
	(175)	(390)	(488)	(0.08)

Note: Standard errors in parentheses.

site is $1,085. The marginal willingness to pay for one less non-NPL CERCLA site, RCRA site, or permit compliance system (PCS) site within a quarter-mile of the house is $1,588. An additional printed word about any of the Superfund sites decreases a house's price by $0.19.

Replacing the variables that measure the risk signals with the actual risk does not result in markedly different estimates for the willingness to pay for the Superfund-related attributes. The estimates from equation 2 of table 8.1 indicate that the marginal willingness to pay for an additional mile from the closest site is $859. The marginal willingness to pay for one less non-NPL CERCLA site, RCRA site, or PCS site within a quarter-mile of the house is $1,486. An additional printed word about any of the Superfund sites decreases a house's price by $0.17. With the average newspaper article on the local Superfund sites being 550 words in length, the price decrease is $94 per article.

The results indicate that a house sold before the release of the EPA risk information on the closest site sold for $661 more than one sold after the information was made public. Thus, while the impact of risk on housing prices diminishes after the release of the Remedial Investigation, housing prices nonetheless decrease after the release of the Remedial Investigation.[26]

The coefficient estimates from equation 3 of table 8.1 yield very similar estimates of marginal willingness to pay for the various attributes. The marginal willingness to pay for an additional mile from the closest site is

$857. A house sold before the release of the Remedial Investigation for the closest site sold for $756 more than one sold after the Remedial Investigation was made public.

The marginal willingness to pay for a unit reduction of a non-NPL CERCLA site, RCRA site, or PCS site within a quarter-mile of the house is $1,486. This estimate for the value of a removal of one non-NPL CERCLA site, RCRA site, or PCS site within a quarter-mile of the house is equivalent to a cancer risk reduction of 1.7×10^{-5}.[27] Of the 850 RCRA sites studied in a Regulatory Impact Analysis, 640 of the sites had risk estimates between 1.0×10^{-6} and 1.0×10^{-4}. Housing price reactions to RCRA sites imply resident assessments of risk similar to those estimates in the RCRA Regulatory Impact Analysis. For comparison, the mean level of risk from a Greater Grand Rapids Superfund site within 0.25 mile is 1.16×10^{-4}.

The Box-Cox coefficient estimates yield slightly different estimates of the marginal willingness to pay for attributes. The marginal willingness to pay for an additional mile from the closest site is $627. The marginal willingness to pay for one less non-NPL CERCLA site, RCRA site, or PCS site within a quarter-mile of the house is $1,982. An additional printed word about any of the sites decreases the price by $0.16. A house sold before the release of the EPA's Remedial Investigation for the closest site sold for $520 more than one sold after the Remedial Investigation was made public.

Our estimates indicate that removing a hazardous waste site that is not a Superfund site yields a benefit between $1,486 and $1,982 for a household within a quarter-mile of the site. Using the other estimated coefficients for the *Sites* variables, we find that the average benefit of removing a site (to a resident within one mile of the site) ranges from $385 to $714. These estimates are similar to those found in Stock (1991), who estimated the benefit to an average household in suburban Boston from removing the Nyanza hazardous waste site (located in Ashland, Massachusetts). His unrestricted OLS model found a benefit ranging from $487 to $885, and his nonparametric model found a benefit ranging from $155 to $161 (all estimates converted to 1996 dollars).[28]

Assessing the cost-effectiveness of the EPA's Superfund program requires comparing the costs of the program with the benefits accrued from the reduction in the health risk. Previous studies have suggested that people overreact to the threats from hazardous wastes, resulting in an inefficient outcome in which the EPA spends too much on remediation.

Pressures for public spending on safety, however, may be quite different from private willingness to pay amounts. Our results suggest that residents have heightened perceptions of the risks from Superfund sites before they receive the information provided in the Remedial Investigation. When the residents are informed of the risks through the EPA's Remedial Investigation, and when they must spend their own funds to avoid the Superfund risks, their willingness to pay is similar to trade-offs made in other encounters with risk, such as those made in labor market decisions.

Before the EPA releases the Remedial Investigation the estimated willingness to pay for a risk reduction implies an upper-bound benefit of cleaning up the six sites ranging between $9.1 million and $10.1 million for a reduction of the mean level of cancer risk. For comparison, the total present value cost of the EPA's remediation plans for the six neighborhood Superfund sites is $56.8 million. Had the EPA only undertaken institutional controls for the remediation, the total present value cost would be $5.4 million, a figure more consistent with values implied by residents' willingness to pay to avoid Superfund risk.

The housing choices in the Greater Grand Rapids housing market provide evidence on private valuation of Superfund risk reduction. The findings indicate that, after the EPA releases its Remedial Investigation, the trade-off between cancer risk and housing prices is similar in magnitude to the trade-off between mortality risk and wages found in previous labor market studies. This similarity suggests that there appears to be no evidence that people substantially overestimate the risk of cancer when making informed decisions for which they must pay for greater safety.

Our analysis suggests that EPA information reduces residents' biased estimation of the risks from hazardous waste sites. These results contradict previous studies that suggest that people either have alarmist reactions to risk information or no reaction at all to the information.[29] We show that uninformed residents overestimate the level of risk, yet they exhibit the ability to learn from information presented by the EPA. Though previous work suggests that biased perceptions make greater risk information harmful or ineffective, we show that large gains from learning can take place once the public receives expert risk information. In the following chapter we explore the implications for Superfund of regulatory reforms aimed at providing legislators, residents, interest groups, and the general public with even more information about Superfund risks and regulator treatment of those risks.

Implementing Risk Reforms in Site Remediations

Hazardous wastes often top the list of people's environmental concerns, but the Superfund program itself has few enthusiasts. Although less than two decades old, the program has already undergone one major legislative overhaul and is due for yet another. Since the early years of the program, the pace of cleanup efforts has escalated. But progress in site cleanups has raised questions about how much is being spent and what is being accomplished.

At a superficial level, EPA seems to be undertaking the kind of policy analysis that would lead to sensible decisions. For each site it commissions an expensive study of risks and costs. Calculated, maximum lifetime cancer risks at Superfund sites, which average 0.07 for our sample, are extremely high relative to risks addressed through other regulatory programs. Moreover the stated policy risk triggers—10^{-6} cancer risk for discretionary cleanup and 10^{-4} for mandatory cleanup—would seem to weed out some of the most inefficient remediation efforts. The results, however, fall short of any reasonable level of accomplishment for the $20 billion expended on cleanups from 1981 to 1992. How did EPA go wrong?

In thinking about risk, EPA regulators focused on situations that might best be thought of as "nearly" worst case scenarios. Moreover, it did so on a parameter by parameter basis, compounding the conservatism biases. Analysis of three of the biased parameters, which is only a partial adjustment for the total biases, indicates that EPA overestimates risks by a factor of almost 30 and that there is more than a 99 percent chance that the actual site risks are smaller than those calculated by EPA. These biases differ by site, so no simple adjustment will suffice other than redoing the analysis correctly.

The more glaring error in determining which risks are consequential is a sin of omission. Populations often do not matter to the EPA. Large groups exposed to risk may receive the same weight in many remediation decisions as does a single individual. Indeed a hypothetically exposed person who could come into contact with the chemicals if land use changed in the future may receive the same weight as does a large population currently residing on-site. Risk exposures vary considerably across sites. At most sites in our sample fewer than 0.1 cases of cancer will arise over the next thirty years. We propose that prevention of expected cases of cancer be the way that benefits are measured. This metric recognizes both risk probabilities and sizes of exposed populations. If other benefit components such as reducing noncancer health effects are identified as remediation goals, a similar comprehensive approach is warranted for measuring these components as well.

Costs should enter policy decisions as well. Currently the EPA acts almost as if cost does not matter, perhaps in part because of congressional instructions to pursue a more stringent remediation policy. The result is that cleanups are grossly inefficient. At present, 95 percent of the cleanup dollars are spent to cleanup 0.5 percent of the expected cancer risks. This level of performance is far worse than Supreme Court Justice Breyer feared when he hypothesized that 90 percent of the costs were being incurred to address the last 10 percent of the risk. To prevent such inefficiencies, EPA should select cleanups based on site level benefit–cost tests.

Even in absolute terms, the performance of Superfund is shocking. The median cost per case of cancer prevented numbers in the billions, and the cost per case is about $140 million or more for 95 percent of all cleanup expenditures. This waste of cleanup resources is not simply a financial matter. Every time EPA chooses to clean up a site where there are no real risks rather than using society's resources to address risks that pose real threats to actual populations, the agency in effect fails to save statistical lives. This low level of performance is not entirely a matter of agency choice. EPA's decisions are subject to legislative constraints and the influence of political pressures. In this chapter we explore the role of these influences within the broader context of reform.

What accounts for this apparent level of inefficiency in site remediations? One answer lies in the legislative language creating the program's mandate. The statutory language does not mention costs and cost-effectiveness; rather, it directs the agency to focus on threats to human health and the environment. This omission does not, however, prevent EPA from balancing risk and cost, though it may contribute to the substantial emphasis on risk. Concern with risk does not, however, fully explain EPA's neglect of population exposures and inattention to actual, as compared to hypothetical, risks. Other answers may lie in the influence of risk biases and politics on the implementation of site cleanups. Our analysis of selection of risk cleanup targets indicates that the decisions reflect risk biases such as the anchoring phenomenon and excessive attention to highly publicized hazards. Remediations have benefits concentrated in the immediate area of the site and costs dispersed nationwide across taxpayers and consumers. Residents consequently have an incentive to press for stringent cleanups even if they are extremely costly, for they bear few of the direct costs. Our work indicates that political action by residents around sites exerts a perverse influence. Residents influence cleanups most when site risks are low and the costs per cancer case avoided are high. Our analysis of housing prices around Superfund sites indicates that when their own money is involved people are more willing to balance risk and cost concerns. After the release of the EPA's risk information, residents are willing to pay to avoid site cancer risks in amounts similar to the value of life estimates from labor market studies. Yet, when regulators commit general revenue funds or industry resources to avert cancers, the political marketplace results in cost per cancer case avoided orders of magnitude greater than that observed in the economic marketplace.

Environmental regulation involves a principal-agent relationship between multiple principals (e.g., House members, senators, the president) and the Environmental Protection Agency. In a world where information is costly to assemble and assess, agents will always enjoy some ability to take actions and generate results that principals might not approve. EPA has some discretion both to do well and to do ill, relative to the guidance given to it. In the language of political economy, this means that regulators derive part of their power from hidden action and hidden information.[1] One way to change the behavior of regulators is to provide more explicit directions to guide their decision making and to make their decisions more open to public scrutiny. Recent congressional efforts to change the implementation of regulations have focused on the use of risk assessment and benefit–cost analysis to alter policy decisions. In this chapter we explore how these proposed reforms could affect the remediation decisions we have examined at our sample of 150 NPL sites. The results underscore how changes in risk assessment and management could target Superfund resources more effectively without sacrificing the protection of human health.

9.1 Regulatory Reform

Several bills designed to increase the role of risk assessment and benefit–cost analysis in regulatory decision making were introduced during the 104th Congress, and at least one such proposal remained active in the 105th Congress. Many of the proposals would have greatly altered regulatory agencies' current practices. Some risk reform proposals would have required federal regulatory agencies to use central tendency estimates to estimate levels of risk exposure—instead of the conservative assumptions they often use today. Some bills sought to have agencies clearly articulate the assumptions embedded in risk assessments and benefit–cost analysis, so they can be analyzed and debated by the regulatory community.[2] With respect to benefit–cost analysis, some bills also included a supermandate provision that would have required benefit–cost analysis. The super-mandate provision would have trumped existing statutes which prohibited balancing of benefits and costs and removed the loopholes in the executive orders that have exempted agencies from basing policy on a benefit–cost test when doing so conflicts with the agency's legislative mandate.[3] Another, more limited, proposal would have required EPA analysts to undertake an explicit benefit–cost analysis for Superfund site cleanups that cost more than $5 million.[4]

The congressional battle over these and other regulatory reforms ignited a debate about how such procedural reforms would affect regulatory policy. Proponents of the reform bills argued that the reforms would enhance efficiency. Many of the proposed reforms reflect economists' views that regulation would be more efficient if federal agencies based regulatory decisions on analyses that consider a range of assumptions, explained the risks their regulations address in terms of risks assumed to exist in other areas of our lives, and explicitly balanced the benefits and costs of the rules they proposed.[5] Scholars such as Cass Sunstein make the case that benefit–cost analysis can systematically produce information on the impacts of regulatory decisions, focus attention on such decisions' intended and unintended effects, and assist agencies in recognizing both the quantified and unquantified effects of regulatory decisions.[6]

In contrast, many opponents of regulatory reform saw the proposed changes as a thinly veiled attempt to reduce rather than improve regulation, noting that regulatory reform coincided with the first election of a Republican House in forty years. Reform opponents have offered a number of critiques of the reform bills: Benefit–cost analysis would weaken regulatory protection if costs of regulation are more easily quantified than the benefits, the lack of knowledge in areas such as epidemiology and toxicology may cause risks to human health to be underestimated, and the divergence of public perceptions and expert analyses may result in the assessments of risk experts overriding the "preferences" of those affected by a regulation.[7] When these critiques are made, they are often not well documented.

Reform opponents also argued the bills presented many procedural problems. Some bills explicitly provided for judicial challenges to the economic analyses, which would lead to increased litigation and unnecessary involvement of the courts in regulatory decision making.[8] The establishment of peer review panels to evaluate the scientific bases of regulatory proposals would add additional delays. The increase in reporting requirements for regulators spurred by the detailed retrospective regulatory assessments and other reports to Congress required by some bills, coupled with proposed cuts in agency budgets, would lead to regulatory gridlock.[9] These features, however, are not essential to the kinds of reform proposals we advocate. Indeed the main problem with the reform effort may have been that it was overly ambitious and needlessly burdensome.

The conflicting views of the regulatory reforms, either as efficiency-enhancing or strategically burdensome, reflect a broader controversy over the general role of the administrative procedures that govern regulatory action. Traditional legal theories hold that legislation such as the Administrative Procedure Act establishes a framework to ensure openness, fairness, and public participation in rulemaking. Under this view the rule-making process itself is a normative good, since people value the democratic method of decision making embodied in the open and participatory process, and the information exchange generated by mechanisms such as notice and comment rule making generally improves the rule-making outcomes.[10]

A more recent literature describes administrative procedures as an instrument of political control. This theory, associated most strongly with the trio Mathew McCubbins, Roger Noll, and Barry Weingast, describes how members of Congress attempt to use administrative procedures, such as the design of the regulatory decision-making environment, to achieve political ends.[11] Legislated administrative procedures help reelection-oriented Congress members serve the interests of their constituents, including voters and campaign donors. Congress members design the administrative procedures governing the implementation of legislation so that particular groups may participate and particular viewpoints are advantaged. Examples of the strategic use of administrative procedures include requirement of a particular burden of proof, mandating agencies consider the environmental impacts of their actions, and providing avenues for public participation in federal agency decision making.[12]

In this chapter we explore the issues raised in the debate over regulatory reform by examining the potential effects of implementing a mix of the proposed reforms within the Superfund program, one of the most highly visible and controversial environmental programs. We first review EPA's current risk assessment procedures and other practices relating to Superfund implementation, which allows us to offer a qualitative description of how various proposed benefit–cost and risk assessment changes would have affected EPA's analyses and decisions under the Superfund program. We then provide quantitative data revealing the effects that different proposed policy reforms would have had on the Superfund program, had they been implemented. For our nationwide sample of 150 sites where the EPA made cleanup decisions in 1991–92, we examine how the sites selected for remediation would have been evaluated, and how remediation decisions would have changed if various benefit–cost and risk assessment reforms had been in place. This examination demonstrates the potential gains in efficiency which can be achieved within the Superfund program through regulatory reform and indicates the degree to which implementation of such reform is feasible. These results demonstrate that the application of benefit–cost principles at the Superfund site level could provide greater protection of human health and the environment through a program focused on the balancing of real risks against cleanup costs. The calculations we present document the extent to which the EPA can reduce cleanup expenditures without jeopardizing the objective of reducing risks. Our risk analysis is conservative, since our assessments of reductions in site risks from remediation do not include any countervailing increases in risks that may arise because of the increased risks to workers undertaking the remediations.[13]

9.2 Review of Current EPA Implementation

As we stressed in chapters 2 and 3, the EPA conducts an individual risk assessment for each site on the National Priorities List (NPL), the set of sites that qualify for remediation funds. EPA analysts assess chemical concentrations at the site and then estimate the corresponding health risks associated with the site.[14] The health risk estimate is comprised of both calculations of individual lifetime excess cancer risks (LECRs) as well as health risks due to exposure to chemicals associated with other adverse health effects.

It is important to note that EPA bases its assessments of risk in the Superfund program on the calculated risk levels to a potentially exposed individual. The agency does not explicitly consider the *number* of potentially exposed individuals in its calculation of cancer risks. In addition, while EPA does not explicitly state the degree of conservatism represented in its risk estimates, an examination of the agency's assumptions in chapters 2 and 3 reveals that it often uses very conservative parameter values in its risk assessments.[15] For example, in an analysis of health risks associated with groundwater contaminants at Superfund sites where future residential development is feasible, EPA analysts will simply assume such development will take place, without considering the *likelihood* of such development. Such use of conservative assumptions prompted Supreme Court Justice Breyer's concerns described in chapter 5 with the wisdom of the Superfund approach.[16]

During the early implementation of the Superfund program, some critics noted that EPA officials used the latitude provided by legislation to reach cleanup agreements that were highly favorable to polluters.[17] In response to the agency's implementation of the program, Congress passed the Superfund Amendments and Reauthorization Act (SARA).[18] This bill directs EPA to pursue remedies that "permanently and significantly [reduce] the volume, toxicity, or mobility of hazardous substances," thus discouraging the selection of less costly remedies such as institutional controls, containment, or removal.[19] SARA also requires the EPA to adopt as Superfund site cleanup standards those federal environmental standards from other programs that are "applicable or relevant and appropriate" (ARARs), and any state environmental standards that are more stringent than the federal standards.[20]

A 1991 EPA guidance memo further restricts the latitude of site managers in making cleanup decisions. It states that if the cumulative lifetime excess cancer risk for an individual is less than 10^{-4} and the hazard quotient is less than one (meaning the chemical exposure level for noncancer risks is below the "no-risk" threshold), then cleanup "generally is not warranted unless there are adverse environmental impacts."[21] While the directive provides that EPA regional officials may choose to clean up sites where cancer risks are between 10^{-4} and 10^{-6}, it requires site managers to explain why action is necessary if they choose to clean up.[22] These guidance directives reflect internal EPA policy decisions and are indicative of the kinds of policy directives that can be achieved administratively without any legislative changes. Site managers' cleanup decisions are guided also by the EPA's National Contingency Plan, which offers criteria for the site managers to use in selecting cleanup remedies.[23] Site managers may consider long-term effectiveness and permanence, reduction of toxicity, mobility, or volume, short-term effectiveness, implementability, cost, state acceptance, and community acceptance in developing a remediation plan, as long as the plan protects human health and the environment and complies with applicable environmental standards from other environmental programs.[24]

9.3 How Would the Superfund Program Change under Proposed Reforms?

If the cost–benefit and risk assessment reforms debated in Congress were implemented within EPA's Superfund program, the nature of EPA's analyses and decisions would change substantially.[25] To illustrate how EPA's assessment of risks could change under proposed reforms, we consider EPA's calculation of lifetime excess cancer risks for an adult Superfund site resident exposed to groundwater contaminated with the chemical trichloroethylene (TCE).[26] The current EPA risk assessment guidelines, outlined in the Human Health Evaluation Manual, encourage risk analysts to estimate the "reasonable maximum exposure" at a site.[27] In assessing the chemical concentration of TCE at the site, the analyst would use the 95th percentile of the mean concentration or the maximum concentration detected, whichever is lower. The analyst would then make assumptions, in accordance with "reasonable maximum exposure" guidelines, regarding parameters such as frequency of exposure (typically 350 to 365 days per year, an upper-bound estimation), daily ingestion of groundwater (2.0 liters per day for adults, approximately the 90th percentile), and the number of years exposed to the contamination (thirty years, approximately the 95th percentile).[28]

EPA's assessment of how likely it is that a chemical will cause cancer also includes conservative assumptions. To assess this propensity, EPA analysts use a figure called the chemical's "slope factor," which is an upper-bound estimate of the probability of development of cancer per unit intake of the chemical over a lifetime. This number, obtained from an EPA database representing the agency's assessment of the research literature on chemical toxicity, may include built-in safety factors of 10 or 100 due to low dose extrapolation or the assumption that animal data apply to human reactions.[29] EPA analysts combine all of these assumptions to yield an estimate of the probability the on-site resident will contract cancer based on consumption of groundwater contaminated with TCE.

In contrast, in risk assessments conducted under the proposed reforms, EPA would use a range of estimates regarding any one parameter and would produce as a result a range of estimates of cancer risk from TCE. One proposed bill, acknowledging that parameters comprising cancer risk estimates are better conveyed as distributions, would require agencies to present risk estimates based on central tendency. For example, it would require EPA analysts to calculate risk estimates using mean or median parameter values, even if analysts also choose to use more conservative assumptions in calculations.[30]

Since EPA's current guidelines encourage analysts to use differing degrees of conservatism for different parameters, the degree of conservatism represented in the ultimate risk assessment is unclear. Under the reform proposals one could actually quantify the degree of conservatism embedded in a risk estimate. This could be done by applying Monte Carlo analysis to the approach described above. As we demonstrated in chapter 3, in a Monte Carlo analysis an analyst randomly picks a point on the distribution of each parameter, estimates the lifetime excess cancer risk based on these points, and then repeats the process over and over to develop an estimate of the distribution of the lifetime excess cancer risk from TCE. Such an approach would enable analysts to identify the degree of conservatism embodied in different points on the overall risk distribution in Superfund site analyses.

Under other proposed risk assessment reforms, EPA's exposure characterization would change dramatically. For example, where future residential development on a Superfund site is feasible, the reforms could require EPA analysts to incorporate the likelihood of different exposure scenarios in their estimates of individual risk levels, rather than automatically assuming that such development will take place.[31] These estimates of individual risk could then be combined with census data on surrounding populations living on and near a contaminated site, yielding a distribution of estimates for the number of cancer cases arising from site contamination and the number of individuals likely to be exposed to "unsafe" levels of noncancer risks.[32] These calculations of population risk would provide more information than the EPA's current practice of estimating risks to a potentially exposed individual.

Risk management in Superfund—the process of determining what remedy will be selected at a site—would also radically change under the proposed reforms. For example, one proposal, which is in line with our recommendations, would require EPA to choose site remedies based on benefit–cost analysis of site cleanups.[33] EPA would explicitly consider and balance remediation costs with cancer and noncancer risks, calculating indicators such as the cost per cancer case averted in agency analysis.[34] The benefit–cost analysis would indicate the additional cost of meeting more stringent cleanup targets and establish trade-offs embodied in the selection of permanent remedies such as treatment of contamination instead of the use of institutional controls (such as deed restrictions that prohibit future residential use), containment, or removal of wastes. Cleanup standards would change dramatically if the supermandate provision described above were implemented, allowing this benefit–cost framework to supersede the requirement that the EPA use ARARs as cleanup goals. As a practical matter, such requirement could eliminate over 95 percent of current Superfund remediation expenditures. Cleanup remedies would also shift to more cost-efficient alternatives than those currently selected.

While many analysts have speculated about the impacts of regulatory reform on environmental policy, to date no one has estimated quantitatively how these proposals would affect the implementation of the Superfund program. In the following section we use extensive risk and cost data from a sample of Superfund sites to explore how regulatory decision making would change under various benefit–cost and risk assessment reforms.

We should note that it is not clear how participants in the political process would ultimately respond to information provided by benefit–cost analysis. Evidence of extremely large expenditures to avert a statistical cancer case could result in environmental cleanup dollars being shifted from inefficient to efficient remediations. This same evidence, however, might spur the passage of legislative standards that would demand the use of particularly stringent cleanup standards, even if they were demonstrably inefficient. In our assessment we adopt an optimistic view of the implementation of benefit–cost analysis and explore how this analytical tool could lead to wiser environmental spending.

9.4   Empirical Analysis of the Effect of Reforms on the Superfund Program

In this section we examine three different scenarios representing variations on EPA regulatory policy regarding which Superfund sites qualify for remediation; two of these scenarios reflect implementation of the proposed regulatory reform measures. The first scenario—the "current policy" scenario—is the structure under existing risk assessment guidelines, and it provides the baseline for discussion. The second scenario—the "no-ARARs" scenario—assumes that risk managers make decisions regarding which sites to remediate based on risk considerations alone, rather than on the basis of existing ARARs. Environmental standards from other state and federal programs are thus no longer binding constraints. In this scenario we assume that EPA remediates sites with cumulative individual risk of at least 10^{-4}, which represents a risk cutoff based on current EPA guidelines.[35] The third scenario—the "no future on-site residents" scenario—assumes everything in the "no-ARARs" scenario and imposes the additional assumption that risk assessment reforms require EPA analysts to perform risk assessments that assume no new residents will move onto the Superfund site. This scenario thus precludes EPA from including hypothetical, future on-site resident risks in their risk assessments.[36]

We then cross the three scenarios with an additional element of regulatory reform: the requirement that EPA analysts undertake an explicit benefit–cost analysis for site cleanups exceeding $5 million and not remediate sites for which the costs of remediation exceed the benefits.[37] The $5 million threshold itself is an implicit benefit–cost decision, for it suggests that the transaction costs associated with benefit–cost analysis are more likely to yield higher net benefits at sites with large resource expenditures than at those with lower costs of remediation. We examine this assumption and the relative benefit–cost performance of sites above and below the $5 million cost cutoff.

In analyzing this matrix of risk reform scenarios crossed with benefit–cost reform, we consider several dimensions. First, we examine what percentage of sites have remediation costs exceeding $5 million. Second, we consider the cleanup costs and health risks associated with each Superfund site, and determine which sites would pass a benefit–cost test (meaning which site cleanups would have costs per cancer case averted lower than specific levels). Related questions under this second dimension are: Is there a difference, above or below the $5 million threshold, in terms of the desirability of the remediation decisions? Are the cleanups that cost less than $5 million (and thus are not subject to benefit–cost analysis) more or less cost-effective? In other words, are the cleanups that cost less than $5 million cleaning up at a lower or higher cost per cancer avoided than those cleanups that cost more than $5 million? Third, we examine how these policy analysis concerns interact with issues pertaining to environmental equity. For example, will hazardous waste sites with higher minority populations be disproportionately affected by a policy based on benefit–cost concerns? Finally, we consider what general policy prescriptions can be offered regarding the effective targeting of resources to clean up hazardous waste sites.

Our analysis of the benefit–cost trade-offs begins with assumptions that greatly overstate the attractiveness of the cleanup. In particular, we initially take EPA's cancer exposure assumptions at face value even though they overstate the actual risk. Moreover we assume that all cancer risks incurred over the thirty-year exposure period occur without the discounting of deferred effects. These assumptions are not sound economics, but they are consistent with the conservative policy approach used by EPA. Even with these generous assumptions, the EPA cleanups do not fare well on a benefit–cost basis. We then assess the effect of incorporating more realistic mean risk assumptions as well as incorporating a latency period (ten years) and the role of discounting of benefits (3 percent) into the analysis. In all cases we recognize two key components that do not currently affect EPA's formal policy tests—size of exposed populations and costs per cancer case averted.

Our analysis, outlined below, demonstrates that there are few Superfund remediations for which the benefits of cleanup exceed the remediation costs. From a sample of 150 sites where EPA made remediation decisions in 1991–92, we collected extensive data on individual risk levels, cleanup costs, and remediation cleanup targets. As indicated in chapter 4, we then used the individual chemical concentration data collected by the EPA to estimate the expected number of cancer cases arising at a site over the course of thirty years, and generated estimates of noncancer effects by calculating the number of individuals exposed to levels above the no observable adverse effects level (NOAEL) or the lowest observed adverse effects level (LOAEL) (e.g., sites for which the chemical exposure exceeds the exposure threshold above which noncancer risks becomes a concern).[38]

We employed two reference points to judge the cost-effectiveness of Superfund cleanups: $5 million and $100 million in cleanup costs per cancer case averted. The $5 million figure represents the midpoint of the range of estimates for the implicit value of a statistical life using evidence from the labor market wage–risk trade-offs.[39] This value is in the general range of figures used by other federal agencies and by EPA in its benefit–cost analyses. The second reference point, $100 million, is a useful cutoff level because due to the influence of agencies' restrictive legislative mandates the Office of Management and Budget has never rejected a proposed regulation with a cost per life saved below $100 million.[40] The $100 million figure also exceeds the value at which there will be net adverse mortality costs associated with the regulation (due to diversion of resources from other health-enhancing uses) that exceed the direct risk reduction effects.[41]

As we noted in chapter 5, the individual lifetime excess cancer risks estimated by the EPA at the 150 sites we examined are extremely high relative to risks regulated in other programs; though if one changes the assumptions about future land use, the risk estimates drop dramatically. By EPA's current calculations, among a set of 145 sites, 126 had individual lifetime excess cancer risks that were greater than or equal to 10^{-4}. If we match the chemical concentrations at these sites with information on populations that would be exposed under current land uses, the cancer risks from Superfund sites appear much different. At the 150 sites examined, over a thirty-year period, there would be 731 excess cancer cases estimated to arise from contamination. Of this amount, 652 are concentrated at one site, the Westinghouse site in Sunnyvale, California (notable for a high concentration of polychlorinated biphenyls [PCBs]). The median number of cancer cases per site averted by remediation is 0.017. Only ten out of 150 sites had one or more expected cancer cases estimated to arise over thirty years.

Our results from chapter 5 also demonstrate that the cost-effectiveness of remediating the 150 sites sampled is quite low. If one matches cancers with remediation expenditures, the median cost per discounted cancer case averted is $388 million. Overall, only 44 out of the 145 sites had a cost per cancer averted less than $100 million. These costs are particularly dramatic considering that these numbers were calculated using the relatively conservative exposure parameters chosen by the EPA, and also do not account for the time lag before the cancer cases occur. If one assumes mean chemical concentration and a ten-year latency period for the onset of cancers, and discounts costs as well as benefits at a rate of 3 percent, the median cost per discounted cancer case averted is $7.2 billion. Viewed from the perspective of cost per cancer case averted, there is thus substantial opportunity for regulatory reform to improve the implementation of the Superfund program.

We evaluate the consequences of various regulatory reforms (represented by the "no-ARARs" scenario and the "no future on-site residents" scenario, outlined above) along the following dimensions: (1) the number of sites qualifying for remediation, (2) total remediation expenditures, (3) expected cancers averted by remediation, (4) populations protected from noncancer effects, and (5) environmental equity. Our results demonstrate that the adoption of the proposed regulatory reforms would save a great deal of money and foster environmental equity while sacrificing little in the way of mitigated health risks.

Number of Sites That Would Qualify for Remediation

Table 9.1 details the number of sites that would qualify for remediation under the three different scenarios. The table demonstrates that changing risk assessment and benefit–cost practices would radically change the number of sites subject to remediation.

First, as outlined above, table 9.1 demonstrates that the cost-effectiveness of the remediation path chosen under EPA's current regulatory regime (i.e., the cost per cancer case averted for the alternative selected at the site) is quite low, particularly for sites with total cleanup costs exceeding $5 million. Of the 150 sites in the sample, we were able to estimate a cost per cancer case avoided at 145 sites. Of these 145 sites, 100 sites, or 69 percent, had total expected cleanup costs exceeding $5 million and thus would be subject to benefit–cost analysis under the proposed regulatory reforms. Most of the remediation at the sites in this subset would not pass a benefit–cost test, so different remediation strategies would have to be considered if regulatory reforms were adopted. Only 5 percent of these 100 sites have a cost per case of cancer averted under $5 million. Twenty-six percent of the 100 sites have a cost per cancer case averted less than $100 million.[42]

The results are somewhat better for the forty-five sites (see table 9.1, panel B) where total costs are sufficiently low that benefit–cost analysis would not be required by the proposed regulatory reforms. For this group, 40 percent (eighteen sites) had cleanups chosen with costs less than $100 million per cancer case averted, and 18 percent (eight sites) had cleanups that cost less than $5 million per case of cancer averted. These numbers suggest that the sites that are exempted from benefit–cost analysis because of their lower costs have greater likelihood of passing this benefit–cost test. The exemption would consequently not lead to disproportionate inefficiencies.

Current Superfund law requires the agency to use state or federal ARARs as cleanup goals. These cleanup standards, however, could be overridden by evidence derived from benefit–cost analysis if regulatory reform legislation trumped existing statutes. If current ARARs were ignored, and action were taken only at sites where cancer risks were at least 10^{-4}, the number of sites qualifying for remediation would drop from 145 to 126. Of the 126 sites that would be addressed if ARARs could be disregarded, 91 sites had costs sufficient to warrant conducting a benefit–cost analysis under the proposed reforms. Only 24 of these sites had cleanup remedies chosen that would pass a benefit–cost test based on the $100 million cost per cancer case averted threshold.

Existing Superfund risk assessment guidelines encourage analysts to consider exposure pathways for onsite residents at Superfund sites, even if the area today is uninhabited or used as an industrial site. Table 9.1 indicates that if EPA analysts considered only actual risks based on current land use patterns, rather than risks based on future, hypothetical onsite residents (as the case would be under the "no future on-site residents" scenario), a remediation policy of cleaning up sites with risks of at least 10^{-4} would yield a total of 86 sites subject to remediation out of 145.[43] Of the 68 sites where the costs would warrant benefit–cost analysis, just over a quarter have a cleanup costs under $100 million per cancer case averted; only 6 percent would have a cleanup cost under $5 million per case of cancer averted.

Total Expenditures for Remediation of Superfund Sites
Implementing regulatory reforms requiring benefit–cost analysis would decrease the number of sites that would be remediated, substantially decreasing the total expenditures for the Superfund program. Table 9.2 examines the cost levels for the different site groups considered in table 9.1. A total of $2.2 billion will be spent in remediation costs at the 145 sites under current policy. If the remedies selected remain unchanged, but the number of sites remediated declined because decisions regarding which sites to clean up were made only on the basis of cancer risks rather than ARARs, as would be the case under the "no ARARs" scenario, $2.0 billion would be spent on cleanup. Cleanup costs drop to $1.6 billion if potential risks from future on-site residents do not trigger cleanups.

As one would expect, the total remediation costs are much greater at sites above the $5 million total cleanup cost trigger: $2.1 billion versus $82.2 million, despite the fact that one-third of the sites fall below the $5 million threshold. By focusing on the two-thirds of the sites with expenditures large enough to warrant a benefit–cost analysis, the EPA would

Table 9.1
Number of sites qualifying for remediation under different policy analysis criteria

a. Sites with cleanup costs over $5 million

	Total number of sites qualifying for remediation	Number of sites with total cleanup costs over $5 million	Percentage of sites with total cleanup costs over $5 million	Of sites with total cleanup costs over $5 million, number with cost per cancer case averted under $5 million	Of sites with total cleanup costs over $5 million, percentage with cost per cancer case averted under $5 million	Of sites with total cleanup costs over $5 million, number with cost per cancer case averted under $100 million	Of sites with total cleanup costs over $5 million, percentage with cost per cancer case averted under $100 million
Current policy[a]	145	100	69	5	5	26	26
No ARARs[b]	126	91	72	4	4	24	26
No future on-site residents[c]	86	68	79	4	6	19	28

b. Sites with cleanup costs under $5 million

	Total number of sites qualifying for remediation	Number of sites with total cleanup costs under $5 million	Percentage of sites with total cleanup costs under $5 million	Of sites with total cleanup costs under $5 million, number with cost per cancer case averted under $5 million	Of sites with total cleanup costs under $5 million, percentage with cost per cancer case averted under $5 million	Of sites with total cleanup costs under $5 million, number with cost per cancer case averted under $100 million	Of sites with total cleanup costs under $5 million, percentage with cost per cancer case averted under $100 million
Current policy[a]	145	45	31	8	18	18	40
No ARARs[b]	126	35	28	5	14	15	43
No future on-site residents[c]	86	18	21	3	17	8	44

a. All sites in risk sample.
b. Sites with cumulative risks of at least 10^{-4}.
c. Sites with cumulative risk of at least 10^{-4} assuming no risks to future on-site residents.

Table 9.2
Summed cleanup costs (1993 $) of sites under different policy analysis criteria

a. Sites with cleanup costs over $5 million

	Total cost of remediating all sites in simulation	Total cost of remediating all sites with individual cleanup costs over $5 million	Total cost of remediating all sites with individual cleanup costs over $5 million and cost per cancer case averted under $5 million	Total cost of remediating all sites with individual cleanup costs over $5 million and cost per cancer case averted under $100 million
Current policy[a]	$2.16 billion	$2.08 billion	$71.6 million	$593 million
No ARARs[b]	$2.01 billion	$1.94 billion	$52.6 million	$567 million
No future on-site residents[c]	$1.59 billion	$1.55 billion	$52.6 million	$482 million

b. Sites with cleanup costs under $5 million

	Total cost of remediating all sites in simulation	Total cost of remediating all sites with individual cleanup costs under $5 million	Total cost of remediating all sites with individual cleanup costs under $5 million and cost per cancer case averted under $5 million	Total cost of remediating all sites with individual cleanup costs under $5 million and cost per cancer case averted under $100 million
Current policy[a]	$2.16 billion	$82.2 million	$3.54 million	$25.0 million
No ARARs[b]	$2.01 billion	$69.9 million	$3.54 million	$25.0 million
No future on-site residents[c]	$1.59 billion	$41.8 million	$3.54 million	$17.4 million

a. All sites in risk sample.
b. Sites with cumulative risks of at least 10^{-4}.
c. Sites with cumulative risk of at least 10^{-4} assuming no risks to future on-site residents.

examine 96 percent of expenditures. Within each scenario a small percentage of the total expenditures is spent at sites where the currently selected remedy yields a cost per cancer case averted that passes a benefit–cost test. For the larger sites with costs above $5 million, a total of $72 million is spent at sites with a cleanup cost per cancer case averted below $5 million, and $593 million is spent at sites with a cleanup cost per cancer case averted below $100 million. Over $1.4 billion in costs at these larger sites is spent to reduce cancers at a cost above $100 million per cancer case averted. For the smaller scale sites with a total cleanup costs less than $5 million, $3.5 million is spent at sites where a remediation cost per case of cancer averted is below $5 million, and $25 million is spent to reduce cancer cases at a cost below $100 million per cancer case averted. The remaining $57 million is spent on cancer prevention above $100 million per case averted.

More widespread use of benefit–cost analysis in determining which sites to remediate thus offers the potential for large savings in the Superfund program. If EPA decisions were made based on actual risks (rather than ARARs), the number of sites remediated drops from 145 to 126 and expenditures drop by $150 million. Ruling out hypothetical risks to future on-site residents reduces the number of sites to 86, cutting cleanup costs by an additional $400 million. If one recalculates the cleanup costs of the sites that do not pass the benefit–cost test, and assumes alternative remedies instead of the remedy actually implemented, costs would drop even further.

Expected Health Problems Averted by Remediation

Under the reform scenarios, while both the number of sites that would qualify for remediation and the total Superfund expenditures would dramatically decrease, the vast majority of cancer cases would still be averted since the sites that would qualify for remediation are the sites that pose greater cancer risks (see table 9.3). Remediation of the full sample of 145 sites would avoid 731 estimated cancers arising over thirty years from site contamination. Basing decisions to remediate on risk levels of 10^{-4} or higher reduces the number of sites remediated to 126, but would still avert 713 cancers. Ruling out remediations based on risks to future on-site residents reduces the number of sites remediated from 145 to 86 but does not significantly affect the number of cancer cases averted, which would shrink to only 710. Even when remediation decisions are generally based on current land uses rather than hypothetical future residential use, the

Table 9.3
Expected cancer cases averted under different policy analysis criteria

a. Sites with cleanup costs over $5 million

	Total cancer cases averted in all sites in simulation	Total cancer cases averted in all sites with cleanup costs over $5 million	Total cancer cases averted in all sites with cleanup costs over $5 million and cost per cancer case averted under $5 million	Total cancer cases averted in all sites with cleanup costs over $5 million and cost per cancer case averted under $100 million
Current policy[a]	731	728	704	726
No ARARs[b]	713	710	686	708
No future on-site residents[c]	710	708	686	706

b. Sites with cleanup costs under $5 million

	Total cancer cases averted in all sites in simulation	Total cancer cases averted in all sites with cleanup costs under $5 million	Total cancer cases averted in all sites with cleanup costs under $5 million and cost per cancer case averted under $5 million	Total cancer cases averted in all sites with cleanup costs under $5 million and cost per cancer case averted under $100 million
Current policy[a]	2	2	1	2
No ARARs[b]	2	2	1	2
No future on-site residents[c]	2	2	1	2

a. All sites in risk sample.
b. Sites with cumulative risks of at least 10^{-4}.
c. Sites with cumulative risk of at least 10^{-4} assuming no risks to future on-site residents.

cleanups avert the vast majority of cancers arising from the full sample of sites.

All but two of the total cancer cases averted are at sites with costs that would warrant a benefit–cost test. Perhaps most striking is that the requirement of a benefit–cost test for sites with total cleanup costs over $5 million captures most of the cases of cancer that could be prevented. If EPA remediated only those sites subject to benefit–cost analysis which could be cleaned up for less than $5 million per cancer case averted, 704 of the expected 731 cancer cases would be averted. With a $100 million cost per case cutoff, 726 out of the 731 expected cases would be prevented.

Implementation of a benefit–cost test would yield similar results for exposure to noncancer health risks, even though the test focuses on cancer effects. As table 9.4 illustrates, regulatory reform would reduce expenditures while still protecting a significant number of residents from exposure to noncancer risks. For the sample of 145 sites, 113,000 residents living within one mile of a contaminated site face exposure to at least one chemical with a chemical exposure level above the no risk threshold. For the "no-ARARs" scenario, the number of those protected drops by only 3,000 people to 110,000. Remediation of sites under the "no future on-site resident scenario" would continue to protect 97,000 people (86 percent of the original number protected by remediation of 145 sites). Restricting site cleanups to those that passed a benefit–cost test would address most of these noncancer exposures. For example, remediating only those sites that can be cleaned up for less than $5 million per cancer case averted would protect 70,500 (68,000 plus 2,500) people from noncancer risks; remediating only those sites that can be cleaned up for less than $100 million per cancer case averted protects over 100,000 (97,000 plus 3,400) of the 113,000 people exposed to such health risks.

Because cancer and noncancer health risks exhibit a strong correlation, the vast majority of noncancer exposures can be averted by remediating sites that pass a benefit–cost analysis where the cost per cancer case averted is less than $100 million. However, in a full benefit–cost analysis, EPA decision makers would collect more information on the magnitudes and harms of noncancer effects. This might lead to even more noncancer effects being addressed at the sample sites.

Natural Resource Considerations
Proposed Superfund polices such as cleaning up sites on the basis of risk levels rather than ARARs, excluding hypothetical future risks, and

Table 9.4
Exposed populations under different policy analysis criteria

a. Sites with cleanup costs over $5 million

	Total exposed population in all sites in simulation	Total exposed population in all sites with cleanup costs over $5 million	Total exposed population in all sites with cleanup costs over $5 million and cost per cancer case averted under $5 million	Total exposed population in all sites with cleanup costs over $5 million and cost per cancer case averted under $100 million
Current policy[a]	113,000	109,000	68,000	97,000
No ARARs[b]	110,000	107,000	68,000	94,000
No future on-site residents[c]	97,000	94,000	68,000	86,000

b. Sites with cleanup costs under $5 million

	Total exposed population in all sites in simulation	Total exposed population in all sites with cleanup costs under $5 million	Total exposed population in all sites with cleanup costs under $5 million and cost per cancer case averted under $5 million	Total exposed population in all sites with cleanup costs under $5 million and cost per cancer case averted under $100 million
Current policy[a]	113,000	3,700	2,500	3,400
No ARARs[b]	110,000	3,500	2,400	3,300
No future on-site residents[c]	97,000	2,900	2,400	2,700

a. All sites in risk sample.
b. Sites with cumulative risks of at least 10^{-4}.
c. Sites with cumulative risk of at least 10^{-4} assuming no risks to future on-site residents.

imposing benefit–cost tests to determine what sites to remediate all decrease remediation costs while preserving high levels of protection from cancer and noncancer risks. Two additional criteria are relevant in evaluating policy choices: the prevention of natural resources damage and the exposure of different demographic groups to different levels of health risks (i.e., environmental equity). According to EPA survey data, environmental concerns served as the basis for cleanup goals at only 21 of the 145 sample sites.[44] If potential on-site residents did not drive remediation decisions, only 8 of the 21 sites would still be protected. Of the 21 sites with assessed risks relating to natural resource damage, only 4 were cleaned up at a cost per cancer averted of less than $100 million. These numbers suggest that since natural resource damages may not be strongly linked to cancer risks, adequate protection against natural resources damage would require that risk analysts explicitly incorporate measures of natural resource damages into remediation decisions.[45] Current EPA assessments of the desirability of cleanups do not document these damages to an extent that is sufficient to determine whether they provide an adequate basis for cleanup action.

Environmental Equity Concerns

Critics of risk assessment frequently conjecture that basing policies on efficiency concerns will generate policies that have a negative impact on minority communities.[46] Such criticisms may be especially relevant to the Superfund effort since current Superfund guidelines do not incorporate synergistic effects of exposures to multiple chemicals (due to a lack of toxicity data).[47] Risks to minorities, who are more likely to experience multiple exposures, may therefore be undercounted.[48] And while some communities may benefit from hiring technical expertise to critique EPA's analysis, minority communities are typically less able to afford such consultation. Although Superfund has a technical assistance program that funds analysis for local communities, our research indicates that EPA is less likely to award such grants to minority communities.

The proposed risk reform legislation, however, will not disproportionately harm minority populations. For the purpose of this assessment we define the minority population around a site as the total population minus non-Hispanic whites. Minorities would thus include African Americans, Hispanics, Asians, American Indians, and those defined as other races in the census. Table 9.5 reveals that for each policy scenario the minority population percentage is very similar. At the 146 sites that would be

Table 9.5
Interaction between minority population and different policy analysis alternatives

a. Sites with cleanup costs over $5 million

	Mean minority population (as % of site population) in all sites in simulation	Mean minority population (as % of site population) in all sites with cleanup costs over $5 million	Mean minority population (as % of site population) in all sites with cleanup costs over $5 million and cost per cancer case averted under $5 million	Mean minority population (as % of site population) in all sites with cleanup costs over $5 million and cost per cancer case averted under $100 million
Current policy[a]	17	18	32	26
No ARARs[b]	17	17	39	25
No future on-site residents[c]	16	17	39	22

b. Sites with cleanup costs under $5 million

	Mean minority population (as % of site population) in all sites in simulation	Mean minority population (as % of site population) in all sites with cleanup costs under $5 million	Mean minority population (as % of site population) in all sites with cleanup costs under $5 million and cost per cancer case averted under $5 million	Mean minority population (as % of site population) in all sites with cleanup costs under $5 million and cost per cancer case averted under $100 million
Current policy[a]	17	14	17	12
No ARARs[b]	17	15	34	13
No future on-site residents[c]	16	12	25	13

a. All sites in risk sample.
b. Sites with cumulative risks of at least 10^{-4}.
c. Sites with cumulative risk of at least 10^{-4} assuming no risks to future on-site residents.

remediated under the current policy scenario, the mean minority population is 17 percent.[49] The mean minority population is also 17 percent at the 126 sites remediated under the "no-ARARs" scenario, and 16 percent for the policy scenario assuming "no future on-site residents." The mean minority population percentage at sites subject to a benefit–cost test is also virtually identical to the overall minority percentages at these sites.

A different pattern emerges with respect to the mean minority percentage at sites that pass a benefit–cost test. At those sites with cleanup costs greater than $5 million, which pass a cost–benefit test assuming a saved life is worth $5 million, the mean minority percentage ranges from 32 to 39 percent. For smaller scale sites that are not subject to a benefit–cost test but would pass a benefit–cost test assuming a saved life is worth $5 million, the mean minority percentage ranges from 17 to 34 percent. The departure from the overall mean minority percentages is less dramatic for the larger set of sites that pass a benefit–cost test assuming a saved life is worth $100 million. Nevertheless, even for this high cutoff, minorities are not disadvantaged by a regulatory scenario that requires benefit–cost analysis to determine which sites are remediated: The sites that pass the benefit–cost test, and therefore are remediated, have higher mean minority population percentages than those sites with cleanups that do not pass a benefit–cost test.

Implementation of risk assessment and benefit–cost analysis requirements would also benefit minority populations by overriding some of the discretionary elements of the Superfund program which allow constituent pressures to trigger policy actions. Such discretionary elements can leave minority communities at a disadvantage if such communities are less likely to engage in collective action to pressure regulators or if their actions are met with less response.[50] We have found evidence that this is the case. The process by which sites are placed on the National Priorities List, the set of sites that qualify for remediation funds, is influenced by community pressure. Controlling for a measure of local levels of pollution, we have found that hazardous sites in communities with higher percentages of minorities were less likely to be placed on the NPL. In addition Superfund site residents in high minority, lower voter turnout sites are less likely to receive the technical assistance grants administered by the agency.[51]

Table 9.5 indicates that if the regulatory playing field were leveled so that site remediation decisions were based only on risks and costs rather than on community pressure or other factors, minority populations would not be harmed. The mean minority population percentage is actually much higher at the sites where remediations would be implemented based on benefit–cost analysis alone. Those smaller scale sites not subject to a benefit–cost test have slightly lower minority population percentages. In sum, risk assessment and benefit–cost analysis may reduce environmental inequities by reducing the role for constituent pressure in remediations and by focusing attention on high health risks, which often occur in minority communities. Basing cleanup decisions on the merits as reflected by assessments of costs and benefits is the risk policy analogue of equal opportunity policies in the labor market. Equal risk protection may thus ameliorate the environmental inequities that result from the powerful influences of political forces.

Accounting for Changes in Risk Assumptions

In the preceding analysis in the chapter we have treated the way that risks are calculated—hazard identification, exposure assessment and dose response—as a given and examined how changes in risk characterization and risk management rules altered site remedy decisions. This subsection quantifies how additional changes in EPA's risk assessment calculations would alter Superfund decision making.

As noted above, if Congress adopted the risk reform provisions, EPA's calculation of risks would change in at least three ways. First, the reforms could require EPA to use population risks, rather than individual risks, as the basis of its risk assessments. Second, the requirement that agencies report risk estimates based on central tendencies would shift EPA's risk assessment analyses away from the use of reasonable maximum exposure scenarios to those based on mean assumptions. Third, the reforms would require EPA to assess risk not as a single point estimate but as a probability distribution.

Our analysis in chapter 3 demonstrates that the use of central tendency estimates in risk assessment greatly alters the ascertained magnitude of individual risks and population risks. For 141 sites, we recalculated EPA estimates of soil and groundwater ingestion risks (which account for 40 percent of the exposure pathways at these Superfund sites). If one examines the maximum ingestion pathways at the 67 sites where estimates of average chemical concentrations were available, the magnitude of the individual risks calculated are quite large (mean 0.038, median 0.0019). Classifying these sites on the basis of maximum ingestion risks, 94 percent would fall in EPA's current range requiring remediation (risk at least

10^{-4}), 5 percent would be in the discretionary range (10^{-4} to 10^{-6}), and 1 percent in the range where remediation is generally not pursued under current guidelines.[52] But if one uses mean estimates for the ingestion rates, exposure duration, and contaminant concentration parameters, the magnitude of the maximum ingestion risks drops substantially. The mean of the maximum ingestion risks using current EPA guidelines is twenty times larger than that derived from central tendency estimates (0.0019). The median risk calculated under EPA guidelines is also greater than that estimated with central tendency assumptions (0.00011). If EPA cleaned up sites based on maximum ingestion-risk levels calculated under central tendencies, 54 percent would fall into the remediation category of risks in excess of 10^{-4}, 43 percent would be in the discretionary zone of risks between 10^{-4} and 10^{-6}, and 3 percent would be in the category of risks below 10^{-6} where remediations are not generally pursued. A shift to central tendencies would thus place a substantial percentage of sites in the discretionary zone.

The number of cancer cases expected to arise also changes drastically if one uses assumptions less conservative than used by the EPA. If exposure and intake parameters are set at conservative values, chapter 4 indicates there are 731 cancer cases estimated to arise at the 145 sites over the next thirty years.[53] Under a different set of assumptions that the intake rate/bodyweight ratio and chemical contaminant values are at their means, that cancer occurs with a ten-year latency, and that cancer cases are discounted at 3 percent per year (since individuals value cases differently depending on whether they are averted now or in the future), the estimated number of cancer cases changes from 698 to 204 cases at the 99 sites where average concentrations were available.

Our data also demonstrate that the combination of conservative assumptions results in highly conservative estimates of the risks arising at Superfund sites. Monte Carlo analysis offers another way to quantify the degree of conservatism embedded in the EPA's RME scenario. To explore this, we calculated a distribution of ingestion risks arising at 86 sites using information on the distributions of exposure parameters and chemical concentrations. For the "reasonable maximum exposure" ingestion pathways calculated under EPA guidelines, nearly two-thirds were in the 99th percentile of the distributions calculated under Monte Carlo analysis.

A Note on Remedy Selections
The Superfund Amendments and Reauthorization Act directed the EPA to select remedies that "permanently and significantly reduce the volume,

toxicity, or mobility of hazardous substances."[54] This requirement constrains the agency to favor permanent treatment of contaminants at a site over potentially less costly remedies, such as institutional controls, containment, or removal of waste. Nevertheless, the diversity of remedies that have been selected, detailed in table 9.6, demonstrates that site managers do enjoy some discretion over the selection of remedies.

Table 9.6 explores how remedy selection varies across different categories of sites. Specifically, institutional controls and removals were more likely at sites where total cleanup costs were below $5 million than at those where expenditures exceeded $5 million.[55] In terms of cost-effectiveness, sites that were cleaned up at less than $100 million per cancer case avoided were much more likely to deal with soil contamination through institutional controls or removals than through treatment. The same holds true for groundwater remedies: Sites that passed a very loosely defined benefit–cost test (with the assumption that a life is worth $100 million) were more likely to deal with groundwater contamination through institutional controls. At some sites multiple remedies that use similar technologies but vary in price were proposed to deal with contamination. At sites with expenditures less than $5 million, the less expensive soil alternative was chosen 52 percent of the time, while at more expensive sites the cheaper soil alternative was only chosen 33 percent of the time. There is thus some room for additional discretion to be used to reduce costs under current guidelines, despite the statutorily mandated preference for permanence which restricts the types of alternatives considered and chosen at sites.

Of the 145 sites in our sample, only 44 had a cost per cancer case avoided less than $100 million under current remedy selections. Of the 101 sites that did not meet this cutoff, 14 had considered but not chosen remedies that, if chosen, would have resulted in a cost per cancer averted of less than $100 million. At the remainder of the sites, none of the remedies proposed by EPA would result in a cost per cancer averted of less than $100 million. To achieve greater efficiencies in cleanup at Superfund sites, regulatory reform would have to allow equal consideration of all possible remedies rather than strongly favoring permanent treatment.

One of our principal policy recommendations is that EPA adopt more flexibility in its cleanup decisions, permitting less stringent cleanups in situations where more limited policy options, such as institutional controls, have a much stronger performance from a benefit–cost standpoint. As our analyses in chapters 5 and 8 make clear, when it is others' money

Table 9.6
Selection of remediation alternatives

Sites with soil or groundwater contamination addressed	Sites with cleanup costs under $5 million	Sites with cleanup costs over $5 million	Sites with cost per cancer case averted under $100 million	Sites with cost per cancer case averted over $100 million
Soil				
Total number	45	164	26	69
Percentage of total number				
Institutional Controls	13%	4%	19%	3%
Containment	16%	22%	8%	24%
Removal	11%	4%	15%	5%
Treatment	56%	64%	50%	65%
Containment with Removal	4%	6%	8%	3%
Groundwater				
Total number	58	166	34	77
Percentage of total number				
Institutional Controls	52%	25%	47%	22%
Treatment	48%	75%	53%	78%

that is being spent, it is easier to be much more demanding with respect to cleanup stringency than would be the case if it were one's own funds being spent. Residents' housing price valuations of cancer risks are dwarfed by the magnitudes of expenditures mandated for Superfund cleanups, indicating the disparity between private valuation of the benefits and the cost-effectiveness of government expenditure efforts.

Another contrast that highlights the inefficiency in cleanup policies is to examine what the government itself does when its own funds are being used to fund a hazardous waste cleanup. Consider the case of a hazardous waste site in South Boston that is slated to become the site of a new convention center.[56] The city of Boston is now purchasing this site under the rules of eminent domain. The site itself would probably rank among the more dangerous waste sites in our sample. Regulators have documented the presence of PCB contaminants at the site. The hazards were so severe that pools of oil containing hazardous levels of PCBs were discovered in neighboring properties, and even residents two blocks away have reported that oil odors were coming from the site. The city now plans to address the risks at the worst part of the site, which is a junkyard, by capping the site with a thick barrier. The current estimate is that cleanup costs will be a minimum of $500,000, though the figure could climb to as high a several million dollars. Even this upper bound cost estimate is still an order of magnitude smaller than the average cleanup costs when private funds are typically used. Boston's decision not to use the most ambitious cleanup option typically required of private parties is not irresponsible, but in fact reflects the kinds of policy flexibility that should be extended more broadly.

9.5   Conclusions

The current policy approach used in the Superfund program is a peculiar halfway house. EPA devotes substantial effort to identifying chemicals at a site and ascertaining their potential risks. It also assesses costs of a range of remedies in considerable detail. However, many key elements are missing in the agency's analysis. There is no explicit consideration of the size of the population at risk in final remediation decisions. Risks to a single individual have the same weight as risks to a large exposed population. Actual and hypothetical exposures to chemicals receive equal weight so that risks to a person who, in the future, may choose to live near a currently uninhabited Superfund site receive the same weight as risks to large populations that are currently involuntarily exposed. EPA also reports the conservative risk assessment value for each site, without focusing its policy attention on the expected risk level or most likely risk scenarios. Finally, explicit trade-offs that balance benefits and costs do not enter remediation decisions. These problems arise in part because of decision-making constraints in the Superfund legislation and in part because of the way regulators have implemented the program.

The cleanup decisions analyzed here were made in 1991 and 1992. Since 1993 the EPA has undertaken three waves of administrative reforms of the Superfund program, though none of them fully addresses the kinds of issues we have raised.[57] Most of the reforms have focused on more expeditious cleanup efforts rather than incorporation of benefit–cost concerns or the role of exposed populations. According to the agency's 1997 assessment of these reforms, the changes in policy have resulted in a number of program improvements: increased the speed of cleanups so that construction has been completed at 498 NPL sites, authorized potentially responsible parties to conduct or pay for nearly 70 percent of long-term cleanups, taken more than 15,000 small contributors out of the Superfund liability disputes, engineered a reduction in future Superfund costs of over $900 million, and led to the evaluation and archiving of 30,454 sites in the national tracking system for hazardous waste sites.[58] Reforms that focused explicitly on cleanup policies included the creation of a National Remedy Review Board (NRRB) to examine site decisions in order to "promote cost-effectiveness and national consistency in remedy selection," the issuance of guidance on remedy selection rules of thumb, the updating of remedy decisions when new information becomes available, and the ranking of sites based on risk.[59] The agency also began to examine how the risk assessment process could be improved upon, identifying four major areas for improvement and study: "community involvement in the risk assessment process; land use considerations; establishing background for risk assessment purposes; and uncertainty/probabilistic analysis."[60]

These changes may ultimately reduce the transaction costs of the cleanup process, and conceivably may target resources more effectively. Even if fully implemented, however, these changes in policy would not explicitly require the agency to calculate risks on a population basis, present risk estimates to the public based on a variety of parameter assumptions, and make cleanup decisions on the basis of cost-effectiveness considerations such as the cost per cancer case avoided. During the course of our research, which was funded by the agency, we had a series of presentations at the Superfund office and elsewhere at EPA. The officials there had strong beliefs that our policy proposals would require a fundamental shift in EPA policy, which they would not consider in the absence of the passage of regulatory reform legislation or a Superfund reform bill that mandated such an approach.[61] A principal goal of this book is to demonstrate that such fundamental shifts in policy evaluation are feasible and to indicate how such changes will affect cleanup actions and their consequences.

Our data show that the core economic elements of the proposed regulatory reform bills would dramatically alter EPA's policy choices. Put simply, the reforms would require that agency regulations maximize the net gain to society (benefits less costs) using plausible risk assumptions. Sound risk analysis and benefit–cost analysis would force wiser spending and eliminate many of the problems that decrease the overall performance of those potentially desirable regulatory efforts such as hazardous waste cleanup.

Consider how benefit–cost analysis would help one answer how effectively EPA has targeted its expenditures to reduce risks. For the most effective 5 percent of cleanup expenditures, through remediation EPA eliminates 99.47 percent of the cancer risks averted. All expenditures beyond that level will have cleanup costs per discounted case of cancer averted in excess of $140 million. Potentially EPA can generate virtually all the gains in reduced risk at a fraction of the cleanup costs. *At present, 95 percent of the expenditures at Superfund sites are devoted to eliminating only 0.5 percent of the cancer risk.*[62]

Under risk assessment and risk management reforms, EPA would assess population risks, rather than simply individual risks, from contamination at Superfund sites. The agency would present central tendency estimates so that analysts could see the range of risks at a site.[63] More flexible remedy decisions based on risk levels rather than ARARs would reduce the costs associated with cleanup goals based on standards from other environmental programs, and costs based on the preference for permanent remedies.

Risk reform is inevitably vulnerable to the fear that it will become a vehicle for ignoring environmental hazards rather than remediating them more efficiently. Our analysis shows, however, that there is a wide zone within which risk reforms can improve efficiency without sacrificing human health considerations. In our analysis the shift toward site cleanups based on risk levels alone—rather than ARARs and calculations that include on-site future residents—would drop the number of sites remediated from 145 to 86 and site expenditures from $2.2 billion to $1.6 billion, but would reduce the number of cancer cases averted by only 21 (from 731 to 710) and the number of individuals protected from non-cancer exposures by 16,000 (from 113,000 to 97,000). Our analysis further indicates that calculation of risks based on central tendency would shift a substantial fraction of sites into the cleanup discretionary zone, where EPA site managers currently have the authority to decide whether or not to remediate a site. Removal of preference for permanence would also allow managers to consider more cost-effective alternatives.

The findings for minority populations are perhaps the most telling. Sites that pass a benefit–cost test have a much higher mean minority percentage than the average for the overall set of sites considered. These results help provide an efficiency rationale for the environmental equity movement. If current political pressures lead to neglect of environmental harms in minority communities, as the environmental justice critics note, such communities could benefit from decisions made on the merits of risks. Our data support this: Sites with large minority populations had stronger benefit–cost performance. By focusing on objective measures of risk, benefit–cost analysis will highlight the policy importance of addressing the real risks that minorities may face from hazardous waste sites.

To be more effective, agency risk assessments should include more information—such as calculations of population risks—than they do now. EPA must better document any potentially important natural resource damages, noncancer effects, and synergistic influences. The transaction costs of these new calculations would be vastly offset by the savings afforded by an efficient implementation of the program, not the least of which will be the greater number of lives saved through better targeted policies. Our analysis shows that the government has a tremendous opportunity in the Superfund program both to cut costs and to be more protective of human health. Somewhat paradoxically, EPA's current seemingly uncompromising approach is less protective of life and health than more targeted and balanced policies would be. Real populations now at risk would receive the preference that they should be accorded as compared to hypothetical future populations. At present, EPA has largely succumbed to a variety of irrational biases in terms of how people think about risk as well as to political pressures that force it further away from a cost-effective effort for reducing risk. EPA's neglect of the existence and size of populations now exposed to risk epitomizes the gaps in analytic thinking that could be addressed through a sounder policy analysis approach.

Appendix A: Assessing Human Health Risks and Remediation Costs

This Superfund project began in late 1992 at Duke University under a U.S. EPA Cooperative Agreement. Our purpose was to study the relationship between remediation costs and human health risks at Superfund sites. To do this, we collected site-specific documents that detail both carcinogenic and noncarcinogenic health risks posed by sites as well as the measures that the EPA considered to address these hazards. We used these documents to create databases containing relevant human health risk and remediation cost information. This appendix describes the data collection and summarizes the methodologies used to assess the relationship between human health risks and remediation costs at Superfund sites.

A.1 Sample Construction

As of May 1995 the National Priorities List (NPL) contained 1,302 final or deleted sites, 1,151 of which were nonfederal sites, according to EPA's CERCLIS database. Because no central repository of detailed risk and cost information exists for NPL sites, collecting and analyzing data on all NPL sites was not feasible. Therefore, at the outset of our study, we limited our sample to nonfederal Superfund sites with Records of Decisions (RODs) signed in the years 1991 and 1992, for several reasons: Nonfederal sites are the focus of extensive debate over cleanup policies; the sample size was large enough to allow for statistical analysis, yet small enough to allow us to acquire and enter the data; and the risk assessments for these sites would more likely have used the standardized methodology as set forth in EPA's *Risk Assessment Guidance for Superfund, Volume 1* (U.S. EPA 1989a).

Using EPA's CERCLIS database, we identified all nonfederal NPL sites with RODs signed in 1991 or 1992 that were not later removed from, or in the process of being deleted from, the NPL, and which had not been moved from under the jurisdiction of Superfund to other EPA programs. This produced a list of 289 RODs at 268 sites. We later eliminated twelve RODs because the method of tracking RODs on CERCLIS results in counting certain RODs more than one time if the ROD addressed multiple operable units (OUs). One site was also dropped because neighboring sites in CERCLIS are addressed as if they were a single site for the remedial process. The final sample used in our analysis of remediation costs thus consisted of 277 RODs at 267 sites, representing 23 percent of all nonfederal NPL sites.

The risk sample is a subset of the cost sites, since the greater time requirements needed for entry of a site's detailed human health risk information prevented our analysis of all sites with risk data. Our final risk sample consisted of 150 sites, for which we have all of the quantified risk at the site. Not included in this sample were an additional 20 sites/21 RODs for which we entered risk information on part of the site but were missing portions, such as descriptions of particular operable units at a site, that are necessary to characterize the risk fully. Of the remaining 101 unentered RODs, most were omitted for reasons such as incompatibility with our methodology (e.g., the risks were not presented by pathway), missing or nonstandard baseline risk assessments, or large inconsistencies between the Baseline Risk Assessment and the ROD where the cause of errors could not be identified. The 150 sites that make up our risk sample represent 13 percent of all nonfederal NPL sites.

The data collection process led to the creation of information on human health risks, remediation alternatives and cost, potentially exposed populations, and remediation levels, all of which are discussed below. The primary sources of data for this study were Records of Decisions (RODs), Remedial Investigations (RIs), and Feasibility Studies (FSs). Each remedial cleanup action taken at a site must have a ROD signed by the regional administrator. A ROD explains the process used in making the remediation decision and summarizes the information from the more detailed RI and FS. This summary includes carcinogenic and noncarcinogenic risk pathways of concern, considered and selected remediation alternatives, and explicit chemical and medium specific cleanup levels. The RI/FS supports the ROD, providing details on the extent of contamination, the calculations used in the human health risk assessments, preliminary cleanup goals, and descriptions of remediation actions considered along with a breakdown of their associated costs. The documents were copied from master documents on file at EPA regional offices or administrative dockets, requested through the Freedom of Information Act, or were sent to us through correspondence with site Remedial Project Managers (RPMs).

Human Health Risks
The human health risk database we created characterizes the carcinogenic and noncarcinogenic risks presented in the RODs, capturing the full set of

risk parameters, pathway descriptors, and risk equations used. This level of detail was attempted in order to make it possible to generate a different set of risks through substitution of values for one or more parameter variables. The primary sources of data for the risk database are RODs and RIs. RODs detail the decision-making process for cleanup actions at Superfund sites and summarize the information on which the decision was based. RIs usually contain Baseline Risk Assessments (BLRA) which detail the extent of contamination as well as the specific equations and parameters used in the calculation of health risks. All pathways with cancer risks greater than or equal to 1×10^{-7} and noncancer risks with a hazard index of greater than or equal to 0.1 were entered to ensure the thorough capture of all potential site-related risks. These cutoffs are an order of magnitude lower than the point of departure levels established for cleanup at Superfund sites. For the chemical pathways within these exposure pathways, we entered the chemical level information for cancer and noncancer risks when the risks were greater than or equal to 1×10^{-8} and 0.01, respectively. This sample provided us with over 20,000 chemical level risk observations.

For each chemical level exposure pathway, we collected all relevant data describing the population exposed, the mechanism/type of exposure, and the parameters used in calculating the risk. For the modeled biota and air pathways, we attempted to collect any additional parameters and equations used in the models. Additional data entered included type of exposure point concentration, proxy value for nondetections, and the risk level for any sensitivity analysis conducted in the BLRA.

Remediation Alternatives and Costs

Remediation alternative cost information was taken from the ROD. More detailed figures, such as indirect capital costs and the annual operation and maintenance (O&M) outlays, were usually entered from the detailed cost tables of the FS. If detailed FS costs did not agree with ROD costs, then only those in the ROD were used. We decided that media costs could be successfully collected so long as detailed cost tables were available or an alternative addressed only one medium (i.e., groundwater or soil). All cost figures collected at the alternative level were collected at the media level. Some costs, such as caps or site setup costs, were difficult to identify as soil or groundwater. These costs were coded separately and divided between soil and groundwater during the analysis.

For 14 "no-action" RODs, costs were unavailable, and they were assumed to be 0 as implied in the ROD. A total of 16 percent of our cost observations came from sites where detailed costs tables were not available to facilitate a breakdown of costs by media. For these observations, the division of costs between media was estimated on the basis of the specific types of alternatives considered. Present-value costs were recalculated at all sites using a common set of conditions. When the base year was given for the cost figures, all costs were recalculated to 1993 dollars on the basis of GDP deflators. This information was available for only 31 RODs. For 219 RODs the base year was assumed to be the year that the FS was published. For the remaining 13 RODs no FS was available and the base year was assumed to be the year that the ROD was issued. Present values were recalculated for all RODs at 7 percent, since current EPA directives require that Superfund cost estimates employ a 7 percent discount rate.[1]

Potentially Exposed Populations

To identify populations exposed to hazardous waste, we developed a geographic information systems (GIS) laboratory to overlay and relate spatial data, which allows us to relate areas of Superfund risk with census data to determine potentially exposed populations. Two databases, one containing potentially exposed populations to soil risks and the other containing exposed populations to groundwater risks, were created. For soil risks it was decided to use proximity measures to define persons who are potentially exposed. Rather than choose a single distance from the site, we decided to determine populations living within eight rings, each a given distance from the site boundary. The probability that a person would come on the site was used to determine a fraction of the population in each ring who would be exposed to contamination. The risk to the fraction of the persons in each ring considered exposed was determined with the use of dilution factors (discussed below). For groundwater risks, it was possible to measure directly the exposed population by determining the number of well users living atop areas of aquifer contamination.

Census files provided the population and demographic information necessary for the analysis. PL 94-171 data provided total population, total households, and population by race figures for the 6,961,148 blocks and 226,337 block groups that comprise the United States. 1990 TIGER files (which stands for Topologically Integrated Geographic Encoding and Reference) from the Census Bureau provided a geographic reference to the PL 94-171 block-level data and the STF-3A block group level data. With the TIGER data we created coverages (maps) that delineate the boundaries of census blocks and block groups. All TIGER data were converted to ARC/INFO format on a county by county basis for the entire United States. Coverages were created at the state level for block groups; block coverages were saved at the county level.

Site boundary maps for 1,202 federal and nonfederal Superfund sites were provided by the EPA in ARC/INFO format and served as the basis for determining proximity to sites. Twenty-nine sites were excluded from analysis because of incomplete or missing boundary or census information. Using EPA's CERCLIS database we determined that our remaining sample of 1,173 sites included 96 percent of the 1,224 sites listed on the NPL from the inception of CERCLA to February 11, 1991. Sites listed after this date were not included in our analysis.

Site specific GIS coverages defining the extent of groundwater contamination were created on the basis of maps and figures from site documentation. Data were usually available in the RI, but other sources included RODs and groundwater monitoring reports. Multiple "plumes" are possible at any given site, due in part to noncontiguous areas of contamination and also due to the availability of chemical specific plumes for many sites. A total of 153 "plume maps" detailing contamination at 74 sites were entered.

To calculate potential soil exposures, we used GIS to create rings of a given distance from each Superfund site, at $\frac{1}{4}$, $\frac{1}{2}$, $\frac{3}{4}$, 1, 2, 3, and 4 miles from the boundary of each site. Each ring was then linked to either blocks or block groups by "intersecting" the ring with the appropriate census coverage. For most purposes we used a block-level analysis, where a given ring was intersected with a block coverage. All blocks and portions of blocks that fell within the ring were retained for analysis, and blocks that fell outside of the ring were deleted.

Ring-specific data from the GIS analysis allowed us to examine the population figures attached to each block. While the population for blocks that were entirely captured by the ring was known, the population for partial blocks had to be estimated. It was assumed that the residents of each partial block were spread evenly across the block; thus the population for the area of the block within the ring was determined by multiplying the population of the block times the percentage of the block area that fell within the ring. The population residing in each ring was then calculated by summing the populations in the full and partial blocks. For the 1,193 NPL site sample the database is based on a block group analysis. A separate database was created for the 267 sites in the cost sample (which includes all 150 risk sample sites) and is based on a block-level GIS analysis. Both databases contain total population by ring as well as racial breakdowns and sample data.

The determination of populations exposed to groundwater contamination was considerably more complicated than the method for determining populations exposed to soil contamination. Since groundwater contamination usually flows in a specific direction and for a given distance that varies considerably among sites, a proximity-based methodology (like that for soil) that treats all directions equally is undesirable. Instead, we collected actual plume data and then determined exposed populations using GIS and census data. At sites with more than one plume the plumes were combined to create a total area of groundwater contamination.

Contamination data from sites with complete information were used to fill in holes at the other risk sample sites that did not. Data from 74 sites in the total and partial risk samples with GIS plumes were used to generate a mean plume size. The mean plume size was then applied to the nonplume sites as a fraction of the area of each ring that would be contaminated by the average plume. While most plumes migrate from a site in a single direction, no attempt to assign direction was made when applying the average plume to the 73 sites in the 150-site risk sample lacking plume data. Populations living within the ring were assumed to be evenly distributed throughout the ring, and the fraction of the population living over the contaminated area then served as the potentially exposed population. The total number of persons exposed to groundwater combined this fraction with the fraction of households in each ring which are not connected to a municipal water supply.

Groundwater plumes can change in size and shape over time depending on local conditions. While other analyses of groundwater contamination have assumed that all groundwater plumes continue to grow over time, empirical evidence has led us to believe that this assumption may not be justified. If contaminated groundwater discharges to the surface water, as it does at many sites in our sample, longitudinal growth of the plume is not likely. Contamination of the surface water itself is a possibility in this situation, but dilution may make this contamination insignificant. At many of our sites it was explicitly noted in the RI documentation that systematic declines in contaminant concentrations were noted between groundwater sampling events. At some sites this decline was so pronounced that "natural attenuation" was selected as the groundwater remedy. In light of this evidence, we concluded that an assumption of universal plume growth is not valid. Rather than attempting to predict which plumes will grow and which will shrink, we assumed that all plumes remain constant in size over the thirty-year time frame we use for our estimation.

Groundwater contamination threats to municipal water supplies are present at several NPL sites. However, given the stringent testing requirements that originally brought the contamination to light, it is unlikely that the consumers of the municipal water face any risk from contamination. By law all municipal water companies that serve more than 25 persons must routinely test the quality of the water. If contamination is detected, then action is required by law to protect the quality of the water supply. For this reason all persons connected to municipal water supplies are considered safe from Superfund site related groundwater risks in this analysis.

Remediation Levels

That remediation levels or cleanup standards be met at any Superfund site where the chosen remedy does not remove all contamination is one of the nine criteria for remedy selection specified by SARA in 1986. Remediation levels chosen at a site must fulfill the criteria for applicable or relevant and appropriate (ARAR) standards. These ARARs cover any contaminated media that is to be remediated. For groundwater there are specific federal regulations as part of the Clean Water Act that set maximum contamination limits (MCLs) for chemicals found in drinking water. Remedies at a site must meet federal MCLs or any state regulations that are stricter. For other contaminated media, such as soil or sediment, there are generally no federally mandated levels. Cleanup goals for soil may come from state laws or may emerge from site-level analyses based on potential exposures.

We attempted to collect and classify remediation levels for all 150 sites in our risk sample. Remediation levels are typically found in a section in the ROD or may be present in other site documents, such as the remedial design (RD). Levels were found for 96 groundwater remediation sites and 63 soil remediation sites. Levels were not present for the remaining RODs either because the no-action alternative was chosen, cleanup levels were to be included in a later document, or the levels were not discussed quantitatively. All remediation levels presented at a site were entered, regardless of whether the concentration was binding (i.e., smaller than the exposure concentrations for that site entered in the risk database).

Each remediation level was assigned to a consolidated medium, either groundwater (groundwater, surface water) or soil (made up of soil, sediment, sludge). The "basis" was grouped into three groups: federal, if it involved federal ARARs such as MCLs or EPA directives; state, if it involved state ARARs; or site, if a risk level or modeled concentrations, since they tend to vary from site to site. Once classified, remediation observations were matched with risk data at the chemical level.

Quality Assurance and Quality Control
Quality assurance and quality control (QA/QC) were a top priority in creation of the risk and cost databases. We briefly describe here our quality control efforts.

Since we collected all relevant data used in deriving risk estimates in order to recalculate the chronic daily intake and the final risk values, we were able to check the accuracy of our data by recalculating risk and comparing our risk numbers against numbers listed in the documents at the chemical and pathway level. Errors and discrepancies were usually not entry problems, but differences in rounding methods, internal errors between tables and text, or mistakes in the BLRA's calculation of risks. For problems that could not be corrected, we turned to EPA officials to determine if updates or other data not available to us accounted for the differences, or coded observations to describe the reason for differences between our calculation of risk and that in the BLRA when they could be supported by documentation. For the mean and Monte Carlo analyses, the set of unresolved errors and the set of incorrectly recalculating observations were dropped so that they would not adversely affect the accuracy of the results. In all other analyses, BLRA pathway risks were generally taken at face value.

Three different types of quality control checks were performed on the Superfund site boundary data. Our first verification entailed comparing the CERCLIS identification number that serves as the coverage name for each site in our block-group data against the CERCLIS number for the boundary data associated with each site provided by the EPA. A second check sought to confirm the validity of each CERCLIS number against EPA's CERCLIS database. The final quality check was to verify that each site coverage was located in the correct county, as defined by EPA's

RELAI (also known as the Remedial Project Managers Site) database and other agency information. Three sites in the cost sample were misplaced and the coverages were properly positioned on the basis of site documents. Four other sites did not have coverages among the 1,202 originally provided by EPA. Coverages for these sites were created using ArcEdit and site maps.

Quality checks were performed on our TIGER, STF-3A, and PL 94-171 databases after they were created to verify their accuracy. This involved checking for incorrectly labeled block groups and checking fields used for analysis for internal consistency. The few discrepancies detected were tracked back to the original data and corrected by instructions provided by the Census Bureau. Population counts for block groups were produced using the PL 94-171 data and compared to the STF-3A data as a further quality check of both databases.

Visual checks were used to verify the plume coverages against the source material from which they were created. A more likely source of error pertains to the actual plume data presented in the site documentation. Only a small fraction of the groundwater contaminants presented at the 150 risk sites are represented by plumes in our data. The lack of site-specific plume data at about half of the risk sample sites was also a concern. To address this issue, we collected additional information on these sites without plumes. While most of these sites had no or very limited groundwater contamination, some nonplume sites potentially had sizable plumes contaminating residential wells. Overall, we had plume data for 69 of the 142 sites with groundwater cancer risks. For the 73 sites in our risk sample lacking plume data we assumed each site had a mean area of contaminated groundwater equivalent to the "average" plume size for the 74 sites we had with plume data. This assumption has an additional conservative aspect because this "average" plume is actually four times the size of the median plume and ranks in the 77th percentile for plume size at the 74 plume sites. The 74 sites used to develop a plume average included 69 sites in our final risk sample of 150 sites.

One potential source of error for block analyses comes from the assumption of proportionality, or constant population density, for the "partial" blocks. For rings of less than one mile, most of the data used came from partial blocks. Most sites did not achieve a single full block for the on-site study area. The magnitude of block-level error, fortunately, was relatively small. Concern about partial blocks may be reduced in urban areas, since the areas under scrutiny are very small. Estimates may be more difficult in rural areas where blocks sometimes are several square miles in area.

A second possible source for error was that the detailed census sample data on education and income were only available at the block-group level and that the assumption was made that these sample data were representative of each of the blocks on which they were based. This is a strong assumption, which means the accuracy of sample data that accompany populations for a block-level analysis is decreased. The population and race data, which were at the block level, were not affected by this issue. Note that the census figures used in our analysis have not been fully corrected for underreporting, which is an error associated with census data. The level of underreporting may differ significantly by race, so that estimates of exposed minority populations are likely to under-report the number of exposed individuals.

A.2   Analysis Methodologies

Risk

For our analysis, we refer to two distinct risk databases: the baseline risk assessment (BLRA) data and the standardized risk data. The BLRA information is taken directly from site documents and is, verbatim, the risk data that were available to EPA officials at the time the remediation decisions were made. Thus it is the most appropriate risk information to use when evaluating which factors may have played the most significant role in remediation decisions. The BLRA risk database was also used to examine the effect of using Monte Carlo risk simulations to estimate the sensitivity of the risks that formed the basis of the remedial decision. The second risk database is standardized risk, used to determine estimated cancer cases.

Baseline Human Health Risks   In chapter 2 we analyze the pathway specific risks estimated in EPA site documents. To aggregate these risks and determine the individual risk levels faced by particular populations, we created a "cumulative risk" scenario to assess the cumulative risk possible from all media and routes present at the site. The distribution of sites by risk level is based on the level of the cumulative risk to the potentially exposed individual or population (e.g., current on-site resident adult over 18 years of age) who face the largest risk per site. This maxi-mum cumulative risk based on the BLRA pathways is not equivalent to the maximum individual pathway risk from the baseline risk assessment because at many sites individuals/populations could be exposed additively via a combination of routes.

Several steps were necessary to manipulate and simplify the risk data so that risk could be aggregated to a population. First, we developed a matrix of 24 potentially exposed populations for the following combinations: (Resident/Worker/Other) × (Adult/Child) × (On-site/Off-site) × (Current/Future). The "other" category included trespassers, hunters, recreators, visitors, and any other type of exposed individual from the baseline risk assessment. Since many risk assessments evaluated the carcinogenic risk to children as part of a time-weighted individual's lifetime risk, it was necessary to split the "child" portion of the pathway apart from the "adult" portion.

Second, to classify the media and route codes into a more manageable set of pathway mechanisms, we grouped the dozens of specific media codes into a final set of three categories: soil, groundwater, and biota. Thus there were seven potential pathways by which an individual could be exposed: (Soil/Groundwater) × (Ingestion/Dermal/Inhalation) plus biota ingestion. To develop the cumulative risk to an individual, we then summed the set of unique pathways (out of seven potential) to each of the 24 possible individuals at a site.

We acknowledge that for many sites, the definition of site areas, the nature of exposed individuals, or the professional judgment of the RPM in each instance might preclude the aggregation of pathways in the above manner. However, aggregation of, for example, residential groundwater ingestion risks with soil risks is appropriate at the majority of sites where a resident could conceivably be exposed to multiple contaminants via multiple routes. Thus the cumulative risk scenario represents a conservative bounding scenario appropriate as a starting point for the Monte Carlo analysis, and it presents a useful model for evaluating the end result of changing risk assessment assumptions.

It is difficult to summarize noncancer risks through a single indicator number. The magnitude of a hazard quotient is not a measure of probability, nor does the relative size of a hazard quotient exceeding one have any predictive power. Furthermore, since different chemicals have different toxic effects, and exposure via different routes may affect the body differently, chemical level hazard quotients are rarely aggregated. Nevertheless, we were interested in the relationship between cancer risks and noncancer risks at a site—were the sites with high cancer risks more likely to also have high noncancer risks? In an attempt to identify the role of noncancer risks in remediation decisions, we plotted the distribution of cancer risk levels at all sites where one or more chemical pathways reached or exceeded the threshold hazard quotient of one, five, and ten. All chemical and pathway level data on noncarcinogens were retained from the BLRA database for use in deriving standardized risk pathways for noncarcinogens as well. This allowed us to estimate the magnitude of populations exposed to sites with, for example, a chemical pathway with a hazard quotient greater than one.

The baseline risk data formed the basis for the analysis of individual cancer risk levels in chapters 2 and 3. The assessments of the impact of substitution of mean parameters and the comparison of EPA's reasonable maximum exposure scenarios to Monte Carlo simulations of risk distribution all draw upon these risk data as reported in EPA site-level documents.

Standardized Risk   Although the baseline risk database contains full information on all pathways evaluated in site documents that exceeded the EPA threshold of concern for carcinogenic and noncarcinogenic effects, we found it necessary to create a database of "standardized" risk to estimate expected cancer incidence among populations living near our sample sites. The standardized risk was based directly on the BLRA risk pathway exposure levels but was calculated by running the chemical concentrations at a site through a set of standardized exposure pathways to minimize the effect of differing styles and methodologies used by risk assessors at different sites.

Data generated through the risk assessment process concerning the carcinogenic and noncarcinogenic risks to potential human receptors, as well as any sensitive local ecological areas, play an important role in the risk manager's decision concerning the appropriate action to take at the site. Risk assessments generally do not, however, make quantitative estimates of the numbers of individuals living near a site who are likely to be exposed to these relevant risks; nor do they use risk levels predictively to derive estimates of the cancers expected to develop due to exposure. This is because the risk assessment phase of the site process has traditionally been cost-blind as a matter of policy, and risk assessors were directed to identify the pathways to a reasonable maximally exposed individual. Such individuals might or might not be very numerous around a given site, under existing or hypothetical land use scenarios.

Despite highly developed federal and regional guidelines on performing Superfund risk assessments, the uncertainty currently inherent in health risk assessment has led to considerable variation in how various regional and local EPA officials, as well as potentially responsible parties (PRPs), interpret these guidelines. For example, some risk assessors evaluated a set of indicator pathways for representative age groups, using only the most reliable models (i.e., ingestion). Once they determined that risks from this given media via a given route reached levels of concern (i.e., 1×10^{-4}), they did not thoroughly research other potential pathways, particularly if lower risks were expected. Others attempted to evaluate all potential routes and receptors under various land use alternatives, often incorporating models that were subject to greater uncertainty than the basic ingestion models. In addition some risk assessors divided their "lifetime receptor" into age groups that were inconsistent with the "child" and "adult" receptor populations at other sites. For our purposes of deriving a consistent estimate of population risk, a comprehensive estimate of all the pathways by which a given population may come into contact with site contaminants—not just the principal, most likely, or most accurate—was necessary.

Another factor that highlighted the need to standardize risk before making intersite risk comparisons was the continuously improving data on chemical toxicity. Risk assessments performed earlier may have toxicities different than those used for the same chemicals in later assessments. For these reasons, and others, we developed a more standardized methodology for comparing risks across sites by deriving a database of receptor point, medium-specific chemical contaminant concentrations based on the concentrations used in the risk pathways from the risk assessments. In addition we derived a chemical toxicity database based on the most recent and accurate toxic data from EPA's Integrated Risk Information System (IRIS) or, in the absence of these data, the most commonly used toxicities for each chemical in our sample. We then applied several standardized risk pathway scenarios to these sites in order to characterize the population risks.

The reference doses and cancer slope factors used for the standardized risk database were derived, for each ingestion, inhalation, or dermal route, by their highest frequency of use per site within our existing sample. These toxicities were then checked against IRIS, and corrected with more recent information. In a few cases chemicals with interim toxicities sometimes used in risk assessments which had been later classified by the EPA as Class D carcinogens ("Not classifiable as to human carcinogenicity (inadequate or no evidence)") in EPA's *Health Effects Assessments, Summary Tables, FY 1994* (U.S. EPA, 1994), were dropped from the analysis. Dermal permeability constants (for groundwater) and absorption factors (for soil) were also derived based on the frequency of use in risk assessments. The adherence factor used for the soil dermal pathways was derived from the mean value present in a survey of the dermal pathway literature. For pathways involving volatilization of chemicals in the shower, we classified chemicals as to their "type" (i.e., volatile organic compounds [VOCs], semivolatile organic compounds [SVOCs], or inorganics) based on vapor pressure, frequency of appearance in the risk assessment documents, and classification according to other site and EPA documents. We then only included VOCs in the calculation of risks from shower inhalation.

The concentrations of contaminants in each medium at a given site were derived directly from the baseline risk assessment pathways for use in standardized risk. First, we classified the various specific media into categories of "soil" or "groundwater." A concentration was derived for each chemical present in either or both of these media, assuming at least one pathway for that chemical in the risk assessment met our risk-level entry cutoffs of 1×10^{-8} for carcinogens and 0.01 for noncarcinogens. Since many (about a third) of the risk assessments defined concentrations for multiple areas and media on-site as well as distinguishing between on-site and off-site contamination, we took a mean, a minimum, and a maximum of the on-site exposure concentrations used, as well as the mean, the minimum, and the maximum of the average concentrations in each medium (if they were given). Each unique sample concentration was weighted equally in determining this mean, so no area of the site is counted more heavily than another. This results in extremely high exposure concentrations at a few sites where pathways were evaluated for "hot spots" at the sites.

In EPA risk assessments as well as in debates over Superfund cleanups, residential risks often drive policy choice and remediation. The vast majority of risk assessments evaluate some type of potential exposure to on-site or off-site residents, typically groundwater ingestion by on-site residents (current or future) or soil ingestion. At more than half of the sites, however, exposure to residents via the inhalation and/or dermal pathways is not evaluated. The lack of these pathways is not necessarily due to the assumption that they do not exist but that the models for risk via these routes are subject to much greater uncertainty. To avoid underestimating population risks, we developed an inhalation, dermal, and an ingestion pathway for each medium (soil and groundwater). Therefore at any site where both soil and groundwater contamination are present, we evaluated six pathways for each resident: for soil, inhalation of dust, incidental outdoor ingestion, and dermal contact while outdoors; for groundwater, drinking water ingestion, shower VOC inhalation, and shower dermal exposure.

In order to calculate the annual risks over the time period of our analysis to the populations in various age groups for which we have census data, we classified receptor populations either into six child age groups of three year duration each, or as an over-18 adult. Pathway parameter values for each age group were based on EPA references or other sources. For ingestion and inhalation intake rate, we used Monte Carlo means and 95 percent UCLs based on our survey of the literature on intake rate, evaluated in conjunction with mean body weight. For dermal exposure, we used the mean and 95 percent UCL for surface areas in conjunction with reasonable percentages of skin exposed to soil. Exposure frequency was held at 350 days/year, the standard residential frequency used in EPA risk assessments. The Respirable Particulate Fraction dust model most frequently referred to from a survey of sites was used to generate a rough estimate of dust loads in on-site air, with the contaminant fraction of the dust in direct proportion to that present in soil. Groundwater VOC inhalation was based on the Andelman shower model, conservatively assuming a 75 percent volatilization rate in the shower, as well as average values for shower size, shower duration, and time in the shower room. These values were then inserted into the basic equations for determining LECR (Lifetime Excess Cancer Risk) found in EPA's 1989 *Risk Assessment Guidance for Superfund, Volume 1* (U.S. EPA 1989).

By combining these standardized pathways with our chemical concentration database and with the chemical-specific toxicities and constants for each route, we generated a database for our sample of 150 risk sites which contained, for each chemical, annual carcinogenic risk probabilities as well as annual hazard index figures. For each unique route-specific chemical risk in seven age groups, we generated a set of risk numbers for several scenarios, ranging from a reasonable scenario using mean concentrations and parameter values to an upper-bound plausible scenario using maximum concentration and upperbound parameter values.

Since the concentrations used to derive the pathway risks in the standardized database are the same as those used in the baseline risk assessments, the relative positions of sites in the sample ranked according to maximum risk pathways are roughly equivalent in both databases, once standardized risk is converted from annual risk to lifetime exposures. However, the standardization and creation of comprehensive risk across the sample did result in some shifts in relative risk between the two risk databases. One reason why standardized risk differs slightly from baseline risk results from all areas defined in the baseline risk assessments being weighted equally in deriving exposure point means. The evaluation of pathways specific "hot spots" at a small number of sites resulted in elevated standardized risk at some of those sites.

The standardized risk database is not used here to estimate the number of cancers expected among site workers, due to our concerns about the differing quality of estimates of worker populations, and because worker safety generally falls under the jurisdiction of other federal programs. However, our initial analysis of parameter distributions and risks demonstrated that risks to on-site and off-site workers are often substantial, responsible for the maximum pathway risk at several sites. Since the majority of sites are inactive or purely industrial or commercial in land use, workers are a more probable potentially exposed population than residents. If the cost per estimated cancer averted is intended as a benchmark of whether more expensive remedial alternatives are worthwhile at sites, neglecting to include on-site worker risks—or the risks to remediation workers which would result from remedial activities—could significantly influence conclusions about whether the benefits of cleanup outweigh the costs.

Estimating Cancer Cases: Combining Population Estimates with Standardized Risk Data

GIS block-level population data were combined with the carcinogenic risk probabilities to generate estimates of the number of cancers likely to arise from a given site. The time frame of the exposure duration was set at thirty years because it represented the block of time generally accepted by risk assessors as "current"; it corresponded to the time frame for most cost projections, and it minimized uncertainty regarding future land uses and changes in policy. The basic formula for estimating the number of cancers expected in any given year near a Superfund site is as follows:

$$ECR \times \text{Population} = \text{Expected cancers}, \tag{A.1}$$

where the ECR is the annual excess cancer risk, or probability of cancer resulting from a one-year exposure duration, and the population is the number of people exposed via the given contaminant pathway.

For the sake of simplicity, we considered three standardized risk scenarios: Case 1, as the base case for comparison to EPA risk models, used the 95th upper confidence level (UCL) exposure parameters with the chemical's reasonable maximum exposure (RME) concentration (the 95th UCL of the mean detected concentration or the maximum concentration, whichever is less). Case 2 also used the 95th UCL parameters with the mean exposure concentration to derive ECR, but only for the subset of sites where mean contaminant concentrations had been given for all contaminated media. Case 3 used mean parameters and mean contaminant concentrations from the Case 2 sample sites to predict a "mean" risk applicable to a population. The basic formula for expected cancers above was also modified as described below to account for the different mechanisms affecting exposure to soil and groundwater, in the areas on-site and in the off-site rings out to four miles.

To refine our estimate of on-site populations in the risk sample of 150 sites, we combined EPA RELAI data with GIS block data. If RELAI listed any on-site land use except "industrial" or "other," the on-site land use was assumed to be residential, and census block populations were distributed evenly throughout the rings defined for each site. However, if RELAI listed no use for the site other than "industrial" or "other," this was assumed to preclude residential use, and census block population figures were redistributed evenly throughout the rings excluding the on-site land area. Only eighteen of the 150 risk sample sites were listed in RELAI as having residential use. Note that at 9 of the sites where the BLRA listed current on-site residential risks, RELAI listed only industrial or other uses.

To estimate the proportion of the on-site risk likely to affect populations living in each ring around the site, we developed separate exposure assumptions for soil and groundwater outlined below.

Soil dilution factors were developed according to methodologies outlined by EPA's Office of Emergency and Remedial Response for use in the 1990 Hazard Ranking System to estimate the probability that individuals in nearby populations would come on-site and thereby be exposed to on-site contamination (U.S. EPA 1990c). This probability is assumed to decline over a one-mile radius, and individuals living beyond this radius are assumed to have a negligible probability of visiting the site. Separate dilution factors were developed for inhalation of dust versus ingestion and dermal contact with soil. Dilution factors for the air pathway were estimated using the Industrial Source Long-Term (ISLT) air transport model (U.S. EPA 1990c). The model combines conservative assumptions from the 1990 HRS with the least conservative wind stability class to generate distance-dependent dilution factors. These ring dilution factors were then multiplied times the basic formula for expected cancers to approximate the number of expected cancers in a given ring.

Our GIS data permitted us to use maps to form a reliable estimate of the number of people living directly above groundwater plumes at 69 of our risk sample sites. As noted above, exposed populations for the remainder of the sites were determined based on a plume of average size. Thus the formula for determining expected cancers due to groundwater exposure is

Population exposed $\times$ ECR = Expected cancers.   (A.2)

"Population exposed" is the number of people living above the plume area not connected to municipal water supply according to 1990 Census data. The smallest level of detail of each observation was the annual expected rate of cancer from one chemical to one individual in one of seven age groups via one medium and route combination. We linearly aggregated these annual cancer counts to form population estimates of, for example, the number of cancers expected to develop over thirty years among adults in the on-site ring.

Our analysis assumes a time horizon of thirty years, where current land use at any site, as well as population growth trends based on the 1980 to 1990 census figures, were assumed to remain constant. While it is inappropriate to assume that land use will remain constant beyond thirty years, it seems appropriate to use current land use as a predictive indicator for a thirty-year period, the time horizon of many cost alternatives as well as the most common exposure duration of adult current risk pathways. Another possible method would take changes in land use into effect by modeling the likelihood that land use at the site will change over time.

A potential flaw in calculating annual cancer risks, multiplying by annual population estimates, and then aggregating over several years is that for very high risks, the linear low-dose cancer risk equation cannot be used. Aggregated cancer risk could exceed one, and the number of cancers predicted over thirty years may be higher than the exposed population in any given year. While this was only a potential problem at a few sites, we made the following adjustments: For risks greater than 1 in 10, the one-hit equation $\text{LECR} = 1 - \exp(-\text{cdi} * \text{tox}))$ was used for all annual risks (where cdi = chronic daily intake and tox = slope factor); any aggregated annual risks to an individual via multiple routes and chemicals that exceeded one were set equal to one; it was assumed that at any time over the thirty years in which a cancer case developed, the affected "person" was replaced in the population by a new individual with zero initial exposure.

To account for population growth each year we used information on the change in U.S. population in the counties where Superfund sites were located over the period 1980 to 1990. Therefore the formula for the number of expected cancers in any given year is

$$\text{Expected cancers} \ (year = n) = \text{Annual ECR} \times \text{Pop } n. \tag{A.3}$$

The above scenario assumes that each cancer predicted by the standardized risk scenarios appears in the initial year of exposure. This is not necessarily the case, since the formula for predicting cancer risk gives a probability of developing cancer over a seventy-year lifetime. In actual cases of exposure to contaminants on which these models are based, there is often a latency period before cancers related to given chemical exposures develop. Latency periods are not well understood and are rarely predictable, vary from chemical to chemical, and may depend on the magnitude of exposure. Therefore we developed two different latency scenarios, a base rate latency of 0 years and a 10 years period assuming that there would be a ten-year gap between exposure to a chemical and development of cancer for all age groups and exposed populations. For the purposes of relating expected cancers to the costs expended for their prevention and the higher value the public places on averting immediate risks over future ones, we also developed a scenario that combined the ten-year cancer latency with a discount rate of 3 percent and mean parameters and exposure concentrations. We then examined the effect of discounting on expected cancer counts over the thirty-year time horizon of our model.

Note that our calculations focus on chemical concentrations after sites may have already experienced removal actions. The EPA's removal program is designed as a short-term response to address immediate threats to public health at a site, while the long-term remedial response program aims to remove remaining contamination. Our study focuses only on the remedial program because these actions have historically engendered more controversy due to the higher costs, protracted cleanup periods, and litigation and because the detailed risk and cost data collected for this study are not available for the removal program. Neither the risk nor the cost database addresses removal actions. However, excluding removal information could in some cases result in an incomplete or inaccurate picture of the relationship of costs to risks, since removals that took place following the RI/FS sampling may have reduced the actual risks and costs.

Equity Analyses

The data in chapter 7 show that minorities constitute a disproportionate percentage of the populations living within four miles of NPL sites. For some minority groups, particularly Asians, and Hispanics, the probability of an individual living within four miles of a site was markedly elevated. At the same time the majority of sites are surrounded by white populations in concentrations higher than their nationwide percentage. These seemingly contradictory conclusions can be reconciled based on our finding that the highest population sites have a disproportionate number of minority residents within four miles. These findings are not surprising in that they are consistent with the distribution of demographic groups in the U.S. population with the most densely populated areas containing the largest percentage of minorities.

Having established that minorities are more likely to live proximate to Superfund sites, we then took the next step to investigate why. Two immediate possibilities deserve attention. The first is that given a significantly large area, sites are more likely to be located in the part of that area that has more minorities. Our data suggest that the trend of declining minority population percentages as one moves further from a site visible in the ring data out to four miles does not continue to the ten mile ring. For most of the sites the minority percentage of the population is greater for the ten-mile ring than it is for the four-mile ring. Further analysis is needed to study the possibility that Superfund sites may lie within sub-areas of more minorities.

A second possibility is that sites are more likely to be located in densely populated areas, and thus potentially expose large numbers of minorities due to the urban nature of both Superfund sites and minority populations. This urban explanation can potentially be examined by comparing the density distribution of block groups in the United States with NPL sites against block groups that do not host NPL sites. Findings were not consistent with the hypothesis that a disproportionate number of urban NPL sites accounts for the disproportionate number of minorities exposed. The mean density for block groups with NPL sites is actually lower than the mean density of block groups without NPL sites.

The distribution of the total number of expected cancer cases makes it difficult to draw conclusions about the demographic breakdown of those cancers. Results show that a disproportionate percentage (43 percent) of the potential cancers affect minorities. Yet when the Westinghouse site is removed from the analysis, the results shift (16 percent of expected cancers are among minority groups). The distribution of risks across the 150 sites used in the analysis presents the same problem as does the distribution of cancers, though to a slightly lesser degree. Risks vary across six orders of magnitude so that the risks at the highest risk sites are 1,000,000 times greater than risks at the lowest risk site. There are also several different measures of risk available for analysis. The measures most used in the text involve the maximum cumulative carcinogenic risk that any population is exposed to according to the EPA site risk assessment. A maximum hazard quotient is a measure of noncarcinogenic risk that can also be considered. Noncarcinogenic risk is higher at the sites with the highest population density level and highest minority composition, consistent with findings for carcinogenic risk.

One potential error when addressing the issue of cumulative populations near NPL sites involves double counting populations. If the study area involves a four-mile ring around all NPL sites, then special attention must be given to those populations within four miles of two or more sites. One method to resolve this problem is to create a single study area that is the union of all four-mile rings. Though the ability to perform a site-specific analysis is lost, the cumulative population will be correct. If double counting is present, then the total population within four miles of the 1,193 sites analyzed is 84 million. The correct figure, reported in chapter 7, is 51 million.

Cost

Costs were analyzed at three different levels: alternative, ROD, and site. The alternative level was useful to examine the costs of technologies selected as compared to the costs of technologies that were considered but ultimately dismissed. There are approximately 1,750 cost observations at the alternative level. The ROD level takes only those alternatives selected. At sites where more than one alternative is selected (often because one alternative addresses groundwater while the other addresses soil contamination), these costs are summed to arrive at the ROD cost. One observation is available for each ROD at this level, so the total is 277. Costs for all site RODs are combined at the site level for a total of 267 site-level cost observations.

The only difficulty in bringing the alternative level data to the ROD level involves determining which alternatives were selected in the ROD. For fifteen RODs this determination was problematic because a final decision between two very similar alternatives (or separately costed options within an alternative) was not made. In these cases a mean cost between the two contending alternatives was used. The site cost is the sum of the cost of all RODs—those before our sample, those in our sample, and those presumed to occur after our sample. A cost growth figure is also needed for some analysis to adjust estimated costs to actual costs. Two-thirds of the necessary RODs, those from our sample period and prior to our sample period, were immediately available. Costs for future RODs, however, had to be estimated.

Using data from site documentation, a total of 109 RODs were anticipated at 91 sites after 1992 for sites in our sample. Further investigation showed that these RODs would involve 66 soil actions and 78 groundwater actions. These figures were verified by the CERCLIS and RELAI databases. Average costs were determined for future soil actions and future groundwater actions on the basis of RODs in our sample. With these data, we applied the average cost to each future ROD (for both soil and groundwater) to arrive at a total cost for future RODs at each site. The average cost applied to the future RODs was based on an analysis of 93 sample RODs that were not the first ROD for a site. This selection was performed to recognize the fact that all future RODs are at least the second ROD in a site's remedial process and our analyses show that the first ROD performed at a site is significantly cheaper than later RODs.

Data necessary to address the final issue, cost growth, were taken from an EPA database called RATRENDS. A total of 208 RODs dating from 1982 to 1992 are listed in the database, each with the ROD estimate of capital costs and final capital cost expenditures. The mean growth between ROD estimated costs and actual costs was 133 percent for the raw data. We began our analysis by adjusting all costs to 1993 dollars. With this adjustment the mean growth factor declined to 109 percent (median = 33 percent). A strong negative correlation was found between capital cost and cost growth, so four cost growth factors were produced for four different ranges of capital costs ($0 to $99,999, $100,000 to $999,999, $1,000,000 to $9,999,999, and $10 million or more). Because no data about operation and maintenance (O&M) growth were available, we assumed that O&M growth was equal to capital cost growth.

Cost growth was thus applied on a site by site basis for all sample and presample RODs. The growth that resulted for sample RODs was 42 percent, while for presample RODs the cumulative effect was 29 percent. Future RODs were grown by a default 50 percent (a figure chosen to represent the uncertainty of future growth yet remain close to what current growth data suggest). The total growth at the site level was 42 percent, bringing the mean site cost from $18.2 to $25.8 million. This final site cost estimate is comparable to those of other studies of Superfund site costs done by both the Congressional Budget Office in 1994 ($24.5 million) and by Russell et al. in 1991 ($30.9 million).

Appendix B: Sample Description

Our research focuses on data from all nonfederal Superfund sites where Records of Decisions (RODs) were signed in 1991 and 1992. Since estimated remedy costs were available at each site, the analyses of remedy selection costs and simulation of site costs under different policy alternatives are based on data from the 277 RODs signed at the 267 nonfederal sites in 1991 and 1992. The risk analysis proceeds from a sample of 160 RODS signed at 150 sites from the larger pool of 267 sites where RODs were signed during this time period. A subset of sites was chosen for the risk analysis because of the cost of assembling the data and incomplete risk assessments at some sites. This appendix compares the full nonfederal NPL sites to both the cost sample and risk sample. The analysis reveals that the 1991 and 1992 sites analyzed are similar to the rest of the sites on the NPL in terms of regional site distribution and factors associated with cleanup costs and factors associated with hazards to human health.

Assessing how comparable the sites in our analysis are to other nonfederal sites on the NPL might first appear problematic, for if we had easily available information on risks and costs on all NPL sites we would work with a census rather than a sample of the sites. Fortunately, two EPA databases provide information on the full NPL that allow us to compare some characteristics across samples of sites. RELAI (also known as the Remedial Project Managers Site Database) is a database derived from a 1993 survey of remedial project managers in the summer of 1993 that asked EPA personnel involved with each site to estimate cleanup costs and site factors associated with risks. The NPL Characterization database contains rough estimates of the populations surrounding Superfund sites. Data from these two sources on the full NPL thus allow us to examine how the sites in our analyses compare to other sites.

A sample of 267 sites forms the basis of the cost analysis, while 150 sites are used to describe risks to human health at Superfund sites. The following tables will present information on the full set of nonfederal NPL sites, the 267 sites in the cost analysis, and the 150 sites in the risk analysis. For each factor involving the distribution of sites across a set of categories, chi square statistics are presented for the cost sample and the risk sample to test the null hypothesis that inclusion in the particular sample is independent of the characteristic considered. Although we do not present the full data for the contingency tables for each classification variable (i.e., we show the frequency for the sites in the cost sample but do not report the frequency for the sites not in the sample), the chi square statistic reported tests whether the frequency distributions for sites in the sample and sites outside the sample indicate that inclusion in the sample is independent of the variable analyzed. For continuous variables, the mean from those in the analysis sample is compared to the mean in those not in the analysis sample. Treating these as sample means from two underlying populations (e.g., the type of sites likely to be included in the cost analysis and the type not likely to be included), we report the results of difference of means tests.

Table B.1 reveals that the regional distribution of sites in the cost and risk samples from RODs signed in 1991 and 1992 mirrors the distribution of sites across the country for the full set of 1,124 nonfederal NPL sites in the RELAI database. The top three regions on the full nonfederal NPL in terms of percentage of sites are region 5 (23.0 percent), region 2 (17.3 percent), and region 3 (13.8 percent). The same three regions head the distribution of sites in the cost set (region 5, 23.2 percent; region 2 18.7 percent; region 3 16.1 percent) and the risk set (region 5, 24.7 percent; region 2 20.0 percent; region 3 17.3 percent). Chi square tests for both the cost and risk samples indicate that the inclusion of sites in either sample is independent of the regional distribution of sites.

Chapter 5 presents analysis of the costs of selected remedies at the 267 sites with RODs signed in 1991 and 1992, yet this raises the question of how representative these sites are of cleanup costs of NPL sites. The RELAI survey contains questions about site costs that help answer this. Site managers were asked to estimate whether total site costs were expected to exceed $20 million and to determine the likely dollar value ranges of operable unit capital costs and operation and maintenance costs. Table B.2 compares the responses of these questions for the full nonfederal NPL, for sites included in the costs analysis versus those not included, and for sites included in the risk analysis versus those not included. Note that the number of sites in each sample varies with the question because not all site managers responded to particular questions.

For the full nonfederal NPL, 24.3 percent of the sites were estimated to have total site costs exceeding $20 million, compared to 20.6 percent for the cost sample and 15.9 percent for the risk sample. The chi square test indicates (at the 1 and 5 percent level of significance) that inclusion in the

Table B.1
Comparison of regional distribution

EPA region	Entire nonfederal NPL		Cost sites		Risk sites	
	Frequency	Percent	Frequency	Percent	Frequency	Percent
1	77	6.8	14	5.2	9	6.0
2	195	17.3	50	18.7	30	20.0
3	155	13.8	43	16.1	26	17.3
4	148	13.1	35	13.1	19	12.7
5	259	23.0	62	23.2	37	24.7
6	67	6.0	10	3.8	4	2.7
7	56	5.0	13	4.9	6	4.0
8	35	3.1	9	3.4	2	1.3
9	84	7.5	21	7.9	13	8.7
10	50	4.4	10	3.8	4	2.7
Total	1126		267		150	
Chi square			6.349		9.438	
Degrees of freedom			9		9	
p value			0.705		0.398	

Note: States in EPA Regions are:

Region 1: Connecticut, Maine, Massachusetts, New Hampshire, Rhode Island, Vermont

Region 2: New York, New Jersey, Puerto Rico

Region 3: Deleware, Pennsylvania, Virginia, West Virginia

Region 4: Alabama, Florida, Georgia, Kentucky, Mississippi, North Carolina, South Carolina, Tennessee

Region 5: Illinois, Indiana, Michigan, Minnesota, Ohio, Wisconsin

Region 6: Arkansas, Louisiana, New Mexico, Oklahoma, Texas

Region 7: Iowa, Kansas, Missouri, Nebraska

Region 8: Colorado, Montana, North Dakota, South Dakota, Utah, Wyoming

Region 9: Arizona, California, Hawaii, Nevada

Region 10: Alaska, Idaho, Oregon, Washington

cost sample is independent of cost size, but this cannot be said for the risk sample (which contains a smaller percentage of high-cost sites). In terms of the overall distribution of operable unit current expected capital costs, the rank of cost categories is similar for the full NPL, the sites in the cost sample, and the sites in the risk sample. Note that the tables report the distribution of the number of operable units in a given category, since the RELAI question referred to operable unit costs rather than site costs. For the full NPL, operable units with costs in the $1,000,001–$3,000,000 range account for 19.2 percent, followed by 16.6 percent for sites

Table B.2
Comparison of cost magnitudes

a. Is total site cost estimated to be >$20 million?

	Entire nonfederal NPL		Cost sites		Risk sites	
	Frequency	Percent	Frequency	Percent	Frequency	Percent
Yes	231	24.3	52	20.6	23	15.9
No	718	75.7	201	79.4	122	84.1
Total	949		253		145	
Chi square			2.688		6.682	
Degrees of freedom			1		1	
p value			0.101		0.010	

b. Operable unit capital cost

	Entire nonfederal NPL		Cost sites		Risk sites	
	Frequency	Percent	Frequency	Percent	Frequency	Percent
<100,000	71	5.4	22	5.4	12	5.7
$100,001–$500,000	73	5.6	33	8.1	19	9.1
$500,001–$1,000,000	101	7.7	29	7.1	16	7.7
$1,000,001–$3,000,000	253	19.2	89	21.8	49	23.4
$3,000,001–$5,000,000	186	14.1	58	14.2	28	13.4
$5,000,001–$10,000,000	218	16.6	64	15.7	35	16.7
$10,000,001–$15,000,000	124	9.4	46	11.3	23	11.0
$15,000,001–$20,000,000	84	6.4	25	6.1	8	3.8

	Entire nonfederal NPL		Cost sites		Risk sites	
	Frequency	Percent	Frequency	Percent	Frequency	Percent
$20,000,001–$40,000,000	122	9.3	27	6.6	12	5.7
$40,0000,001–$100,000,000	66	5.0	13	3.2	7	3.3
>$100,0000,001	16	1.2	2	0.5	0	0
Total operable units	1314		408		181	
Chi square	23.118		19.194			
Degrees of freedom	10		10			
p value	0.017		0.058			

c. Operable unit operation and maintenance cost

	Entire nonfederal NPL		Cost sites		Risk sites	
	Frequency	Percent	Frequency	Percent	Frequency	Percent
0	78	8.3	20	6.4	7	4.0
$500–1,000	20	2.1	3	1.0	1	0.6
$1,001–5,000	16	1.7	4	1.3	2	1.1
$5,001–20,000	39	4.1	16	5.1	11	6.2
$20,001–100,000	93	9.8	33	10.5	20	11.3
$100,001–1,000,000	245	25.9	74	23.6	43	24.3
$1,000,001–5,000,000	227	24.0	82	26.2	46	26.0
$5,000,001–20,000,000	167	17.7	61	19.5	35	19.8
>$20,000,000	60	6.3	20	6.4	12	6.8
Total operable units	945		313		177	
Chi square	9.486		11.715			
Degrees of freedom	8		8			
p value	0.303		0.164			

$5,000,001–$10,000,000 and 14.1 percent for sites in the $3,000,001–$5,000,000 range. The percentage distribution for these three categories are 21.8, 15.7, and 14.2 for the cost sample and 23.4, 16.7, and 13.4 for the risk sample. The operable unit operation and maintenance costs also show similar distributions for the full NPL sites and the cost and risk samples. Chi square tests indicate that inclusion in the cost analysis is independent of operable unit operation and maintenance cost and that the same is true for inclusion in the risk sample. Both samples fail the chi square test for the distribution of capital costs.

Table B.3 offers information about factors likely to influence costs at Superfund sites. DNAPL (dense nonaqueous phase liquid) contamination often prolongs the cleanup time frame for groundwater contamination and complicates remediation in other ways. Site managers were asked in the RELAI survey to express whether DNAPLs had been identified at a site and if they had not whether the likelihood that they were present in groundwater zone at the site was high, medium, low, or unknown. For the responses among the full NPL set, 14.2 percent of the sites had DNAPLs identified and the distribution of sites across the likelihood categories was 34.9, 20.3, and 30.6 percent for those sites answering ($N = 281$). For the cost sample there were fewer definite sites with DNAPLs (8.1 percent), which was also true for the risk sample (7.4 percent). Chi square tests indicate the inclusion in either sample, however, is independent of DNAPL presence or likelihood.

The number of potentially responsible parties may also be related to site costs. Sites with more PRPs could entail more transaction costs to settle because of litigation over liability and coordination costs in remedy study and implementation. Table B.3 shows that for the full nonfederal NPL, 18.1 percent of the sites were estimated to have a single PRP, 42.3 percent had 2–10 PRPs, and 18.4 percent had 11–50. On the other end of the transaction cost spectrum, 1.6 percent of the sites were estimated to have more than 1,000 PRPs. The distribution of PRPs at the cost sites and risk sites is similarly concentrated in the low end of PRP count categories, with 43.2 percent of the cost sample and 43.5 percent of the risk sample sites having an estimated number of 2–10 PRPs. In terms of sites with 1,000 or more PRPs, these sites make up 1.5 percent of the cost sample and 2.0 percent of the risk sample. Chi square tests indicate that inclusion in either sample is independent of the estimated universe of PRPs at a site.

Overall, tables B.2 and B.3 indicate that conclusions about cost drawn from the cost sample are likely to be similar to those that would be drawn if full cost data were available on the full NPL. The full nonfederal NPL

Table B.3
Comparison of cost factors

a. Likelihood of dense nonaqueous phase liquid contamination (DNAPL)

	Entire nonfederal NPL		Cost sites		Risk sites	
	Frequency	Percent	Frequency	Percent	Frequency	Percent
Definite	40	14.2	7	8.1	4	7.4
High	98	34.9	31	36.1	17	31.5
Medium	57	20.3	20	23.3	14	25.9
Low	86	30.6	28	32.6	19	35.2
Total	281		86		54	
Chi square			3.977		3.917	
Degrees of freedom			3		3	
p value			0.264		0.271	

b. Estimated number of potentially responsible parties

	Entire nonfederal NPL		Cost sites		Risk sites	
	Frequency	Percent	Frequency	Percent	Frequency	Percent
0	17	1.6	0	0	0	0
1	192	18.1	46	17.8	30	20.4
2–10	448	42.3	112	43.2	64	43.5
11–50	195	18.4	55	21.2	31	21.1
51–100	64	6.0	15	5.8	7	4.8
101–500	101	9.5	25	9.7	11	7.5
501–1000	24	2.3	2	0.8	1	0.7
>1000	17	1.6	4	1.5	3	2.0
Total	1058		259		147	
Chi square			10.503		7.263	
Degrees of freedom			7		7	
p value			0.162		0.402	

contains a slightly higher percentage of sites estimated by EPA personnel in the RELAI survey to have costs greater than $20 million, but the lower percentage of sites for which this was true for RODs signed in 1991 and 1992 could be in part because these sites were not as far along in the remediation pipeline as the cleanups at earlier sites. This could also indicate that fewer large cost sites were coming on line in the later years (a point made by the CBO in their analysis of Superfund site cost projections). According to a CBO Study (1994, 21) on the costs of cleaning up nonfederal Superfund sites:

The available data suggest that the distribution of NPL sites is changing. In particular, the incidence of so-called mega-sites appears to be declining. Defining a mega-site as one with cleanup costs of $50 million or more (as estimated in the records of decision), EPA staff know or expect 44 of the 711 nonfederal sites proposed for the NPL through October 1984 to be mega-sites, a ratio of 6.2 percent. The same can be said of only 0 .9 percent (4 of 438) of the nonfederal sites proposed since 1984.

For factors related to transaction costs and cleanup costs that are available for the full NPL and the cost sample the distributions are extremely similar. The risk sample, which is used primarily to make statements about risks to human health, is also similar to the full NPL in terms of cost factors. This is helpful to the analysis since the cost and risk data are combined in chapter 5 to make statements about the cost per cancer case averted across sites. The risk sample does contain a much lower percentage (15.9 percent) of sites with costs estimated to be greater than $20 million than the full NPL (24.3 percent), so the costs per cancer case averted based on the risk sites may be lacking information on this tradeoff at the more expensive sites.

Risk assessments conducted at Superfund sites provide detailed information on levels of individual lifetime excess cancer risks, but the data are not combined with information on populations surrounding sites to produce estimates of excess cancer cases arising from contamination. While individual risk level data are not readily available for the full NPL, we can compare sites in terms of potentially exposed populations to determine if the cost and (especially) the risk samples are similar to the full nonfederal NPL. Table B.4 provides information from RELAI on the presence of a groundwater operable unit at a site, number of people served by water supply wells in the aquifer pertaining to the site, and whether any wells were shut down or replaced at the site.

For the full nonfederal NPL, the RELAI surveys indicate that 83.2 percent of the sites had RODs addressing or expected to address groundwater cleanup, compared to 87.4 percent for the cost sample and 90.1 percent for the risk sample. Among those sites with groundwater contamination where the EPA estimated the number of people using the aquifer, for the full NPL, 29.6 percent of the sites had 0 people estimated to be served by the aquifer while 9.2 percent had more than 100,000 people served. This compared to 26.7 percent serving 0 people and 8.6 percent for aquifers serving more than 100,000 in the risk sample. Among those answering whether there were any wells that had been shut down or

Table B.4
Comparison of groundwater characteristics

a. Presence of groundwater operable unit for the site?

	Entire nonfederal NPL		Cost sites		Risk sites	
	Frequency	Percent	Frequency	Percent	Frequency	Percent
Yes	790	83.2	215	87.4	127	90.1
No	159	16.8	31	12.6	14	9.9
Total	949		246		141	
Chi square			4.106		5.531	
Degrees of freedom			1		1	
p value			0.043		0.019	

b. Number of people using aquifer

	Entire nonfederal NPL		Cost sites		Risk sites	
	Frequency	Percent	Frequency	Percent	Frequency	Percent
0	199	29.6	57	30.2	28	26.7
1–24	75	11.1	24	12.7	11	10.5
25–100	59	8.8	13	6.9	7	6.7
101–500	46	6.8	10	5.3	4	3.8
501–1,000	24	3.6	3	1.6	2	1.9
1,001–5,000	56	8.3	21	11.1	14	13.3
5,001–10,000	48	7.1	15	7.9	9	8.6
10,001–100,000	104	15.5	31	16.4	21	20.0
>100,000	62	9.2	15	7.9	9	8.6
Total	673		189		105	
Chi square			8.787		9.497	
Degrees of freedom			8		8	
p value			0.361		0.302	

c. Were any wells shut down or replaced?

	Entire nonfederal NPL		Cost sites		Risk sites	
	Frequency	Percent	Frequency	Percent	Frequency	Percent
Yes	313	35.7	76	34.4	37	29.1
No	563	64.3	145	65.6	90	70.9
Total	876		221		127	
Chi square			0.232		2.815	
Degrees of freedom			1		1	
p value			0.630		0.093	

Table B.5
Analysis of populations on or near Superfund sites

	In cost sample?			In risk sample?		
	N	Mean	Standard deviation	N	Mean	Standard deviation
Population within 1 mile						
Yes	162	5345	14555	89	4466	8133
No	534	6450	44153	607	6466	41965
Total	696	6193		696	6193	
t statistic		0.496			1.037	
p value		0.620			0.300	
Population within 3 miles						
Yes	192	43990	87319	112	40951	83240
No	570	54242	279019	650	53503	263275
Total	762	51659		762	51659	
t statistic		0.772			0.967	
p value		0.440			0.334	
Population affected by drinking water impacts						
Yes	257	90970	662198	146	66355	292590
No	799	41762	223913	910	51713	392865
Total	1056	53738		1056	53738	
t statistic		−1.170			−0.533	
p value		0.243			0.595	

Source: NPL Characterization database.

replaced at the site, for the full NPL there were 35.7 percent of the sites where this had occurred, versus 34.4 percent for the cost sample and 29.1 percent for the risk sample. The chi square tests for the groundwater estimates in table B.4 indicate that sample sites were slightly less likely to have groundwater operable units. Inclusion in the risk or cost sample, however, was independent of factors such as the number of people using the aquifer or whether wells had been shut down.

Table B.5 contains means of variables from the NPL Characterization database relating to exposed populations. In our analysis in chapter 4 estimating expected cancer cases at sites, we use site boundaries, 1990 census data, and GIS technology to calculate the populations around sites. We the use the rougher data estimates from the NPL Characterization database here, however, to compare population distributions, since this information is available for the broader set of NPL sites. In terms of populations within one mile of the site, the mean for the full nonfederal

NPL is 6,200, versus 5,300 for sites in the cost sample and 4,500 for the risk sample. For populations within three miles of the sites, the means are 51,700 for the full nonfederal NPL, 44,000 for the cost sample, and 41,400 for the risk sample. For estimated populations affected by drinking water impacts, the full NPL mean is 53,700, versus 91,000 for the cost analysis and 66,400 for the risk analysis. For each of these risk factors relating to population size, one cannot reject the hypothesis at the 1 or 5 percent level that the means are equal for the sites in the sample analyzed and the sites outside the sample analyzed.

Overall, these comparisons of site characteristics, factors associated with estimated cleanup costs, and factors associated with human health risks indicate that the sites selected for analysis in our study are similar to the rest of the nonfederal NPL sites.

Notes

Chapter 1

1. See U.S. Environmental Protection Agency (U.S. EPA 1987).

2. Cost estimates for Superfund cleanups are presented in Congressional Budget Office (1994).

3. A 1997 EPA report estimated that future remedial action costs starting from the end of fiscal 1997 for currently listed or proposed nonfederal sites on the National Priorities List (i.e., the sites qualifying for federal remediation funds) would be $6.7 billion. See Bureau of National Affairs (1997) and U.S. EPA (1997a).

4. See Doty and Travis (1989), Church and Nakamura (1993), and Barnett (1994) for research on program management and decision rules. Acton and Dixon (1992) focus on the role of transaction costs in site remediation. Hird (1990, 1994), Zimmerman (1993), and Gupta, Van Houtven, and Cropper (1996) analyze the potential impact of congressional oversight or neighborhood composition on site cleanups. Burmaster and Harris (1993) and Hamilton and Viscusi (1995) analyze the way risk assessments are conducted in the program, while works by the National Research Council (1991) and Johnson (1995) analyze the nature of site risks. Probst and Portney (1991), Probst, Fullerton, Litan, and Portney (1995), Revesz and Stewart (1995), and Sigman (1998) examine the impact of funding mechanisms on program operation. Aggregate cost estimates are offered in CBO (1994) and Russell and David (1995).

5. The official title of the bill establishing the Superfund program to cleanup hazardous waste sites was the Comprehensive Environmental Response, Compensation, and Liability Act of 1980 (CERCLA). See Parisi (1980) and Chemical Week (1980) for descriptions of the Superfund legislation as it was debated and passed.

6. Describing a congressional hearing at which Administrator Gorsuch appeared in 1983, one observer noted "Senators from both parties raised the stakes in the controversy over the Environmental Protection Agency yesterday, accusing Administrator Anne M. Gorsuch of seeking to dismantle her agency and undermining federal laws through budget cuts and mismanagement." See Russakoff (1983, A1). An internal EPA report on Superfund implementation in 1983 declared "It is clear ... the agency never mobilized its full resources to implement the program in a coordinated way" (Santos 1983).

7. For analyses of these problems with the program's operation, see Barnett (1994), Hird (1994), and Church and Nakamura (1993).

8. Eleven sites in the United States were listed by the EPA as having construction activities completed by October 17, 1986, the date of passage of the Superfund reform legislation (see U.S. EPA 1997b). Buckley (1986) discusses political economy aspects of early Superfund implementation and reform.

9. See 42 USC 9621(b)(1).

10. See U.S. EPA (1990a, 8713).

11. Diamond and Hausman (1994).

12. Section 104(a) of CERCLA authorizes government activity whenever "(A) any hazardous substance is released … or (B) there is a release … of any pollutant or contaminant which may present an imminent and substantial danger to the public health or welfare … to protect the public health or welfare or the environment."

13. Noll and Krier (1990) and Spitzer (1990) provide excellent discussions about how risk perceptions may influence risk policies.

14. Hird (1994, 215).

15. See Hersh et al. (1997) for analysis of future land use at Superfund sites.

16. Becker (1983), Wittman (1989), and Lott (1997) examine the degree that democracy generates efficient outcomes.

17. Our analysis does not address the contentious issues raised by liability rules and funding mechanisms, which have been examined extensively elsewhere (Church and Nakamura 1993; Probst and Portney 1991; Probst, Fullerton, Litan, and Portney 1995; Revesz and Stewart 1995).

18. See U.S. EPA (1994a).

19. See U.S. EPA (1990b, 1994a, c).

20. See U.S. EPA (1989a).

21. See 42 USC 9601(23).

22. See U.S. EPA (1991b).

23. See Viscusi (1996) for evidence on individual annual risk levels subject to final, proposed, or rejected rules across different federal programs. We find that the mean of the maximum cumulative lifetime excess cancer risk to an individual at the 150 Superfund sites in our sample is 0.07. This is greater than all but 3 of the 33 regulated or potentially regulated risks (converted to a lifetime basis) examined in Viscusi (1996). The median of these 33 lifetime cancer risks is 0.003, more than an order of magnitude less than the Superfund risks estimated with the EPA's risk assessment methodology.

24. See U.S. EPA (1993b).

25. See Nichols and Zeckhauser (1986).

26. See U.S. EPA (1989a, 6–19).

27. The EPA's Hazard Ranking System (HRS) score for a site is based in part on the number of individuals surrounding a site. The HRS is used to determine that sites qualify for placement on the National Priorities List (NPL), and thereby qualify for remediation funds. See EPA (1990c). In the analysis that forms the basis for the remediation decision at a site, however, the agency does not require an assessment that determines population risks, such as the number of expected cancer cases likely to arise at a site.

28. For discussions of academic research on environmental equity, see Been (1995). Chapter 7 offers more discussion of such research. Executive Order 12898 issued in 1994 explicitly focused attention of federal regulators on environmental equity. EO 12898 requires agencies to "identify and address … disproportionately high and adverse human health or environmental impacts" on minority populations. While the order requires federal agencies to consider environmental equity concerns in their actions, its implementation has been slowed by uncertainty over definitions such as what constitutes "disproportionate impact." See BNA (1994).

29. Costs of site remediation are spread across taxpayers since part of the Superfund is paid for through general tax revenues and targeted taxes on specific petroleum and chemical products. Private expenditures to engage in liability litigation and contribute to site cleanups may also generate higher product costs for consumers. For a discussion of Superfund funding issues, see Probst et al. (1995). Note that residents may bear another form of costs from site remediations if cleanups themselves generate human health risks. For discussion of such risk–risk trade-offs in regulatory policy, see Graham and Wiener (1995).

30. See Lichtenstein et al. (1978) and Tversky and Kahneman (1982).

31. Most estimates cluster in the $3 million to $7 million range per statistical life saved. See Viscusi (1992a) for a complete survey. Note that individuals may perceive potential cancers from Superfund sites as arising with some time lag.

Chapter 2

1. The data produced by actions and studies at Superfund sites have generated debates over the progress and stringency of cleanups (Doty and Travis 1989; Hird 1990), the assumptions employed in the exposure scenarios analyzed (Versar 1991; Burmaster and Harris 1993; Environ 1993; Hazardous Waste Cleanup Project 1993; U.S. EPA 1993a), and the costs of reducing these risks (Russell, Colglazier, and English 1991; Acton and Dixon 1992; Gupta, Van Houtven, and Cropper 1996). Walker, Sadowitz, and Graham (1995) focus explicitly on the nature of risks identified in Superfund site risk assessments.

2. One commentator, for example, has questioned EPA's $9.3 million expenditure to clean a swamp site so that it is not only safe for children to eat dirt for 70 days per year, but for 260 days per year. See Stroup (1993). Breyer (1993) and Schneider (1993) also contain discussions about the magnitude of site risks and stringency of cleanup targets.

3. For the full National Contingency Plan, see 55 Federal Register 8665–8865, March 8,1990. The risk assessment requirement is in Section 33.430(d)(4).

4. U.S. EPA (1991b).

5. U.S. EPA (1989a, 1-1).

6. U.S. EPA (1988a, 1-1).

7. In Hamilton and Viscusi (1994, 1995) current potential risks were treated as current risks if they were classified as current by the risk assessments at sites.

8. U.S. EPA (1989a, 6-7).

9. We often use body-weight assumptions in risk assessments to classify risk pathways as relating to an adult or child, with an adult pathway defined as involving a person weighing 59 kg or higher.

10. See appendixes A and B for a more detailed description of the sample construction and risk estimation methodology.

11. See U.S. EPA (1989a, 1989b).

12. See U.S. EPA, Region I (1991, table 5).

13. Hamilton and Viscusi (1994, 1995) focused on an intermediate sample numbering 77 sites. This chapter reflects analysis of the final risk sample of 150 sites. As indicated, the Hydro-Flex site is dropped from the total pathway analysis because it did not meet the risk-level cutoff used for this analysis.

14. U.S. Department of Commerce (1992, 19, table 19). Statistics are for 1991. EPA may be making a special effort to identify potential routes of exposure for children because they are a sensitive subpopulation due to their greater sensitivity to chemical exposures, and due to certain child behaviors, such as soil ingestion, that increase exposure. The higher number of risk pathways pertaining to children may also be a function of the fact that children have a higher intake-to-body-weight ratio than adults for pathways such as groundwater and soil ingestion.

15. See Viscusi (1992b).

16. The Westinghouse site also accounts for a substantial portion of the expected cancer cases arising at the sample sites (see chapter 4).

17. The difference of means test for different pathways compared in this analysis are: current (1.4e-3) versus future pathways (1.2e-2) $t = 5.1$; adult (1.1e-2) versus child (5.4e-3) $t = 1.9$; resident (1.1e-2) versus nonresident (2.4e-3) $t = 4.2$; current resident (1.4e-3) versus future resident (1.4e-2) $t = 4.9$; on-site populations (1.1e-2) versus off-site residents (1.1e-2) $t = 0.08$; on-site media (9.9e-3) versus off-site media (4.6e-3) $t = 1.7$; ingestion (1.2e-2) versus noningestion (5.1e-3) $t = 2.5$.

18. The National Oil and Hazardous Substances Pollution Contingency Plan of 1990 is codified in the *Code of Federal Regulations*: 40 CFR Section 300.430 (e)(2)(I)(A)(2) 1993. See also 55 *Federal Register* 8665-8865, March 8, 1990.

19. Vinyl chloride, for example, is subject to regulation under CERCLA, the Clean Air Act, the Clean Water Act, and OSHA exposure standards. PCBs are targeted under CERCLA, the Clean Air Act, the Toxic Substance Control Act, and the Water Pollution Control Act. See Hamilton and Viscusi, 1994.

20. U.S. EPA (1993b).

21. Note that arsenic is often treated within the same ROD at a site as a carcinogen and as a source of noncarcinogenic risk. In terms of being mentioned in noncarcinogenic risk pathways, it is the most frequently occurring chemical in risk assessments in our sample (appearing at 100 out of 150 sites).

Chapter 3

1. Bills of the 104th Congress with such provisions included HR690, HR2500, S291, S343, and S1285.

2. Reviews of risk assessment practices and conservatism appear in Graham et al. (1989), Latin (1988), and Lave et al. (1988).

3. This is essentially the distinction between type II and type I errors drawn in statistics and econometrics. See Krier (1990) and National Research Council/National Academy of Sciences (1994) among others. It has been argued that these false negatives may be catastrophic so policy should therefore be biased in favor of false positives (Page 1978).

4. Viscusi, Magat, and Huber (1991).

5. See Noll and Krier (1990) for a review. There is some evidence that EPA resource allocation is more aligned with the public's perceptions of risk rather than with expert opinions (U.S. EPA 1987).

6. Both major cost–benefit bills in the 104th Congress (HR690, S343) emphasized the importance of identifying policy assumptions. S343 stressed that preference be given to

assumptions that represent plausible or realistic inferences. S343, Section 633(a)(3), would have required the use of the "best estimate" for each parameter. HR2500 and S1285 called for reliance on unbiased and scientifically objective risk assessments, with Section 403 of S1285 specifically focusing on the estimation of central estimates of risk.

7. U.S. EPA (1989a, 6-19).

8. U.S. EPA (1989a, 6-5).

9. Appendix 2, U.S. EPA (1991a). Proposed legislation in Congress suggested the use of the 90th percentile as a goal for probabilistic risk estimates (HR 2500).

10. For the list of criteria in evaluating remedial actions, see 40 C. F. R. 300.430 (e)(9)(iii). In terms of binding cleanup goals established at Superfund sites, we find in chapter 5 that goals based on state environmental standards result in lower residual risks targeted to remain after cleanups.

11. See U.S. EPA (1991b).

12. For example, Environ Corporation (1993) found that interim exposure values using EPA risk assessment are significantly greater than the 95th percentile of a distribution generated by Monte Carlo simulation. A similar result was obtained by Chemical Manufacturers Association (1991). Cullen (1994) cites several examples in which similar conservative point estimates are greater than the 99th percentile of a simulated distribution. Using a slightly different RME, Finley and Paustenbach (1994) estimate the RME in the 99th percentile for the case of groundwater contamination, and in the 99.9th percentile for risks arising from dioxin emissions in the food chain. In contrast, Smith (1994), in an example using Monte Carlo simulation to estimate potential risks from a Superfund site, finds RME risks to be between the 90th and 95th percentile.

13. Nichols and Zeckhauser (1986), Bogen (1994), and Burmaster and Harris (1993), among others, critique this approach. Some, however, question whether "conservative" risk estimates are really excessively conservative. See Finkel (1989), for example. Other observers simply note that it is unclear exactly what the RME is (Hird 1994).

14. The linear equation is a simplification of the underlying model. For risks greater than 0.01 EPA Risk Assessment Guidelines recommend the use of what is called a "one-hit" equation that better estimates risks from relatively high doses. Slightly different from the linear form, the risk from any given contaminant is calculated using the equation:

$$\text{LECR}_{ij} = 1 - \exp(-\text{HIF}_j \times \text{CC}_{ij} \times \text{Tox}_{ij}).$$

These contaminant level risks are then summed to obtain the risk for a given pathway. We use each equation where appropriate.

15. Treating the pathway risk as a summation of individual contaminant risks ignores synergistic effects of chemical mixtures, so this equation may be interpreted to be less conservative than it would be otherwise (Finkel 1989). Of course, the relationship between contaminants might be antagonistic so that summation would over-estimate health effects. See Seed et al. (1995) for a review of risk assessment and chemical mixtures. The fact that not every possible contaminant is included in risk estimates will also tend to reduce potential conservatism.

16. Even exposure frequency could be viewed as an upper bound. The number of days per year a resident is assumed to be exposed to ingestion risks is typically 350 to 365. Due to the lack of reliable data for this variable, we do not change this value.

17. In particular, our choice for exposure duration is recommended by Finley et al. (1994), and our choice for groundwater ingestion rates is derived from the recommended source. Child soil ingestion data come from a more recent study by Stanek and Calabrese (1995). There are relatively little data on adult residential soil ingestion rates, and no recommendation is made for this value. Our choice is based on the best available data.

18. It is difficult to determine how often this is the case for Superfund sites because assessments often report that exposure concentration is the RME value without specifying if this is the sample maximum or the 95th UCL on the mean estimate.

19. Note that it is possible that the site document numbers that are calculated with the parameter estimates may diverge from EPA default values, but a careful comparison of the two sets of estimates indicates that most of the site risk assessments are consistent with the use of default EPA values. The average of the figures reported in the site documents was 1.3×10^{-2}. When we re-estimated these risks using EPA recommended guidelines, the average of these conservative risks was 1.1×10^{-2}. A test of equality of the means yields a t-statistic of 0.38, which implies that risks reported in site documents were calculated using EPA's stated conservative guidelines.

20. See U.S. EPA (1991b).

21. U.S. EPA (1991b, 4).

22. We note that this ratio of expected values is not the same as the expected value of the ratio, namely $E(\text{conservative})/E(\text{central}) \neq E (\text{conservative}/\text{central})$.

23. Lung cancer risks from cigarette smoking are currently estimated as ranging from 0.06 to 0.13. Overall lifetime mortality risks from cigarette smoking are somewhat larger, between 0.18 and 0.36. See Viscusi (1992b). As other comparisons, annual job fatality risks are below 1×10^{-4} and the risk threshold for many other federal risk policies is between 1×10^{-5} and 1×10^{-6}. See Viscusi (1992a).

24. See Goodman and Krusk (1979).

25. It should be noted that the risk manager is currently constrained by the legislation that authorizes Superfund, for example, requirements that cleanups comply with ARARs.

26. If these parameters are lognormally distributed, then Pearson correlation coefficients can frequently be used to impose the correct covariance structure. Pearson correlation coefficients do not often survive transformations of the parameters, but Iman and Conover (1982) have illustrated that Spearman rank-order correlation coefficients may be preserved for any transformation of random variables.

27. Elliott (1992) also includes an interesting application to risk management by applying probabilistic risk estimates to an expected-value approach to achieving compliance with standards.

28. Ingestion rate distributions were required for water and soil ingestion by adult and child residents. Ingestion of tap water per day is taken from Roseberry and Burmaster (1992), which is a lognormal parameterization of data reported in Ershow and Cantor (1989). Roseberry and Burmaster also provide estimates on total water ingestion that includes that taken in from foods, but the data on tap water are relevant for this pathway. RME water ingestion rates have a default value of 2 L/day for adults and 1 L/day for children. Soil ingestion rates for children were taken from Stanek and Calabrese (1995), and those for adults are from Calabrese et al. (1990). The former data are relatively new and differ substantially from earlier estimates (Calabrese et al. 1989), although they are derived from the same dataset. The default RME value soil ingestion is 200 mg/day for children and 100 mg/day

for adults. Because the distributions found in the literature did not precisely match the age descriptions found in the site documents, assumptions had to be made in assigning distributions to risk pathways. These assumptions were generally conservative, erring toward overestimating the resulting risk. For example, if the specified age group in the risk assessment was "age 1–18," then that pathway was assigned the (larger) water ingestion rate for 11–20 year olds, instead of that for 1–10 year olds. If the same age group was defined for a soil pathway, the (larger) "child" rate for incidental soil ingestion was used in the simulation. These assumptions will tend to bias positively the simulated risk estimates. The distribution for exposure duration is taken from U.S. EPA (1991a) and durations for child age groups are assumed to be equal to those of adults, but truncated at the span of the age group. For example, if the age group is "1–18" as above, the distribution is truncated at 17 years. Distributions for body weight were created by weighting the distributions for constituent spans. For example the body weight of 4–8 had a cumulative distribution function that was weighted equally between that for 4–6 year olds and that for 6–8 year olds.

The values for the (normal) distribution for adult body weight come from Biorby and Finley (1993), with a mean of 72 kg and a standard deviation of 15.9 years. The RME value is 70 kg. For child body weight (RME value of 15 kg), evidence on the distribution comes from the U.S. EPA (1991a).

29. See Smith (1995).

30. See U.S. EPA (1992a).

31. See Dockins (1996, 67).

32. See Gilbert (1987) for several alternatives.

33. There were four cases to be considered with the site specific data: mean value arithmetic, RME value = 95 upper confidence limit on the mean; mean value arithmetic, RME value = maximum detected or unspecified; mean geometric, RME value = based on geometric mean; and a normal distribution specified as the basis for sample statistics. See Dockins (1996) for details on how each case was handled in the distribution of exposure concentration estimates.

34. For ingestion pathways such as the ones used here it seems unlikely that exposure parameters are highly correlated, but it is not known how neglecting these correlations affects the final risk estimates.

Chapter 4

1. The number of people surrounding a Superfund site is incorporated in the EPA's Hazard Ranking System (HRS) score, the indicator score that the agency uses to determine which sites qualify for inclusion on the National Priorities List. But the agency's subsequent assessment of characteristics at a site focuses on individual level cancer risks, not the expected number of cancer cases at a site (which would invoke an explicit calculation of exposed populations).

2. Although one might be reluctant to discount cases of cancer, the willingness to pay to prevent cases of cancer in the future is a monetary amount. For benefit–cost analysis, one is, in effect, simply discounting the willingness to pay associated with these future cases of cancer that are prevented. If one were to assume that no discounting of remote cases of cancer is desirable, then one would be led to very irrational policies if the efficacy of policies in reducing cancer is constant or increasing. With constant efficacy, one would be indifferent to an indefinite postponement of any cancer reduction effort. With policies that increase in

their efficacy over time, it is always optimal to defer policy actions until some future juncture. The use of a discount rate is a reflection of the importance society places on preventing cases of cancer now rather than deferring such actions to the future.

3. See U.S. EPA (1993b).

4. See U.S. EPA (1988b).

5. Evidence of groundwater use was derived from Census STF-3A block-group data question H23, Source of Water. Public water supplies are defined as those serving five or more houses. See appendix A.

6. See U.S. Department of Commerce (1996).

7. See U.S. EPA (1988b).

8. See U.S. EPA (1990c).

9. See appendix A for more detail on this methodology. Note that we assume that the plume size stays constant for thirty years, that individuals are exposed to either RME or mean concentrations, and that there is no dilution within the plume.

10. See Travis, Scofield, and Blaylock (1993), Graham and Wiener (1995), and Applegate and Wesloh (1998).

11. See Johnson (1993, 1995).

Chapter 5

1. 42 U.S.C. at 9601(23).

2. 42 U.S.C. at 9621(d)(2)(A)(ii).

3. The nine criteria for evaluating remedial actions are (1) overall protection of human health and the environment; (2) compliance with applicable or relevant and appropriate requirements (ARARs); (3) long-term effectiveness and permanence; (4) reduction of toxicity, mobility, or volume; (5) short-term effectiveness; (6) implementability; (7) cost; (8) state acceptance; (9) community acceptance. See 40 CFR at 300.430(e)(9)(iii).

4. For analysis of the benefits of removal actions, see EPA (1994). Recent analyses of remediation costs include CBO (1994), National Strategies (1995), and Russell and Davis (1995). Dixon, Drezner, and Hammitt (1993) and Dixon (1994) focus on transaction costs at sites. The overall market for remediation services, of which Superfund is only a small part, is described in EPA (1997a).

5. The site cost estimate of $18.1 million (pre-cost growth) is based on our analysis that indicates a mean site cost of $10.4 million from 1991–92 RODS at our sites, $3.0 million from RODs before 1991, and $4.7 million from RODs anticipated at these sites after 1992. Factoring in cost growth boosts the mean site cost to $25.7 million. Of the sample we analyzed of 267 nonfederal sites with a ROD in 1991–92, 93 had a ROD signed prior to 1991, while at 105 sites there was at least 1 ROD anticipated after 1992. If one excludes 19 "no-action" sites from the mean cost estimates, the "post-cost growth" site mean cost rises from $25.7 million to $27.7 million. Unless otherwise noted, the cost figures we discuss in this chapter reflect a 7 percent discount rate, are expressed in 1993 dollars, and are not adjusted to take into account likely increases in costs between estimation in site documents and implementation (i.e., are pre-cost growth).

6. For soil, institutional controls could involve construction of a fence, restrictions on land use, sediment monitoring; containment might involve placing a cap on contaminated soil; removal could entail removal of contaminated soil to a landfill or treatment and storage facility; and treatment could involve incineration or solidification and in-situ stabilization of the soil. For groundwater, institutional controls might involve provision of alternate water supplies, restrictions on land use or groundwater use, or groundwater monitoring; treatment could involve pumping and treating the water through air stripping or chemical precipitation.

7. Russell and Davis (1995) also estimate that remediation expenditures would drop if requirements for permanent cleanups and the ARAR cleanup standards were removed.

8. See Viscusi (1992a) for a review of this literature.

9. See Viscusi (1992a).

10. See Viscusi (1994a, b) for a discussion of these concepts and a review.

11. See Breyer (1993, 11–12).

12. See Stewart (1993).

13. See Zimmerman (1993) and Hird (1993, 1994) for examinations of environmental equity and Superfund.

Chapter 6

1. See Viscusi (1992a, 51–74).

2. See Kahneman, Slovic, and Tversky (1982).

3. See US EPA (1987) for a report on this survey evidence.

4. This theme is also articulated in Zeckhauser and Viscusi (1990). Noll (1989) provides a more general assessment of the interaction between political concerns and regulatory policy, which is a central theme of this chapter.

5. Political factors have long played a prominent role in local hazardous waste policies. See, among others, Kunreuther and Easterling (1990, 1992), Kunreuther and Gowda (1990), and Cohen (1981).

6. See Travis et al. (1987, 418).

7. For simplicity we focus on the benefits of cancer reduction since most policy action triggers are tied to cancer effects rather than other benefits from site remediation.

8. See Desvousges et al. (1992), Portney (1994), Diamond and Hausman (1994), and Hanemann (1994), who discuss such influences.

9. See Peter J. Huber (1967) and William H. Rogers (1993) for discussion of this procedure. Clusters were based on unique pathways defined by site, exposure medium, time frame, exposure location, and age of the potentially exposed population.

10. Although the number of variables was great, multicollinearity was not a major problem in the target risk analysis with large sample size, and only minor amendments were needed for the cost per cancer case analysis.

11. Gupta, Van Houtven, and Cropper (1996) find that the agency's decision about the permanence of a site remediation is affected by factors such as cleanup costs.

12. See Gupta et al. (1995).

13. See chapter 2 for documentation of the future-oriented nature of residential pathways.

14. "Facilities" is a count of the number of times a facility tracked under the EPA's Toxics Release Inventory, Resource Conservation and Recovery Act (Biennial Reporting System), Aerometric Information Retrieval System, CERCLIS, or Permit Compliance Systems (wastewater) was located within one mile of a given CERCLIS site. Facilities falling under the jurisdiction of multiple regulatory programs would therefore be double counted, but this actually occurred at only a small fraction of sites.

15. See Hamilton (1993, 1995) for evidence of the impact of collective action on polluter (rather than regulator) behavior.

16. These variables, which are not reported, are a series of EPA regional dummy variables to control for regional differences in site characteristics and policy decisions.

17. See chapter 2 for documentation of the dominance of hypothetical future on-site resident scenarios in the EPA risk assessments.

18. Though site-level media coverage could be viewed as endogenous, we lack good instruments to estimate coverage. Dropping this variable leaves the other results unchanged in terms of their statistical significance, sign, and general magnitude. The endogeneity of variables such as media coverage and hazard ranking score (HRS) means that the coefficients estimated for variables likely to influence coverage or the HRS will only capture the partial effects of these variables. Consider the case of measuring the influence of chemical toxicity, which can affect a site's HRS. The toxicity elasticity presented will only be a partial elasticity based on holding constant the HRS. The total elasticity would reflect a direct effect and an indirect effect through the influence of the HRS.

19. To the extent that environmental group membership and legislator votes reflect the values that residents place on the environment, then these variables could also represent values an efficiency-minded regulator would consider in making cleanup decisions. The significance of the voter turnout variable represents a political bias, however, since it reflects the likelihood a regulator will face local scrutiny or pressure.

20. These results reflect EPA's risk assessment practices and have not been adjusted to reflect the "conservatism" practices that lead to an upward bias in the risk estimates. This is similar to the median cost per cancer case averted of $388 million we found for the larger sample of 145 sites.

21. See Koenker and Bassett (1978) for further discussion as well as Buchinsky (1994). We use a bootstrap estimator to obtain the value of the asymptotic standard errors.

22. See Zimmerman (1993), Hird (1993, 1994), Gupta, Van Houtven, and Cropper (1995, 1996).

23. See Becker (1983), Wittman (1989, 1995), and Lott (1997).

Chapter 7

1. See Kohlhase (1991), Kiel and McClain (1995), and our analysis in chapter 8 for information on how housing prices respond to environmental risks and other disamenities.

2. Been (1994) emphasizes how changes in environmental risk may lead to changes in housing prices and therefore changes in residential demographics.

3. For overviews of the research and policy issues involved in analyzing environmental equity, see Cole (1992), Bryant and Mohai (1992), Been (1993), Lazarus (1993), Bullard (1993), and Petrikin (1995).

4. Hamilton (1995) discusses how differences in collective action across neighborhoods may affect the degree that particular areas are targeted for the expansion of hazardous waste processing capacity test.

5. For research on hazardous waste facilities, see Commission on Racial Justice (1987) (which also contains analysis of CERCLIS sites), Bullard (1990), Hamilton (1993, 1995), Anderton et al. (1994a, b), Anderson, Anderton, and Oakes (1994), Goldman and Fitton (1994), Been (1995), and Been and Gupta (1997). For analysis of the release of toxic chemicals by manufacturing facilities, see Goldman (1994), Hersh (1995), Perlin et al. (1995), and Bowen et al. (1995), and Brooks and Sethi (1997). Recent research about how to measure environmental equity includes Zimmerman (1994), Boerner and Lambert (1995), Pollock and Vittas (1995), Anderton (1996), Yandle and Burton (1996a, 1996b), Bullard (1996), Mohai (1996), and Barkenbus, Peretz, and Rubin (1996). Discussions of policy issues in this area include Blais (1996), Centner, Kriesel, and Keeler (1996), Kuehn (1996), Graham and Grills (1997), Lambert and Boerner (1997), and Shanklin (1997).

6. Anderton, Oakes, and Egan (1997, 23).

7. The estimate of 51 million people living within four miles of NPL sites does take into account the fact that some individuals may live within four miles of more than one Superfund site. In order to eliminate double counting of these individuals in the derivation of the 51 million figure, we created joint geographic coverages based on the union of all overlapping site boundaries or proximity rings and then combined these joint coverages with census variables weighted according to the portion of the block group or block-level census tract which fell within a given proximity ring. However, since combining sites in this way precludes site-level analysis, the term "site level" refers to analysis where each site is associated with a given coverage without regard to overlaps, so a given individual may contribute information to site data at more than one site.

8. See Kohlhase (1991).

9. Note that although Hispanic populations are counted separately in the census, "Hispanic" is considered an ethnic rather than a racial classification. Roughly 52 percent of Hispanics are identified as white in the census, while 48 percent of Hispanics are included in the "other" racial category. In these tables whites include both Hispanic and non-Hispanic members. The all minority classification refers to the set of the population that excludes non-Hispanic whites. The national figures presented in table 7.1 fail to convey the large regional variation in the composition of "minority" populations. For example, Asians make up less than 2 percent of the population in most regions but account for 10 percent of the total population in region 9 (which includes California). In EPA regions 7 and 9, Hispanics make up more than 17 percent of the population, or more than half of the minority populations in these regions, compared to only one third of the minority population nationwide. Similarly blacks account for as little as 2 percent of the population in region 8 (15 percent of total minority population), and up to 20 percent of the population (or 80 percent of the minorities) in region 4, which includes southern states. The proportion of Native Americans ranges from less than 5 percent of the minority population in the east and midwest (or 0.5 percent of the total population) to 20 percent of the minority population in region 10 (or 2.5 percent of total population).

10. Minority population, defined as total population minus non-Hispanic whites, declines from 35.1 percent of on-site residents (or 32.4 percent of residents within a quarter mile of one or more Superfund sites) to 29.5 percent in the one- to two-mile range to 27.6 percent of the population within three to four miles. This result holds for each racial and ethnic group

with the notable exception of blacks, who constitute between 9 and 10 percent of the population within a quarter mile, while accounting for between 12 and 13 percent of residents living within two to four miles of one or more Superfund sites. This is roughly equivalent to their national population percentage of 12 percent.

11. Ring trends for site-level means provide additional confirmation of the income and housing price gradients predicted by theories of environmental amenities. Income steadily increases with distance from the site. Mean incomes grow from $36,770 for the 0.25 ring (i.e., populations living between the site boundary and the 0.25 ring boundary) to $37,400 for the 0.75–1 mile ring to $39,170 for the 3–4 mile ring. The same pattern is apparent in housing values, which increase from $97,850 in the 0.25 ring to $99,770 for the 0.75–1 mile ring to $108,560 for the 3–4 mile ring.

12. See Mauderly (1993), Blancato (1994), and Krishnan and Brodeur (1994).

13. National Research Council (1991).

14. We repeated our analysis of exposures to polluting facilities for 36,901 sites listed in CERCLIS, which includes both sites on the NPL and sites not on this list. The mean number of polluting sources for minority residents living within 1 mile of these sites was 14.8 versus 9.1 for white residents. By demographic group, these figures were 5.9 for Native Americans, 11.7 for blacks, 19.3 for Asians, 19.7 for Hispanics, and 20.6 for other demographic groups. Both of these counts and the ones reported in the text exclude the Superfund site the residents live near from this measure of "other polluting" sources.

15. Mean population density averages 300 persons per square mile for sites classified as "rural" according to EPA site survey data, 1400–1600 for sites classified as "suburban," and 3,000+ for sites classified as "urban." Thus a population density of 2,000 persons per square mile might fall somewhere between suburban and urban. If one divided the sample by median density (590 persons per square mile), the mean of the maximum cumulative individual risks for the more densely populated half of the sample is 0.098, compared to 0.041 for the less densely populated half ($t = 1.7$). Splitting the sample by mean density (1,290 persons per square mile) also results in significantly ($t = 1.7$) higher risk for the set of 51 sites where population density exceeds the mean (0.118 versus 0.045 maximum cumulative individual risk).

16. See Scholz (1986, 1991), Gupta, Van Houtven, and Cropper (1995, 1996), and Hamilton (1995).

17. McCubbins and Schwartz (1984) distinguish between police patrol versus fire alarm regulatory strategies.

18. See Barnett (1994).

19. Anderton, Oakes, and Egan (1997) examine potential differences between NPL and non-NPL sites. They find using census tract data that NPL neighborhoods have a lower percentage of black and Hispanic residents when compared to areas with CERCLIS sites not on the NPL. They note that it is difficult to draw conclusions about the impact of resident composition on EPA decisions about whether to include a CERCLIS site on the NPL because of the lack of risk data on CERCLIS sites.

20. There are some instances in which area residents reject the strict cleanup alternatives chosen by the EPA and oppose their implementation (see Williams 1993). This may be correlated with Senate membership on the environmental oversight committee.

21. E.O. 12898 requires federal agencies to "identify and address . . . disproportionately high and adverse human health or environmental impacts" on minority populations. While the

order requires federal agencies to consider environmental equity concerns in their actions, its implementation has been slowed by uncertainty over definitions over issues such as what constitutes "disproportionate impact." See Bureau of National Affairs (1994).

Chapter 8

1. See the EPA Report (1987) for a summary of the survey conducted by the Roper Organization and for the expert panel rankings. For more details on the analysis discussed in this chapter, see Gayer, Hamilton, and Viscusi (1998a).

2. Portney (1981) was the first researcher to publish estimates of the value of life using a hedonic property model. He coupled the estimate of the price gradient with respect to total dustfall (obtained from a study on Allegheny County, Pennsylvania) with a separate EPA study relating total particulate concentration to mortality rates. By linking the study on dustfall with the study on particulate concentration he demonstrated that the ratio of these two estimates is a measure of the statistical value of life, which he found to be $0.3 million (1996 dollars).

3. See Lichtenstein et al. (1978) and Tversky and Kahneman (1982).

4. Note that the comparison is between values placed on mortality risk and values placed on cancer risk—in which type of cancer, latency period, and probability of death are considerations.

5. On the overestimation of small risks, see Lichtenstein et al. (1978). Kunreuther et al. (1978) note that small unidentified risks may be ignored. For evidence on the overestimation of risks at Superfund sites, see Gayer, Hamilton, and Viscusi (1998b).

6. This particular re-parameterization of the Bayesian learning model with a beta distribution was introduced by Viscusi (1979).

7. We assume that the probabilities p, q, and r are independent. Situations with overlapping information also can lead to an identical functional form for estimation.

8. We assume that only the closest site contributes visual disamenities.

9. In order to estimate the welfare effects of a nonmarginal change in a characteristic, we would need to know the willingness-to-pay function. The endogeneity of marginal prices and quantities limits the use of instrumental variables in a two-stage estimation of willingness to pay. Bartik (1987) suggested using data from multiple markets in order to estimate the structural equations. This approach results in identified structural equations only if consumer preferences are assumed the same across markets, while the price function is assumed to differ due to differences in the matching process (see Kahn and Lang 1988). It is difficult to assume that preferences are homogeneous across housing markets. However, Epple (1987) showed that—even using multiple markets—there are very strong orthogonality conditions that must be met in order to identify the equations. Bartik (1988) and Palmquist (1992) demonstrated that for local disamenities (e.g., Superfund sites), the slope of the hedonic price function is an approximate measure of the willingness to pay for a nonmarginal change.

10. See Bartik and Smith (1987) for a review.

11. The omitted city dummy variable is for Grand Rapids, and the omitted annual dummy variable is for 1988.

12. As we indicated in chapter 2, sites placed on the National Priorities List (NPL) qualify for federal remediation funds. NPL sites undergo a site characterization process known as

the Remedial Investigation and Feasibility Study (RI/FS). The RI/FS contains a baseline risk assessment and provides regional EPA decision makers with a quantitative assessment of human health risk at a site, a description of remedial action objectives, and an analysis of the alternatives proposed to reach these objectives. After evaluating an RI/FS, the EPA selects a remedial action and then documents the reasons for its selection in the Record of Decision.

13. Other studies have considered the effect that information has on the hedonic gradient— although not in a Bayesian framework. Kohlhase (1991) found that a positive relationship between distance to the closest site and the price of the house occurred only after the site was placed on the EPA's National Priorities List. Michaels and Smith (1990) found that for certain submarkets, the price–distance gradient changes slope depending on whether or not the house was sold within six months of the discovery of hazardous waste at the closest site. Kiel and McClain (1995) found no price–distance relationship before the construction of an incinerator, even though there were rumors of its imminent construction. However, they found a positive price–distance relationship during the construction phase, and also throughout the duration of the operation of the incinerator.

14. Most previous hedonic studies have used distance (from the house to the disamenity) as a proxy for both the (nonrisky) aesthetic and (risky) health effects of the disamenity. Where more than one disamenity is present, studies have typically used the distance to the closest site as a proxy. Michaels and Smith (1990) and Harrison and Stock (1984) examined alternative measures of distance. Note that even though we control for cancer risks generated at a site, the difficulty of indexing noncancer health risks means that the distance variable may also reflect in part past reactions to those health effects.

15. The Spartan site contains only a qualitative analysis, which does not contain pathway risk estimates.

16. The price and structural data come from the Multiple Listing Service of the Grand Rapids Society of Realtors. Additionally the GIS analysis determined the longitude and latitude coordinates of the houses and computed the distances of each house to the neighborhood Superfund sites. The GIS capabilities also linked each house to the demographic data of its census tract, city, and school district.

17. The CERCLA data are maintained by the EPA's Office of Solid Waste and Emergency Response. RCRA refers to the Resource Conservation and Recovery Act, and these data are also maintained by the EPA's Office of Solid Waste and Emergency Response. PCS refers to the EPA's Permit Compliance System, which tracks the National Pollutant Discharge Elimination System program under the Clean Water Act.

18. We examine only cancer risk. For noncarcinogenic risk, the EPA's assessment entails computing the ratio of a chemical's calculated exposure intake to its reference dose, the level of exposure thought to be without appreciable risk of noncancer effects. A ratio above 1 for a chemical triggers greater scrutiny. Because noncancer risk varies in its severity (e.g., from skin rashes to reproductive damage), there is no way to summarize accurately the aggregate noncancer risk arising from multiple chemicals at a given site.

19. The cancer risk estimate is for an individual residing in the house. EPA guidance indicates that a *site* risk greater than 10^{-4} generally warrants action and that a site risk between 10^{-4} and 10^{-6} is allowed discretion in the remediation consideration. The household risk used in this chapter couples the site risk estimates with dilution estimates.

20. Cropper, Deck, and McConnell (1988) found that a linear Box-Cox model performs well in a housing market when all attributes are observed and also in the presence of specification error.

21. For each of the sites, the costs (converted to 1996 dollars) of the proposed remediation plans are as follows: Butterworth, $19.4 million; Chem-Central, $2.6 million; Folkertsma, $1.9 million; H. Brown, $18.8 million; Kentwood, $7.1 million; Organic Chemical, $7.4. The costs of the institutional controls had they been implemented are as follows: Butterworth, $2.3 million; Chem-Central, $0.6 million; Folkertsma, $0.7 million; H. Brown, $0.6 million; Kentwood, $0.7 million; Organic Chemical, $0.6 million. One reason for the high cleanup costs could be the EPA's preference for more permanent remediation actions, even though the benefits of permanence are still uncertain. Gupta, Van Houtven, and Cropper (1996) show that the premium that the EPA places on on-site incineration of waste (over and above the cost of capping it) is $12 million at small sites and up to $40 million at large sites (1987 dollars).

22. Estimates are computed at the mean housing price.

23. Slovic and Fischhoff (1982) and Tversky and Kahneman (1982) offer explanations of the cognitive heuristics that can lead to risk perception biases.

24. For example, Viscusi (1981) estimated value-of-life at $7.8 million, Garen (1988) at $16.1 million, Moore and Viscusi (1988) at $8.7 million (all estimates converted to 1996 dollars). See Viscusi (1992a) for a complete survey.

25. The marginal prices are evaluated at the mean housing price. All figures are in 1996 dollars.

26. The marginal value of a house sold after the release of the Remedial Investigation is computed using the price gradient with respect to the dummy variable (i.e., $\partial h/\partial After$) and is evaluated at the mean level of risk. This net impact of the dummy variable differs from the analysis of the change in the impact of risk on prices after the release of the Remedial Investigation, which is represented by the interaction term.

27. This estimate was determined by taking the mean willingness to pay for removal of a non-NPL CERCLA, RCRA, or PCS site and calculating the Superfund cancer risk which yields the same mean willingness to pay.

28. Stock (1991) estimated that the total value of a cleanup of the Ashland site ranged from $7 million to $42 million (in 1996 dollars).

29. See, for example, Morgan et al. (1985) and Nisbett and Ross (1980).

Chapter 9

1. For a discussion of the principal-agent relationship in politics, see Kiewet and McCubbins (1991) and Miller (1992).

2. H.R. 1022, 104th Congress, 1st Session. § 105(2) (1995).

3. See BNA (1995f), and Executive Order No. 12,291, 3 C.F.R. 638 (1993), reprinted in 5 U.S.C. § 601 (1994).

4. H.R. 1022, 104th Congress § 204 (1995).

5. H.R. 1022. §§ 105(3), 201(a)(4) (1995).

6. See Sunstein (1996b).

7. See BNA (1995b), BNA (1995e), and Sunstein (1996b, 265).

8. See BNA (1995g) and BNA (1995c).

9. See BNA (1995c).

10. See Aranson et al. (1982), Farina (1989), Stewart (1975), Wiley (1986), and Mashaw (1985).

11. See McCubbins et al. (1987, 1989, 1992), Horn and Shepsle (1989), and Macey (1992).

12. For example, under the Federal Food, Drug and Cosmetic Act a company must prove a drug is safe before bringing it to market, while under the Toxic Substances Control Act the EPA must prove a chemical is harmful to prevent its marketing. See McCubbins et al. (1987). The National Environmental Policy Act requires that regulators at least develop information on the environmental impacts of their decisions. See 42 U.S.C. 4321–4370 (1994). The Emergency Planning and Community Right-to-Know Act (EPCRA) allows interested parties to petition the EPA to remove chemicals from the list which governs industry pollution reporting in the Toxics Release Inventory program. In one instance, for example, the EPA removed the reporting requirement under EPCRA for the chemical di-n-octyl (DnOP) after the Vista Chemical Company petitioned for its removal. See BNA (1993).

13. See Miller (1996). He notes that work by J. Paul Leigh indicates that "the risk of fatality to the average cleanup worker—a dump truck driver involved in a collision or a laborer run over by a bulldozer, for example—is considerably larger than the cancer risks to individual residents that might result from exposures to the sites."

14. See U.S. EPA (1991b). The most precisely quantified risks are the excess cancer risks for carcinogens, which are expressed in terms of a lifetime incremental cancer probability. The noncancer risk from a given chemical is expressed as a hazard quotient, defined as the calculated exposure intake divided by the chemical's reference dose (e.g., its highest no-observed-adverse-effect level). Within a particular exposure pathway, the noncancer hazard quotients for different chemicals are added to yield an overall pathway hazard index. While the hazard index "sums" information on noncancer exposures, the fact that the severity of health consequences (e.g., skin rashes or birth defects) differs for each chemical makes aggregation of noncancer risks difficult. Moreover, the existence of a nonzero risk does not indicate the magnitude of the risk, so the *degree* of hazard in terms of the probability of risk is not clear for noncancer exposures. For a further description of the Superfund risk assessment process, see chapter 2.

15. The degree of conservatism adopted in risk assessment in Superfund reflects agency choices, since legislation does not require the EPA to focus on "reasonable maximum exposures" or on risks to a hypothetical or actual exposed individual rather than risks to the entire population. In fact, the risk management goals established by Congress for the Superfund program are extremely vague: the legislation calls for actions "as may be necessary to prevent, minimize, or mitigate damage to the public health or welfare or the environment." See Public Law No. 96-510, 94 Statute 2767 (1980) (codified as amended at 42 U.S.C. §§ 9601–9675 (1988 & Supp. IV 1992)), § 104(a).

16. Breyer (1993, 11–12).

17. See Davis (1983). Also see Hamilton (1996) and Hamilton and Schroeder (1994) (providing evidence on how EPA has used discretion in enunciating and enforcing hazardous waste laws).

18. Superfund Amendments and Reauthorization Act (SARA), Public Law No. 99-499, 100 Stat. 1613 § 9621(b)(1) (1986) (amending U.S.C. §§ 9601–9675 (1988 and Supp. IV 1992).

19. Ibid.

20. SARA § 9621 (d)(2)(A).

21. See U.S. EPA (1991b, 1).

22. See U.S. EPA (1991b, 4).

23. 40 C.F.R. § 300 (1995).

24. 40 C.F.R. § 300.430(e)(9) (1995) .

25. In our analysis, we combine a mix of individual proposals from the array of proposed bills in order to examine the potential impacts of regulatory reform.

26. In an analysis of risk assessments in chapter 2, we found that TCE was the second most frequently occurring carcinogen at our sample of 150 sites. TCE accounted for 7 percent of the total chemical cancer pathways at these sites. For an example of Superfund site remediation involving TCE groundwater contamination, see BNA (1989).

27. See U.S. EPA (1989a, 6-4). The degree of conservatism this exposure level embodies is not specified. Default assumptions for risk assessment parameters reflect different degrees of conservatism depending on the parameter.

28. Mean values for these parameter values include 1.4 liters for daily ingestion of water and nine years for exposure duration. For a discussion of the impact of conservatism on the magnitude of Superfund risk assessment, see chapter 3.

29. See U.S. EPA (1989a, 7-11).

30. H.R. 1022, 104th Congress § 110 (1995).

31. Cancer and noncancer risks at Superfund sites arise from several sources—dermal exposure, ingestion, or inhalation of contaminated soil and water as people use a site as residents, workers, recreational users, and trespassers.

32. Estimating the expected number of cancer cases would involve assumptions about contaminant plume size, groundwater use, and the dispersion of contaminants as one gets farther from the site. See chapter 4 and appendices A and B.

33. The use of benefit–cost analysis would automatically alter EPA's focus from individual risks to population risks; the agency would explicitly be concerned both about the magnitude of individual risks as well as the number of individuals exposed.

34. The evaluations of reductions in noncancer risks, since these range from skin rashes to reproductive effects, will be particularly difficult. In addition these risks are stated as ratios of exposure rather than probabilities of experiencing the adverse effect. See U.S. EPA (1989a, 8-15).

An ideal benefit–cost analysis of a proposed Superfund remediation would go beyond mere calculation of the cost per cancer case averted. It would also quantify natural resource damages and, to the extent possible (perhaps through contingent valuation), monetization of them. The analysis would explore synergistic effects of exposure to multiple chemicals, though there currently exist little data on the toxicity of combinations of chemicals arising at Superfund sites. The analysis would also explore differences in the efficacy of cleanup alternatives. For example, what is the probability that institutional controls will not succeed in restricting access to a site? What is the chance that a landfill containment will leak over thirty years, or the likelihood that a removal action will result in contamination as the waste is being transported off-site? Differences in the contribution of the site to a community's economic output, such as the loss that would occur if institutional controls caused land to lie fallow or the gain realized from future site use if the land were made suitable for residential development, would also be part of the analysis. Both Senate bill 343 and House bill 9 at one time contained or considered benefit–cost provisions that would supersede any existing laws. House bill 9 was passed by the House. See BNA (1995a, d).

35. The 10^{-4} risk figure would not be pertinent if benefit–cost analysis were our sole guide. It may, for example, be worthwhile to eliminate risks smaller than 10^{-4} if the exposed population is large and the costs of risk reduction are low. In our analysis we use a risk cutoff to demonstrate how remediations might change if attention were focused on a given level of risk. We then add in benefit–cost considerations explicitly by calculating the cost per cancer case averted at sites. Unless noted otherwise, our cost estimates use a 7 percent discount rate, are expressed in 1993 dollars, and are pre-cost growth (i.e., do not reflect likely growth in costs as measures are implemented.)

36. Zoning restrictions could, for example, prevent development of hazardous waste sites for residential use. An alternative approach would be to estimate the probability of future, on-site residents at sites that currently do not have on-site residents.

37. While EPA may have considered options with different costs in determining cleanup remedies, the cost of cleanup at each site in our analysis is based on the actual remedy EPA selected for the site. Costs are expressed in 1993 dollars and are discounted at a 7 percent rate. Although the decisions regarding sites to remediate are based on risk levels rather than ARARs in our "no-ARARs" and "no future on-site residents" scenarios, ARARs may still have an impact on the *costs* of remediations examined at these sites. The result is reached because current expenditures may be influenced by the requirement to meet state or federal ARARs.

38. We used a thirty-year period because it is the time horizon used by the EPA in its risk assessments. Our estimates of cancer cases averted by remediation were derived by combining site level data on chemical concentration with information on contaminant plume size, data on groundwater use, and site population figures. For a description of our methodology, see chapter 4 and appendixes A and B. The cancer case estimates in this chapter are based on the case 1 scenario in chapter 4.

39. For instance, a worker who receives $500 extra compensation to face an annual fatality risk of 1/10,000 would have an implicit value per statistical life of $5 million, that is, $500 divided by the 1/10,000 probability to yield a value per unit risk of $5 million. This approach is recommended for conducting benefit–cost analysis throughout the federal government by the U.S. Office of Management and Budget (OMB). See OMB (1993). For a review of this approach, see Viscusi (1992a).

40. See Viscusi (1992a).

41. See Viscusi (1994a); see also Lutter and Morrall (1994), Sunstein (1996a), and Viscusi (1994b).

42. Note that these estimates utilize EPA assumptions of conservative risk levels and do not discount deferred cases of cancer. Thus, even under procedures that overstate actual cost-effectiveness, few cleanups pass a benefit–cost test.

43. A more sophisticated application of risk assessment would estimate the probability that residents would move onsite in the future, based on surrounding land uses and trends in residential growth in the area. This probability would then be multiplied by the future onsite resident risk, to yield an expected risk for this population. The role of policy decisions (e.g., zoning restrictions) in influencing this probability would merit consideration as well.

44. Search of RELAI, Remedial Project Managers Site Database (U.S. EPA 1993b).

45. For a discussion of natural resource damages and Superfund, see Stewart (1995).

46. See Kuehn (1996, 106–107).

47. In chapter 7, we find that for residents living within one mile of Superfund sites, the mean number of polluting facilities/sites tracked in five different EPA pollution databases within one mile of these Superfund sites was 11.4 for minority residents versus 6.3 for white residents. Minorities are thus more likely to bear a burden from synergistic effects from these multiple sources of pollution. For an additional discussion of environmental equity and Superfund, see Hird (1994) who found that the number of sites in a county on the National Priorities List (i.e., the hazardous waste sites qualifying for federal cleanup money under Superfund) increased with the nonwhite population percentage. Zimmerman (1993) found that the percentages of blacks and Hispanics of the aggregate populations of communities with NPL sites were higher than their national population percentage. See also Been (1994) and Lazarus (1993).

48. See Hamilton and Viscusi (1997b).

49. The mean minority population is the average of the population percentages in the given subsample of sites.

50. See Hamilton (1995), which demonstrates that firms calculating where to expand hazardous waste processing capacity are more likely to target areas with lower levels of potential political activity.

51. See chapter 7.

52. This sample of 67 sites excluded those sites where the EPA chose to take no action. If those no-action sites were included, the mean risk for the 76 sites would be 0.034 and the median risk would be 0.0015.

53. See chapter 4.

54. SARA, 42 U.S.C. § 9621(b)(1) (1994).

55. This pattern is especially pronounced for groundwater contaminants. At roughly half of the sites involving groundwater contamination where expenditures were less than $5 million, EPA addressed contamination through institutional controls. Of the more expensive sites with groundwater contamination, EPA selected treatment remedies for 75 percent of the sites.

56. This discussion is based on Leung (1998).

57. See EPA (1998a). For a discussion of the degree that the reforms have been implemented successfully, see Information Access Company (1995a, 1995b, 1996) and Bureau of National Affairs (1997b, c, d).

58. U.S. EPA (1988a, 2).

59. See U.S. EPA (1998a, 21). This report indicates the NRRB had reviewed decisions at 20 sites, which the agency estimated resulted in savings of $31.5 million. From the updating of remedy selection decisions to take into account "significant new scientific information, technological advancements, or other considerations," the agency estimated that it achieved in fiscal year 1997 over $360 million in future cost reductions at more than 60 sites (U.S. EPA 1998a, 23). The agency also created a National Risk-Based Priority Panel to rank sites based on risk, which in fiscal year 1997 evaluated over 50 Superfund projects.

60. U.S. EPA (1998a, 32). Note that in 1995 the EPA issued a directive to regional offices indicating factors officials could take into account when determining future probable land use, including "the site's location and current use; vulnerability of groundwater; and proximity to wetlands, floodplains, and critical habitats" (Dunsky 1995).

61. In commenting on the release of the report (U.S. EPA 1998a) on EPA's Superfund administrative reforms, EPA Administrator Carol Browner noted that "in addition to these administrative reforms, we still need a new law to make the program work even better" (U.S. EPA 1998b, 1). For discussion of possible reforms of EPA procedures, see Geltman and Skroback (1998).

62. These calculations assume a 3 percent discount rate for costs and cancers, a ten-year latency period for the onset of cancers, and average exposure concentrations and intake parameters.

63. This is a process that Monte Carlo analysis would also advance.

Appendix A

1. OMB Circular No. A-904 issued October 29, 1992 changed federal government practice of using a 10 percent discount rate to 7 percent. In response EPA revised its guidance for conducting RI/FSs by calling for the use of a 7 percent rate instead of the 5 percent rate published in a 1988 guidance. See Office of Management and Budget (1992).

Bibliography

Acton, Jan P. and Lloyd S. Dixon. 1992. *Superfund and Transaction Costs: The Experiences of Insurers and Very Large Industrial Firms.* Santa Monica, CA: Rand, Institute for Civil Justice.

American Industrial Health Council (AIHC). 1994. *Exposure Factors Sourcebook.* Washington, DC: American Industrial Health Council.

Anderson, Andy B., Douglas L. Anderton, and John Michael Oakes. 1994. Environmental equity: Evaluating TSDF siting over the past two decades. *Waste Age* (July): 83–100.

Anderton, Douglas L. 1996. Methodological issues in the spatiotemporal analysis of environmental equity. *Social Science Quarterly* 77(3): 508–15.

Anderton, Douglas L., Andy B. Anderson, John Michael Oakes, and Michael R. Fraser. 1994a. Environmental equity: The demographics of dumping. *Demography* 31(2): 229–48.

Anderton, Douglas L., Andy B. Anderson, Peter H. Rossi, John Michael Oakes, Michael R. Fraser, Eleanor W. Weber, and Michael J. Calabrese. 1994b. Hazardous waste facilities: "Environmental equity" issues in metropolitan areas. *Evaluation Review* 18(2): 123–40.

Anderton, Douglas L., John Michael Oakes, and Karla L. Egan. 1997. Environmental equity in Superfund: Demographics of the discovery and prioritization of abandoned toxic waste sites. *Evaluation Review* 21(1): 3–26.

Applegate, John S., and Steven M. Wesloh. 1998. Short changing short-term risk: A study of Superfund remedy selection. *Yale Journal on Regulation* 15: 269–327.

Aranson, Peter H., Ernest Gelhorn, and Glen O. Robinson. 1982. A theory of legislative delegation. *Cornell Law Review* 68(November): 1–67.

Arrow, Kenneth J. 1982. Risk perception in psychology and economics. *Economic Inquiry* 20: 1–9.

Arrow, Kenneth J., Maureen L. Cropper, George C. Eads, Robert W. Hahn, Lester B. Lave, Roger G. Noll, Paul R. Portney, Milton Russell, Richard Schmalensee, V. Kerry Smith, and Robert N. Stavins. 1996. *Benefit–Cost Analysis in Environmental, Health, and Safety Regulation: A Statement of Principles.* Washington, DC: AEI Press.

Bailey, Martin J., Richard F. Muth, and Hugh O. Nourse. 1963. A regression method for real estate price index construction. *Journal of the American Statistical Association* 58: 933–42.

Barkenbus, Jack N., Jean H. Perez, and Jonathan D. Rubin. 1996. More on the agenda. *Social Science Quarterly* 77(3): 516–19.

Barnard, Robert C. 1995. Risk assessment: The default conservatism controversy. *Regulatory Toxicology and Pharmacology* 21: 431–38.

Barnett, Harold C. 1994. *Toxic Debts and the Superfund Dilemma.* Chapel Hill: University of North Carolina Press.

Bartik, Timothy J. 1987. The estimation of demand parameters with single market data: The problems caused by unobserved tastes. *Journal of Political Economy* 95: 81–88.

Bartik, Timothy J. 1988. Measuring the benefits of amenity improvements in hedonic price models. *Land Economics* 64(2): 172–83.

Bartik, Timothy J., and V. Kerry Smith. 1987. Urban amenities and public policy. In E. S. Mills, ed., *Handbook on Urban Economics* 1207–54. Amsterdam: North-Holland.

Baumol, William J., and Wallace E. Oates. 1988. *The Theory of Environmental Policy*. 2d ed. New York: Cambridge University Press.

Bawn, Kathleen. 1995. Political control versus expertise: Congressional choices about administrative procedures. *American Political Science Review* 89(1): 62–73.

Becker, Gary S. 1983. A theory of competition among pressure groups for political influence. *Quarterly Journal of Economics* 98: 371–99.

Been, Vicki. 1993. What's fairness got to do with it? Environmental justice and the siting of locally undesirable land uses. *Cornell Law Review* 78 (September): 1001–85.

Been, Vicki. 1994. Locally undesirable land uses in minority neighborhoods: Disproportionate siting or market dynamics? *Yale Law Journal* 103 (April): 1383–1422.

Been, Vicki. 1995. Analyzing evidence of environmental justice. *Journal of Land Use and Environmental Law* 11(1): 1–36.

Been, Vicki, with Francis Gupta. 1997. Coming to the nuisance or going to the barrios? A longitudinal analysis of environmental justice claims. *Ecology Law Quarterly* 24: 1.

Beider, Perry. 1994. *Analyzing the Duration of Cleanup at Sites on Superfund's National Priorities List*. Washington, DC: Congressional Budget Office.

Binder, S., D. Sokal, and D. Maugham. 1986. Estimating soil ingestion: The use of tracer elements in estimating the amount of soil ingested by young children. *Archives of Environmental Health* 41: 341–45.

Blais, Lynn E. 1996. Environmental racism reconsidered. *North Carolina Law Review* 75: 75.

Blancato, J. N. 1994. Pharmacokinetics, chemical interactions, and toxicological risk assessment in perspective. *Quality Management in Pharmaceutical Development: From Molecular Design to Drug Approval, Drug Information Journal* 28(4): 133–37.

Blomquist, Glenn C. 1979. Value of life saving: Implications of consumption activity. *Journal of Political Economy* 96: 675–700.

Boerner, Christopher, and Thomas Lambert. 1995. Environmental justice. *Public Interest* (Winter): 61–83.

Bogen, Kenneth T. 1994. A note on compounded conservatism. *Risk Analysis* 14(4): 379–81.

Bowen, William M., Mark J. Salling, Kingsley E. Haynes, and Ellen J. Cryan. 1995. Toward environmental justice: Spatial equity in Ohio and Cleveland. *Annals of the Association of American Geographers* 85(4): 641–63.

Boyd, James. 1998. Searching for the profit in pollution prevention: Case studies in the corporate evaluation of environmental opportunities. Discussion paper 98-30. Washington, DC: Resources for the Future.

Boyd, James, Winston Harrington, Molly Macauley, and Mary Elizabeth Calhoon. 1994. The impact of uncertain environmental liability on industrial real estate development: Developing a framework for analysis. Discussion paper 94-03 REV. Washington, DC: Resources for the Future.

Brehm, John, and Scott Gates. 1997. *Working, Shirking, and Sabotage: Bureaucratic Response to a Democratic Public*. Ann Arbor University of Michigan Press.

Breyer, Stephen. 1993. *Breaking the Vicious Circle: Toward Effective Risk Regulation*. Cambridge: Harvard University Press.

Brooks, Nancy, and Rajiv Sethi. 1997. The distribution of pollution: Community characteristics and exposure to air toxics. *Journal of Environmental Economics and Management* 32: 233–50.

Brown, Donald A. 1988. Superfund cleanups, ethics, and environmental risk assessment. *Environmental Affairs* 16: 181–98.

Bryant, Bunyan, and Paul Mohai, eds. 1992. *Race and the Incidence of Environmental Hazards: A Time for Discourse*. Boulder, CO: Westview Press.

Buchinsky, Moshe. 1994. Changes in the U.S. Wage Structure 1963–1987: Application of Quantile Regression. *Econometrica* 62(2): 405–408.

Buckley, James R. 1986. The political economy of Superfund implementation. *Southern California Law Review* 59(4): 875–909.

Bullard, Robert D. 1990. *Dumping in Dixie: Race, Class, and Environmental Quality*. Boulder, CO: Westview Press.

Bullard, Robert D. 1993. ed. *Confronting Environmental Racism*. Boston: South End Press.

Bullard, Robert D. 1996. Environmental justice: It's more than waste facility siting. *Social Science Quarterly* 77(3): 493–99.

Bureau of National Affairs (BNA). 1989. Parties agree to pay over $1 million to contain TCE plume in municipal wells. *Environment Reporter* 19: 2267 (Feb. 17).

Bureau of National Affairs (BNA). 1993. Facilities no longer required to report DnOP on EPCRA's toxic release inventory. *Chemical Regulation Reporter* 17: 1238 (Oct. 8).

Bureau of National Affairs (BNA). 1994. Environmental justice: Difficulty predicted for demonstrating effectiveness of Clinton executive order. *BNA Environment Daily* (Dec. 8).

Bureau of National Affairs (BNA). 1995a. Compromise to address "Supermandate" adopted by Senate in regulatory bill. *Environment Reporter*. 26: 566 (July 14, 1995).

Bureau of National Affairs (BNA). 1995b. GOP Contract would undermine enforcement of environmental regulations, groups say. *Environment Reporter* 25: 1691 (Jan. 6).

Bureau of National Affairs (BNA). 1995c. House bill's risk provisions called "prescription for gridlock," by Chafee. *Environment Reporter* 25: 2037 (Feb. 24).

Bureau of National Affairs (BNA). 1995d. House considering broad mandate to apply Cost–Benefit provision to all laws. *Chemical Regulation Reporter* 18: 1478 (Jan. 13).

Bureau of National Affairs (BNA). 1995e. Regulatory reform poses threat to environmental justice, activists say. *Environment Reporter* 25: 2119 (Mar. 3)

Bureau of National Affairs (BNA). 1995f. Risk assessment: House considering broad mandate to apply cost–benefit provision to all laws. *Chemical Regulation Reporter* 18: 1478 (Jan. 13).

Bureau of National Affairs (BNA). 1995g. Unintended consequences for business predicted if existing legislation enacted. *Chemical Regulation Reporter* 19: 201 (May 19).

Bureau of National Affairs (BNA). 1997a. Hazardous waste: Report examines remediation techniques, contract work of national cleanup market. *Environment Reporter* 28(14): 644.

Bureau of National Affairs (BNA). 1997b. Superfund: Administrative reforms prove helpful, should be expanded, CMA report says. *Environment Reporter* 27(50): 2641 (Apr. 25).

Bureau of National Affairs (BNA). 1997c. Superfund: Faster cleanup times required by EPA to meet recent projections, GAO Reports. *Environment Reporter* 28(24): 1216 (Oct. 17).

Bureau of National Affairs (BNA). 1997d. Superfund: Savings of reforms exceed $600 million in two years, EPA says in program report. *Environment Reporter* 28(25): 1249 (Oct. 24).

Burmaster, David E., and Robert H. Harris. 1993. The magnitude of compounding conservatisms in superfund risk assessments. *Risk Analysis* 13(2) 131–34.

Calabrese, E. J., R. Barnes, E. J. Stanek, III, H. Pastides, C. E. Gilbert, P. Veneman, X. Wang, A. Lasztity, and P. T. Kostecki. 1989. How much soil do young children ingest: An epidemiological study. *Regulatory Toxicology and Pharmacology* 10: 123–37.

Calabrese, E. J., E. J. Stanek, III, C. E. Gilbert, and R. M. Barnes. 1990. Preliminary adult soil ingestion estimates: Results of a pilot study. *Regulatory Toxicology and Pharmacology* 12: 88–95.

Camerer, Colin F., and Howard Kunreuther. 1989. Decision processes for low probability events: Policy implications. *Journal of Policy Analysis and Management* 8(4): 565–92.

Caputo, Michael R., and James E. Wilen. 1995. Optimal cleanup of hazardous wastes. *International Economic Review* 36(1): 217–43.

Centner, Terence J., William Kriesel, and Andrew G. Kreeler. 1996. Environmental justice and toxic releases: Establishing evidence of discriminatory effect based on race and not income. *Wisconsin Environmental Law Journal* 3: 119.

Chemical Manufacturers Association. 1991. *Analysis of the Impact of Exposure Assumptions on Risk Assessment of Chemicals in the Environment.* Springfield, VA: Risk Focus, Versar, Inc.

Chemical Week. 1980. Superfund: How it will work, what it will cost. *Chemical Week* (Dec. 17): 38.

Chertow, Marain R., and Daniel C. Esty. 1997. *Thinking Ecologically.* New Haven: Yale University Press.

Church, Thomas W., and Robert T. Nakamura. 1993. *Cleaning up the Mess: Implementation Strategies under Superfund.* Washington, DC: Brookings Institution.

Clean Sites. 1990. *Hazardous Waste Sites and the Rural Poor: A Preliminary Assessment.* Alexandria, VA: Clean Sites, Inc.

Coase, Ronald. 1960. The problem of social cost. *Journal of Law and Economics* 3 (October): 1–44.

Coates, Dennis, Victoria Heid, and Michael Munger. 1994. Not equitable, not efficient: U.S. policy on low-level radioactive waste disposal. *Journal of Policy Analysis and Management* 13(3): 526–38.

Coglianese, Cary. 1997. Assessing consensus: The promise and performance of negotiated rulemaking. *Duke Law Journal* 46(6): 1255.

Cohen, Linda. 1981. Who pays the bill: Insuring against the risks from low level nuclear waste disposal. *Natural Resources Journal* 21(4): 773–87.

Cohen, Mark. 1999. Enforcement of environmental policy. In Hank Folmer and Tom Tietenberg, eds., *International Yearbook of Environmental and Resource Economics,* vol. 3. Northampton, MA: Edward Elgar, forthcoming.

Cole, Luke W. 1992. Empowerment as the key to environmental protection: The need for environmental poverty law. *Ecology Law Quarterly* 19(4): 619–83.

Combs, B., and Paul Slovic. 1979. Causes of death: Biased newspaper coverage and biased judgments. *Journalism Quarterly* 56: 837–43.

Commission for Racial Justice. 1987. *Toxic Wastes and Race in the United States: A National Report on the Racial and Socioeconomic Characteristics of Communities with Hazardous Waste Sites.* New York: Commission for Racial Justice, United Church of Christ.

Congressional Budget Office. 1994. *The Total Costs of Cleaning Up Nonfederal Superfund Sites.* Washington, DC: Government Printing Office.

Covello, Vincent T., and Merkhofer, Miley W. 1993. *Risk Assessment Methods: Approaches for Assessing Health and Environmental Risks*, New York: Plenum Press.

Crandall, Robert W., Christopher DeMuth, Robert W. Hahn, Robert E. Litan, Pietro S. Nivola, and Paul R. Portney. 1997. *An Agenda for Federal Regulatory Reform.* Washington, DC: American Enterprise Institute for Public Policy Research/Brookings Institution.

Cranor, Carl F. 1990. Scientific conventions, ethics and legal institutions. *Risk: Issues in Health and Safety* 1: 155.

Cropper, Maureen L., Leland B. Deck, and Kenneth E. McConnell. 1988. On the choice of functional form for hedonic price functions. *Review of Economics and Statistics* 70(4): 668–75.

Cropper, Maureen L., William N. Evans, Stephen J. Berardi, Maria M. Ducla-Soares, and Paul R. Portney. 1992. The determinants of pesticide regulation: A statistical analysis of EPA decision making. *Journal of Political Economy* 100(1): 175–97.

Cullen, Alison C. 1994. Measures of compounding conservatism in probabilistic risk assessment. *Risk Analysis* 14(4): 389–93.

Davies, J. Clarence (Terry), and Jan Mazure. 1997. *Regulating Pollution: Does the U.S. System Work?* Internet Edition. Washington, DC: Resources for the Future.

Davis, Joseph A. 1983. House subcommittees begin reviewing EPA documents; two more officials are fired. *Congressional Quarterly Weekly* 41: 411–12.

Desvousges, William H., F. Reed Johnson, Richard W. Dunford, Kevin J. Boyle, Sara P. Hudson, and K. Nicole Wilson. 1992. Measuring natural resources damages with contingent valuation: Tests of validity and reliability. Paper presented at the Cambridge Economics, Inc., Symposium, Contingent Valuation: A Critical Assessment, April 1992, Washington, DC.

Diamond, Peter, and Jerry Hausman. 1994. Contingent valuation: Is some number better than no number? *Journal of Economic Perspectives* 8(4): 45–64.

Dixon, Lloyd S. 1994. Fixing superfund: The impact of the proposed superfund reform act of 1994 on transaction costs. Paper presented at American Institute Conference, Reforming Superfund, Washington DC, June 3.

Dixon, Lloyd S., and James K. Hammitt. 1993. *Private-Sector Cleanup Expenditures and Transaction Costs at 19 Superfund Sites.* Santa Monica, CA: Rand Corporation.

Dockins, P. Christen. 1996. What's worst? Who's first? Conservatism, risk assessment and priorities at hazardous waste sites. Doctoral dissertation. Department of Economics. Duke University, Durham, NC.

Dockins, P. Christen, James T. Hamilton, and W. Kip Viscusi. 1997. The costs of conservative risk assessment: Monte Carlo evidence from Superfund sites. Working paper. Department of Economics Duke University, Durham, NC.

Doty, Carolyn B., and Curtis C. Travis. 1989. The Superfund remedial action decision process: A review of fifty Records of Decision. *Journal of the Air Pollution Control Association* 39: 1535–42.

Dunsky, Christopher J. 1995. EPA directives outline CERCLA reforms. *Michigan Environmental Compliance Update* 6(5).

Environ Corporation. 1993. *A Comparison of Monte Carlo Simulation-Based Exposure Estimates with Estimates Calculated Using EPA and Suggested Michigan Manufacturers Association Exposure Factors.* Princeton, NJ: Environ Corporation.

Epple, Dennis. 1987. Hedonic prices and implicit markets: Estimating demand and supply functions for differentiated products. *Journal of Political Economy* 95: 59–80.

Ershow, A. G., and K. P. Cantor. 1989. *Total Water and Tapwater Intake in the United States: Population-Based Estimates of Quantities and Sources.* Bethesda, MD: National Cancer Institute, 263-MD-810264.

Esty, Daniel C. 1996. Revitalizing environmental federalism. *Michigan Law Review 95: 570–638.*

Farber, Daniel A. 1992. Politics and procedure in environmental law. *Journal of Law, Economics and Organization* 8(1): 59–81.

Farina, Cynthia. 1989. Statutory interpretation and the balance of power in the administrative state. *Columbia Law Review* 89(Mar.): 452–528.

Ferris, Deeohn. 1994. Communities of color and hazardous waste cleanup: Expanding public participation in the federal Superfund program. *Fordham Urban Law Journal* 21: 671–87.

Finkel, Adam M. 1989. Is risk assessment really too conservative? Revising the revisionists. *Columbia Journal of Environmental Law* 14: 427–67.

Finkel, Adam M., and Dominic Golding, eds. 1994. *Worst Things First? The Debate over Risk-Based National Environmental Priorities*, Washington, DC: Resources for the Future.

Finley, Brent, Deborah Proctor, Paul Scott, Natalie Harrington, Dennis Paustenbach, and Paul Price. 1994. Recommended distributions for exposure factors frequently used in health risk assessment. *Risk Analysis* 14(4): 533–53.

Finley, Brent, and Dennis Paustenbach. 1994. The benefits of probabilistic exposure assessment: Three case studies involving contaminated air, water, and soil. *Risk Analysis* 14(1): 53–73.

Fix, Michael, and Raymond J. Struyk, eds. 1993. *Clear and Convincing Evidence: Measurement of Discrimination in America.* Washington, DC: Urban Institute Press.

Flynn, James, Paul Slovic, and C. K. Mertz. 1994. Gender, race, and perception of environmental health risks. *Risk Analysis* 14(6): 1101–1107.

Forsyth, Margaret. 1997. The economics of site investigation for groundwater protection: Sequential decision making under uncertainty. *Journal of Environmental Economics and Management* 34: 1–31.

Foster, Kenneth R., D. Bernstein, and Peter W. Huber, eds. 1993. *Phantom Risk: Scientific Inference and the Law.* Cambridge: MIT Press.

Fullerton, Don, and Seng-Su Tsang. 1996. Should environmental costs be paid by the polluter or by the beneficiary? The case of CERCLA and Superfund. *Public Economics Review* (June): 85–127.

Garen, John. 1988. Compensating Wage Differentials and the Endogeneity of Job Riskiness. *Review of Economics and Statistics* 70(1): 9–16.

Gayer, Ted, James T. Hamilton, and W. Kip Viscusi. 1998a. Private values of risk tradeoffs at Superfund sites: Housing market evidence on learning about risk. Working paper. Public Policy Institute. Georgetown University. Washington, DC.

Gayer, Ted, James T. Hamilton, and W. Kip Viscusi. 1998b. Market evidence on learning about cancer risks: A repeat sales housing market analysis. Working paper. Public Policy Institute. Georgetown University Washington, DC.

Geltman, Elizabeth Glass, and Andrew E. Skroback. 1998. Reinventing the EPA to conform with the new American environmentality. *Columbia Journal of Environmental Law* 23: 1–52.

Ghosh, Debapriya, Dennis Lees, and William Seal. 1975. Optimal motorway speed and some valuations of time and life. *Manchester School of Economics and Social Studies* 43: 134–43.

Goldman, Benjamin A. 1994. *Not Just Prosperity: Achieving Sustainability with Environmental Justice.* Vienna, VA: National Wildlife Federation.

Goldman, Benjamin A., and Jaura J. Fitton. 1994. Toxic waste and race revisited. An update of the 1987 report on the racial and socioeconomic characteristics of communities with hazardous waste sites. Washington, DC: Center for Policy Alternatives.

Goodman, Leo A., and William H. Kruskal. 1979. *Measures of Association for Cross Classifications.* New York: Springer-Verlag.

Graham, Carolyn, and Jennifer B. Grills. 1997. Comment: Environmental justice: Survey of federal and state responses. *Villanova Environmental Law Journal* 8: 237–258.

Graham, John D. 1991. *Harnessing Science for Environmental Regulation,* New York: Praeger Publishers.

Graham, John D. 1995. Historical perspective on risk assessment in the federal government. *Toxicology* 102: 29–52.

Graham, John D., and Jonathan Baert Wiener. 1995. *Risk versus Risk: Tradeoffs in Protecting Health and Environment.* Cambridge: Harvard University Press.

Graham, John D., Laura C. Green, and Marc J. Roberts. 1989. *In Search of Safety: Chemicals and Cancer Risk.* Cambridge: Harvard University Press.

Greene, William H. 1993. *Econometric Analysis.* 2d ed. New York: Macmillan.

Gupta, Shreekant, George Van Houtven, and Maureen L. Cropper. 1995. Do benefits and costs matter in environmental regulation? An analysis of EPA decisions under Superfund. In ed. Richard L. Revesz and Richard B. Stewart, eds., *Analyzing Superfund: Economics, Science, Law.* Washington, DC: Resources for the Future.

Gupta, Shreekant, George Van Houtven, and Maureen L. Cropper. 1996. Paying for permanence: An economic analysis of EPA's cleanup decisions at Superfund sites. *Rand Journal of Economics* 27(3): 563–82.

Hahn, Robert William. 1996. *Risks, Costs, and Lives Saved: Getting Better Results from Regulation.* New York: Oxford University Press.

Hahn, Robert William. 1997. Achieving real regulatory reform. *University of Chicago Legal Forum* 1997: 143–57.

Hahn, Robert William. 1998. An analysis of the first government report on the benefits and costs of regulation. Working paper E-98-05. Belfer Center for Science and International Affairs. John F. Kennedy School of Government. Harvard University.

Hahn, Robert W., and John A. Hird. 1991. The costs and benefits of regulation: Review and synthesis. *Yale Journal on Regulation* 8: 233–78.

Hahn, Robert W., and Robert E. Litan. 1997. *Improving Regulatory Accountability*. Washington, DC: American Enterprise Institute for Public Policy Research/Brookings Institution.

Hamilton, James T. 1993. Politics and social costs: Estimating the impact of collective action on hazardous waste facilities. *Rand Journal of Economics* 24(1): 101–25.

Hamilton, James T. 1994. Information provision and pollution reduction: Does pollution reporting lead firms to consider the risks of their pollutants? Working paper. Sanford Institute of Public Policy. Duke University, Durham, NC.

Hamilton, James T. 1995. Testing for environmental racism: Prejudice, profits, power? *Journal of Policy Analysis and Management* 14(1): 107–32.

Hamilton, James T. 1996. Going by the (informal) book: The EPA's use of informal rules in enforcing hazardous waste laws. In Gary Libecap, ed., *Reinventing Government and the Problem of Bureaucracy*. Greenwich, CT: JAI Press, 109–55.

Hamilton, James T. 1997. Taxes, torts, and the toxics release inventory: Congressional voting on instruments to control pollution. *Economic Inquiry* 35: 745–62.

Hamilton, James T., and Christopher H. Schroeder. 1994. Strategic regulators and the choice of rulemaking procedures: The selection of formal vs. informal rules in regulating hazardous waste. *Law and Contemporary Problems* 57(2): 111–60.

Hamilton, James T., and W. Kip Viscusi. 1994. Human health risk assessments for Superfund. *Ecology Law Quarterly* 21(3): 573–641.

Hamilton, James T., and W. Kip Viscusi. 1995. The magnitude and policy implications of health risks from hazardous waste sites. In Richard L. Revesz and Richard B. Stewart, eds., *Analyzing Superfund: Economics, Science, and Law*. Washington, DC: Resources for the Future, 55–81.

Hamilton, James T., and W. Kip Viscusi. 1997a. How costly is "clean"? An analysis of the benefits and costs of Superfund site remediations. *Journal of Policy Analysis and Management*, forthcoming.

Hamilton, James T., and W. Kip Viscusi. 1997b. Estimating Environmental Equity: Who Bears Risks at Superfund Sites? Working paper. Sanford Institute of Public Policy. Duke University, Durham, NC.

Hamilton, James T., and W. Kip Viscusi. 1997c. The benefits and costs of regulatory reforms for Superfund. *Stanford Environmental Law Journal* 16(2): 159–98.

Hanemann, Michael W. 1994. Valuing the environment through contingent valuation. *Journal of Economic Perspectives* 8(4): 19–43.

Harper, Carolyn R., and David Zilberman. 1992. Pesticides and worker safety. *American Journal of Agricultural Economics* (February): 68–78.

Harper, Richard K., and Stephen C. Adams. 1996. CERCLA and deep pockets: Market response to the Superfund program. *Contemporary Economic Policy* 14: 107–15.

Harris, W. E. 1993. Low-dose risks and authoritative misinformation. Parts I and II. *Risk Abstracts* 10(2, 3): 1–5, 1–5.

Harrison, David, Jr., and James H. Stock. 1984. Hedonic housing value, local public goods, and the benefits of hazardous waste cleanup. Working paper. Energy and Environmental Policy Center. Harvard University.

Hartman, Raymond S., Michael J. Doane, and Chi Seung Woo. 1991. Consumer rationality and the status quo. *Quarterly Journal of Economics* 106(1): 141–62.

Hazardous Waste Cleanup Project. 1993. *Exaggerating Risk: How EPA's Risk Assessments Distort the Facts at Superfund Sites throughout the United States.* Washington, DC: Morgan, Lewrs, and Bockius.

Heinzerling, Lisa. 1998. Regulatory costs of mythic proportions. *Yale Law Journal* 107: 1981–2070.

Helland, Eric. 1998a. Prosecutorial Discretion at the EPA: Was Ann Gorsuch an environmentalist? Working paper. Department of Economics. Ball State University, Muncie, IN.

Helland, Eric. 1998b. The revealed preferences of state EPAs: Stringency, enforcement and substitution. *Journal of Environmental Economics and Management* 35: 242–61.

Hersh, Robert. 1995. Race and industrial hazards: An historical geography of the Pittsburgh region, 1900–1990. Discussion paper. Resources for the Future, Washington, DC.

Hersh, Robert, Katherine Probst, Kris Wernstedt, and Jan Mazurek. 1997. *Linking Land Use and Superfund Cleanups: Uncharted Territory* Washington, DC: Resources for the Future.

Hird, John A. 1990. Superfund Expenditures and Cleanup Priorities: Distributive Politics or the Public Interest? *Journal of Policy Analysis and Management* 9(4): 455–83.

Hird, John A. 1993. Environmental policy and equity: The case of Superfund. *Journal of Policy Analysis and Management* 12(2): 323–43.

Hird, John A. 1994. *Superfund: The Political Economy of Environmental Risk.* Baltimore: Johns Hopkins University Press.

Horn, Murray J., and Kenneth A. Shepsle. 1989. Commentary on administrative arrangements and the political control of agencies: Administrative process and organizational form as legislative responses to agency costs. *Virginia Law Review* 75(2): 499–508.

Huber, Peter J. 1967. The behavior of maximum likelihood estimates under non-standard conditions. In *Proceedings of the Fifth Berkeley Symposium in Mathematical Sciences and Probability*, vol. 1. Berkeley: University of California Press, 221–33.

Information Access Company. 1995a. Superfund reform: Amid skepticism, EPA takes step away from pump-and-treat systems. *Ground Water Monitor* 11 (Apr. 6).

Information Access Company. 1995b. EPA Superfund measures barely touch fundamental problems, reformer says. *Hazardous Waste News* (October 9).

Information Access Company. 1996. Clinton administration unveils own superfund plans. *Chemical Marketing Reporter* 249 (June 10): 3.

Israeli, M., and C. B. Nelson. 1992. Distribution and expected time of residence for U.S. households. *Risk Analysis* 7: 519–29.

Jasanoff, Susan. 1993. Relating risk assessment and risk management. *EPA Journal* 19: 35–37.

Johnson, Barry L. 1993. Testimony before Senate subcommittee on Superfund, recycling, and solid waste management, May 6, 1993. Agency for Toxic Substances and Disease Registry, Atlanta, GA.

Johnson, Barry L. 1995. Nature, extent and impact of superfund hazardous waste sites. *Chemosphere* 31: 2415–28.

Johnson, B. B., and Paul Slovic. 1994. "Improving" risk communication and risk management: Legislated solutions or legislated disasters? *Risk Analysis* 14: 905–906.

Kahn, S., and K. Lang. 1988. Efficient estimation of structural hedonic systems. *International Economic Review* 29(1): 157–66.

Kahneman, Daniel, Paul Slovic, and Amos Tversky. 1982. *Judgment under Uncertainty: Heuristics and Biases.* New York: Cambridge University Press.

Kahneman, Daniel, and Amos Tversky. 1979. Prospect theory: An analysis of decision under risk. *Econometrica* 47: 263–92.

Kiel, Katherine A. 1995. Measuring the impact of the discovery and cleaning of identified hazardous waste sites on house values. *Land Economics* 71(4): 428–35.

Kiel, Katherine A., and Katherine T. McClain. 1995. House prices during siting decision stages: The case of an incinerator from rumor through operation. *Journal of Environmental Economics and Management* 28: 241–55.

Kiewet, D. Roderick, and Mathew D. McCubbins. 1991. *The Logic of Delegation: Congressional Parties and the Appropriations Process.* Chicago: University of Chicago Press.

Koenker, Roger, and Gilbert Bassett, Jr. 1978. Regression quantiles. *Econometrica* 50(1): 43–61.

Kohlhase, Janet E. 1991. The impact of toxic waste sites on housing values. *Journal of Urban Economics* 30: 1–26.

Krier, James E. 1990. Risk and design. *Journal of Legal Studies* 19: 781–90.

Krishnan, K., and J. Brodeur. 1994. Toxic interactions among environmental pollutants: Corroborating laboratory observations with human experience. *Quality Management in Pharmaceutical Development: From Molecular Design to Drug Approval, Drug Information Journal* 28(4): 11–17.

Kuehn, Robert B. 1996. The environmental justice implications of quantitative risk assessment. *University of Illinois Law Review* 1996(1): 103–72.

Kunreuther, Howard H., Ralph Ginsberg, L. Miller, Phillip Sagi, Paul Slovic, B. Borkan, and N. Katz. 1978. *Disaster Insurance Protection: Public Policy Lessons.* New York: Wiley.

Kunreuther, Howard, and Douglas Easterling. 1990. Are risk–benefit tradeoffs possible in siting hazardous facilities? *American Economic Review* 80(2): 252–56.

Kunreuther, Howard, and Douglas Easterling. 1992. Gaining acceptance for noxious facilities with economic incentives. In Daniel W. Bromley and Kathleen Segerson, eds., *The Social Response to Environmental Risk: Policy Formulation in an Age of Uncertainty.* Norwell, MA: Kluwer Academic, 151–86.

Kunreuther, Howard, and Rajeev Gowda. 1990. *Integrating Insurance and Risk Management for Hazardous Wastes.* Norwell, MA: Kluwer Academic.

Lambert, Thomas, and Christopher Boerner. 1997. Environmental inequity: Economic causes, economic solutions. *Yale Journal on Regulation* 14: 195.

Latin, Howard. 1988. Good science, bad regulation, and toxic risk assessment. *Yale Journal on Regulation* 5: 89–148.

Lave, Lester, Fanny K. Ennever, Herbert S. Rosenkranz, and Gilbert S. Omenn. 1988. Information value of the rodent bioassay. *Nature* 336: 631–33.

Lavelle, Marianne, and Marianne Coyle. 1992. Unequal protection. The racial divide in environmental law. *National Law Journal*, Special Investigation (Sept. 21).

Lazarus, Richard J. 1993. Pursuing "environmental justice": The distributional effects of environmental protection. *Northwestern University Law Review* 87(3): 787–857.

League of Conservation Voters. 1994. The Greenbook and 1994 National Environmental Scorecard. On-line versions available at *http://www.lcv.org*.

Levinson, Arik. 1997. A note on environmental federalism: Interpreting some contradictory results. *Journal of Environmental Economics and Management* 33(3): 359–66.

Leung, Shirley. 1998. Convention-center site to get overdue cleanup. *Wall Street Journal* (July 1): NE1, NE3.

Lichtenberg, Erik, and David Zilberman. 1988. Efficient regulation of environmental health risks. *Quarterly Journal of Economics* 103(1): 167–78.

Lichtenberg, Erik, David Zilberman, and Kenneth T. Bogen. 1989. Regulating environmental health risks under uncertainty: Groundwater contamination in California. *Journal of Environmental Economics and Management* 17: 22–34.

Lichtenstein, Sarah, Paul Slovic, Baruch Fischhoff, Mark Layman, and B. Combs. 1978. Judged frequency of lethal events. *Journal of Experimental Psychology: Human Learning and Memory* 4: 551–78.

Lott, John R. 1997. Does political reform increase wealth? Or, why the difference between the Chicago and Virginia schools is really an elasticity question. *Public Choice* 91: 219–27.

Lutter, Randall, and John F. Morrall, III. 1994. Health-health analysis: A new way to evaluate health and safety regulations. *Journal of Risk and Uncertainty* 8: 34, 49–50.

Macey, Jonathan R. 1992. Organizational design and political control of administrative agencies. *Journal of Law, Economics and Organization* 8: 93.

Magat, Wesley A., Alan J. Krupnick, and Winston Harrington. 1986. *Rules in the Making: A Statistical Analysis of Regulatory Agency Behavior*. Washington, DC: Resources for the Future.

Margolis, Howard. 1996. *Dealing with Risk: Why the Public and Experts Disagree on Environmental Issues*. Chicago: University of Chicago Press.

Mashaw, Jerry. 1985. Prodelegation: Why administrators should make political decisions. *Journal of Law, Economics and Organization* 1(1): 81–100.

Mauderly, J. L. 1993. Toxicological approaches to complex mixtures. *Environmental Health Perspectives Supplement*. 101(4): 155–65.

Mazmanian, Daniel, and David Morell. 1992. *Beyond Superfailure: America's Toxics Policy for the 1990s*. San Francisco: Westview Press.

Mazurek, Jan, and Robert Hersh. 1997. *Land Use and Remedy Selection: Experience from the Field—The Abex Site*. Washington, DC: Resources for the Future.

McClelland, G. H., W. D. Schulze, and Brian Hurd. 1990. The effect of risk beliefs on property values: A case study of a hazardous waste site. *Risk Analysis* 10(4): 485–97.

McCubbins, Mathew D., Roger G. Noll, and Barry Weingast. 1987. Administrative procedures as instruments of political control. *Journal of Law, Economics and Organization* 3: 243–77.

McCubbins, Mathew D., Roger G. Noll, and Barry Weingast. 1989. Structure and Process, Politics and Policy: Administrative Arrangements and the Political Control of Agencies. *Virginia Law Review* 75(2): 431–82.

McCubbins, Mathew D., Roger G. Noll, and Barry Weingast. 1992. Positive canons: The role of legislative bargains in statutory interpretation. *Georgetown Law Journal* 80(3): 705–42.

McCubbins, Mathew, and Thomas Schwarz. 1984. Congressional oversight overlooked: Police patrols versus fire alarms. *American Journal of Political Science* 28: 165–79.

Michaels, R. Gregory, and V. Kerry Smith. 1990. Market segmentation and valuing amenities with hedonic models: The case of hazardous waste sites. *Journal of Urban Economics* 28: 223–42.

Miller, Gary J. 1992. *Managerial Dilemmas: The Political Economy of Hierarchy*. New York: Cambridge University Press.

Miller, Henry I. 1996. Superfund's big risks. *Journal of Commerce* (Sept. 25): 6A.

Mohai, Paul. 1996. Environmental justice or analytic justice? Reexamining historical hazardous waste landfill siting patterns in metropolitan Texas. *Social Science Quarterly* 77(3): 500–507.

Moolenaar, Robert J. 1994. Default assumptions in carcinogenic risk assessment used by regulatory agencies. *Regulatory Toxicology and Pharmacology* 20: S135–S141.

Moore, Michael J., and W. Kip Viscusi. 1988. The quantity-adjusted value of life. *Economic Inquiry* 26(3): 369–88.

Morgan, M. Granger. 1994. Quantitative risk ranking: More promise than the critics suggest. In Adam M. Finkel and Dominic Golding, eds., *Worst Things First? The Debate over Risk-Based National Environmental Priorities*. Washington, DC: Resources for the Future.

Morgan, M. Granger, et al. 1985. Powerline frequency and magnetic fields: A pilot study of risk perception. *Risk Analysis* 5: 139–49.

Morgan, M. Granger, and Max Henrion. 1990. *Uncertainty: A Guide to Dealing with Uncertainty in Quantitative Risk and Policy Analysis*. New York: Cambridge University Press.

Morgenstern, Richard D., ed. 1997. *Economic Analyses at EPA: Assessing Regulatory Impact*. Washington, DC: Resources for the Future.

Munnell, Alicia H., Geoffrey M. B. Tootell, Lynn E. Browne, and James McEneaney. 1996. Mortgage lending in Boston: Interpreting HMDA data. *American Economic Review* 86(1): 25–53.

Muoghalu, Michael, and John E. Rogers. 1992. The economic impact of Superfund's litigation on the value of the firm: An empirical analysis. *Journal of Economics and Finance* 16(3): 73–87.

National Research Council. 1991. *Environmental Epidemiology: Public Health and Hazardous Waste*. Washington, DC: National Academy Press.

National Research Council/National Academy of Sciences. 1983. *Risk Assessment in the Federal Government: Managing the Process*. Washington, DC: National Academy Press.

National Research Council/National Academy of Sciences. 1994. *Science and Judgment in Risk Assessment*. Washington, DC: National Academy Press.

National Strategies. 1995. *The Costs of Superfund and Proposed Reforms*. Washington, DC: National Strategies, Inc.

Nichols, Albert L., and Richard J. Zeckhauser. 1986. The perils of prudence: How conservative risk assessments distort regulation. *Regulation* 10: 13–24.

Nisbett, Richard, and Lee Ross. 1980. *Human Inference: Strategies and Shortcomings of Social Judgment*. Englewood Cliffs, NJ: Prentice Hall.

Noll, Roger G. 1989. Economic perspectives on the politics of regulation. In Richard Schmalensee and Robert D. Willig, eds., *Handbook of Industrial Organization*, vol. 2. New York: Elsevier Science, 1253–87.

Noll, Roger G., and James E. Krier. 1990. Some implications of cognitive psychology for risk regulation. *Journal of Legal Studies* 19: 747–79.

Office of Management and Budget. 1992. Revisions to OMB Circular No. A-94 on guidelines and discount rates for benefit–cost analysis. 57 *Federal Register* 53, 519.

Office of Management and Budget. 1993. *Regulatory Program of the United States Government. April 1, 1992–March 31, 1993, Appendix V*. Washington, DC: Government Printing Office.

Olson, Mancur. 1971. *The Logic of Collective Action: Public Goods and the Theory of Groups*. Cambridge: Harvard University Press.

Olson, Mary. 1996. Substitution in regulatory agencies: FDA enforcement alternatives. *Journal of Law, Economics and Organization* 12(2): 376–407.

Page, Talbot. 1978. A generic view of toxic chemicals and similar risks. *Ecology Law Quarterly* 7: 207–44.

Palmquist, Raymond B. 1979. Hedonic price and depreciation indexes for residential housing: A comment. *Journal of Urban Economics* 6: 267–71.

Palmquist, Raymond B. 1982. Measuring environmental effects on property values without hedonic regressions. *Journal of Urban Economics* 6: 267–71.

Palmquist, Raymond B. 1992. Valuing localized externalities. *Journal of Urban Economics* 31: 59–68.

Parisi, Anthony J. 1980. Who pays? Cleanup up the Love Canals. *New York Times* (June 8): C1.

Paustenbach, Dennis J. 1995. Retrospective on U.S. health risk assessment: How others can benefit. *Risk: Health, Safety and Environment* 6: 283–332.

Percival, Robert V., and Christopher Schroeder. 1996. *Environmental Regulation: Law, Science, and Policy*. Boston: Little, Brown.

Perlin, Susan A., R. Woodrow Setzer, John Creason, and Ken Sexton. 1995. Distribution of industrial air emissions by income and race in the United States: An approach using the toxic release inventory. *Environmental Science and Technology* 29(1): 69–80.

Petrikin, Johnathan (ed.). 1995. Environmental Justice. San Diego, CA: Greenhaven Press.

Pollock, Phillip H., III, and M. Elliot Vittas. 1995. Who bears the burdens of environmental pollution? Race, ethnicity, and environmental equity in Florida. *Social Science Quarterly* 77(2): 294–310.

Portney, Paul R. 1981. Housing prices, health effects, and valuing reductions in risk of death. *Journal of Environmental Economics and Management* 8: 72–78.

Portney, Paul R. 1994. The contingent valuation debate: Why economists should care. *Journal of Economic Perspectives* 8(4): 3–17.

Pratt, John W., Howard Raiffa, and Robert Schlaifer. 1995. *Introduction to Statistical Decision Theory*. Cambridge: MIT Press.

President William Jefferson Clinton. Executive Order. 1994. Federal actions to address environmental justice in minority populations and low-income populations. Executive Order 12898. 59 *Federal Register* 7629 (Feb. 11).

Probst, Katherine N., and Paul R. Portney. 1991. *Assigning Liability for Superfund Cleanups: An Analysis of Policy Options* Washington, DC: Resources for the Future.

Probst, Katherine N., Don Fullerton, Robert E. Litan, and Paul R. Portney. 1995. *Footing the Bill for Superfund Cleanups: Who Pays and How?* Washington, DC: Brookings Institution/Resources for the Future.

Rabe, Barry G. 1990. Legislative incapacity: The congressional role in environmental policymaking and the case of Superfund. *Journal of Health Politics, Policy and Law* 15: 571–89.

Rausser, Gordon C., and Leo K. Simon. 1998. Information asymmetries, uncertainties, and cleanup delays at Superfund sites. *Journal of Environmental Economics and Management* 35: 48–68.

Revesz, Richard L. 1997a. Environmental regulation, ideology, and the D.C. circuit. *Virginia Law Review* 83(8): .

Revesz, Richard L. 1997b. The race to the bottom and federal environmental regulation: A response to critics. *Minnesota Law Review* 82: 535–564.

Revesz, Richard L., and Richard B. Stewart, eds. 1995. *Analyzing Superfund: Economics, Science, and Law*. Washington, DC: Resources for the Future.

Ringquist, Evan J. 1993. *Environmental Protection at the State Level: Politics and Progress in Controlling Pollution*. Armonk, NY: M.E. Sharpe.

Rogers, William H. 1993. Regression Standard Errors in Clustered Samples. *Stata Technical Bulletin* 13: 19–23.

Rosenberry, A. M., and D. E. Burmaster. 1992. Lognormal distributions for water intake by children and adults. *Risk Analysis* 12: 99–104.

Rosen, S. 1974. Hedonic prices and implicit markets: Product differentiation in pure competition. *Journal of Political Economy* 82: 34–55.

Rosenthal, Alan, John D. Graham, and George M. Gray. 1992. Legislating acceptable cancer risk from exposure to toxic chemicals. *Ecology Law Quarterly* 19: 269–362.

Russell, Milton, E. W. Colglazier, and Mary R. English. 1991. *Hazardous Waste Remediation: The Task Ahead*. Knoxville, TN: University of Tennessee, Waste Management Research and Education Institute.

Russell, Milton, and Kimberly L. Davis. 1995. *Resource Requirements for NPL Sites: Phase II Interim Report*. Knoxville, TN: Joint Institute for Energy and Environment.

Russakoff, Dale. 1983. EPA chief is assailed at hearing; Gorsuch decries "Political" goals behind criticism. *Washington Post* (Feb. 16): A1.

Samuelson, William, and Richard Zeckhauser. 1988. Status quo bias in decision making. *Journal of Risk and Uncertainty* 1: 7–59.

Santos, Lori. 1983. EPA report hits management. *UPI News* (May 11).

Schneider, Keith. 1993. New View Calls Environmental Policy Misguided. *New York Times* (Mar. 21): D3.

Scholz, John T., Jim Twombly, and Barbara Headrick. 1991. Street-level political controls over federal bureaucracy. *American Political Science Review* 85: 829–50.

Scholz, John T., and Feng Heng Wei. 1986. Regulatory enforcement in a federalist system. *American Political Science Review* 80: 1249–70.

Schulze, William, et al. 1994. *An Evaluation of Public Preferences for Superfund Site Cleanup: A Preliminary Assessment*, vol 1. Boulder, CO: Center for Economic Analysis, University of Colorado.

Seed, Jennifer, Ronald P. Brown, Stephen S. Olin, and Jeffery A. Foran. 1995. Chemical mixtures: Current risk assessment methodologies and future directions. *Regulatory Toxicology and Pharmacology* 22: 76–94.

Shanklin, Carita. Comment: Pathfinder: Environmental justice. *Ecology Law Quarterly* 24: 333.

Shere, Mark Eliot. 1995. The myth of meaningful environmental risk assessment. *Harvard Environmental Law Review* 19(2): 409–92.

Shrader-Frechette. 1995. Evaluating the expertise of experts. *Risk: Health, Safety, and Environment* 6: 115.

Sigman, Hilary. 1998a. Liability Funding and Superfund Clean-up Remedies. *Journal of Environmental Economics and Management* 35: 205–24.

Sigman, Hilary. 1998b. Midnight dumping: Public policies and illegal disposing of used oil. *Rand Journal of Economics* 28(1): 157–78.

Slovic, Paul. 1986. Informing and educating the public about risk. *Risk Analysis* 6(4): 403–15.

Slovic, Paul, Baruch Fischhoff, and Sarah Lichtenstein. 1982. Facts versus fears: Understanding perceived risks. In Daniel Kahneman, Paul Slovic, and Amos Tversky, eds., *Judgment Under Uncertainty: Heuristics and Biases*. Cambridge: Cambridge University Press.

Slovic, Paul, Baruch Fischhoff, and Sarah Lichtenstein. 1982. Why study risk perception? *Risk Analysis* 2(2): 83–93.

Slovic, Paul, and Sarah Lichtenstein. 1971. Comparison of Bayesian and regression approaches to the study of information processing and judgement. *Organizational Behavior and Human Performance* 6: 649–744.

Smith, A. E., P. B. Ryan and J. S. Evans. 1992. The effect of neglecting correlations when propagating uncertainty and estimating population distribution of risk. *Risk Analysis* 12: 467–74.

Smith, Roy. 1994. Use of Monte Carlo simulation for human exposure assessment at a superfund site. *Risk Analysis* 14: 433–39.

Smith, V. Kerry, William H. Desvousges, Ann Fisher, and F. Reed Johnson. 1988. Learning about radon's risk. *Journal of Risk and Uncertainty* 1: 233–58.

Spence, David B. 1997. Administrative law and agency policy-making: Rethinking the positive theory of political control. *Yale Journal on Regulation* 14: 407.

Spence, David B. 1998. Imposing individual liability as a legislative policy choice: Holmesian "intuitions" and Superfund reform. Working paper. Graduate School and College of Business. University of Texas, Austin.

Spitzer, Matthew L. 1990. Some implications of cognitive psychology for risk regulation: Comment. *Journal of Legal Studies* 19(2), Part 2: 801–808.

Stanek, Edward J., III, and Edward J. Calabrese. 1991. A guide to interpreting soil ingestion studies: Development of a model to estimate the soil ingestion detection level of soil ingestion studies. *Regulatory Toxicology and Pharmacology* 13: 263–77.

Stanek, Edward J., III, and Edward J. Calabrese. 1995. Daily estimates of soil ingestion in children. *Environmental Health Perspectives* 103: 276–85.

Stavins, Robert N. 1996. Correlated uncertainty and policy instrument choice. *Journal of Environmental Economics and Management* 30(2): 218–32.

Stewart, Richard B. 1975. The reformation of American administrative Law. *Harvard. Law Review* 88(8): 1667–1813.

Stewart, Richard B. 1995. Liability for natural resource injury: Beyond tort. In Richard L. Revesz and Richard B. Stewart eds., *Analyzing Superfund: Economics, Science, and Law* Washington, DC: Resources for the Future.

Stiglitz, Joseph. 1998. Distinguished lecture on economics in government: The private uses of public interests: Incentives and institutions. *Journal of Economic Perspectives* 12(2): 3–22.

Stock, James H. 1989. Nonparametric policy analysis. *Journal of the American Statistical Association* 84(406): 567–75.

Stöhrer, Gerhard. 1995. Realistic risk assessment. *Regulatory Toxicology and Pharmacology* 22: 118–21.

Stroup, Richard L. 1994. Newly vulnerable to Superfund's claws. *Wall Street Journal* (Jan. 4): A10.

Sunstein, Cass R. 1996a. Health–health analysis. *University of Chicago Law Review* 63(4): 1533–71.

Sunstein, Cass R. 1996b. Legislative forward: Congress, constitutional moments, and the cost-benefit state. *Stanford Law Review* 48(Jan.): 247–309.

Tengs, Tammy O., Miriam E. Adams, Joseph S. Pliskin, Dana Gelb Safran, Joanna E. Siegel, Milton C. Weinstein, and John D. Graham. 1994. Five-hundred life saving interventions and their cost-effectiveness. *Risk Analysis* 15(3): 369.

Travis, Curtis C., Samantha A. Richter, Edmund A. C. Crouch, Richard Wilson, and Ernest D. Klema. 1987. Cancer risk management: A review of 132 federal regulatory Decisions. *Environmental Science and Technology* 21(5): 415–20.

Travis, Curtis C., Patricia A. Scofield, and Bonnie P. Blaylock. 1993. Evaluation of remediation worker risk at radioactively contaminated sites. *Journal of Hazardous Materials* 35: 387–401.

Tversky, Amos, and Daniel Kahneman. 1973. Availability: A heuristic for judging frequency and probability. *Cognitive Psychology* 5: 207–32.

Upton, Arthur C. and Eden Graber, eds. 1993. *Staying Healthy in A Risky Environment: The New York University Medical Center Family Guide*. New York: Simon and Schuster.

U.S. Department of Commerce. 1994. *Statistical Abstract of the United States, 1994.* Washington, DC: Government Printing Office.

U.S. Department of Commerce. 1996. *Summary Tape File 3 Technical Documentation*. Department of Commerce, Bureau of the Census. Available online at www.census.gov.

U.S. Environmental Protection Agency. 1987. *Unfinished Business: A Comparative Assessment of Environmental Problems*. Washington, DC: Government Printing Office.

U.S. Environmental Protection Agency. 1988a. *CERCLA Compliance with Other Laws Manual: Interim Final*. Washington, DC: U.S. EPA, Office of Emergency and Remedial Response.

U.S. Environmental Protection Agency. 1988b. Hazardous ranking system revisions technical support document. CERCLA Docket No. 105 NCP-HRS-10-1 Washington, DC: U.S. EPA.

U.S. Environmental Protection Agency. 1989a. *Risk Assessment Guidance for Superfund, Volume 1: Human Health Evaluation Manual (Part A), Interim Final*. Washington, DC: U.S. EPA, Office of Emergency and Remedial Response OSWER Directive 9285.701A, EPA/540/1-89/002.

U.S. Environmental Protection Agency. 1989b. *Risk Assessment Guidance for Superfund: Volume I: Human Health Evaluation Manual (Part C, Risk Evaluation of Remedial Alternatives), Interim*. Publication 9285.7-01B. Washington, DC: U.S. EPA, Office of Emergency and Remedial Response.

U.S. Environmental Protection Agency. 1990a. National oil and hazardous substances pollution contingency plan. *Federal Register* 55: 8666–865.

U.S. Environmental Protection Agency. 1990b. *Progress toward Implementing Superfund Fiscal Year 1989: Report to Congress*. Washington, DC: U.S. EPA, Office of Emergency and Remedial Response. EPA/540/8-90/017.

U.S. Environmental Protection Agency. 1990c. Hazard Ranking System. *Federal Register* 55: 51532–667.

U.S. Environmental Protection Agency. 1991a. *Exposure Factors Handbook*. Washington, DC: U.S. EPA, Office of Health and Environmental Assessment. EPA/600/08-89/043.

U.S. Environmental Protection Agency. 1991b. *Role of the Baseline Risk Assessment in Superfund Remedy Selections Decisions*. Directive 9355 0-30. (Apr. 22). Memo from Don Clay, Assistant Administrator, to directors of regional hazardous waste divisions. Washington, DC: U.S. EPA, Office of Solid Waste and Emergency Response.

U.S. Environmental Protection Agency. 1992a. Memorandum from F. Henry Habicht, II on behalf of the Agency's Risk Assessment Council, Deputy Administrator, EPA to assistant and Regional Administrators, EPA Guidance on Risk Characterization for Risk Managers and Risk Assessors. Washington, DC: U.S. EPA.

U.S. Environmental Protection Agency. 1992b. *Monte Carlo Approach to Simulating Residential Occupancy Periods and Its Application to the General U.S. Population*. Washington, DC: U.S. EPA, Office of Air Quality 450/3-92-011.

U.S. Environmental Protection Agency. 1993a. *A SAB Report: Superfund Site Health Risk Assessment Guidelines*. EPA-SAB-EHC-93-007. Washington, DC: U.S. EPA, Science Advisory Board.

U.S. Environmental Protection Agency. 1993b. *Remedial Project Managers Site Database (RELAI)* Washington, DC: U.S. EPA, Office of Emergency and Remedial Response.

U.S. Environmental Protection Agency. 1994a. *A Report on State/Territory Non-NPL Hazardous Waste Site Cleanup Efforts for the Period 1980–1992*, Washington, DC: U.S. EPA, Office of Solid Waste and Emergency Response EPA540/R-94/001.

U.S. Environmental Protection Agency. 1994b. *Health Effects Assessment Summary Tables FY-1994 Annual.* Washington, DC: U.S. EPA, Office of Solid Waste and Emergency Response, EPA540/R-94/059.

U.S. Environmental Protection Agency. 1994c. *Estimating Potential Casualties from Acute Events at Emergency Response Sites, Technical Appendices, Draft.* Washington, DC: U.S. EPA, Office of Emergency and Remedial Response.

U.S. Environmental Protection Agency. 1995. *Integrated Risk Information System* (IRIS) database, July 1995. Washington, DC: U.S. EPA.

U.S. Environmental Protection Agency. 1996. *Proposed Guidelines for Carcinogen Risk Assessment.* Washington, DC: U.S. EPA, Office of Research and Development. EPA/600/P-92/003C.

U.S. Environmental Protection Agency. 1997a. *Cleaning up the Nation's Waste Sites: Markets and Technology Trends, 1996 Edition.* Washington, DC: U.S. EPA, Office of Solid Waste and Emergency Response.

U.S. Environmental Protection Agency. 1997b. Construction completions at National Priorities List (NPL) sites. On-line data from USEPA's Superfund website, http://www.epa.gov/superfund/oerr/impm/products/npl/nplccl.htm, Washington, DC: U.S. EPA.

U.S. Environmental Protection Agency. 1998a. *Superfund Administrative Reforms Annual Report, 1997.* Washington, DC: U.S. EPA.

U.S. Environmental Protection Agency. 1998b. *EPA Delivers on Superfund Reform Progress Making 1997 a Standout Year for Faster Cleanups at Lower Costs.* Headquarters press release, Feb. 3.

U.S. General Accounting Office. 1993. *Environmental Protection Issues.* Washington, DC: U.S. GAO, GAO/OGC-93-16TR.

U.S. General Accounting Office. 1994a. *Superfund: EPA's Community Relations Efforts Could Be More Effective.* Washington, DC: U.S. GAO, GAO/RCED-94-156.

U.S. General Accounting Office. 1994b. *Superfund: Estimates of Number of Future Sites Vary.* Washington, DC: U.S. GAO, GAO/RCED-95-18.

U.S. General Accounting Office. 1994c. *Superfund: Improved Reviews and Guidance Could Reduce Inconsistencies in Risk Assessments.* Washington, DC: U.S. GAO, GAO/RCED-94-220.

U.S. General Accounting Office. 1994d. *Superfund: Reauthorization and Risk Prioritization Issues.* Washington, DC: U.S. GAO, GAO/T-RCED-94-250.

U.S. General Accounting Office. 1995a. *EPA's Use of Risk Assessments in Cleanup Decisions.* Washington, DC: U.S. GAO, GAO/T-RCED-95-231.

U.S. General Accounting Office. 1995b. *Superfund: Operations and Maintenance Activities Will Require Billions of Dollars.* Washington, DC: U.S. GAO, GAO/RCED-95-259.

U.S. General Accounting Office. 1995c. *Superfund: Risk Assessment Assumptions and Issues.* Washington, DC: U.S. GAO, GAO/T-RCED-95-206.

U.S. General Accounting Office. 1996a. *Superfund: How States Establish and Apply Environmental Standards When Cleaning up Sites*. Washington, DC: U.S. GAO, GAO/RCED-96-70FS.

U.S. General Accounting Office. 1996b. *Superfund: Implications of Key Reauthorization Issues*. Washington, DC: U.S. GAO, GAO/T-RCED-96-145.

U.S. General Accounting Office. 1996c. *Superfund: More Emphasis Needed on Risk Reduction*. Washington, DC: U.S. GAO, GAO/T-RCED-96-168.

Van Houtven, George, and Maureen L. Cropper. 1996. When is a life too costly to save? The evidence from U.S. environmental regulations. *Journal of Environmental Economics and Management* 30: 348–68.

Versar, Inc. 1991. *Analysis of the Impact of Exposure Assumptions on Risk Assessment of Chemicals in the Environment*. Springfield, VA: Versar, Inc.

Viscusi, W. Kip. 1979. *Employment Hazards: An Investigation of Market Performance*. Cambridge: Harvard University Press.

Viscusi, W. Kip. 1981. Occupational Safety and Health Regulation: Its Impact and Policy Alternatives. In J. Crecine (ed.), *Research in Public Policy Analysis and Management*. Greenwich, CT: JAI Press, 281–99.

Viscusi, W. Kip. 1983. *Risk by Choice*. Cambridge: Harvard University Press.

Viscusi, W. Kip. 1989. Prospective Reference Theory: Toward an Explanation of the Paradoxes. *Journal of Risk and Uncertainty* 2(3): 235–64.

Viscusi, W. Kip. 1992a. *Fatal Tradeoffs: Public and Private Responsibilities for Risk*, New York: Oxford University Press.

Viscusi, W. Kip. 1992b. *Smoking: Making the Risky Decision*. New York: Oxford University Press.

Viscusi, W. Kip. 1994a. Mortality effects of regulatory costs and policy evaluation criteria. *Rand Journal of Economics* 25: 94–109.

Viscusi, W. Kip. 1994b. Risk–risk analysis. *Journal of Risk & Uncertainty* 8: 5–17.

Viscusi, W. Kip. 1995. Carcinogen regulation: Risk characteristics and biases in policy decisions. *American Economic Review* 85(2): 50–54.

Viscusi, W. Kip. 1996. Regulating the regulators. *University of Chicago Law Review* 63: 1423–61.

Viscusi, W. Kip. 1998. How do judges think about risk? Working paper. Harvard Law School. Forthcoming in the *American Law and Economics Review* (1999).

Viscusi, W. Kip, and James T. Hamilton. 1996. Cleaning up Superfund. *The Public Interest*, 124 (Summer): 52–60.

Viscusi, W. Kip, and James T. Hamilton. 1998. Are risk regulators rational? Evidence from hazardous waste cleanup decisions. *American Economic Review*, forthcoming.

Viscusi, W. Kip, James T. Hamilton, and P. Christen Dockins. 1997. Conservative versus mean risk assessments: Implications for Superfund policies. *Journal of Environmental Economics and Management* 34: 187–206.

Viscusi, W. Kip, and Wesley A. Magat. 1987. *Learning about Risks: Consumer and Worker Responses to Hazard Information*. Cambridge: Harvard University Press.

Viscusi, W. Kip, and Wesley A. Magat. 1992. Bayesian decisions with ambiguous belief aversion. *Journal of Risk and Uncertainty* 5(4): 371–87.

Viscusi, W. Kip, Wesley A. Magat, and Joel Huber. 1987. An investigation of the rationality of consumer valuations of multiple health risks. *Rand Journal of Economics* 18(4): 465–79.

Viscusi, W. Kip, Wesley A. Magat, and Joel Huber. 1991. Communication of ambiguous risk information. *Theory and Decision* 31: 159–73.

Viscusi, W. Kip, and Charles J. O'Connor. 1984. Adaptive responses to chemical labeling: Are workers Bayesian decision makers? *American Economic Review* 74: 942–56.

Walker, Katherine D., March Sadowitz, and John D. Graham. 1995. Confronting Superfund mythology: The case of risk assessment and management. In Richard L. Revesz and Richard B. Steward, eds., *Analyzing Superfund: Economics, Science, and Law.* Washington, DC: Resources for the Future.

Wernstedt, Kris, and Katherine N. Probst. 1997a. *Land Use and Remedy Selection: Experience from the Field—The Fort Ord Site.* Washington, DC: Resources for the Future.

Wernstedt, Kris, and Katherine N. Probst. 1997b. *Land Use and Remedy Selection: Experience from the Field—The Industri-Plex Site.* Washington, DC: Resources for the Future.

White, Halbert. 1980. A heteroskedasticity–consistent covariance matrix estimator and a direct test for heteroskedasticity. *Econometrica* 48: 817–38.

Wiener, Jonathan Baert. 1998. Global environmental regulation: Instrument choice in legal context. *Yale Law Journal*, forthcoming.

Wiley, John S., Jr. 1986. A capture theory of antitrust federalism, *Harvard Law Review* 99: 713.

Williams, Ted. 1993. The sabotage of Superfund: The federal program has cost billions, cleaned up little, and satisfied no one. *Audubon* 95(4): 30.

Wittman, Donald. 1989. Why democracies produce efficient results. *Journal of Political Economy* 97: 1395–1424.

Wittman, Donald. 1995. *The Myth of Democratic Failure: Why Political Institutions Are Efficient.* Chicago: University of Chicago Press.

Wood, B. Dan, and Richard W. Waterman. 1994. *Bureaucratic Dynamics.* San Francisco: Westview Press.

Yandle, Tracy, and Dudley Burton. 1996. Reexamining environmental justice: A statistical analysis of historical hazardous waste landfill siting patterns in metropolitan Texas. *Social Science Quarterly* 77(3): 477–92.

Yandle, Tracy, and Dudley Burton. 1996. Methodological approaches to environmental justice: A rejoinder. *Social Science Quarterly* 77(3): 520–27.

Zeckhauser, Richard J., and W. Kip Viscusi. 1990. Risk within reason. *Science* 248(4955): 559–64.

Zerbe, Richard O., Jr. 1998. Is cost–benefit analysis legal? Three rules. *Journal of Policy Analysis and Management* 17(3): 419–56.

Zimmerman, Rae. 1993. Social equity and environmental risk. *Risk Analysis* 13: 649–66.

Zimmerman, Rae. 1994. Issues of clarification in environmental equity: How we manage is how we measure. *Fordham Urban Law Journal* 21: 633–661.

Index

90–10 principle, 124–25

Acton, Jan P., 281, 283
Administrative Procedure Act, 215
Aerometric Information Retrieval System, 172, 290
Agency for Toxic Substances and Disease Registry (ATSDR), 107
Ambiguity aversion, 61
Anchoring effect, 18, 133, 137, 145
Anderton, Douglas L., 162, 291
Applegate, John S., 288
Applicable or relevant and appropriate requirements (ARARs), 4, 6, 10, 16, 22, 26, 29, 63, 110, 140, 217, 220–21, 224–25, 229, 231, 235, 242, 251–52
Aranson, Peter H., 296
ARC/INFO, 249
Arsenic, 49, 284
Availability heuristic, 18, 133, 138, 145–46, 154

Barnett, Harold C., 281, 292
Bartik, Timothy J., 293
Baseline risk assessment (BLRA), 10, 26–28, 31, 131, 145, 246–47, 252, 254, 256, 259–61
Bassett, Gilbert, Jr., 290
Bayesian learning, 190, 192–98
Becker, Gary S., 282, 290
Been, Vicki, 282, 290–91, 299
Benefit-cost analysis, 3, 21, 134, 213–214, 216, 220, 222, 235, 242, 287
Beorner, Christopher, 291
Bi-annual reporting system, 172
Biorby, 287
Blais, Lynne E., 291
Blancato, J. N., 292
Blaylock, Bonnie P., 288
Block group analysis (census), 15, 18, 91, 93, 96, 102, 132, 148, 200, 206, 249, 253, 261–63, 265
Blomquist, Glenn C., 206
Boerner, Christopher, 291
Bofors Nobel, 94, 102–104

Bogen, Kenneth T., 285
Boston, Massachusetts, 209
Bowen, William M., 291
Box-Cox model, 204–205, 207, 209
Breyer, Stephen, 124–25, 212, 217, 283, 289, 296
Brodeur, J., 292
Brooks, Nancy, 291
Bryant, Bunyan, 290
Buckley, James R., 281
Bullard, Robert D., 290–91
Bureau of Labor Statistics, 195
Burmaster, David E., 82, 281, 283, 285–86
Burton, Dudley, 291

Calabrese, E. J., 67, 286
California, 15, 173–74, 223
Cancer
  cases avoided, 91–108, 148, 229–31
  latency, 15–16, 92, 101, 103, 105, 121, 148, 237, 263
  risks, 3, 10, 40, 92 (*see also* Lifetime excess cancer risk)
Cantor, K. P., 286
Carter administration, 3
Census data, 9, 93, 102, 132, 148, 187, 219
Centner, Terence J., 291
CERCLIS, 162, 172, 178, 245, 249, 252, 266, 290–91
Chemical Manufacturers Association, 285
Church, Thomas W., 281–82
Clean Air Act, 29
Clean sites, 162
Clean Water Act, 29, 114
Cleanup costs, 15, 16, 225–29
Cleanup standards, 114, 116, 160, 182, 251
Cleanup targets, 116, 133
Coase theorem, 158
Cohen, Mark, 289
Cole, Luke W., 290
Colglazier, E. W., 283
Collective action, 189. *See also* Voter turnout
Combs, B., 204
Commission on Racial Justice, 291

Compounding conservatism, 63, 82–83, 127
Comprehensive Environmental Response, Compensation, and Recovery Act of 1980 (CERCLA), 3, 6, 10, 26, 109, 111, 199, 208–209, 249
Congressional Budget Office (CBO), 267, 275, 281, 288
Conservatism, 2, 59, 61, 89, 107, 109
  and risk assessment, 12, 14–15, 20, 22, 57, 59–90, 92, 103, 105, 107, 117, 119, 127, 140, 148, 174, 211, 214, 217, 219, 222, 237, 241
  and risk assessment (costs), 108–28
Containment, 113, 238
Contaminant concentration, 67, 74
Contingent valuation, 134
Cost effectiveness, 2, 7, 15, 110, 117–26, 150–53, 223
Cost per cancer case avoided, 16, 20, 119–27, 132–33, 135–36, 148–51, 154, 160, 182, 189, 212, 223–24, 229
Coyle, Marianne, 131, 163
Cropper, Maureen L., 113, 130–31, 139, 153, 163, 281, 283, 289–290, 292, 294–95
Cullen, Alison C., 285
Current risks, 30, 36, 38, 47, 123, 176

Davis, Joseph A., 296
Davis, Kimberly L., 281, 288–89
Deck, Leland B., 294
Dense nonaqueous phase liquid (DNAPL), 274
Dermal exposure, 15
Desvousges, William H., 289
Diamond, Peter, 281, 289
Dilution factor, 98–99, 200, 262
Dixon, Lloyd S., 281, 283, 288
Dockins, P. Christen, 59, 287
Doty, Carolyn B., 281, 283
Drezmer, 288

Easterling, Douglas, 289
Ecological damage, 122, 126, 128, 231–33
Egan, Karla L., 162, 291
Egleton township, 102
Elliott, 83, 286
Ellsberg paradox, 61
English, Mary R., 283
Environmental equity, 18–19, 21, 139, 147, 157–88, 233–36, 243, 264–65

Environmental group membership, 154, 182
Environmental Protection Agency (EPA), 116, 121, 222
  costs of Superfund cleanup, 1
  decisions, 132, 145
  guidelines, 82, 135, 139, 217
  information, 210
  political factors, 17, 131–33, 139, 150, 153–54
  prioritization, 80
  remedy selection, 183, 236–37
  responses, 176
  risk analyses, 56
  risk management, 219
  technical assistance grants, 183
Epple, Dennis, 293
Ershow, A. G., 286
Executive Order 12898, 186, 282, 292
Expected cancer cases, 15, 173, 229
Expected utility, 129, 130, 193
Exposed population, 15, 163, 248, 262, 278
Exposure route, 11, 31, 38

Feasibility study (FS), 8–9, 28–29, 32, 102, 200, 246–48, 264
Finkel, Adam M., 285
Finley, Brent, 67, 83, 285–87
Fire-alarm model, 158, 177, 183
Fischhoff, Baruch, 295
Flynn, James, 147
Franklin Square, 94
Fullerton, Don, 281–82
Future residents, 46, 52, 223
Future risks, 11–12, 14, 21, 30, 36, 38, 41–42, 44, 46–47, 51–52, 56–57, 137, 148, 176

Garen, John, 295
Gayer, Ted, 189, 293
Genzale Plating Company, 94–101
Geographic Information System (GIS), vii, 2, 9, 15, 18, 20, 91, 93, 102, 104, 127, 132, 148, 164, 173, 187, 248–51, 260–63, 278, 294
Ghosh, Debapriya, 206
Gilbert, C. E., 287
Goodman, Leo A., 286
Gorsuch, Anne M., 3
Gowda, Rajeev, 289
Graham, John D., 283–84, 288, 291

Greater Grand Rapids area, 20, 189–91, 196, 198, 200, 205, 209–10
Grills, Jennifer B., 291
Groundwater
  characteristics, 277
  contamination, 33
  exposure, 104
  ingestion, 13, 38, 67, 75, 88
  risks, 34, 101–103
  treatment, 113
Gupta, Shreekant, 113, 131, 139, 163, 281, 283, 289–92, 295

Hamilton, James T., 7, 147, 281, 283, 290–93, 296, 299
Hammitt, James K., 288
Hanemann, Michael W., 289
Harris, W. E., 82, 281, 283, 285
Harrison, David, Jr., 294
Hausman, Jerry, 281, 289
Hawkins, 83
Hazard index, 33, 42
Hazard quotient, 10, 26–29, 33, 42, 53–56, 123–24, 217, 255, 265
Hazard ranking system (HRS), 8, 138, 162, 177, 195, 261–62, 282, 287
Hedonic price model, 164, 191, 193–99, 201, 293
Hersh, Robert, 282, 291
Hird, John A., 6, 131, 139, 161–62, 171, 281–83, 285, 289–90, 299
Horn, Murray J., 5, 296
Hot spots, 105, 258, 260
Housing price effects, 187, 189–210, 240
Huber, Joel C., 284
Huber, Peter J., 289
Human Health Evaluation Manual, 218
Human intake factor (HIF), 64
Hurd, Brian, 189
Hypothetical risks, 12, 14, 18, 22, 25, 36, 91, 145, 176, 211–12, 229

Ingestion rate, 69
Inhalation, 15
Inorganic compound, 136, 258
Institutional controls, 113, 121, 206, 220, 238
Integrated risk information system (IRIS), 28, 257
Involuntary risks, 118

Johnson, Barry L., 281

Kahn, S., 293
Kahneman, Daniel, 283, 289, 293, 295
Keeler, Andrew G., 291
Kiel, Katherine A., 205, 290, 294
Kiewet, D. Roderick, 295
Koenker, Roger, 290
Kohlhase, Janet E., 205, 290–91, 294
Krier, James, 60, 130, 282, 284
Kriesel, William, 291
Krishnan, K., 292
Kruskal, William H., 286
Kuehn, Robert B., 291, 298
Kunreuther, Howard H., 289, 293

Lambert, Thomas, 291
Land use, 30, 36
Lang, K., 293
Latin, Howard, 284
Lave, Lester, 284
Lavelle, Marianne, 131, 163
Lazarus, Richard J., 290, 299
League of Conservation Voters (LCV), 5, 139, 147
Lees, Dennis, 206
Leung, Shirley, 299
Lichtenstein, Sarah, 283, 293
Lifetime excess cancer risk (LECR), 11–12, 64–65, 68, 216, 218, 259, 263
Litan, Robert E., 281–82
Long Island, New York, 94
Lott, John R., 282, 290
Love Canal, New York, 3, 25–26
Lowell, Massachusetts, 32
Lowest observed adverse effect level (LOAEL), 28–29, 222
Lutter, Randall, 298

Macey, Jonathan R., 296
Magat, Wesley A., 284
Mashaw, Jerry, 296
Mauderly, J. L., 292
Maximum contaminant levels, 116, 251–52
Maximum cumulative cancer risks, 11, 50, 52, 57, 176
Maximum ingestion risk, 88
Maximum pathway risks , 75–78, 149
McClain, Katherine T., 205, 290, 294
McClelland, G. H., 189
McConnell, Kenneth E., 294
McCubbins, Mathew D., 158, 215, 292, 295–296

Media citations, 146, 151
Mertz, C. K., 147
Methylene chloride, 84
Michaels, R. Gregory, 294
Miller, Gary J., 295
Miller, Henry I., 296
Minorities, 19, 131, 147, 157–62, 165, 174, 176, 187
  population, 138–39, 235
  risks to, 162, 165, 174, 176, 187
Mohai, Paul, 290–91
Monte Carlo analysis, 2, 14, 60, 63, 82–83, 86, 127, 219, 237, 252, 254–56, 259, 285
Moore, Michael J., 295
Morgan, M. Granger, 295
Morrall, John F., III, 298
Muskegon, Michigan, 102

Nakamura, Robert T., 281–82
Nassau County, 96
National Oil and Hazardous Substances Pollution Contingency Plan of 1990, 4, 26, 46, 217, 284
National Priorities List (NPL), 8–9, 11, 25, 91, 110, 138, 160–64, 168, 171–74, 177–79, 183, 195, 197, 199, 203, 209, 216, 235, 241, 245–46, 250–51, 264–65, 269–71, 274, 276, 279, 282
National Remedy Review Board, 241
National Research Council, 281
Natural resources damage, 233
Newspaper publicity, 202, 204, 208
Nichols, Albert L., 282, 285
Nisbett, Richard, 295
No observed adverse effect level (NOAEL), 28, 222
Noll, Roger, 60, 130, 215, 282, 284, 289
Noncancer risk, 28, 53, 105, 107, 128, 231
Nyanza site, 209

Oakes, John Michael, 162, 291
Office of Emergency and Remedial Response (OERR), 261
Office of Environmental Equity, 157
Office of Management and Budget (OMB), 118–19, 223, 298, 300
Office of Solid Waste and Emergency Response (OSWER), 10, 26, 294
On-site populations, 38
On-site risks, 12, 39, 50

Palmquist, 293
Parameter distributions, 67
Pathway risk, 40–56, 64
Paustenbach, Dennis J., 83, 285
PCBs, 41, 49, 105, 137, 223, 240
Perlin, Susan A., 291
Permit compliance system (PCS), 172, 208–209
Pesticide registration, 130
Petrikin, Johnathan, 290
Plumes, groundwater, 93, 164, 200, 250
Population risks, 15, 248–51
Portney, Paul R., 281–82, 289, 293
Potentially responsible parties (PRP), 257, 274
Principal-agent relationship, 3, 5, 213
Probst, Katherine N., 281–83
Public opinion polls, 1, 129, 211

Quantile regressions, 151–54

Rabe, Barry G., 111
RATRENDS database, 266
Reagan, Ronald, 5
Reasonable maximum exposure (RME), 13, 26, 32, 60, 62–65, 67, 74, 84–89, 92, 96–97, 99, 101, 105, 127, 218, 237, 261, 285, 287
Record of Decision (ROD), 8–9, 28, 31–33, 69, 92, 102, 110, 112–14, 126, 133, 179, 245–48, 251, 265–67, 269–70, 275
Reference dose, 28
Reference risk effect, 131
Regulatory reform policies , 213–16
RELAI database, 253, 261, 266, 269–71, 275–76
Remedial action / feasibility study (RI/FS), 8, 28, 200
Remedial investigation (RI), 8–9, 20, 28–29, 32, 102, 191, 194–201, 203–207, 209–10, 246–47, 264
Remedial project managers, 246
Remediation costs, 111, 113–14, 119, 212, 247–48, 265–67
Remediation effects on health risks, 229–31
Remedy selections, 110, 121
Removal actions, 8, 179
Removals, 113, 238
Representativeness heuristic, 138, 146
Residential populations, 36, 40, 47

Resource Conservation and Recovery Act
  (RCRA), 29, 172, 178, 199, 208–209,
  290
Revesz, Richard L., 281–82
Risk Assessment Guidance for Superfund
  (RAGS), 9, 27, 30, 32, 62, 221, 245, 259
Risk
  assessment, 10, 59, 176, 188, 213
  biases, 6, 17, 130, 153
  pathway, 10–11, 14, 25–26, 29–40, 67, 74–
    75, 133, 256–60
  perception biases, 17, 146, 154, 191
  reform, 21, 242
  threshold, 63
  uncertainty, 60, 82
  variability, 60–61, 82
    money trade-off, 191
    risk analysis, 119
Rogers, William H., 289
Rosen, Sherwin, 193
Rosenberry, A. M., 286
Ross, Lee, 295
Russell, Milton, 267, 281, 283, 288–89

Sadowitz, March, 283
Safe Drinking Water Act, 29
Samuelson, William, 131
Scholz, John T., 292
Schroeder, Christopher H., 296
Schulze, William, 189
Schwarz, Thomas, 158, 292
Scofield, Patricia A., 288
Scope effect, 6, 134–35, 138
Seal, William, 206
Seed, Jennifer, 285
Semivolatile organic compounds (SVOC),
  258
Senate Environmental Affairs Committee,
  182
Sensitivity analysis, 75
Sethi, Rajiv, 291
Shanklin, Carita, 291
Shepsle, Kenneth A., 5, 296
Sigman, Hilary, 281
Silresim site, 32
Slope factor, 218
Slovic, Paul, 147, 204, 289, 295
Smith, Roy, 84, 285, 287, 293–94
Soil exposure risks , 94–101
Soil ingestion, 13, 33, 38, 67, 75, 88
South Boston, Massachusetts, 240

Spitzer, Matthew L., 282
Stanek, Edward J., 286
Status quo bias, 131
Stewart, Richard B., 281–82, 289, 296, 298
Stock, James H., 209, 294–95
Sunnyvale, California, 173, 223
Sunstein, Cass R., 214, 295, 298
Superfund Amendments and Reauthorization Act of 1986 (SARA), 4–5, 7, 22,
  26, 109, 111, 113, 121, 123, 217, 237,
  251, 296
Superfund
  cancer risks, 2
  cleanup policies, 109
  decision making, 17
  expenditures, 1, 229
  legislation, 1, 3
  reauthorization, 62
  how clean is clean, 130
  legislative mandate, 4
  remediation policy, 63
  remedies, 121
Synergistic effects, 233
Synthetic chemicals, 130

Target risk , 17, 128–40, 142–48, 153, 189
TCE (trichloroethylene), 218–19, 297
TIGER files, 248, 253
Toxics Release Inventory (TRI), 172, 178,
  290
Travis, Curtis C., 131, 281, 283, 288–89
Treatment, 238
Trichloroethylene (TCE), 218
Tversky, Amos, 283, 289, 293, 295

U.S. Bureau of Census, 200
U.S. Department of Transportation, 118
United States v. Ottati & Goss, 124

Value of life estimates, 20–21, 118, 124, 191,
  206, 213
Van Houtven, George, 113, 130–31, 139,
  163, 281, 283, 289–90, 292, 295
Viscusi, W. Kip, 130–31, 153, 206, 281–84,
  286, 289, 293, 295, 298–99
Volatile organic compound (VOC), 136, 258
Voter turnout, 17, 133, 146–48, 154, 183,
  186, 235

Walker, Katherine D., 283
Weingast, Barry, 215

Wesloh, Steven M., 288
Westinghouse Electric site, 15, 41, 104–105,
    173–74, 186, 223, 265, 284
Whitmyre, 83
Wiener, Jonathan Baert, 283, 288
Wiley, John S., Jr., 296
Williams, Ted, 292
Wittman, Donald, 282, 290

Yandle, Tracy, 291

Zeckhauser, Richard, 131, 282, 285, 289
Zimmerman, Rae, 131, 161–62, 281, 289–
    91, 299